THE
MUGHAL
EMPERORS

Francis Robinson

THE
MUGHAL
EMPERORS

AND THE ISLAMIC DYNASTIES OF
INDIA, IRAN AND CENTRAL ASIA, 1206–1925

with 238 illustrations, 123 in color

Thames & Hudson

CONTENTS

(*Half-title*) Jade pendant made for Shah Jahan. India, dated 1637/38.

(*Frontispiece*) Shah Jahan receives his three eldest sons and Asaf Khan during his accession ceremonies. Agra, Diwan-i Am, 8 March 1628. *Padshahnama* folio 50B, painted by Bichitr, *c.* 1630.

IL KHANS, MUZAFFARIDS AND TIMURIDS
1256–1506

The establishment of the Mongol Il Khans in power in Iran, their conversion to Islam, their decline into local lordships, and the recreation of a vast empire centred on Samarqand by Timur and his successors.

Special Features
The Composite Bow • The Tomb of Oljaitu at Sultaniya • Rashid al-Din • Jalairid Baghdad • Clothing Buildings in Ceramic Tiles • Hafiz • Samarqand • The Artistic Patronage of Gawhar Shad and her Son, Baisunqur • Ulugh Beg, Astronomer • Qara Qoyunlu and Aq Qoyunlu Confederations • Mir Ali Shir Nawai'i • Bihzad, the Master Painter

THE SULTANS OF DELHI
1206–1526

How Turks from Central Asia created a Muslim empire in India in the 13th century based on Delhi, which came by the mid-14th century to rule almost all the subcontinent. In the 15th century it divided into a number of competing local sultanates.

Special Feature
Six Regional Sultanates

First published in 2007 in hardcover in the United States of America by Thames & Hudson Inc., 500 Fifth Avenue, New York, New York 10110

thamesandhudsonusa.com

Library of Congress Catalog Card Number 2006908250

ISBN 978-0-500-25134-8

Printed and bound in Singapore by Craft Print International Ltd.

Timur

THE MUGHALS
1526–1858

Babur's attempts to recreate the empire of his ancestor, Timur, led to the establishment of Mughal rule in India. After a brief reassertion of Suri Afghan power, the Mughals – Akbar, Jahangir, Shah Jahan and Awrangzeb – rule one of the world's great empires, which suffers a long decline from the early 18th century to the mid-19th century.

Special Features
Babur and Gunpowder • Babur's Gardens • Babur's Memoirs •
The Suri Sultans of Delhi • Hamida Begum • Fatehpur Sikri • Akbar and
Technology • Akbar and Mughal Painting • Akbar and his Mother •
Jahangir and Painting • Nur Jahan • Shahjahanabad Delhi •
The Taj Mahal • Jahanara Begum • The Battle of Panipat, 1761

Akbar

THE SAFAVIDS, AFSHARIDS,
ZANDS AND QAJARS
1501–1925

This shows how in the region once ruled by the Il Khans, the Safavids laid the foundations of the modern Iranian state, the Afsharids and Zands sustained these foundations through the 18th century, and the Qajars developed them in the 19th century, and defended them in the context of the imperialism of the British and the Russians.

Special Features
Early Safavid Painting • Riza Abbasi: Artist • Isfahan • The Maidan •
Malik Jahan, Mahd-i Ulya

Muhammad Shah

Nasir al-Din

PREFACE: MUGHAL LIVES

A mihrab indicating the direction of prayer in the Imamzada Yahya at Varamin, Iran. It is made of lustre-painted tilework dated 1305 and crafted by Yusuf bin Ali bin Muhammad from the family of Abu Tahir, which was famed for its lustre pottery. Il Khanid rule saw the rapid development of the clothing of buildings in ceramic tiles.

IN THE WEST THE TERM 'MUGHAL', usually spelled Mogul, means a man of great power. The history of the word explains why this is so. In India, 'Mughal' refers to India's greatest dynasty, which lasted from 1526 to 1858. In the Persian language the term 'Mughal' in the plural means Mongols, the people who in the 13th and 14th centuries had a devastating impact on Asia as they set out to conquer the world. This book embraces those Muslim rulers from the 13th to the 20th centuries whose reigns and lands were affected by Mongol/Mughal power, and who all shared the persianate high civilization which flourished from Iran and Central Asia, through Afghanistan to northern and central India. The main dynasties were the Il Khans, Timurids, Safavids and Qajars in Iran and in India the Delhi Sultans and Mughals.

Some of the rulers are known beyond the realms of scholarship: the Il Khan Hulagu, grandson of Chingiz (Genghis) Khan, who in 1258 destroyed the Abbasid Caliphate; Timur (Tamerlane), whose name still brings with it the memory of a life of remorseless conquest; Shah Abbas, who in Isfahan brought the greatness of early modern Iran to its peak; Akbar, who fashioned an ideal of inclusive government for India; and Shah Jahan, who left India – and the world – its finest monument, the Taj Mahal. We are fortunate that the chroniclers have had much to say not just about these men, but about almost all those whom we cover. Through their eyes we can engage with these rulers, these 'Mughals', as military leaders, administrators, patrons of the arts, and confronters of the challenges of their times. We can also glimpse, on occasion, their lives as lovers, husbands, fathers, sons and brothers.

All these rulers, from the Il Khans and Delhi Sultans in the 13th century to the Qajar rulers of Iran in the 19th century, were confronted by the same problem: how, in a pre-industrial society, to build up and maintain strong central power. One key necessity was money. For much of our period, down to the raids of Nadir Shah and Ahmad Abdali into India in the mid-18th century, rulers set out to obtain money by conquest, returning with huge baggage trains loaded with treasure. By the time of the Safavids and Mughals, however, it was increasingly realized that the encouragement of agriculture and trade, allied to fair taxation, might offer a more sustainable way of maintaining central power.

The second key necessity was maintaining the loyalty of nobles and ministers. Fear and reward played their part. But other elements also reinforced the crude use of stick and carrot: the very early Safavids used Sufi religious leadership to cement loyalties, while later Safavids used slavery; the Mughals developed the concept of the imperial household, to which all nobles belonged. Both dynasties experimented with forms of the 'divine right' to rule, whether it was the Safavid idea that they were reincarnations or representatives of the 'Hidden' Shia Imam, or the Mughal ideology that their divine right to rule came down to them from the mythical Mongol queen Alanqoa through the bloodline of Chingiz Khan.

Three themes emerge in Mughal lives which might overturn some common preconceptions about Islam, as actually lived. First, Islam, and

The Mughal emperors had a profound sense of being part of a tradition of might and power which reached back to the Mongols. Thus, in the *Akbarnama* Abul Fadl traced Mughal ancestry back through Timur and Chingiz Khan to the mythical Mongol Queen, Alanqoa (see also pp. 49, 121). This led to a tradition in painting of portraying dynastic succession. Here, Timur sits in the centre flanked by his successors down to Awrangzeb.

the range of ideas it offers, were consistently made subordinate to the requirements of power. The Il Khan ruler Ghazan chose to become a Muslim because it was politically convenient. The first Safavid Shah set out to convert Iran to Shiism to bring ideological strength to his regime. Arguably, the Mughals in India were strong when they ran a regime inclusive of all faiths, and became weaker as they became more exclusively Islamic. Secondly, almost all these Muslim rulers indulged seriously in mood-enhancing drugs. Opium was a favourite, but for most the drug of choice was alcohol, which was enjoyed often in large quantities by men and women. Several died from its effects. In the case of some, the chroniclers hint that their addiction was not without guilt. Thus the chronicler Afif shows us the Delhi Sultan Firuz Shah guiltily pushing his drinks tray underneath his bed as a courtier comes to see him.

Thirdly, women often play a prominent part in affairs. They are patrons of architecture, investors in business, central figures in court politics, players in succession struggles, and at times they even came to rule, with the approval of some at least of their menfolk, as did Raziya in the Delhi Sultanate and Nur Jahan under the Mughals. What is evident, too, at least from the records of the Mughal royal family, is the great respect which the male members have for their womenfolk: Babur would set aside Friday afternoons in Agra to visit his aunts; Akbar's love for his mother, and hers for him, leaps from the pages of Abul Fadl's history; Jahangir confides to his memoirs his admiration for Nur Jahan's many gifts; and Awrangzeb honours his sister, Jahanara, even though she opposed him in the bloody struggle to succeed Shah Jahan.

INTRODUCTION: CHINGIZ KHAN AND THE RISE OF THE MONGOL LAND EMPIRE

When Chingiz Khan rose from the degree of manhood, he became in the onslaught like a roaring lion and in the mêlée like a trenchant sword; in the subjugation of his foes his rigour and severity had the taste of poison, and in the humbling of the pride of each lord of fortune his harshness and ferocity did the work of Fate.

Juwaini

IN THE 13TH CENTURY THE MONGOLS ruled the greatest land empire the world has seen. At its furthest extent it stretched from Korea in the east to Poland in the west, from the Arctic in the north to Turkey and Iran in the south. This was the last and the largest of the movements of the barbarian nomads of Central Asia against the settled regions on their frontiers. They transformed the political landscape, for instance by destroying the wealth of Iraq, laying the foundations of modern Iran and creating the conditions for the widespread dispersal of Turkish peoples in Central and Western Asia. They greatly enhanced the fortunes of Islam in Asia and reduced those of Christianity, but in the process Islam lost much of its openness to a free spirit of enquiry, and weaknesses developed which in the long run were to see it fall behind the West.

The man who led the Mongols to make this extraordinary mark on history was Temuchin. Born around 1167, he was a Mongol and a member of a minor tribe amongst the peoples of the steppe. His father, Yesughi, a lesser chieftain of noble descent, was killed when Temuchin was young, and in consequence his upbringing was harsh and difficult. Such were Temuchin's qualities, however – his courage, his charisma and his capacity for leadership – that he was able to gather a large group of young warriors around him. Eventually, he came to be recognized as Khan, or Lord, of the Mongols, and it is probably at this time he adopted the title Chingiz, meaning Oceanic, and hence Genghis Khan as he is commonly known to English speakers. Then, one by one, he set about subduing the tribes of Central Asia until in 1206 he was acclaimed supreme Khan. There followed a great assault on the settled areas beyond the steppe. In 1211 he began a conquest of China which was not completed until seven years after his death. In 1218 he attacked the Islamic world, destroying the empire of the Khwarazm Shah in Transoxania, Khurasan and Iran. Although he died in 1227, from the effects of a fall from his horse while on his way to campaign in China, his empire continued to expand, its limits not being fixed until 1260 in West Asia and 1279 in East Asia.

At the heart of the reasons for Mongol success was the Mongol army. All male Mongols up to the age of 60 were liable for military service, and all Turco-Mongol tribes were organized into a unified military structure. Estimates vary as to its size; at times it could certainly have numbered 100,000 men, although if some chroniclers are to be believed there were armies seven or eight times as large. It was highly organized on a decimal basis, the key unit being 1,000 men. The main formations were of light cavalry, armed with a compound bow which was much more powerful

Chingiz Khan was arguably the greatest conqueror in world history. All the rulers in this book, except the early Delhi Sultans, were to some extent affected by his legacy. Here, he is painted in old age, from a series of idealized paintings of the Mongol rulers in the Chinese imperial portrait gallery.

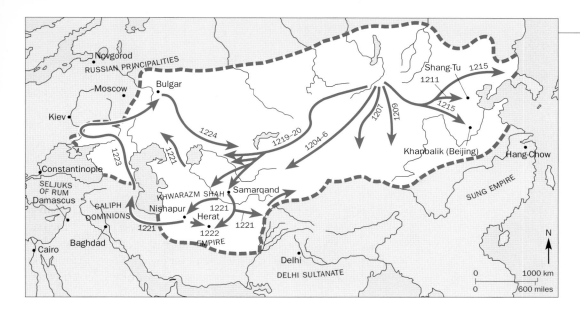

From 1206, when he was proclaimed supreme Khan of the Mongols of Central Asia, to 1227, when he died, Chingiz Khan created an empire which stretched from China through European Russia to Mesopotamia.

Pages 10–11 This double-page spread from the *Padshahnama* of Shah Jahan depicts the wedding procession of his eldest son, Dara Shikoh. We are left in no doubt of the wealth and magnificence of the Mughals, descendants of the Mongol rulers.

than the English longbow (see p. 21). This was a highly trained and extremely manoeuvrable force, which used a wide range of well-synchronized tactics including encirclement and surprise. Particularly important was the use of terror. The inhabitants of cities that resisted were massacred en masse to encourage others to submit without a fight. Having acquired their empire, the Mongols ruled it with utter pragmatism, their aim being to enrich themselves, within reason, and to stay in power.

Over their own time and over those who succeeded them the Mongols cast a great shadow. On the death of Chingiz Khan, the empire came to be divided amongst his sons. We are interested in their impact in lands where Muslims lived – Iran, Transoxania and India, where amongst the Persian-speaking elite they were known as Mughals. Their armies were a constant threat to the peoples and the rulers of the Delhi Sultanate. Their will to power and the magic of their bloodline was inspiration to the Il Khans in Iran, to Timur and his successors in Iran, Transoxania and Afghanistan, and to the great Mughal dynasty in India from 1526 to 1858. The Safavids who ruled in Iran from 1501, and based their regime on a special alliance with Shia Islam, paid little attention to the great military and political achievements of the Turco-Mongol past. Their artistic patronage, on the other hand, was profoundly influenced by the brilliance and achievements of the Timurid courts. They provided a fresh flowering of genius in the arts, the resonances of which were felt down to the 20th century.

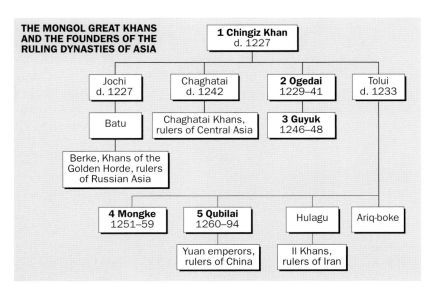

TEXTUAL SOURCES

The textual sources are considerable and wide-ranging in type and it is useful to consider some of the categories involved. One of great importance is the production of scholar civil servants who wrote histories of their times and often of people they knew well, such as Juwaini and Rashid al-Din for the Il Khans, Barani for the Khaljis and Tughluqids of Delhi, Abul Fadl for the early Mughals, and Malcolm for 18th- and 19th-century Iran. Some rulers, particularly the Mughals, were notable memoirists themselves, thus this book is illuminated by the personal insights of Babur, Gulbadan Begum and Jahangir, as well as the glimpses of character and personality revealed in the letters of Awrangzeb.

A small category is that of Muslim travellers, although it does contain the major figure of the 14th-century traveller Ibn Battuta. A large category is that of Western travellers in the Mughal world: representatives of Western powers such as Sir Thomas Roe and the Sherley brothers, Christian missionaries such as the Jesuits in India and the Carmelites in Iran, travellers seeking their fortune like Niccolao Manucci and Sir John (Jean) Chardin, and Western women including Emily Eden and Harriet Tytler, who in the 19th century bring a critical eye to bear on the activities of their menfolk. The portraits below are of just a few of the authors of the main sources.

Abul Fadl (Fazl)

Born in 1551 and murdered 1602, Abul Fadl came from a leading family of learning, developing his career as an author, liberal thinker and secretary to the Mughal emperor, Akbar. Presented at court in 1574, his liberal scholarship, embracing Greek thought and Sufism, and highly critical of the narrow-minded positions of the ulama (scholars), endeared him to Akbar. His masterwork was the *Akbarnama*, a monumental history of the Mughals and Akbar's reign, which emphasizes the divine nature of Akbar's kingship. The third volume, the *Ain-i Akbari*, is a detailed statement of imperial regulations with much information on geography and religious and social life. He also translated into Persian the Bible and the *Mahabharata*, the great Hindu epic. Out of jealousy he was murdered at the instigation of Akbar's son Salim (Jahangir).

Ziya al-Din Barani

Born c. 1285 and died c. 1357, Ziya al-Din Barani came from a family prominent in administration under the Shamsids and Khaljis of the Delhi Sultanate, and was himself for 17 years and three months the boon companion of Muhammad bin Tughluq. Soon after Firuz Shah Tughluq came to power he was banished from court, perhaps because of his involvement in the attempt of Khwaja-yi Jahan to place a minor son of Muhammad bin Tughluq on the throne. He spent his retirement producing two major works: the *Fatawa-yi Jahandari*, a book of advice for kings, counselling them to enforce the holy law, and his *Tarikh-i Firuz Shahi*, covering the period from Balban to the sixth year of Firuz Shah's reign, which is a didactic work demonstrating what happens when the advice of the *Fatawa-yi Jahandari* is not followed.

The Carmelites

Around 1209 the Carmelite Order was formed out of Christian hermits on Mount Carmel in Palestine. Their primary object was to achieve mystic union of the soul with God through love and contemplation; their secondary object was to be socially useful. In the late 16th century the Discalced (barefoot except for sandals) Friars expressed interest in missionary work. In 1604 Pope Clement VIII dispatched some on a mission to the court of Shah Abbas at Isfahan, as part of a series of papal overtures to the Safavid Shahs. They arrived in 1607. A *Chronicle of the Carmelites* is a compilation of their letters to Rome down to the late 18th century from their houses in Iran, Iraq and Goa.

Gulbadan Begum

Gulbadan, daughter of the Mughal emperor Babur, was born in Kabul c. 1523 and died at Agra in 1603. After his conquest of India she joined Babur in Agra. Although she gives excellent descriptions in her book of the exile of her half-brother, Humayun, in Sind and Iran, it seems she spent the whole period from 1540 to 1557 in Kabul, probably deriving her descriptions from her half-sister-in-law, Hamida. Between 1573 and 1582 she led the women of Akbar's household on their pilgrimage to Mecca. She wrote the *Humayunnama* at the behest of her nephew, the emperor Akbar, who was one of those to carry her bier after she died.

Ibn Battuta

This well-known Muslim traveller was born in Tangier on 25 February 1304 and died either in 1368/69 or 1377. Between 1325 and 1353 he travelled the Muslim world from West Africa to China, staying at the Il Khanid court in 1326 and at Muhammad bin Tughluq's court between 1333 and 1342. On his return to Morocco he dictated his *Rihla*, or book of travels, to a scholar commissioned by the Marinid Sultan of Morocco. It is one of the world's best-known travel books.

Ala al-Din Juwaini

Ala al-Din Juwaini, who was born in 1226 and died in 1283, came from a leading family of Iranian scholar administrators from the town of Juwain, close to Shiraz. When Hulagu entered Khurasan, he joined the Il Khan's service, drawing up the terms of the surrender of the Ismaili (Assassin) leader, Rukn al-Din. After the capture of Baghdad in 1258, he was made governor of Iraq-i Arab and Khuzistan. Towards the end of his life he became embroiled in charges of embezzlement. His *History of the World Conqueror* is both a classic of Iranian literature and the main source for the rise of the Mongols.

Sir John Malcolm

Sir John Malcolm was born in 1769 and died in 1833. He joined the East India Company aged 13, his precocious talents leading to his sobriquet 'Boy' Malcolm. He led East India Company missions to the Qajar court in 1800–01, 1808 and 1810; in 1801 he concluded the first treaty between Britain and Iran. In 1815 his *History of Persia* appeared to an excellent reception; other major works of history followed. He ended his Indian service as Governor of Bombay. In Iran he is remembered, among other things, for introducing the potato, which was known as 'Malcolm's plum'.

Niccolao Manucci

Niccolao Manucci was born in 1639 and died in 1717. In 1653 he left Venice to seek his fortune in the East. He visited Isfahan in 1654–55 and arrived in India in January 1656. He enlisted in Dara Shikoh's service as an artillery man, later witnessing the crumbling of Dara's fortunes. He refused to serve under Awrangzeb, whom he disliked. In the 1660s he adopted medicine as a profession, after various vicissitudes entering the service of a Mughal prince. From 1681 he served the British in Madras, where he came to own property. His history, *Storio do Mogor*, was first published in English in 1907 by William Irvine from manuscripts in Italian, French and Portuguese.

Note on transliteration and sources: Where a name has gained a widely accepted form in English, e.g. Safavid, it is spelled thus. Otherwise transliteration follows that of the *Encyclopaedia of Islam,* 1st edition, with the usual changes of q for ḳ and j for dj (so Quran not Koran, and Jahan rather than Djahan); this would appear to offer the best compromise between consistency and accessibility, although some words may initially appear a little strange. Again, to aid accessibility, the spelling of names in quotations has been made consistent, for the most part, with that in the text. Finally, it should be clear that this work rests on that of large numbers of scholars in the field: all are listed in the Select Bibliography.

Abul Fadl, Akbar's secretary and a gifted writer, presents his masterwork, the Akbarnama, *to his master. From this book much can be learned about Akbar's times, the working of the court and India in his day.*

THE IL KHANS 1256–1340	THE MUZAFFARIDS 1314–93	THE TIMURIDS 1370–1506

THE IL KHANS
1256–1340

THE INFIDEL IL KHANS 1256–95	Mubariz al-Din Muhammad 1314–58	Timur 1370–1405
Hulagu 1256–65	Shah-i Shuja 1358–84	Khalil Sultan 1405–09
Abaqa 1265–82	The Last Muzaffarids 1384–93	Shah Rukh 1409–47
Teguder (Ahmad) 1282–84		Ulugh Beg 1447–49
Arghun 1284–91		Abd al-Latif 1449–50
Gaikhatu 1291–95		Abd Allah Mirza 1450–51
Baidu 1295		Abu Said 1451–69

THE MUSLIM IL KHANS
1295–1340

		Sultan Husain Baiqara 1469–1506
Muhammad Ghazan 1295–1304		
Oljaitu 1304–16		
Abu Said 1316–35		
The Last Il Khanids 1335–40		

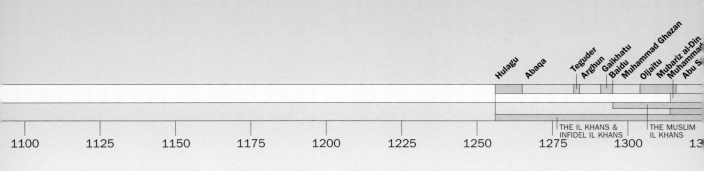

Hulagu

Timur

Ulugh Beg

Sultan Husain Baiqara

IL KHANS, MUZAFFARIDS AND TIMURIDS
1256–1506

T HE IL KHANS, OR SUBORDINATE LORDS, were descended from Chingiz
Khan through his son Tolui. They established Mongol rule in Iran
and Iraq. In the beginning, the impact of Mongol rule was largely destruc-
tive: there were great massacres, irrigation systems were destroyed and
the peasantry were oppressed, as the Mongols concentrated on extracting
as much wealth as they could for themselves. From the time of the Il
Khan Ghazan, however, the Mongols made their crucial conversion to
Islam and began to work to rebuild the prosperity of the region. Throughout this period the Il Khanid lands were part of a vast Asian empire.
Political, religious and cultural barriers were lowered and Iran was open
to influences from Europe through to China.

After the collapse of the Il Khanid state in the 1330s, a local lord,
Mubariz al-Din Muhammad, managed to establish his dynasty, known as
the Muzaffarids after his father, at Shiraz, extending his rule throughout
much of central Iran. In 1384 the Muzaffarids were brushed aside as
Timur, usually known as Tamerlane to the English-speaking world, the
last mighty Mongol conqueror, carved out his empire which stretched
from Baghdad to Delhi and from the Aral Sea to the Indian Ocean. One of
the greatest generals in history, his career was one of victory after victory.
His successors, the Timurids, ruled a smaller empire, at times consisting
of no more than Transoxania and Khurasan, but they presided over brilliant courts in which the arts and sciences flourished.

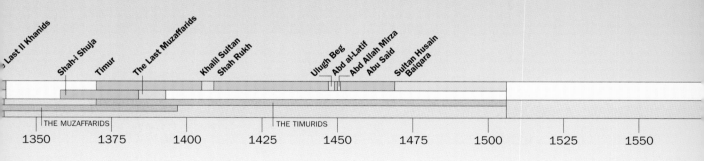

The Last Il Khanids

Shah-i Shuja

Timur

The Last Muzaffarids

Khalil Sultan
Shah Rukh

Ulugh Beg
Abd al-Latif
Abd Allah Mirza
Abu Said

Sultan Husain
Baiqara

THE MUZAFFARIDS

THE TIMURIDS

1350 1375 1400 1425 1450 1475 1500 1525 1550

THE INFIDEL IL KHANS
1256–95

Hulagu
1256–65

Abaqa
1265–82

Hulagu, grandson of Chingiz Khan, was the founder of the Il Khanid dynasty of Iran. Here, in a portrait drawn centuries after his death, he sits enjoying a drink, with his waterpipe, composite bow and broad-headed arrows by his side.

HULAGU	
Born c. 1217	Mangu Timur, Yashmut, Hulaju, Sharbawej, Taghai Timur
Father Tolui, youngest son of Chingiz Khan	*Daughters* Bulughan Aka, Jemi, Manglukan, Tutukaj, Tarakai, Kutlukan, Baba
Mother Sorghanghatani Beki, a Christian	
Wives Doquz Khatun, Kuik Khatun, Oljai, Kutui Khatun, Mertai Khatun, Yisut Khatun, plus 12 concubines	*Died* 8 February 1265
	Buried On the mountainous island of Shahu in Lake Urmiya; several beautiful young women of the court were, according to Mongol custom, buried alive with him
Sons Abaqa, Jumkur, Tekshin, Taraqai, Tuzin, Teguder (Ahmad), Ajai, Kuikurtai, Yesudar,	

HULAGU

The Lord of the Face of the Earth, Mongke Khan, had seen in the character of his brother Hulagu the indications of sovereignty and had detected in his enterprises the practices of conquest ... [he] charged him with the conquest of the Western parts.

Juwaini

HULAGU WAS AN ABLE AND RUTHLESS WARRIOR in the mould of his grandfather Chingiz Khan. Born around 1217, his name meant 'the one in excess', and from early on it was evident that he was well named. When Chingiz Khan first took him and his elder brother, Qubilai Khan – who was later to rule China – hunting with their bows, the 11-year-old Qubilai shot a hare while the 9-year-old Hulagu killed a goat, indicating his tendency to excess. He was well-educated, as Mongol princes went, and in later life gave important patronage to the great Muslim scientist Nasir al-Din Tusi.

At the gathering of Mongol leaders in 1251, another of Hulagu's brothers, the Great Khan Mongke, ordered him to expand Mongol power from 'the banks of the Amu Darya river to the ends of the lands of Egypt'. After Chingiz Khan had swept through the region several decades earlier, Mongol authority had not been established absolutely. In some areas, for instance Herat, there were vassals who acknowledged Mongol authority,

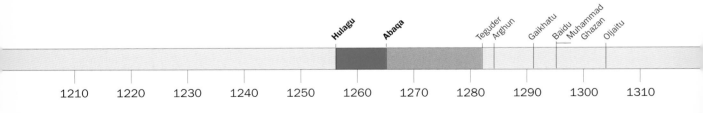

Hulagu Abaqa Teguder Arghun Gaikhatu Baidu Muhammad Ghazan Oljaitu

1210   1220   1230   1240   1250   1260   1270   1280   1290   1300   1310

THE IL KHANID ARMY

By all accounts the Il Khanid armies were vast and impressive. They looked 'like a mountain of iron', declared the historian Juwaini, describing their advance on the castles of the Assassins.

'The valleys and mountains billowed with the great masses of men. The hills which had held their heads so high and had such strong hearts now lay trampled with broken necks under the hooves of horses and camels. And from the din of the braying of those camels and the noise of pipe and kettle-drum the ears of the world were deafened, and from the neighing of the horses and the flashing of the lances the hearts and eyes of the foe were blinded.'

Juwaini

while in others there was resistance, for instance from the Ismaili Assassins who occupied a string of castles in the Alburz mountains south of the Caspian Sea, and the Abbasid Caliph of Baghdad, who ruled much of Iraq. Further west the descendants of Saladin ruled Syria, Crusader states still hung on in the Levant and the Mamluks, a regime of military slaves, had just come to power in Egypt.

The campaigns of Hulagu

Hulagu's first objective was to destroy the Ismaili Assassins, who had been foolish enough, according to William of Rubruck, to send 400 Assassins in disguise to kill the Great Khan. His second was to persuade the Abbasid Caliph to submit, and if he did not, to destroy him. After much feasting in the company of the Great Khan, and burdened with many gifts, in 1253 Hulagu set out from Mongolia. Those who resisted discovered that he was as ruthless as his grandfather: 'the rabble of that place', Juwaini records, 'put up some resistance until on the seventh day the army penetrated the inner town and razed its walls to the ground. They drove all the men and women out into the open country and spared no one over ten years of age except the younger women.'

A contemporary historian described the sack of Baghdad in 1258 thus: '... they swept through the city like hungry falcons attacking a flight of doves, or like raging wolves attacking sheep, with loose rein and shameless faces, murdering and spreading fear.... Beds and cushions made of gold and encrusted with jewels were cut to pieces with knives and torn to shreds; those hidden behind the veils of the great harem ... were dragged like the hair of the idols through the streets and alleys, each of them becoming a plaything in the hands of a Tatar monster....' Ibn Wassaf.

NASIR AL-DIN TUSI

Nasir al-Din, who was born in Tus in 1201 and died in Baghdad in 1275, was a Shia scholar of the first importance in the fields of mathematics, geometry, astronomy, philosophy and theology. Much of his early life was spent in the service of Ismaili (a Shia sect) rulers, including some 20 years at the court of the Assassins at Alamut. He was sent to negotiate, unsuccessfully, on behalf of the Assassins with Hulagu, and later joined the Il Khan on his campaign to destroy the Caliphate. In 1259, at Maragha near Tabriz, he began the construction of the first known observatory in the Muslim world. Maragha became a great centre of scholarship; its library was much enriched by the conquests of Hulagu. Nasir al-Din published across a vast range of subjects; some of his output is read to this day. Among his more notable works were his astronomical tables *al-Zij al-Il Khani*, and his *Akhlaq-i Nasiri*, an ethical work embracing politics, influenced both by Ismaili ideology and by Platonic and neo-Platonic ideas, as well as Aristotle's *Nicomachean Ethics*. Among his more notable achievements, and of his circle, was to make substantial steps towards undermining the geocentric theory of planetary motion.

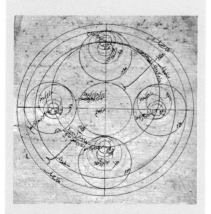

Detail of an illustration to Tusi's Majmuah which marks a major step away from the geocentric theory of interplanetary motion and towards the heliocentric theory.

In 1256 Hulagu confronted the Assassins. Terrified by the size of the Mongol army and by the effectiveness of its siege engines, the Grandmaster of the Order, Rukn al-Din, surrendered and ordered his remaining fortresses to do likewise. He was given permission to visit the Great Khan in Mongolia, who treated him with disdain. On his way back he was 'kicked to pulp and then put to the sword by his escort'. Most of the remaining Assassins fled to India where in the 19th century they came to be led by the Aga Khan.

In 1258 Hulagu turned his attention to Baghdad. The Caliph refused to submit. Hulagu besieged the city; the Caliph surrendered. One Iranian historian, though not a contemporary, put the numbers massacred by the Mongols at 800,000; Hulagu himself reckoned the figure to be 200,000. The Caliph was executed. Tales vary as to how he met his end, but the most credible version has him being rolled up in a carpet and kicked to death, the Mongols not wishing to shed noble blood. Thus died the last of the Abbasid Caliphs, who for nearly 500 years had been the successors of the Prophet Muhammad as leaders, nominal for the most part, of the Muslim community. This brutal act was well received by the Shia enemies of the Sunni Caliph, and by the Crusaders too, but it shocked the Sunni world, and did not meet with the approval of Hulagu's cousin, Berke, Khan of the Golden Horde (Horde means camp): 'he has sacked all the cities of the Muslims', Berke declared, 'and, without consulting his kinsmen, has brought about the death of the Caliph. With the help of God I will call him to account for so much innocent blood.'

In 1260 Hulagu moved on into Syria. He conquered Aleppo and received the submission of the Christian rulers of Antioch and Tripoli. His Mongol troops then entered Damascus, led by three Christians: Bohemond of Antioch, King Hethoum of Cilician Armenia, and his Nestorian general, Kit-buqa. Some have thought that this was potentially a decisive moment in world history, when Christians and Mongols might have worked together to drive Muslim power out of the Levant and defeat the Mamluks in Egypt. But, at this very moment, the Great Khan Mongke died in China, and Hulagu's brothers, Qubilai and Ariq-boke, competed for the succession. Hulagu moved out of Syria into Azarbaijan in order to keep an eye on his rival, Berke – but the serious lack of grazing in Syria seems to have been a further reason for moving a sizeable part of the Mongol army to the northeast. Kit-buqa was left with depleted forces to face the Mamluks. At Ain Jalut (the Spring of Galilee) he was defeated and killed. For the rest of the century Syria was to be the furthest point of Il Khanid expansion in the west.

The remainder of Hulagu's life saw an inconclusive struggle with Berke and the Golden Horde on the western shores of the Caspian. By 1264 the Il Khanid lands reached from the Amu Darya in the east to Syria and half-way into Anatolia in the west. Six months before his death, Hulagu was even negotiating a marriage with the illegitimate daughter of the Byzantine emperor, Michael Palaeologus. After his death at Maragha in 1265, he was buried on an island in Lake Urmiya. Following Mongol tradition

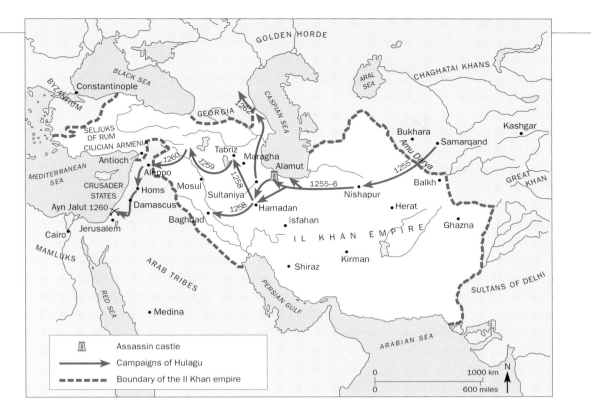

The Il Khan empire in the second half of the 13th century; it was fashioned by the campaigns of Hulagu.

several beautiful young women of the court were buried with him. In the same year his devoted Christian wife, Doquz Khatun, who had done much to patronize eastern Christians throughout his reign, was buried with him. In laying the foundation of the Il Khanid state, Hulagu paved the way for the Safavid state, and ultimately the modern Iranian state.

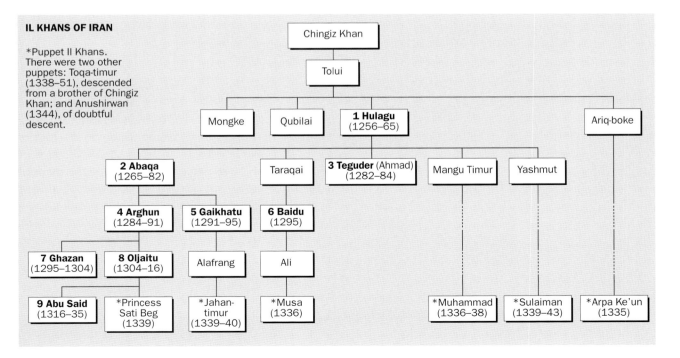

IL KHANS OF IRAN

*Puppet Il Khans. There were two other puppets: Toqa-timur (1338–51), descended from a brother of Chingiz Khan; and Anushirwan (1344), of doubtful descent.

Chingiz Khan

Tolui

Mongke — Qubilai — **1 Hulagu** (1256–65) — Ariq-boke

2 Abaqa (1265–82) — Taraqai — **3 Teguder** (Ahmad) (1282–84) — Mangu Timur — Yashmut

4 Arghun (1284–91) — **5 Gaikhatu** (1291–95) — **6 Baidu** (1295)

7 Ghazan (1295–1304) — **8 Oljaitu** (1304–16) — Alafrang — Ali

9 Abu Said (1316–35) — *Princess Sati Beg (1339) — *Jahan-timur (1339–40) — *Musa (1336) — *Muhammad (1336–38) — *Sulaiman (1339–43) — *Arpa Ke'un (1335)

ABAQA

[He was] good, generous, and clement, soft and modest, a lover of justice, charitable to the poor, and so forgiving that whatever a man's faults he would not sacrifice his life.

The Georgian Chronicle, summarized by Howorth

AFTER HULAGU DIED, HIS ELDEST SON, ABAQA, was invited by his father's leading followers to ascend the throne. Abaqa was careful to stipulate that he would do so only with the approval of the Great Khan, his uncle Qubilai, now all the greater for being the conqueror of China. After the approval was given, he ruled in the name of the Great Khan and there was always a Mongol ambassador, appointed by Qubilai, at the Il Khanid court. This was important as the Il Khanids were in danger of a pincer movement from the alliance of the Mamluks in the west and the Golden Horde in the north. Abaqa endeavoured further to strengthen his position by marrying the same illegitimate daughter of the Byzantine emperor, Michael Palaeologus in whom his father had been interested. He continued his father's policies of supporting Nestorian Christians and also Buddhists.

Abaqa sits on the right of a raised dais, as we look at it, with his son Arghun. During his reign, Abaqa had diplomatic relations with the Mongol rulers of China, the Byzantine Emperor and the Pope.

Abaqa soon found himself continuing his father's struggle with Berke of the Golden Horde. In the summer of 1265, at the head of 300,000 horsemen, he faced Berke, also at the head of a large army, across the river Kur in the southern Caucasus. A mighty clash was only avoided through the death of Berke. Then, the Chaghatai Khan, Baraq, who controlled the region to the east of Transoxania, began to pay serious attention to the Il Khanid territories, eventually allying with Qaidu, the rival of the Great Khan Qubilai. In 1269, Baraq seized parts of Khurasan and Afghanistan, cutting Abaqa's lines of communication with the Great Khan. In July 1270, by dint of feeding Baraq's spies false information, Abaqa was able to defeat him on ground of his own choosing outside Herat. Some further resistance from a Chaghatai officer led to another campaign in 1272–73, during which Bukhara was sacked and burned. From this time on, apart from minor invasions in the time of Oljaitu, the eastern frontiers of Iran remained largely untouched until the invasion of Timur.

THE COMPOSITE BOW

The key weapon of the Mongol and Il Khanid horsemen was the Central Asian composite bow. It was much shorter than the English longbow, and therefore suitable for use on horseback, and more powerful, with twice the range of the longbow, a flatter trajectory and greater accuracy. It was built around a wooden core with the addition of horn, sinew and fish glue. It worked best if kept constantly strung, hence its distinctive bow case. The 'Mongolian' release using a thumb-ring, as opposed to the 'Mediterranean' release using the fingers, enabled it to be pulled back further.

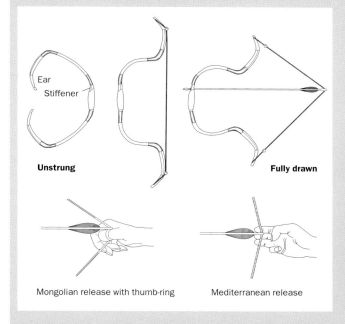

Ear
Stiffener

Unstrung

Fully drawn

Mongolian release with thumb-ring

Mediterranean release

Prince Bahram Gur slays a dragon using a composite bow from a Shahnama *of 1371 (Shiraz). It shows how well the composite bow was adapted for use on horseback.*

ABAQA	
Born	Palaeologus,
1234	betrothed to
Father	Hulagu, who died
Hulagu	before the marriage
Mother	could be
Yisut	consummated),
Wives	plus 3 concubines
Oljai (father's	*Sons*
widow), Durji	Arghun, Gaikhatu
Khatun, Tokini,	*Enthroned*
Nukdai, Iltirmish,	19 June 1265
Padishah Khatun,	*Died*
Mertai (father's	1 April 1282 in
widow), Kutui	*delirium tremens*
(father's widow),	after a drinking bout
Tudai, Bulaghan,	*Buried*
Maria Despina	Alongside his father
(daughter of	on the island of
Byzantine emperor,	Shahu, Lake Urmiya
Michael VIII	

The considerable attention which Abaqa paid to the northeast of Iran encouraged the Mamluks to move against Mongol interests in the west. In 1268 they captured Antioch from the Crusaders, laid waste Cilician Armenia and eventually, in 1277, destroyed the Mongol forces at Albulustan. When Abaqa later saw the battlefield he is said to have wept over the piles of Mongol dead. He sought alliances in Europe to strengthen his position: in 1274, for instance, two Mongol ambassadors met Pope Gregory X at the Second Council of Lyons. But when it came to the crucial moment, the only assistance he could get was from Cilician Armenia. In September 1281, Mongol forces under his brother, Mongke-Timur, were crushed at Hims in Syria.

Strangely, Abaqa did not take personal charge of the campaign at this point, preferring to devote his energies to a major hunting expedition. It was not until the spring of 1282 that he set out to avenge his brother's defeat. But on 1 April he died, apparently of *delirium tremens* after a heavy drinking bout. He was laid to rest next to his father on the island of Shahu in Lake Urmiya.

Teguder (Ahmad)
1282–84

Arghun
1284–91

Gaikhatu
1291–95

Baidu
1295

Arghun: the success of his reign in internal matters was much helped by his Jewish viziers.

TEGUDER (AHMAD)	
Born	*Sons*
?	Kaplanshi,
Baptized	Arslanshi, Nukajiyeh
Nicholas Teguder	*Daughters*
Khan (a Nestorian	Six
Christian)	*Enthroned*
Father	21 June 1282
Hulagu	*Died*
Mother	10 August 1284;
Doquz Khatun	executed on the
Wives	orders of his
Doquz Khatun (the	nephew Arghun by
Konkurat), Ermeni,	having his back
Tukakun Khatun,	broken
Baitegin, Ilkotlogh,	*Buried*
Tudai Khatun	Kara Kapchilghai

TEGUDER (AHMAD)

In the name of God, the most clement and pitiful.... The Firman of Ahmad to the Sultan of Egypt. The Supreme Being worthy of all praise has, by his grace and by the light of his direction for a long time, and since our youth, caused us to know his divinity, to confess unity, to proclaim Muhammad.

Teguder to the Mamluk Sultan of Egypt.

THE MONGOL PRINCES AND CHIEFS now chose Teguder as Il Khan. He was Hulagu's eldest surviving son by a Nestorian Christian wife, Doquz Khatun, and he had been baptized with the name Nicholas. The decision was taken in spite of Abaqa's preference for his eldest son, Arghun – the Il Khanid court soon came to regret it. Some have thought that Teguder's difficulties stemmed from his conversion to Islam and his adoption of the name Ahmad, along with the Muslim title of Sultan or King. This seems unlikely, as religion was not of great importance to the Mongols. Much more significant were a key policy failure and a poor sense of power.

In the teeth of opposition from his princes, Teguder sent two embassies to establish friendly relations with Egypt. They failed in

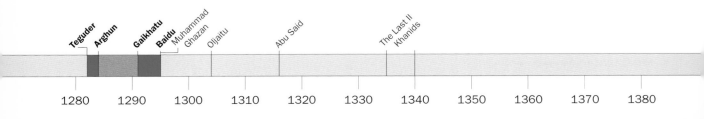

Teguder Arghun Gaikhatu Baidu Muhammad Ghazan Oljaitu Abu Said The Last Il Khanids

1280 1290 1300 1310 1320 1330 1340 1350 1360 1370 1380

ARGHUN	
Born c. 1258 *Father* Abaqa *Mother* Katmish Ikaji (concubine) *Wives* Kutlugh, Oljatai, Uruk, Seljuq, Bulughan (widow of Abaqa), Bulughan II (Kongurut), Mertai (widow of both Hulagu and Abaqa), Tudai (widow of Teguder Ahmad), Kultuk Ikaji	*Sons* Ghazan, Oljaitu, Khatai Oghul *Daughters* Oljaitai, Oljai Timur, Kutlugh Timur *Enthroned* 11 August 1284 *Died* 10 March 1291, probably from medicines designed to prolong his life *Buried* Last Il Khan to have a secret burial, this time close to Sujas in Azarbaijan

Detail of a letter in the Uighur script from the Il Khan Arghun to Philippe le Bel of France, dated 1289, part of which reads:

'Through the power of eternal heaven! Under the auspices of the Emperor! [The following are] Our, Arghun's words: O roi de France ... We agree to your proposition which you had conveyed to Us last year through the mission headed by Mar Bar Sauma Sahura: "If the armies of the Il Khan go to war against Egypt, we shall too set out from here to go to war and to attack [the rear of the enemy] in a common operation."'

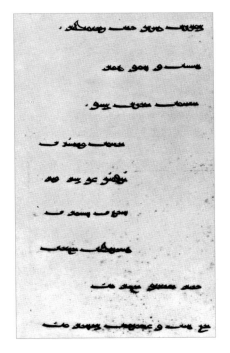

humiliating circumstances. Then, in spring 1284, Arghun, the viceroy of Khurasan, led an army against Teguder. Arghun was captured. But Teguder made two mistakes – he spared Arghun's life and failed to realize the extent of his nephew's support amongst his own following.

Arghun escaped and set about dispatching the supporters of Teguder. 'At night', as the historian Rashid al-Din wrote, 'Arghun was a prisoner, and in the morning he was monarch of the face of the earth.' Teguder was captured and executed by having his back broken, a form of execution which, like being kicked to death in a carpet, avoided the spilling of noble blood.

ARGHUN

And when Arghun had done as you have heard, and remained in possession of the Royal Palace, all the Barons of the different provinces, who had been subject to his father Abaqa came and performed homage before him, and obeyed him, as was his due.

Travels of Marco Polo

ARGHUN WAS ENTHRONED on 11 August 1284, the day after the execution of his uncle; it took a further 20 months for official approval to come through from the Great Khan. Arghun's reign was notable for the viziership of Sad al-Dawlah (Felicity of the State), a Jewish doctor. He first won the confidence of the Il Khan by restoring the economy of Baghdad, and in June 1289 he was apppointed Vizier. He was most able; he restored the state's finances, supported the law, reduced oppression and even facilitated the performance of the pilgrimage to Mecca. But he was also arrogant and made nepotistic appointments, which, together with widespread resentment from both Mongols because he cut down their income and Muslims at being ruled by a Jew, meant that he was able to survive only as long as his master could protect him. He was seized and executed while Arghun was on his deathbed. There followed pogroms against the Jews in Baghdad and Tabriz.

As his father had done, Arghun sought Christian help in fighting the Mamluks. Letters were sent to Popes, to Edward I of England, and to Philippe le Bel of France. That of 1285 to Pope Honorius IV was blunt about his purpose: 'We send you the said messengers and [ask] you to send an expedition and army to the land of Egypt, and it shall be now that we from this side and you from your side shall crush it between us with good men....' Arghun, however, never succeeded in co-ordinating a campaign against the Mamluks.

Arghun was particularly interested in the sciences of his day. On one occasion he is recorded as discussing alchemy with the distinguished scientist, Qutb al-Din Shirazi, and on another, geography. In 1289, persuaded that an Indian yogi had discovered the elixir of life, he began to take a compound of mercury and sulphur on a regular basis. Not surprisingly he fell seriously ill. His shamans diagnosed witchcraft.

Under torture one of his women admitted to giving the Il Khan a love potion, for which she was drowned, along with her maidservants. On 10 May 1291, in his early 30s, Arghun died. He was the last of the Il Khans to be given, following the shamanistic practices of the steppe peoples, a secret burial.

GAIKHATU	
Born	*Sons*
1271; adopted Tibetan Buddhist names: Rin-chen rDorje (precious jewel)	Alafreng, Iranshah, Jiuk Pulad
	Daughters
	Four
Father	*Enthroned*
Abaqa	23 July 1291
Mother	*Died*
Nukdai	26 March 1295; strangled with a bowstring by the supporters of Baidu
Wives	
Aisha, Dundi, Iltirmish, Padishah Khatun, Bulughan II (Kongurut, Arghun's widow), Uruk	*Buried* Karabagh

GAIKHATU

[He was concerned] with nothing except riotous living, and amusement and debauchery. He had no thought for anything except the things that were necessary for Kings and which they were bound to have, and how he could get possession of the sons and daughters of the nobles, and have carnal intercourse with them.... And very many chaste women among the wives and nobles fled from him, and others removed their sons and daughters and sent them away to remote districts. But they were unable to save themselves from his hands, or to escape from the shameful acts which he committed with them.

The Continuator of Barhebraeus

AFTER ARGHUN'S DEATH three candidates for the throne were summoned: his brother Gaikhatu from Anatolia, his cousin Baidu from Baghdad and his son Ghazan from Khurasan. Gaikhatu was chosen by a group of amirs (military commanders) and royal women. He then showed himself merciful in dealing first with those who had murdered his father's vizier and second with those who had subsequently plotted against his own regime. Indeed, one of them, Sadr al-Din Zanjani, he made his vizier on release from prison.

Gaikhatu's reign saw the usual exchanges with the Mamluks, who penetrated as far as the Euphrates and threatened once more that they would make Baghdad the centre of the Islamic world. On the other hand, in 1294, peace was agreed with Toqta, Khan of the Golden Horde, which was to last for several decades. Gaikhatu's reign is most notable, however, for his experiment with paper money. The background seems to have been prodigal spending on the part of the vizier and his Il Khan, combined with an epidemic which wiped out the Mongol herds of sheep. The idea was to introduce paper money modelled after the Chinese *chao* – it even had Chinese figures printed on it alongside the Muslim creed. The money soon caused chaos and Sadr al-Din was forced, after two months, to suppress it. This is the first recorded example of block printing outside China.

On account of his debauchery and extravagance, Gaikhatu was, in all probability, bound to meet an early end. But he himself hastened it through brutality. Insulted by Baidu while sodden with drink, he had his cousin beaten up by his retainers. In the winter of 1294–95 Baidu rebelled and was joined by key amirs who succeeded in capturing Gaikhatu. On 26 March 1295 they strangled him with a bowstring; he was 24.

GAIKHATU'S EXPERIMENT WITH PAPER MONEY

Gaikhatu began the issue of paper money known as *chao*, after its Chinese name, in September 1294, after discussing the issue with Qubilai Khan's representative at the court and braving the criticism of his wiser nobles. On the notes were written several words in Chinese characters: the Muslim profession of faith, Gaikhatu's name, and the note's value, and then the sentence 'The sovereign of the world has issued, in the year 693, this propitious *chao*. Whoever defaces it will be punished with death, with his wives and children, and his goods will be confiscated.' A mint was established in each province, and the use of metal coins forbidden. For a few days the notes were used, but quickly trade came to a standstill as there was no confidence in the currency. Panic followed. Within two months the experiment was ended. It is to be compared with the attempt, some 40 years later, of the Delhi Sultan, Muhammad bin Tughluq, to replace gold and silver with token copper and bronze coinage.

Gaikhatu about to give judgment from his throne. His reign was notable for a disastrous attempt to introduce paper money, following a Chinese precedent.

BAIDU

BAIDU	
Born	*Sons*
?	Kipchak Oghul, Ildar,
Father	Tugal, Ali
Taraqai	*Enthroned*
Mother	April 1295
Foster mother,	*Died*
Maria Despina (wife	4 October 1295;
of Abaqa)	executed on the
Wives	orders of Ghazan
?	

IN APRIL 1295 BAIDU WAS formally made Il Khan near Hamadan, on the great throne on which his predecessors as far back as Abaqa had been enthroned. Arghun's son, Ghazan, decided to challenge Baidu. At the outset of his campaign Ghazan declared his conversion to Islam. This was a calculated move – he had been brought up as a Buddhist and had built temples in Khurasan – but it was one which worked. As a body his amirs converted with him. After observing his first fast of Ramadan, which in that year was from 15 July to 13 August, Ghazan set out to confront his kinsman. His advance was a triumphal progress; Baidu's army melted away and he himself was captured. On 4 October 1295 he was executed in a garden outside Tabriz. Baidu was the last Khan to seek endorsement from the Great Khan and his coins were the last to bear the Great Khan's name. Henceforth Iran was increasingly cut off from China.

THE MUSLIM
IL KHANS
1295–1340

Muhammad Ghazan

1295–1304

MUHAMMAD GHAZAN	
Born 5 November 1271	and Gaikhatu's widow), Tundi,
Name Means the 'tooth', like a tooth in tender flesh	Keremun *Son* Alju
Father Arghun	*Daughter* Kutlugh
Mother Kultuk Ikaji	*Enthroned* 3 November 1295
Wives Kurtika, Bulughan, Eshel, Kokaji, Bulughan II (Arghun	*Died* 11 May 1304 *Buried* Gunbad-i Ali, Tabriz

Opposite Ghazan, with some of his
wives, enthroned before his court.
His reign is marked by his conversion
to Islam. All subsequent rulers of Iran
were to be Muslims.

Muhammad Ghazan

*And the most remarkable thing of all was that within a frame so small,
and ugly almost to monstrosity, there should be assembled nearly all of
the high qualities which nature is wont to associate with a form of symmetry and beauty. In fact amongst all his host of 200,000 Tartars you
should scarcely find one of smaller status or of uglier and meaner aspect
than this Prince.*

King Hethoum of Cilician Armenia

THE ACCESSION OF GHAZAN to the Il Khanid throne was a key moment in
the history of the dynasty; from now on the Il Khans were to behave less
as Mongol despoilers and more as Persian rulers of Iranian society. It was
also an important moment in the history of Iran; from now on Iran had
Muslim rulers who were, from time to time, moved to give a distinctive
Islamic quality to their governance. Ghazan's succession quickly brought
harsher times to non-Muslim faiths. Buddhists, who had been favoured
under the Mongols, were told either to convert to Islam or leave the Sultanate; their temples were destroyed. Jews and Christians became second-
class subjects, forced to wear distinctive clothes and compelled under

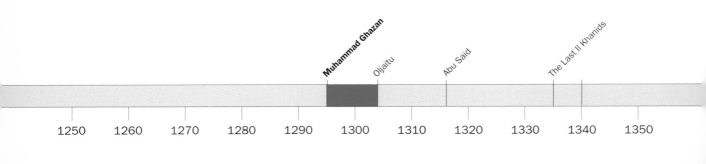

Islamic law to pay the *jizya* or poll tax on protected communities within Islam. They were, nevertheless, still the victims of riots and humiliation.

Ghazan's reasons for becoming a Muslim have often been discussed. One of his three viziers, the historian Rashid al-Din, himself a convert from Judaism, made it the outcome of reflection and revelation. 'With divine help ... he was able, with his sharp eye and correct attitude, to see through the mysteries of these idolatrous practices. He reflected on the different faiths and their adherents; he became enlightened through the light of the religion of Muhammad streaming into his radiant inner being.' Be this as it may, there was short-term advantage in his conversion to Islam during his bid for the Il Khanid throne, and there was long-term sense in identifying, along with other leading Mongols, with the faith of the vast majority of his subjects; indeed, it was a move which was of a piece with this overall approach to the governance of Iran.

'Ghazan', declared Rashid al-Din, 'took the greatest personal interest in the welfare of the state. He sat in person from morning till night, and anything, which was laid before him, he himself corrected in draft. Due to this the empire prospered.' Measures were introduced to restore the economy: the land tax was reformed and its timing regulated; bringing

fresh land under cultivation was encouraged; the system of paying soldiers and officials by giving them drafts to be drawn on local exchequers, and therefore the peasantry, was abolished; taxes on urban crafts and trades were reduced; the coinage was reformed; weights and measures were standardized; paper accounting was introduced in the royal treasury; the court was forbidden to abuse any longer the government courier system; couriers themselves were forbidden to commandeer property for overnight stops; the roads were made safer. Most importantly, a new (to the Mongols, for it had existed in Seljuk times) system was devised for paying the army – from now on agricultural lands (*iqtas*) were assigned to army regiments from which they were to be supported. A full description of these improvements is given by Rashid al-Din, whose policies they also were. Other chroniclers note that Ghazan did indeed achieve an improvement in prosperity, which continued into the time of Oljaitu but did not long outlast the dismissal of Rashid al-Din as vizier in 1317.

Ghazan's conversion to Islam made no difference to Il Khanid policies towards the Mamluks. His campaigns to the west were

NAWRUZ, THE KINGMAKER

Nawruz, the son of a leading Mongol lord of Khurasan, was the key figure in Ghazan's rise to power. During the late 1280s he was competing for power with the future Il Khan in Khurasan and Sistan. Towards the end of 1294, after quarrelling with his local patron, he finally submitted to Ghazan, an act celebrated in a three-day feast. A devout Muslim, it was he who persuaded Ghazan to take the important decision of converting to Islam. After Ghazan came to the throne Nawruz is thought to have been responsible for the subsequent persecution of pagans and Christians. With his power at its peak he deposed and humiliated one of Ghazan's viziers, Sadr al-Din Zanjani, for overreaching his power. But then matters fell apart. Nawruz had been corresponding with the Mamluk Sultan as part of his plan to make Ghazan Il Khan. A series of chances enabled Sadr Al-Din to place forged letters with Nawruz's courier, making him appear disloyal. On their discovery Ghazan had Nawruz's family slaughtered, including women, some of whom were married into his own family. When Nawruz was caught he was cut in two, and his head, for some years, decorated the front of Baghdad prison.

crowned with a great victory in the autumn of 1299 when he crushed the Mamluk army at Hims. Aleppo was captured and the Friday sermon was preached in his name in Damascus. But, as was always the case with Mongol-style armies, the shortage of fodder in Syria forced Ghazan to withdraw. In 1303 he despatched a fresh army to assert his authority over the Mamluks in Syria. But this time the Il Khan forces were humiliated. After a court of enquiry the Il Khan commanders were punished with beating. That winter Ghazan was preparing another invasion of Syria when he was struck down by a serious illness, one symptom of which was inflammation of the eyes. In January 1304 he was much affected by the death of his youngest wife, Keremun. He then sought the company of his favourite wife, Bulughan, who had also been the wife of his father, Arghun, and whom he had married in defiance of Islamic law. On 11 May 1304, aged 33, he died. He was buried in the Gunbad-i Ali, the mausoleum he had created for himself in Tabriz.

Right A charming picture of a lion and a lioness from the *Manafi al-Hayawan* of Ibn Bakhtishu, which was commissioned by Ghazan in 1298 and made in the early Il Khan capital of Maragha. This work of natural history is the earliest surviving Iranian illuminated manuscript.

Opposite Ghazan's funeral was marked by a public procession typical of the Muslim world, as compared with the secret burials of his Mongol and early Il Khan ancestors.

Oljaitu
1304–16

Abu Said
1316–35

OLJAITU	
Born c. 1280	Dunya, Bulughan (widow of Arghun), Terjughan, Iltirmish, Oljai, Siyughetmish, Kutukta
Name Assumed on coming to the throne means 'Fortunate'/ 'Auspicious' in Mongol. Original name was Khar-Banda meaning 'ass herd'. Baptized when young with the Christian name of Nicholas, becoming in turn a Buddhist, a Sunni and then a Shia Muslim	*Sons* Abu Said, Bestam, Bayezid, Taifur, Sulimanshah, Adilshah, Abu Said (II)
Father Arghun	*Daughters* Sati Beg, Dulendi, Fatima, Mihrkutlugh
Mother Uruk Khatun	*Enthroned* 19 May 1304
Wives Maria Despina (widow of Abaqa),	*Died* 17 December 1316 from digestive problems brought on by excess
	Buried In his mausoleum at Sultaniya

OLJAITU

He was good, liberal, and seldom accessible to calumny, but, like all the Mongol princes, he drank spirits to excess, and spent his time chiefly in pleasure.

Continuator of Rashid al-Din, summarized by Howorth.

BEFORE HE DIED, GHAZAN designated his brother Khar-Banda (meaning 'Ass-herd', the name given to him when he was born, following the Mongol custom of naming the child after the first object or person seen by the mother after the birth) as his successor. Although still in Khurasan, Khar-Banda arranged for two potential rivals to be assassinated, and then set off for the Il Khanid heartlands in Azarbaijan. On being enthroned he assumed the name Oljaitu (meaning 'Fortunate' in Mongolian) and in his full title had the somewhat unfortunate Khar-Banda changed to Khuda-Banda, meaning 'Slave of God'.

He quickly made the wise decision of confirming in office his father's able viziers Sad al-Din and Rashid al-Din. Running two viziers side by side was never likely to be a recipe for peace, though it may well have prevented one or the other from becoming over powerful. By 1312 Sad

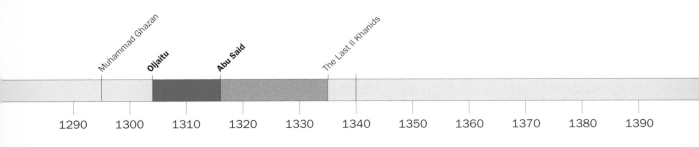

al-Din's arrogance had made him many enemies, the most important of whom was Rashid al-Din, who revealed to Oljaitu the financial dealings of his rival and his associates: Sad al-Din was executed. He was replaced by Taj al-Din Ali Shah, who turned out to be as dishonest as his predecessor. Matters came to light when Taj al-Din was unable to pay the expenses of army operations in Khurasan. This time Oljaitu solved the resulting friction between his viziers by dividing his territories between the two, Taj al-Din getting northwest Iran, Mesopotamia and Asia Minor, and Rashid al-Din central and southern Iran.

Oljaitu had little success in military affairs. He failed, effectively, to bring the Caspian province of Gilan under Il Khanid rule. He did, on the other hand, succeed in imposing his will on the city of Herat, whose Malik (ruler) refused to collaborate with him. But, as for his predecessors, Mamluk power in the west was the big issue. Soon after he came to power he met the ambassadors of the other Mongol Khans, who told him of their agreement to bring to an end the disputes among the descendants of Chingiz Khan. This prompted him to write to the King of France with what might be construed as an offer of joint action against the Mamluks: 'If now there should be good people among you, or among Us, who do not wish to be on good terms, then, with the power of heaven We shall all stand united against them.' But, when it came to the point, Oljaitu had to take the Mamluks on by himself; like his forebears he was never able to co-ordinate the action with European allies which might have transformed the history of West Asia. In October 1312 he crossed the Euphrates, tried to take a town, failed and withdrew. It was the end of the 50-year struggle of the Il Khans with the Mamluks for control of Syria.

Patron of the arts

Oljaitu was more successful as a patron of the arts and as a builder. He patronized the production of magnificent and monumental Qurans, on one of which Ahmad bin Suhrawardi, one of the six pupils of Yaqut, the greatest calligrapher of the medieval Islamic world, worked for four years. He encouraged his vizier Rashid al-Din to continue to write his multi-volume *Compendium of Histories*, which his brother, Ghazan, had first supported. He promoted the highly cultivated atmosphere in which

A page from a magnificent 30-volume manuscript of the Quran commissioned by Oljaitu as an endowment for his mausoleum at Sultaniya. The Quran was calligraphed in 1306–16, probably by two pupils of Yaqut al-Mustasimi (1221–98), regarded by many as the greatest calligrapher of all time. It is one of a series of monumental Qurans commissioned by Oljaitu and his vizier, Rashid al-Din.

THE TOMB OF OLJAITU AT SULTANIYA

The tomb complex of Oljaitu at Sultaniya, which embraced a mosque, madrasa, hospice, hospital, guesthouses and other buildings, gives an idea of the ambitious scale of Il Khanid architecture. Oljaitu's tomb, which is the only part to survive, is a huge octagonal area some 38 m (125 ft) in diameter, supporting a 50-m (165-ft) high dome ringed by eight minarets. The dome was covered in blue-glaze tiles and the interior was decorated in a magnificent scheme of brick and tile. There are few medieval spaces to match its lofty interior.

Right *Vaulting of one of the exterior galleries of Oljaitu's tomb. The decoration was done first in brick and tile, and then soon replaced with the painted plaster seen here, perhaps to celebrate the brief period when Oljaitu was protector of Mecca and Medina.*

Below *Oljaitu's tomb at Sultaniya, on the road between Qazwin and Tabriz. The tomb is the only part of a major complex of buildings, including a mosque, madrasa, hospice, hospital and guesthouse, to survive.* Inset *An axonometric view.*

A stucco mihrab commissioned by Oljaitu for the Friday Mosque at Isfahan. Note the arrangement of a niche within a niche within a rectangular frame. The inscription in the thuluth script includes praise for the 12 imams revered by the Shias.

his vizier might endow a library in Tabriz where his works would be reproduced each year, and in which 220 slaves worked as calligraphers, painters and gilders. But it was as a builder that Oljaitu really made his mark. He completed the new capital in the northwest of Iran, between Qazwin and Tabriz, which had been started by Arghun. Called Sultaniya or 'Imperial', its dimensions, some 30,000 paces in circumference, reflected the Il Khan's imperial vision; it is a major city to this day. At the west of the city was Oljaitu's vast tomb complex. In this he was laid to rest on December 1316, aged 36. He died from digestive problems, following excesses, in particular in drink, to which the house of Chingiz Khan was given.

ABU SAID

A brave and brilliant prince of majestic appearance, generous and witty.

Ibn Taghribirdi

ABU SAID WAS ONLY 11 when his father, Oljaitu, died. It was not until the following year that he reached Sultaniya from Mazandaran, where in the early summer he was enthroned. Seven princes seated him on the throne, and gold and precious stones were scattered over his head. No changes were made in the senior officers of the state. Amir Choban, who

ABU SAID	
Born	*Wives*
2 June 1304	Baghdad Khatun,
Title	Dilshad Khatun,
al-Sultan al-Adil (The	Konkurat, plus
Just Sultan)	others
Father	*Sons*
Oljaitu	None
Mother	*Died*
?	30 November 1335,
	probably poisoned
	by Baghdad Khatun

RASHID AL-DIN

Rashid al-Din (1247–1318) was born in Hamadan to a Jewish family involved in medicine. He trained as a doctor and in that capacity entered the service of the Il Khan court under Abaqa. Aged 30 he converted to Islam, but his Jewish background remained a source of difficulty for the rest of his life. Nevertheless, he rose as an administrator in Il Khanid service and from 1398 to his death was at the head of affairs. In the process he acquired great wealth, founding quarters in both Sultaniya and Tabriz – the deed of endowment for the latter, the *Rab-i Rashidi*, still exists, part in his own hand. Rashid al-Din's fame rests more on his achievement as a historian than as a leading bureaucrat. Ghazan commissioned him to write his *Jami' al-Tawarikh* (*Compendium of Histories*), which is the most important historical source for the Mongol empire. Oljaitu asked him to extend the work so that it eventually became a universal history from the time of Adam. It is, of course, remarkable that such a man, fully engaged in matters of state, should have had time for such an enterprise. He claimed that he wrote on a regular basis between morning prayer and sunrise. He certainly plundered the works of others, Juwaini for instance, and probably used research assistants. He remains, however, an outstanding source for the life of Chingiz Khan and the Il Khanid period.

Mahmud of Ghazni crossing the Ganges, from the history of the Ghaznawids section in the Jami' al-Tawarikh of Rashid al-Din. The painting is done in black ink with colour washes – a Chinese technique. Moreover, the paintings illustrating this section are amongst the largest and most dynamic in the book, indicating the Mongol affinity to the Turkish traditions of conquest, which the Ghaznawids represented and to which they succeeded.

had become Commander-in-Chief under Oljaitu, and to whom the late Il Khan had specifically given responsibility for Abu Said, was confirmed in his office. And so were the two viziers Rashid al-Din and Taj al-Din Ali Shah.

The two-vizier model continued to breed tension; by October 1317 Taj al-Din had succeeded in getting Rashid al-Din dismissed. The following year Choban summoned Rashid al-Din back to his post saying that he was 'as essential to the State as salt to meat'. Taj al-Din began to intrigue against Rashid al-Din again, this time saying that he had prescribed the medicine which had caused Oljaitu's death. The accusation succeeded. On 17 July 1318, the 70-year-old scholar, who had returned to office with the utmost reluctance, was first forced to witness the execution of his son, who had held the cup from which Oljaitu drank, and was then himself executed by being cut in two. His head was carried around Tabriz accompanied by the slogan: 'This is the head of the Jew who has dishonoured the word of God; may God's curse be upon him.'

Amir Choban

Much of Abu Said's reign was taken up by his relationship with Amir Choban and his family. Early on Choban found himself in difficulty when fighting amirs who had rebelled against him on account of his harsh treatment of them. The day was only saved by Abu Said's personal intervention in the battle, and for his conduct he was awarded the title of Bahadur or 'Hero'.

During the 1320s, on the other hand, Abu Said increasingly came to resent the power which Choban wielded in the state – several of the Commander-in-Chief's sons held key positions. He was indignant, too, about the way in which Choban stood in the way of him realizing his passion for Choban's daughter, Baghdad Khatun. He set out to destroy the hold which the house of Choban held on his government. Once the Il Khan made his wishes known, the amirs deserted to his side. Choban took refuge in Herat, but it was no more secure a refuge than it had been for Nawruz some 30 years before. Abu Said ordered the ruler of Herat to execute his guest; he was strangled with a bowstring. One of Choban's fingers was sent to Abu Said, which he ordered to be hung up in the market place of his camp.

From the beginning the Mamluks had been the rock on which Il Khanid ambitions in the west broke. Abu Said's reign saw a friendlier relationship. The evidence came when Timur-tash, governor of Anatolia and one of Choban's surviving sons, fled to Cairo to seek asylum under the Mamluks. At first he was well received by Sultan Nasir, who wrote to Abu Said to ask what he would like done with his guest. The Il Khan demanded his extradition; the Sultan, on reflection, decided that death was the better outcome. Timur-tash's head was stuffed with straw and sent to Abu Said. Arguably, the death of Timur-tash, followed seven years later by that of Abu Said, created the power vacuum in Anatolia which the young Ottoman regime was able to fill.

The end of Abu Said

On 30 November 1335 Abu Said died, in all probability poisoned by his wife Baghdad Khatun. According to Ibn Battuta, Abu Said enjoyed the company of scholars and wrote an elegant hand in both the Mongolian and Arabic scripts. He also played the lute, composed songs and wrote poetry. Ibn Taghribirdi talks of him proscribing strong drink and demolishing churches. But he also continued the Mongol traditions of religious tolerance; it was in his reign that Pope John XII founded the Archbishopric of Sultaniya.

BAGHDAD KHATUN: ABU SAID'S DANGEROUS LOVE

When he was 20, Abu Said conceived a passion for Baghdad Khatun, the daughter of his Commander-in-Chief, Amir Choban, and the wife of one of his greatest amirs, Shaikh Hasan. According to the law or *yasa* of Chingiz Khan, the ruler could have anyone's wife he desired. Choban, however, tried the old trick of separation to bring Abu Said to his senses: the Il Khan was persuaded to spend the winter in Baghdad while the Shaikh and his wife were sent to Qarabagh. But separation had the opposite effect; Abu Said sat in his tent and moped and refused to be distracted by hunting parties. Indeed, his subsequent campaign against the power of Choban and his family in his administration may well have been in part inspired by his anger at Choban's blocking action. After Choban's death in 1327, he immediately demanded the hand of Baghdad Khatun. He now proceeded to marry a woman whose father and several of whose brothers he had caused to be killed. Baghdad quickly demonstrated the ascendancy she had gained over Abu Said by imposing her preferences for the disposal of her father's body, which was to be burial near the tomb of Caliph Uthman in Medina. When Abu Said died in 1334, it was, according to Ibn Battuta, from poison administered by Baghdad Khatun – first because she had been demoted as senior wife in favour of Dilshad Khatun, her niece, and second because she could not forgive the murder of her father and her brothers. As soon as Abu Said was dead, one of the amirs, a Greek eunuch, sought and found Baghdad in her bath and killed her with his mace.

THE LAST IL KHANIDS 1335–40

THE DEATH OF ABU SAID saw the virtual end of the house of Hulagu and the collapse of the Il Khanid state. He was replaced by a Chingizid prince of another line, **Arpa Ke'un**, the great-grandson of Tolui's youngest son, Ariq-boke. He quickly took command of his sultanate, seeing off an Uzbeg threat from the north, putting to death Chingizid princes who might have been rivals, and marrying Princess Sati Beg, sister of Abu Said and widow of Amir Choban. His rule was challenged, however, by Ali Padshah, the governor of Baghdad, who backed an alternative Il Khan, **Musa**, a grandson of Baidu. Arpa Ke'un was defeated by Ali Padshah and killed.

There followed a period in which local lord after local lord put forward claimants to the throne. Shaikh Hasan-i Buzurg, the first husband of Baghdad Khatun, put forward **Muhammad**, the great-grandson of the Great Khan Mongke, installed him in Tabriz and himself married Princess Dilshad, the wife who had displaced Baghdad Khatun in Abu Said's favour. The amirs in Khurasan put forward **Toqa-timur**, a sixth-generation descendant of Chingiz Khan. Then, the son of Timur-tash, **Shaikh Hasan-i Kuchak** (Shaikh Hasan the Little, to distinguish him from Hasan-i Buzurg, the Big), threw his hat into the ring, offering an interesting twist to the game by pretending that his Turkish slave was his father, who had not been killed and had escaped after long confinement by the Mamluks.

The flavour of the time can be seen in Shaikh Hasan-i Buzurg's actions. After his puppet, Muhammad, was killed in battle, he offered Toqa-timur the throne. When this did not work he pushed forward **Jahan-timur**, the grandson of Gaikhatu. But in June 1340 he was defeated by Shaikh Hasan-i Kuchak and fled to Baghdad, where he dumped his candidate and took power for himself, founding the Jalairid dynasty there. In the decade that followed other puppets in Iran such as Sulaiman Khan and Anushirwan Khan were promoted by aspirant power-brokers, but the overthrow of Jahan-timur represented the effective end of the Il Khanid state.

The Il Khans did much to open the lands of Iran to influences from Europe in the west and China in the east. Their patronage helped to develop Iran's distinctive excellence in architecture and the arts of the book. Their power helped shape the lands under one government, which would in large part be the template for Iranian states to follow. It was in their time that Iranian historians forsook writing in Arabic for Persian.

THE DEATH OF SHAIKH HASAN-I KUCHAK

Shaikh Hasan 'the Little' did not live long after defeating Shaikh Hasan 'the Big'. In 1343 his wife Izzat Malik fancied that an intrigue she had had with an enemy of her husband had been discovered. So she took advantage of a time when Shaikh Hasan was very drunk and killed him by crushing his testicles. For her pains she was cut to pieces, some of her body being eaten and the rest fed to pigs.

THE MUZAFFARIDS
1314–93

Mubariz al-Din Muhammad
1314–58

Shah-i Shuja
1358–84

MUBARIZ AL-DIN MUHAMMAD	
Born	*Sons*
c. 1301	Shah-i Shuja, Shah
Father	Mahmud, Shah
Sharaf al-Din	Muzaffar, Sultan
Muzaffar	Imad al-Din Ahmad,
Mother	Abu Yazid
?	*Died*
Wife	1 December 1363
Khan Kutlugh	in prison, after
Makhdum Shah	being blinded by his
	eldest son in 1358

MUBARIZ AL-DIN MUHAMMAD

My elder brother, Shah-i Shuja, one day asked of him 'Have you killed a thousand men with your own hand!' 'No', he replied, 'but I think I may have killed eight hundred'.

Sultan Imad al-Din Ahmad

WITH THE END OF THE IL KHANIDS, power was dispersed amongst a host of local lords. Amongst the most important of these were the Muzaffarids, who ruled in Yazd, Kirman, Shiraz and eventually Isfahan, and the Jalairids, who ruled in Baghdad and Tabriz.

The Muzaffarids were of Arab descent. Long settled in Khurasan, they moved to Yazd at the Mongol conquest, when they entered the service of the local Atabeg. Eventually Sharaf al-Din Muzaffar, after whom the line is named, became governor of Yazd, serving several Il Khans. His son, Mubariz al-Din Muhammad, was brought up at the Il Khanid court. After his father's death, and that of Oljaitu, he returned to Yazd, which he succeeded in wresting from the hands of the Atabeg. Following his capture of Yazd, Mubariz al-Din was assisted by another family of local lords, the Injuids. Subsequently, he found himself competing for power with them.

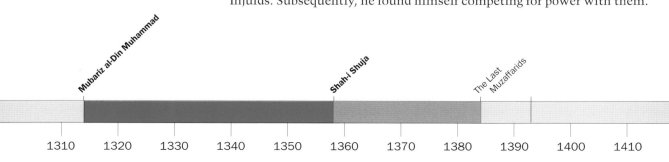

JALAIRID BAGHDAD

Shaikh Hasan-i Buzurg turned his defeat in the power struggle which marked the final Il Khanid years into victory by deposing Jahan-timur and taking power in Baghdad himself. He was a worthy ruler. His great-grandfather, Ilge, was one of Hulagu's generals, and his grandfather and great-uncles were part of the military elite of the Il Khanid empire. His father was married to a sister of the Il Khan, Arghun. Remarkably for someone who played politics in such stormy times he died in his bed. 'No one in his position', declared Ibn Bazzaz, 'has lived to such an age nowadays.' He was succeeded by Shaikh Uwais, the outcome of his marriage to Dilshad Khatun. For most of his reign Uwais was engaged either in struggles amongst the Muzaffarids, or in warfare with the Qara Qoyunlu, the Turkmen federation based on Diyarbakr (see box pp. 64–65), or in attempts to expand his position in Tabriz and Ray. Baghdad remained his capital; he died in Tabriz in 1374. His eldest son, Hasan, failed to please the amirs, who had him killed, and he was succeeded in turn by his second son, Husain.

Husain was soon entangled in fratricidal strife, which came to an end in 1382 when his youngest brother, Sultan Ahmad, defeated and killed him. It was Sultan Ahmad's fortune to face the onslaught of Timur (p. 44). In August 1393 he escaped with his army when Timur appeared by surprise outside Baghdad.

Once Timur had gone, Sultan Ahmad reoccupied his capital. Not surprisingly, this displeased Timur who returned in 1401 to sack the city. Once Timur had departed Sultan Ahmad was again able to return to Baghdad and to remain there until, in 1410, he was defeated by the Qara Qoyunlu. He was strangled and his body left for three days to lie exposed to the elements.

The Jalairids were great patrons of the arts. Shaikh Uwais wrote poetry and practised the arts of calligraphy and painting. Sultan Ahmad, too, was a painter, calligrapher, musician and poet in both Arabic and Persian, whose works were collected in a *Diwan*. Their courts provided a most favourable environment for poetry, architecture and most of all painting. In their time Baghdad and Tabriz were great centres of the arts of the book. It was under Jalairid patronage that the arts of the book broadened from the concerns of the Mongols with the *Shahnama* (the Iranian Book of Kings) and the fate of dynasties, works of history and books of instruction, to embrace romantic and lyrical poetry. Even though the Jalairids spent a great deal of their time at war, they also presided over settled courts in great capital cities. In the last 30 years of their rule the *Khamsa* (Quintet of Epic Poems) of Nizami (*c.* 1140/46–1203) and the *Khusraw-i Shirin* (a famed love story, forming one of Nizami's Quintet) were both the subject of Jalairid studies. The leading painter at the court of Sultan Ahmad was Abd al-Hayy. After he was carried off to Samarqand in 1393 by Timur, his pupil Junaid emerged as the leading painter. He had a hand in the *Khamsa* of Khwaju of Kirman, one of the great achievements of Iranian painting, and in the *Diwan* of Sultan Ahmad. The painting of the Baghdad school came to an end with its sack in 1401. Nevertheless, the achievements of Jalairid patronage look forward to the peaks of Timurid art in 15th-century Herat.

Left *Prince Humay at the gate of Humayun's castle, from the* Diwan *of Khwaju Kirmani completed in Baghdad in 1396. Eight of the nine marvellously executed miniatures in the manuscript are thought to be by the great Jalairid master, Junaid, whose signature is to be found on one of them, for the first time in painting from the Muslim world.*

Above *Pastoral border in the* Diwan *(collected poetry) of Sultan Ahmad, Baghdad c. 1405. This enchanting work gives us a sense of rural life some six centuries ago.*

By 1357 he had come out on top and ruled the rich central areas of Iran, including the key cities of Shiraz, Yazd, Kirman and Isfahan.

Mubariz al-Din was now the most powerful ruler in Iran. He did the natural thing and made a bid to unite his conquests in the south with the old Il Khanid heartlands in the north. He succeeded in capturing Tabriz from the governor who had been placed there by the Khan of the Golden Horde. But his position was not secure and he soon found that he had to retreat in the face of forces from Jalairid Baghdad.

This failure may not have combined well with the unpopularity of his rule in Shiraz. His harsh and intolerant ways had made life in that highly cultivated city intolerable. 'I often saw culprits brought before Muhammad while he was reading the Quran,' declared his constant companion Mawlana Said Lutfullah, 'he used to stop reading, kill them with this own hands, and then resume his pious occupation.' Hafiz, Iran's greatest

CLOTHING BUILDINGS IN CERAMIC TILES

A feature of the Muzaffarid period in central Iran was the move to clothe buildings in coloured tiles. The tomb of Oljaitu at Sultaniya (1307–13) had tiles on just part of the building (see box p. 32). But by the time of the congregational mosques of Yazd, begun in 1325, and of Kirman, c. 1350, surfaces had come to be covered in tile mosaic, featuring calligraphy and complex geometric, floral and vegetal designs in several colours including white. It was in this century that the basis of the repertoire of tilework which was to feature on much Iranian public architecture down to the present was established.

Monumental gateway to the Friday Mosque at Yazd. It was built between 1325 and 1334 by Shams al-Din Nizami who had married a daughter of the vizier Rashid al-Din. It is clothed in tiles.

poet who lived in Shiraz under Mubariz al-Din, railed in poem after poem against the regime's tight hold over behaviour:

> Even though the wine is pleasure-granting and the wind scattering petals
> Don't drink wine at the sound of the harp, for the *muhtasib* [the inspector of markets and morals] is impetuous.

Even his sons came to fear him. In 1358 one, Shah-i Shuja, concerned about the favour which his father was showing to his grandson, Yahya, deposed and blinded him.

SHAH-I SHUJA

At dawn, glad tidings reached my ear from the voice of the Unseen World: It's the time of Shah-i Shuja – drink boldly wine.

Hafiz

IN 1358 SHAH-I SHUJA took power in Shiraz. His brothers Arbakuh and Sultan Imad al-Din Ahmad ruled in Kirman, Shah Mahmud in Isfahan, and his nephew, Shah Yahya, in Yazd. Much of the early part of the reign was taken up with competition for power with his kinsmen. By 1375 Shah-i Shuja seemed to have gained the upper hand with the death of Shah Mahmud. He took the opportunity, as his father had done, of trying to unite his lands in south-central Iran with the old Il Khanid lands in the northwest. Despite a successful campaign in Azarbaijan, however, risings at home forced him to retreat. He tried to bolster his position by marrying his son Zain al-Abidin to the sister of the Jalairid ruler of Baghdad. But this did not prevent the Jalairids from advancing into his territories in northwest Iran and eventually capturing Sultaniya. Shah-i Shuja had just returned from an unsuccessful campaign against Shah Mansur, his ambitious nephew, when he died in October 1384 aged 53.

Shah-i Shuja was a cultivated man who brought an atmosphere of freedom and tolerance to Shiraz. He patronized scholars, in particular Saiyid Sharif al-Jurjani, one of the most important scholars on key texts in the history of Islamic education. A moderate poet, he was the patron and friend of Hafiz, the greatest poet of the Iranian middle ages. When

SHAH-I SHUJA

Born	*Sons*
c. 1331	Sultan Uwais, Zain
Father	al-Abidin, Sultan
Mubariz al-Din	Shibli, Muizz al-din
Muhammad	Jahangir
Mother	*Died*
?	9 October 1384
Wife	
?	

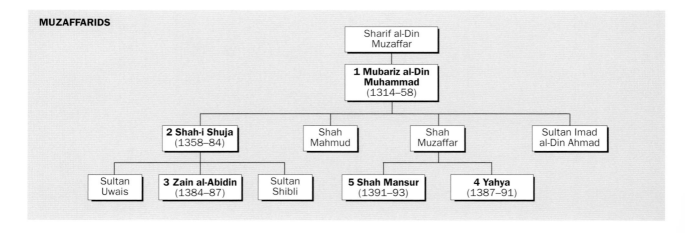

MUZAFFARIDS

- Sharif al-Din Muzaffar
  - **1 Mubariz al-Din Muhammad** (1314–58)
    - **2 Shah-i Shuja** (1358–84)
      - Sultan Uwais
      - **3 Zain al-Abidin** (1384–87)
      - Sultan Shibli
    - Shah Mahmud
    - Shah Muzaffar
      - **5 Shah Mansur** (1391–93)
      - **4 Yahya** (1387–91)
    - Sultan Imad al-Din Ahmad

HAFIZ

Shams al-Din, the poet, was born in Shiraz c. 1325–26 and died c. 1390. For most of his life he moved in the court circle of the Muzaffarids. Among his feats as a boy was the memorization of the Quran, giving him the right to use the title 'Hafiz', which became his pen name. As a young man he is said to have been both a baker and a manuscript copyist, but by the age of 30 he had clearly established himself as a panegyrist. He experienced both the upheavals consequent on the decline of Il Khanid power and the stability and prosperity which came with Muzaffarid rule, in particular the long reign of Shah-i Shuja. These were years which saw his maturity as a poet and his reputation spread both into the Arab lands and into India. Hafiz was the supreme exponent of the *ghazal* or love poem. His fame rests on his collected poems, his *Diwan*, which it is said he put together 20 years before his death. Serious interest was sustained in his work less in Iran than in the Ottoman world and India, whence in the late 18th century it travelled to Europe, inspiring Goethe's *West-östlicher Diwan*, before being taken up again in earnest once more in Iran in the 20th century.

A pencil drawing of Hafiz from the remarkable collection of miniatures and manuscripts made by Richard Johnson (1753–1807) in India. Its presence in the collection indicates the continuing Indian interest in Hafiz. Johnson himself planned to publish an edition of the Diwan *of Hafiz.*

Shah-i Shuja was away fighting his brother Shah Mahmud from 1363 to 1366, Hafiz wrote poems that complained of separation from the 'Friend'. This said, as time went on Shah-i Shuja may have become estranged from Hafiz on the grounds of the weak Islamic character of his poetry. But, if Shah-i Shuja was cultivated, he was also ruthless; for rebellion he put out the eyes of his son Sultan Shibli, as well as those of his father.

THE LAST MUZAFFARIDS 1384–93

SHAH-I SHUJA APPOINTED **Zain al-Abidin** as his successor in Shiraz; he did not enjoy his inheritance for long. For the next nine years his kinsmen fought amongst themselves for the Muzaffarid territories. **Shah Mansur** eventually gained the upper hand, devastating the territories of his rivals, and blinding Zain al-Abidin. These rivalries amongst petty princes were but an enfeebling interlude before the political landscape was transformed by the invasion of Timur at the head of the Chaghatai Turks. He invaded first in 1387, slaughtering the population of Isfahan, plundering Shiraz and receiving homage from the Muzaffarid princes. As was his practice, Timur departed, designating a local prince, in this case Shah-i Shuja's nephew, **Yahya**, as his representative. In 1392 he invaded again. Shah Mansur played the lead role in resisting the Chaghatai army, fighting with great personal courage. Defeated, he was captured while trying to fight his way through to Shiraz and beheaded. Recognizing the situation as hopeless, all the remaining Muzaffarid princes, 17 of them, submitted to Timur. At first they were received with honour. But then, in May 1393, they were all executed. Only Zain al-Abidin and Sultan Shibli, both blind, were spared, to be sent to Samarqand, where they lived out their days in comfort under the clemency of Timur.

THE TIMURIDS
1370–1506

Timur
1370–1405

In 1941 Timur's grave was opened by scientists of the Soviet Archaeological Commission. M. M. Gerasimov reconstructed Timur's head from his skull. He also noted that Timur had a red moustache and three arrow wounds, one of which had fused the knee joint as well as further ones to an elbow and a hand.

TIMUR	
Born	Agha, Sultan Ara
8 April 1336	Agha Nukuz, Nuruz
Father	Agha, plus 26
Amir Taraghai	concubines
Mother	*Sons*
Takina Khatun	Jahangir,
Wives	Miranshah, Umar
Turmush Agha, Uljai	Shaikh, Shah Rukh
Tarkan Agha, Sarai	*Daughters*
Mulk Khanim, Ulus	Aka Biki, Sultan
Agha, Islam Agha,	Bakht Agha, Saadat
Dil Shad Agha,	Sultan, Qutlugh
Tuman Agha, Tukal	Sultan Agha
Khanum, Tughdi	*Enthroned*
Beg, Dawlat Tarkan	9 April 1370
Agha, Burhan Agha,	*Died*
Sultan Agha,	18 February 1405
Janibeg Agha,	*Buried*
Munduz Agha,	Gur-i Amir,
Chulpan Malik	Samarqand
Agha, Bakht Sultan	

TIMUR

Tall and of lofty stature, big in brow and head ... mighty in strength and courage, wonderful in nature, white in colour, mixed with red, but not dark, stout of limb with broad shoulders, thick fingers, long legs, perfect build, long beard, dry hands, lame on the side with eyes like candles, without brilliance, powerful in voice, he did not fear death.... He did not love jest and falsehood; wit and sport please him not; truth, though troublesome to him, pleases him; he was not sad in adversity or joyful in prosperity.

Ahmad ibn Arabshah

WHILE FROM THE 1330s power in the former Il Khanid dominions was dissipated into petty and squabbling lordships, a new force rose from the remains of Mongol might in Transoxania. This was Timur, whose name in Turkish meant iron, and which through the Persian, Timur-i Lang (Timur the Lame), came into English as Tamerlane. An imposing man, one of his legs was rigid and shorter than the other as a result of an arrow wound he received in 1364. Timur was illiterate, but highly intelligent, loving disputations with scholars. He spoke both Persian and Turkish,

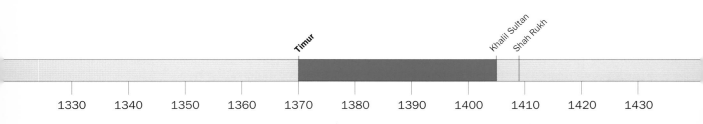

Timur   Khalil Sultan   Shah Rukh

| 1330 | 1340 | 1350 | 1360 | 1370 | 1380 | 1390 | 1400 | 1410 | 1420 | 1430 |

Above Siege of a city from the *Zafarnama* of Sharaf al-Din Yazdi, the official historian of Timur's reign. There are at least 30 known 15th-century copies of the *Zafarnama*, indicating its role in disseminating the record of Timurid power.

Below A battle between Timur and Toqtamish Khan in 1391, from a *Zafarnama* of Sharaf al-Din Yazdi. Note the figure of Timur leading his troops in the upper half of the picture; the role of Timur is emphasized throughout the illustrations to the manuscript.

having a formidable memory for what was read to him; he also had a great appetite for food, drink and women. In matters of the world he was politically gifted and utterly ruthless, and, as one might expect from a keen chess player, he was a brilliant military strategist. Personally brave, he was an awe-inspiring leader, devoted to his troops.

Timur was born on 8 April 1336, in Kish, the modern Shahr-i Sabz, to the south of Samarqand. His family were from the Barlas tribe of the Chaghatai confederation which dominated Transoxania. Turkified Mongols, they were part of the Chaghatai military elite. Timur's father, Amir Taraghai, and his uncle, Hajji Barlas, were joint leaders of the tribe. As a young man Timur had the usual training of his class in horsemanship, archery and surviving hardship. It is said he went in for cattle rustling.

The first step for an ambitious young nomad was to become leader of his tribe. By his early 20s he had taken a step in this direction by gathering a personal following of 300 horsemen. Then, in 1360, he took advantage of a power struggle between his uncle and the Khan of the Chaghatai confederation, which led to an invasion of their lands and the flight of the Hajji, to make a bid for the leadership. In 1361, the Chaghatai Khan recognized his leadership.

The following seven years saw Timur at times allying with the other leading Chaghatai tribal leader, Amir Husain, and at times competing with him for the leadership of the confederation. Much time was spent seeking allies outside Transoxania in Khiva, Khurasan and Badakshan. Occasionally, Timur found himself desperate, his followers having fled and his horse shot from under him. In 1368, however, when Amir Husain set out to assert full sovereignty over the Chaghatai confederation and fortified the city of Balkh as his capital, Timur had his opportunity. Husain's actions brought most of the Chaghatai chiefs to Timur's side. He besieged Balkh, captured Husain, whom he had killed, and, taking command of Husain's troops, emerged as the head of the Chaghatai confederation.

Timur immediately set about strengthening and legitimizing his position. He took four of Husain's wives, but shared the remainder amongst his tribal leaders. He kept for himself the modest title of Amir, leader, but in other ways boosted his prestige by association with the family of Chingiz Khan. One descendant of Chingiz was made into a puppet Khan. One of the four wives he took over from Husain was another descendant, and so he adopted the title of *kuragan*, or son-in-law. He began to make Samarqand, close to the former centre of Chaghatai government, into his royal capital. On 9 April 1370, his government was formally endorsed by the chiefs of the Chaghatai confederation.

Timur's relentless campaigns

Timur spent most of the following 35 years waging war outside Transoxania. In his early campaigns he concentrated on areas dominated by tribal nomads to the north. Between 1370 and 1372 he campaigned against the Eastern Chaghatai Khans who ruled the areas between the Tien Shan

THE INVASION OF INDIA

'The intelligence of these proceedings [his grandson Pir Muhammad's campaigns in Hindustan] being carried to Timur was the cause of his going to Hindustan. Just as that time he had resolved to assemble forces from all his dominions, and to march against China, with the intent of destroying the idol temples, and of raising mosques in their places. He had previously heard that the standards of the faith of Islam had been raised in Delhi and other places, and that its profession of faith was impressed upon the coins, but that the country in general was polluted by the inhabitants being infidels and idolaters. Impelled by the desire of waging a religious war, he resolved to march against Multan and Delhi. He consulted with his nobles and chiefs, and they concurred in the propriety of making the invasion.'

Yazdi

mountains and Lake Balkash. Between 1372 and 1374 he concentrated on the rulers of Khwarazm, who dominated the Farghana valley, Ili and Talas regions. From 1375 to 1377 he allied with Toqtamish, who was descended from Chingiz Khan through his son Jochi, in his attempts to become Khan of the Golden Horde in the lands north of the Aral Sea.

From 1381 Timur concentrated more on settled areas with substantial cities. In the following three years he conquered Khurasan and eastern Iran taking, amongst other cities, Herat and Qandahar. From 1384 to 1388, he campaigned in western Iran and the Caucasus, driving his former protégé, Toqtamish, now Khan of the Golden Horde, out of Azarbaijan and ravaging the Christian kingdom of Georgia for the first of five times. Then, in 1391–92, clearly seeing Toqtamish as his greatest rival, he launched a major campaign against the Golden Horde, ending with victory at Kunduzcha on the Volga river, some 1,000 km (620 miles) east of Moscow, although Toqtamish lived to fight another day.

From 1392 Timur embarked on his five-year campaign in which he destroyed the Muzaffarids, captured Jalairid Baghdad and advanced through the Caucasus, where he defeated Toqtamish at the river Terek and then chased him almost to Moscow – an outcome which led to the Khan being overthrown and the end of the threat from the Golden Horde. In 1398–99 Timur swept into India, defeating Sultan Mahmud Shah, and sacking Delhi (see p. 102). Then, from 1399, with an energy which astonished his contemporaries, and which was extraordinary for a man in his 60s, Timur launched his so-called seven-year campaign. He retook Baghdad, conquered Syria from the Mamluks and defeated outside Ankara the Ottoman Sultan, Bayazid, who subsequently committed

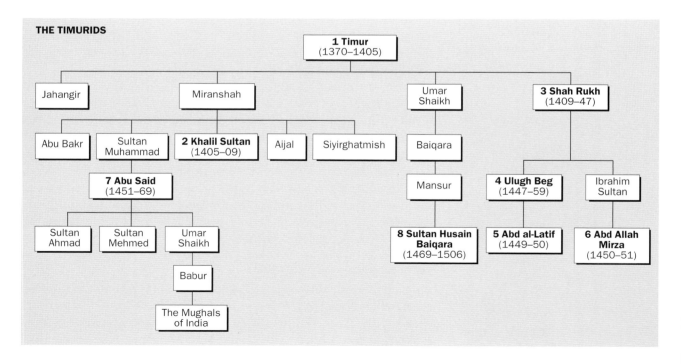

THE TIMURIDS

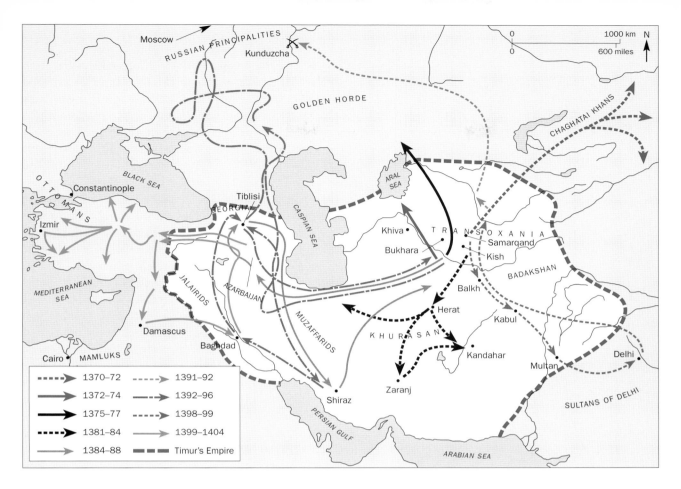

Map of Timur's campaigns.

suicide in captivity. Timur ravaged the Christian-held coast of the Aegean and then returned to Transoxania, dying on 18 February 1405 as he prepared an expedition to China.

Power, prestige and politics

What was the purpose of this career of ceaseless conquest? Certainly, there was the thought of emulating the achievements of Chingiz Khan. The control of potential rivals was arguably the reasoning behind Timur's campaigns against Khwarazm and the Eastern Chaghatais, the elimination of a major military threat the cause of his campaigns against Toqtamish, the assertion of power the driving force of his campaign against the Ottomans, and war against the infidel his declared purpose in his campaign in India. But behind much of his campaigning, and particularly that involving settled areas and great cities, were powerful economic reasons. Transoxania was a poor region. Iran, by comparison, despite the breakdown of order following the end of Il Khanid rule, was wealthy. Timur set out to transfer all that had value to build up Transoxania in general and his capital city of Samarqand in particular. This meant not just treasure but also movable property, from animals to consumables. It also meant people: scholars, artisans, craftsmen and vast numbers of prisoners, all of whom would contribute to Timur's projects.

Timur celebrates his conquest of Delhi in December 1398, from the *Zafarnama* of Sharaf al-Din Yazdi. Just before the battle for the city he had ordered 100,000 Hindu prisoners to be put to the sword.

Timur's economic purpose is underlined by the disciplined and systematic way in which he usually approached cities. One of the rewards of a soldier's life was the sacking of a city, with the opportunities for rape and plunder which came with it. Timur's armies were forbidden to act thus, unless given explicit permission; it reduced the return to his treasury. On approaching a city it would be asked to capitulate and seek immunity from plunder by paying a ransom. The city might then be sealed and tax collectors sent in accompanied by torturers to levy tribute and to force citizens to reveal the economic circumstances of their fellows. All the goods and valuables realized were sent to collection centres, registered and dispatched to Transoxania.

Atrocities and terror played an important part in winning compliance. At the slightest sign of resistance Timur ordered the slaughter of the whole population, which would be accompanied by the rape of women, boys and girls. In 1383, after citizens of Herat had risen against his tax collectors, Timur revived the Mongol custom of erecting towers of skulls outside a city's gates. Many other cities suffered thus. At Isfahan in 1388, after his tax collectors were attacked, Timur's army cut off 70,000 heads. One historian, who walked halfway round the city walls, noted 28 towers of 1,500 skulls each.

Mass slaughter was also used for reasons of security. Just before he fought Mahmud Shah outside Delhi, Timur became worried that the 100,000 prisoners he had taken might endanger the safety of his troops; he ordered that they all be slaughtered. But there were many occasions when Timur seemed to enjoy slaughter for its own sake, and particularly when it involved infidels. In 1386 he dealt with defeated Luristanis, who lived on the borders of Iran and Iraq, by having them pushed over cliffs. In 1387 he did the same to the Armenian Christians of Van. In 1400, when the inhabitants of the Anatolian town of Sivas, which he was besieging, sent out a choir of children singing to win him over, he had them ridden down. After he had captured the city, he ordered that the Christian regiments serving with the Ottomans should be buried alive. 'In a short space of time', he said of an incident on his Indian campaign, 'all the people in the fort were put to the sword, and in the course of one hour the heads of ten thousand infidels were cut off. The sword of Islam was washed in the blood of the infidels....'

Timur used atrocities where he found resistance, but even he set limits. He made a point of sparing, indeed often honouring, the religious classes – saiyids (descendants of the Prophet), qadis (judges) and ulama (scholars). He also spared the urban aristocracy, many of whom were traders, and their servants. Generally, he strove to improve the conditions for trade, and after a welter of destruction was capable of sending forces to rebuild cities and restore agriculture. He knew that the long-term health of Transoxania depended on the continuing wealth of the lands through which his armies marched.

There was, however, another reason for Timur's ceaseless career of conquest. This lay in the measures he had taken to consolidate his sovereignty over the Chaghatai confederation. So that no one in future could rise to power, as he had done, on the basis of tribal loyalties and networks, he transformed the workings of the confederation. In the place of the tribal aristocracy he proposed an elite dependent on him, made up of his personal following and family members. Tribal manpower was transferred to the leadership of this elite. All advancement was dependent on him. Once created, this elite needed to be kept busy and rewarded. His campaigns created continuous occupation, and Timur used a range of techniques designed to prevent the formation of independent power centres. His campaigns also brought the rewards of wealth and manpower, which raised this elite above the old tribal aristocracy. Timur was always actively in command of the Chaghatai confederation.

Timur's army

Timur led an immensely powerful military machine which, during his 1391–92 campaign against Toqtamish, was said to number 200,000 men. At its heart were Chaghatai nomadic horse archers. But, as time went on, it became a great multi-cultural force embracing Muslims, Christians, Shamanists, Turks, Tajiks, Arabs, Georgians and Indians. It was highly organized and, after the Mongol pattern, broken down into units of 1,000, 100 and 10. So, too, were the support troops, such as engineers and infantry. Orders were given by flag and drumbeat; Europeans were very impressed by the unquestioning obedience displayed. Reviews were held on a regular basis to check military skills and preparedness. At one in 1391, during the campaign against Toqtamish, elite troops were armoured from head to foot, carried a spear, sword, dagger, mace, javelin and shield, and rode caparisoned horses. At another in Anatolia in 1402 units were uniformed in different colours with matching equipment and banners. Like all good generals, Timur took great care of his men. They had regular pay and pensions. Loyalty was generously repaid, and there were special rewards, including exemption from tax, for those who distinguished themselves in battle. These special rewards could be passed on to widows or down to descendants. Timur was in no doubt about the importance of respecting and rewarding his men: 'to encourage my officers and my soldiers,' he told his successors in his *Institutions*, 'I have not hoarded gold or jewels for myself. I admit my men to my table and in return they give me their lives in battle.'

This miniature of a warrior on Mount Damavand, the conical mountain in the Alburz range which towers above Tehran, gives a good sense of the weapons and armour used by Timur's army. It comes from the *Collection of Epics* (1397), executed in Shiraz while Timur controlled the city.

Among the many objects commissioned for the Yasawi shrine was this massive bronze basin. It leaves us in no doubt about the connection Timur wished to build between himself and the cult which surrounded the Sufi saint. Its inscription declares: 'The most glorious Amir, the Master of the necks of nations, the one under the especial care of the King, the Merciful, Amir Timur Gurgan [Kuragan], may he be exalted, … ordered the construction of this vessel for drinking on account of the mausoleum of the Shaikh al-Islam, Sultan of Shaikhs in the world, Shaikh Ahmad Yasawi, may God sanctify his dear Soul, in the 20th of Shawwal year 801 [25 June 1399].'

Opposite above After his pilgrimage in 1397, Timur ordered the construction of this massive complex of buildings over the tomb of Shaikh Ahmad Yasawi, north of Tashkent, with its impressive façade and magnificent central dome, whose height of 38 m (126 ft) was Timur's decision.

Religion and the arts

Timur's actions often made him a bad Muslim. He killed many of his co-religionists, and sent more into slavery. He desecrated mosques and killed prayer leaders. He followed Mongol customary law as well as Islamic religious law, and was a conspicuous user of alcohol. Yet, his actions suggest faith as well as *realpolitik*. The reliable historian, Sharaf al-Din Yazdi, ascribes to him a religious motive, amongst others, for his Indian campaign. Moreover, during the campaign he depicts Timur as often trying to save Muslim lives while taking those of Hindus. He commissioned a number of mosques and madrasas (religious seminaries), patronized many ulama, and was particularly interested in Sufis, Muslim mystics. He was a great supporter of the shrine of the Sufi saint, Shaikh Ahmad Yasawi, north of Tashkent, to which he made a pilgrimage in 1397. Timur's own spiritual adviser, Mir Saiyid Baraka, was buried at his feet.

Timur projected himself as a ruler of unparalleled power and prestige. Wall paintings in his palaces showed 'his likeness, now smiling, now austere', his many victories and visits from kings from all directions to pay him tribute. Court ceremonies were designed, as the Spanish ambassador discovered on a visit in 1403, to impose his power upon the visitor. Always interested in history, he had a daily record of his achievements kept which formed the basis of histories designed to enhance the memory of his reign. Samarqand was built as a great capital city, its suburbs named after the capital cities of the Islamic world – many of which he had sacked. His buildings were colossal: a Friday Mosque at Samarqand with an inner courtyard 60 x 90 m (197 x 295 ft), a palace at Kish with a portal 49 m (160 ft) high, a huge bazaar and a citadel, all adorned and furnished by the hundreds of craftsmen he had brought to Transoxania. He also encouraged his womenfolk to build, so his favourite wife, Sarai Mulk Khanim, built a madrasa opposite his Friday Mosque, and his wives and sister built mausolea in the Shah-i Zinda funerary complex.

The death of Timur

Timur's last days went thus. He left Samarqand for China on 27 November 1404. Weather conditions, however, were very severe and by mid-January 1405 he had only reached Utrar some 400 km (250 miles) from Samarqand. Troops and animals had succumbed to the extreme cold; Timur himself was suffering badly. When his courtiers suggested a feast to keep people's spirits up, he agreed. The feast lasted three days, during which Timur drank much alcohol but ate nothing. Afflicted by fever and stomach trouble, he eventually drank himself senseless. When he came round, he said he was about to die. He declared his last will and testament to the nobles and princes around him, making Pir Muhammad, his grandson, his successor on 'the throne of Samarqand', and asking those present to swear to support his decision.

In 1404 Timur had built the Gur-i Amir at Samarqand, a magnificent tomb to commemorate his grandson, Muhammad Sultan, who died from

Below Jade cenotaph which Ulugh Beg had placed over Timur's grave in the Gur-i Amir sometime after 1425. Its inscription traces Timur's ancestry to the mythical Mongol queen Alanqoa, whose children, including Chingiz Khan, were conceived by divine light, which also illuminated their descendants (for Mughal development of this idea see pp. 7 and 121).

wounds received in the battle of Ankara. No one knows if he also intended it for himself, but five days after his death his body was laid there to rest. Above it a cenotaph of jade was eventually placed on which his grandson, Ulugh Beg, had inscribed a record of Timur's descent, both from the mystical Mongol queen, Alanqoa, who also figured in the ancestry of Chingiz Khan, and from Ali, cousin and son-in-law of the Prophet. A month later the formal mourning ceremonies took place, with the whole population of Samarqand wearing black. Alms were distributed, the Quran was read, and animals sacrificed. Then Timur's own drum was brought into the tomb with weeping, 'the sounds of its beats mingled with the cries of mourning. Its skin was then slashed into ribbons so that it might serve no other master.'

Timur was the last great nomad conqueror, who in his own lifetime made the transition from nomadic to settled status. Gunpowder and firearms were soon to put an end to the dominance of the nomadic horse archer. His impact was great. His destruction of the military might of the Golden Horde helped to free Russia from the Mongol yoke. His defeat of Mahmud Shah administered the death blow to the Delhi Sultanate as a major power in India. His defeat of Bayazid allowed Constantinople an extra 50 years of life as the capital of the Byzantine empire. By transporting large quantities of wealth, craftsmen and scholars to Samarqand he made Transoxania and Khurasan for a century the focus of one of the highest expressions of Perso-Islamic culture, which was to influence to a greater or lesser extent the gunpowder empires which flourished from the 16th century onwards: those of the Shaibanid Uzbegs in Transoxania and Khurasan, the Ottomans, the Safavids and the Mughals. To this day his name bears with it the memory of power and ferocity.

SAMARQAND

From the moment that Timur was acknowledged chief of the Chaghatai confederation he began to adorn his capital of Samarqand. Early buildings were put up by his wives and sisters in the Shah-i Zinda (Living King) funerary complex, named after the Prophet's cousin, Quthan ibn Abbas, who brought Islam to Samarqand in 676. He was buried in a shrine at one end of a passage on either side of which stood mausolea, including that of Shad-i Mulk, built by Timur's sister Turkan Aqa for her daughter in 1371–72, and that of Shirin Bika Aqa, another sister, in 1385–86.

Remarkable craftmanship in ceramic tiles, the work of artisans in large part from Iran, is a feature of these mausolea, as it is of many buildings of Timur's Samarqand. A second feature is sheer size. Timur's Friday Mosque, begun in May 1399, was larger than any other in Iran or Transoxania. Indian craftsmen, whom Timur had made a point of sparing the slaughter of his Delhi campaign, were involved in the construction, as were others from Iran and Azerbaijan. One innovation that came with size was the huge entrance gateways of Timur's buildings. In the case of his Friday Mosque, the Spanish Ambassador tells us how Timur found the first version too low, had it knocked down, and personally supervised its rebuilding to its eventual height of 41 m (134 ft). Another innovation was the tiled and ribbed dome. This can be seen to magnificent effect on top of the elongated drum, rising from an octagonal base, which forms Timur's Gur-i Amir

mausoleum, reaching 34 m (111 ft) high. The proportions of the internal chamber are assisted by the use of an internal dome 22 m (72 ft) high. Beneath this lies Timur's jade cenotaph surrounded by seven marble ones of his descendants.

Russian scholars have established that these and other Timurid buildings were designed according to a system of proportions, the plans being laid out on a grid using modules. At this time Samarqand was the leading centre in the world in the exact sciences. It was here that the great mathematician Jamshid Giyath al-Din al-Kashi (d. 1429) calculated the value of pi to unprecedented levels of accuracy.

Left *Part of the Shah-i Zinda funerary complex. It is built around the supposed tomb of Quthan ibn Abbas, a cousin of the Prophet Muhammad. Many of Timur's wives and sisters built tombs there clothed in exquisite tilework.*

Above *The Gur-i Amir, the majestic mausoleum, with a ribbed double dome covered in turquoise tiles, in which Timur and his descendants were buried.*

Opposite left *'Building the Mosque of Samarqand', from the Zafarnama made for Husain Baiqara, Herat.*

Right *Part of the entrance and dome of
Timur's Friday Mosque at Samarqand,
also known as the Bibi Khanum Mosque.
Its massive scale is evident.*

Khalil Sultan
1405–09

Shah Rukh
1409–47

KHALIL SULTAN	
Born	Muhammad Baqir,
c. 1384	Ali
Father	*Sons*
Miranshah	Kichik Agha,
Mother	Shirin Beg Agha,
Minglijak Khatun	Sultan Badi al-Mulk
(concubine)	*Enthroned*
Wives	Seized power in
Jahan Sultan Biki,	1405
Shad Malik Agha,	*Died*
name unknown,	1411
tuqmaq (female	*Buried*
domestic slave)	Ray (Tehran)
Sons	
Burgul, Muhammad	
Bahadur,	

KHALIL SULTAN

It cannot be doubted that Khalil Sultan holds men in his power by clemency and liberality, for though in strength he is lacking and profits little, yet he gains stronger men by goodness of heart and profusion of wealth; but wealth easily vanishes and fails.

Ahmad ibn Arabshah

AFTER TIMUR DIED, THE EXTENT to which the governance of his vast empire had depended on his authority quickly became clear. The princes ignored the arrangements he had made for the succession, pressing forward their own claims and the empire broke up into separate principalities. In 1407 Pir Muhammad, the designated successor, was killed by one of his amirs. By this time there were two key players: Shah Rukh (b. 1377), Timur's fourth son and the governor of Khurasan, and Khalil Sultan (b. 1384), son of Timur's third son, Miranshah. Khalil Sultan had done well in Timur's Indian campaign, after which he had been made governor of Farghana. As soon as Timur died, Khalil Sultan seized Samarqand and set out to use Timur's treasure to buy support. His attempts failed miserably. He permitted his wife, Shad-i Mulk, with whom he was deeply in love, too

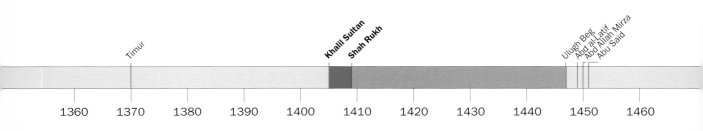

much influence; she cost him much support as she raised the lowly to high positions and showed no respect for Timur's comrades, widows and concubines.

An outbreak of famine fostered popular opposition, and then, on the advice of one of his leading amirs, he made the mistake of leaving Samarqand to claim the rulership of Andijan to the north and to seek military reinforcements. Shah Rukh seized his opportunity. On 13 May 1409, meeting no resistance, he entered Samarqand. Shad-i Mulk fell into his hands. 'They seized Shad-i Mulk', wrote Ibn Arabshah, 'whom they put to shame and abused, prostituting her to her guards.' Khalil Sultan hurried back to rescue his wife. Fortunate not to be killed, he found himself made governor of Ray (Tehran), where in 1411 he died. Shad-i Mulk's response was to kill herself, plunging a dagger into her throat.

SHAH RUKH

... the Shadow of God upon the earth Shahrukh Bahadur Kuragan, he was a king crowned by divine success, propitious fortune and great good luck. He constantly practised justice and had complete compassion toward the elite and common alike. The peace and freedom from want that the peasantry enjoyed during the days of his reign have never been known in any other epoch from the time of Adam until today. His conduct was praiseworthy and he followed the divine law, snatching the ball of propriety from all other sultans.

Dawlatshah

SHAH RUKH IS SAID TO HAVE got his name thus. His father, Timur, was playing chess (the English name is derived from the Persian 'shah', meaning king) and had just castled when the news came that a son had been born. A castle in Persian is *rukh*, hence rook for castle in English. Whatever the truth of this story, there is no doubt that Shah Rukh was a substantially different ruler from his father. Genuinely pious, he saw himself as an Islamic prince, who followed the holy law, rather than as a Khan, who governed by Mongol traditions. It may be for this reason, combined with a certain softness in his character, that Timur had passed him over for the succession, though it may also have been because he was not of the purest lineage – his mother was a slave concubine. When necessary, however, he showed himself to be ruthless.

Politics and diplomacy

Shah Rukh made Herat – his seat as governor of Khurasan and long a centre of Islamic civilization – the capital of the empire. His son, Ulugh Beg, he made governor of Samarqand, where he upheld Mongol traditions. In the early years of his reign Shah Rukh steadily asserted control over Timur's former empire. In 1413 he retook Khwarazm, which had fallen into the hands of the Golden Horde. In the following years he asserted control in central Iran, where he made another son, Ibrahim

THE ARTISTIC PATRONAGE OF GAWHAR SHAD AND HER SON, BAISUNQUR

Shah Rukh's wife Gawhar Shad was not only the most skilful politician of her time, she also left an architectural legacy which more than equalled that of her male relatives. All her buildings were designed by the leading court architect, Qawam al-Din of Shiraz. Today, the one which can still be seen in all its glory is the congregational mosque with two assembly halls that she built for the shrine of Imam Riza (the 8th Imam or leader of the Shia Muslims) at Mashhad. It was marvellously decorated with tiles, and Gawhar Shad's son, Baisunqur, designed the calligraphy which frames the huge portico that

heralds the direction of Mecca. Outside Herat, Gawhar Shad commissioned a major complex including a mosque, a madrasa and a family mausoleum. Much of this was blown up by the British in 1885 because they feared it might provide cover for Russian soldiers. What remains suggests buildings of lavish magnificence, with tilework of the highest class. Baisunqur was the first to be laid to rest in the mausoleum. In 1457 this remarkable woman was murdered by the Timurid Sultan, Abu Said.

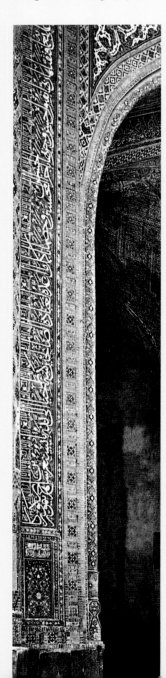

Baisunqur

The leading connoisseur of the book in Shah Rukh's time was his son, Baisunqur. His great opportunity came in 1420 when, aged 23, he was sent to capture Tabriz, till recently the centre of Jalairid artistic patronage, from the Aq Qoyunlu Turkmen. He returned to Herat with manuscripts, calligraphers and painters and set up his library. A report to Baisunqur from Jafar Tabrizi, the director, gives an idea of the work undertaken. There were 22 projects involving 23 artists working on manuscripts, paintings and bindings, as well as tents, buildings and garden design. Of the 20 or so manuscripts associated with Baisunqur, seven are dedicated to him, suggesting his active involvement in their creation. The quality of everything from the paper to the paintings to the bindings bears the mark of the connoisseur.

One of the finest productions with which he was involved was a *Shahnama* (the great Persian epic by Firdawsi).

Jafar Tabrizi, who illustrated the work, dedicates it thus: 'I adorn[ed] the beauties and rarities of these verses and arranged the pearls and jewels of these sentiments for the library of the most mighty Sultan … Baisunqur … may God perpetuate his power.' The scene 'Mourning for Rustam' illustrates the quality of Jafar's work. 'Alike in talent and in the encouragement of talent,' the historian Dawlatshah wrote of Baisunqur, 'he was famous through the world. Calligraphy and poetry were highly esteemed in his time, and scholars and men of talent, attracted by his renown, flocked from all regions and quarters to enter his service….' Unfortunately, Baisunqur's sensual appetites were not restricted to the arts. He was addicted to drink and died aged 36.

Above *Baisunqur seated in a garden, from a* Kalila wa Dimna *of Nizam al-Din Abul Maali Nasr Allah, dated Herat, October 1429. The number of flasks on the table seems fitting for a man addicted to alcohol.*

Left *Mourning for Rustam, from the* Shahnama *commissioned by Baisunqur, Herat 1430. The prince was personally involved in the creation of this manuscript.*

Sultan, governor of eastern Iran and Khuzistan (southern Iraq). Then in Azarbaijan and Mesopotamia he came up against the Turkmen tribesmen of the Qara Qoyunlu (see box p. 64). In 1420 he took Azarbaijan, but could not hold it. He tried again in 1429, and then in 1434–35, when he hit upon the solution of making the brother of the Qara Qoyunlu leader governor of Tabriz. For some time the Ottomans and the Sultans of Delhi, Bengal and Malwa in India recognized Timurid suzeraignty.

Most important were the relations Shah Rukh developed with Ming China. No longer did the Timurids see China, as Timur had done, as a prime destination for a major campaign and booty, regarding it instead as a source of trade and artistic stimulation. The Chinese sought horses, military intelligence and, at this stage, information about the world. The Timurids sought silk and porcelain. Embassies travelled both ways. In 1419, for instance, an embassy of 500 left Herat for Beijing with a painter to keep a record of the two-year journey. Good relations lasted only until 1425, but traffic during these years led to a host of Chinese influences being reintroduced into the art of the region. They had been assimilated once before under Mongol rule, when their cultural weight had been primarily Chinese, but now they were given an Islamic purpose.

As his father had done, Shah Rukh shifted his princes from governorship to governorship, as a way of dealing with insubordination and maintaining control. He dealt with rebellion ruthlessly. One particularly difficult prince was Iskandar Sultan, who was moved from a governorship east of Samarqand to Hamadan and then to Shiraz. From there he attacked Isfahan and Kirman, carrying off women and destroying much. After Shah Rukh had defeated him, he had Iskandar Sultan's 'eyes, which were the envy of blackeyed houris ... stripped of the garb of sight, like the eye of a narcissus.' After Prince Muhammad Baisunqur rebelled, he had all the scholars and nobles who supported him executed.

Despite such displays, and the relative longevity of his reign, Shah Rukh is not seen as a man who dominated his court by force of personality. Nor was he blessed with outstanding political skills. His long reign and the stability that came with it was derived in part from growing prosperity fuelled by trade and in large part from gifted, faithful and long-serving administrators – his chief minister held office for 31 years, his commander-in-chief 35 years and his finance minister 43 years. Most significant, however, was his wife Gawhar Shad. Blessed with considerable political skills, she was a greater influence on government than her husband. Working with key officials and her sons, she was the prime source of continuity at the heart of affairs, as well as the central player in struggles for power. In spite of considerable efforts, however, Gawhar Shad was not able to control disputes over the succession which simmered in Shah Rukh's last years. Her attempts to put her favourite grandson, Ala al-Dawla, in prime position only led to violent opposition from his brothers and cousins. On Shah Rukh's death the struggle for power broke out in earnest, with the outcome that the empire broke into smaller states ruled by Timurid princes or by foreign powers.

Religion and the arts

Shah Rukh's piety was expressed in direct action against those who broke the law; he personally supervised the pouring away of wine which was found in the cellars of both his son Muhammad Juki and his grandson Ala al-Dawla. It was expressed in his harsh treatment of popular Islamic sects, which led to one adherent in February 1427 stabbing him in the stomach as he left Friday prayers in Herat. It was expressed most particularly in the nature of his artistic patronage. He built a madrasa and a khanqah (a Sufi hospice) at Herat, and substantially extended the complex of buildings of the city's great saint, Abd Allah Ansari (see p. 73). He told the emperor of China that he had been ordered by God to build a mosque and a madrasa in every district. His family helped the cause. His wife built magnificent structures in Mashhad and Herat. His son, Ulugh Beg, did the same in Samarqand, while other sons, Ibrahim Sultan and Baisunqur, contributed calligraphy to major religious buildings.

This new religious emphasis was also reflected in princely activity in relation to the Quran. At least five Qurans, which Ibrahim Sultan copied himself, survive in Herat. His brother, Ulugh Beg, was said to have memorized the Quran in seven different readings; he also donated a massive Quran stand, which can still be seen in situ, to his father's mosque in Samarqand.

Shah Rukh's reign lay close to a high point in the arts of book production in the Islamic world. Rulers and princes all had a library, a place where books were calligraphed and adorned. They knew the power of books not just as exemplars of princely taste, but more especially as projectors of the dynastic image. Shah Rukh shared his father's obsession with legitimizing and celebrating his dynasty. The books he commissioned illustrated the continuity from Mongol to Timurid rule, bringing up to date the record of Timurid victories by extending the *Zafarnama* of Shami, first commissioned by Timur. They placed the reign of Shah Rukh in the context of Iran's history, and that of the world from the time of Adam. This dynastic obsession was to run in the family down to the Mughal line which ruled India.

A massive Quran stand which was made for Timur's Friday Mosque in Samarqand *c.* 1405–49. It is emblematic of the emphasis of the early Timurids on size to express their might.

Ulugh Beg
1447–49

Abd al-Latif
1449–50

Abd Allah Mirza
1450–51

Abu Said
1451–69

Opposite Ulugh Beg seated on a carpet, Samarqand, *c.* 1400. As well as being a notable mathematician and astronomer, he was also a great builder, adding many buildings to Samarqand.

ULUGH BEG	
Born	*Sons*
1394	Abd al-Latif, Abd al-
Father	Samad, Abd al-
Shah Rukh	Jabbar, Abd Allah,
Mother	Abd al-Rahman, Abd
Gawhar Shad	al-Aziz, Abd al-Malik,
Wives	Abd al-Razzaq
Aka Biki, Sultan	*Daughters*
Badi al-Mulk, Aqi	Habibe Sultan
Sultan Khanika,	Khanzada Begum,
Husan Nigar	Sultan Bakht, Aq
Khanika, Shukr Bi	Bash, Qutluq Tarkan
Khanika, Mihr	Agha, Sultan Badi
Sultan, Dawlat	al-Mulk, Taghay
Bakht Khatun,	Tarkan, Khanzada
Dawlat Sultan	Agha, Aka Begum,
Khatun, Bakhti Bi	Taghay Shah, Rabie
Khatun, Saadat	Sultan Begum
Bakht Khatun,	*Enthroned*
Wultan Malik,	Struggle for power
Sultanum, name	amongst Timurid
unknown (daughter	princes; no
of Abu al-Khair	apparent formal
Khan), Khatan	enthronement
Khatun, name	*Died*
unknown (daughter	1449, executed at
of Aqile Sultan),	the behest of his
Ruqaiya Khatun	son, Abd al-Latif
Arlat (concubine)	*Buried*
	Gur-i Amir,
	Samarqand

ULUGH BEG

His late Highness Ulugh Begh Kuragan was a learned, just, victorious, and high-minded king. He attained an exalted degree in astronomy and was quite adept at understanding poetry. During his reign scientists were given the greatest respect, and in his time the position of the learned reached exalted heights. In geometry he pointed out the subtlest things, and in cosmography he unlocked the secrets of the Almagest. The learned and wise are agreed that in the history of Islam – nay from the time of Alexander to this moment – there has never reigned a king so wise and learned as Ulugh Beg Kuragan.

Dawlatshah

ULUGH BEG HAD BEEN GOVERNOR of Samarqand for 40 years when Shah Rukh died. Arguably, as Shah Rukh's eldest and only surviving son, he had the strongest claim to succeed. In 1448 he had some success in pressing forward his cause. He defeated Gawhar Shad's candidate, Ala al-Dawla, and occupied Mashhad, while his son, Abd al-Latif, took Herat. But Ulugh Beg failed to understand how far, under his father, Herat in particular and Khurasan in general had become the political centre of gravity. He returned to Samarqand, aiming to make it his capital, taking his father's body with him which he placed in the Gur-i Amir. The return

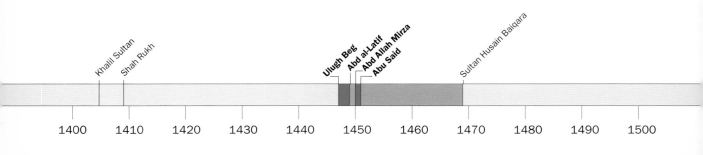

Khalil Sultan | Shah Rukh — Ulugh Beg | Abd al-Latif | Abd Allah Mirza | Abu Said — Sultan Husain Baiqara

1400 1410 1420 1430 1440 1450 1460 1470 1480 1490 1500

ULUGH BEG, ASTRONOMER

Ulugh Beg's most notable achievements were in mathematics and astronomy, in which he led a team of outstanding scholars, including Jamshid Ghiyath al-Din al-Kashi. In decimal fractions and the computation of the value of pi, Ulugh Beg's team produced work which was well ahead of anything known in Europe at the time. For astronomy, Ulugh Beg, who may have been inspired by Nasir al-Din Tusi's observatory at Maragha, which he had seen as a child, built an observatory on a hill outside Samarqand. A circular building three storeys high, it was dominated by a huge mural instrument for measuring the altitude of stars and planets as they crossed the sky. Ulugh Beg and his team composed astronomical tables, the Zij-i Ulugh Beg, which were to replace the earlier tables of Nasir al-Din Tusi. These tables exist in hundreds of copies, indicating how widely they were used; in 1665 they were translated into Latin for European use.

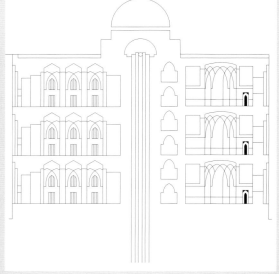

Above *A cross-section of Ulugh Beg's observatory at Samarqand.*

Left *The remains of the meridian transit instrument at Ulugh Beg's observatory of c. 1420, discovered during an excavation in the 20th century.*

Left *A reconstruction of Ulugh Beg's observatory at Samarqand. The development of observatories at Maragha and Samarqand was one of the important achievements of Muslim scientists.*

Below *Amongst the equipment used by Ulugh Beg's astronomers would have been globes like this one, from Iran, 1430–31. They were used for teaching as well as making calculations.*

to Samarqand meant confining his power base to Transoxania. A nephew quickly occupied Khurasan, conquering Herat. Before Ulugh Beg could reoccupy Khurasan, his son, Abd al-Latif, the ruler of Balkh, rebelled against him. Ulugh Beg, it seems, had humiliated his son during his occupation of Herat and then infuriated him by his return to Samarqand. In the war which followed, Ulugh Beg was defeated. Finding himself with the choice of being hunted down like an animal or giving himself up with some dignity, he chose the latter course. His request to make a pilgrimage to Mecca was granted. In his absence, however, his son had him tried and condemned to death. Executioners went in pursuit of the pilgrim and dispatched him.

Ulugh Beg's ultimately fatal preference for Samarqand was of a piece with his ruling style as a prince. He was a strong supporter of Turco-Mongol traditions as opposed to purely Islamic ones. It was he who made the link on his grandfather Timur's cenotaph with the mystical Mongol queen, Alanqoa. He, like his grandfather, issued his decrees in the name of a puppet khan descended from Chingiz Khan. He gave himself the title *kuragan*, as Timur had done, and imposed Mongol taxes on traders and craftsmen in defiance of Islamic law. Under him Samarqand gained a reputation for parties where alcohol and musicians and singers of both sexes were to be found. 'You have destroyed the faith of Muhammad and introduced the customs of infidels', declared the *muhtasib*, or guardian of public morals, as he broke in to one of Ulugh Beg's parties. 'You have won fame through your descent from Saiyids and your learning', Ulugh Beg replied. 'Apparently you also wish to attain martyrdom and therefore utter rude words, but I shall not grant you your wish.'

Ulugh Beg, however, is remembered primarily for his role as a scholar prince. He corresponded with his brother, Baisunqur, about technical matters in poetry. It is fitting that the most significant of his buildings in either Samarqand or Bukhara to survive intact is his madrasa in the former, built between 1417 and 1420, which was a great centre of learning in his time.

ULUGH BEG'S SCIENTIFIC DISPUTATION

Jamshid Ghiyath al-Din al-Kashi, the mathematician, wrote thus to his father about Ulugh Beg's manner of scientific disputation: 'One sees the [royal] presence [Ulugh Beg] exhibiting the extreme of generosity and courtesy. He wants to show the utmost kindness and noble generosity of courtesy to the extent that sometimes in the madrasa between his [royal] presence and one of the students [who is] asking about a problem from any science, there may be so much [mutual] refutation and give and take as cannot be described. This is because he decreed and directed that until a scientific problem penetrates his mind it is not established, and obsequious flattery should not be indulged in, and if sometimes someone accepts blindly he embarrasses him [by saying] you are making us out as ignorant. And for sake of examination of the problem he may [intentionally] insert a mistake into the middle (of the argument). So soon as anyone accepts it he reproaches and shames him.'

A princely couple with attendants, Iran or Central Asia, c. 1425–50. This is a painting on silk, a most luxurious Timurid form, in which the common practice in China was followed.

ABD AL-LATIF	
Born	*Sons*
?	Abd al-Razzaq,
Father	Ahmad, Muhammad
Ulugh Beg	Baqir, Muhammad
Mother	Juki
Ruqaiya Khatun	*Enthroned*
Arlat (concubine)	?
Wives	*Died*
Shah Sultan Agha,	May 1450
name unknown	*Buried*
(daughter of Shah	?
Sultan)	

ABD AL-LATIF

Mirza Abd al-Latif was a ruler known for the delicacy of his nature and sharpness of his mind as well as for his great personal accomplishments. He was inclined to converse with dervishes and hermits, and he sat politely in the assemblies of the shaikhs and the ulama he patronized. However, his temperament was melancholic, he was quick to anger and coarse of speech.

Khwandamir

TWO FURTHER RULERS CAME AND WENT quickly as Timurid princes struggled for the succcession to Timur's empire. Abd al-Latif, who succeeded his father, Ulugh Beg, managed through his pious personal life and the respect he showed to Sufis to win the support of the religious establishment, which his father had not for the most part been able to do. But many of his military commanders could not forget that he had murdered his father (and his brother as well). Within six months he was overthrown.

ABD ALLAH MIRZA	
Born	*Sons*
1432	?
Father	*Enthroned*
Ibrahim Sultan, son	1450, installed as
of Shah Rukh	Sultan by the army
Mother	*Died*
Mihr Sultan Khatun	June 1451,
Wives	executed by Abu
Name unknown	Said
(daughter of Amir	*Buried*
Khudaiquli), name	?
unknown (daughter	
of Ulugh Beg)	

ABD ALLAH MIRZA

Prince Abd Allah b. Ibrahim Sultan b. Shah Rukh Sultan Kuragan was a noble and handsome prince of good character.

Dawlatshah

ABD ALLAH MIRZA, ANOTHER GRANDSON of Shah Rukh, was a supporter of Ulugh Beg and had been imprisoned when he fell. At the overthrow of Abd al-Latif the troops installed him as Sultan, in return for which they received substantial gifts of treasure. Ala al-Dawla, Gawhar Shad's favourite, immediately rose against him, but without success.

Greater danger came from Abu Said, a great-grandson of Timur through Miranshah. His political base was in Bukhara, a centre of Sufis, from whom he derived his support. He had also been imprisoned on Ulugh Beg's death. After the overthrow of Abd al-Latif he was released and proclaimed Sultan. Working with the Uzbeg Khan, Abul Khair, he marched on Samarqand, defeated Abd Allah in June 1451, and had him executed.

ABU SAID

Abu Said was a grandson of Miranshah b. Amir Timur Kuragan. He was a wise and victorious king, magnificent and a good shepherd to his flock. He was also a man of strict and summary justice.

Dawlatshah

IN 1451 ABU SAID WAS ENTHRONED IN HERAT. For most of his reign, up to the winter of 1468–69, he was able to control Khurasan, Mazandaran, western Transoxania and northern Afghanistan. The great empire in Iran and Iraq conquered by Timur 70 years before was lost, however, as the competition amongst the Timurid princes for power there had created the opportunity for the Qara Qoyunlu confederation of Turkmen to invade and take control. The years 1451 to 1458 saw Abu Said competing for control of Khurasan with rival Timurid princes. Their struggles gave Jahan Shah, the Qara Qoyunlu leader, the opportunity to spread his sway further east from his newly won lands in Iran, and in 1458 he invaded Khurasan, taking Herat.

Soon, however, revolts back in the Qara Qoyunlu homelands of Azarbaijan forced Jahan Shah to retreat, but he remained strong enough to resist Abu Said's demand that all former Timurid possessions be returned, recognizing Abu Said's authority only in Khurasan. From now on Abu Said's relations with Jahan Shah improved, each seeing good relations with the other as a means to help them maintain control of their own territories.

In the 1460s Abu Said was dealing with the predatory ambitions of one Timurid prince in Mazandaran, with those of another in Transoxania,

Here again we see Chinese influence in this fur-capped notable, from Iran or Central Asia, *c.* 1425–50, who shows off his finery, which was either made in, or inspired by, China.

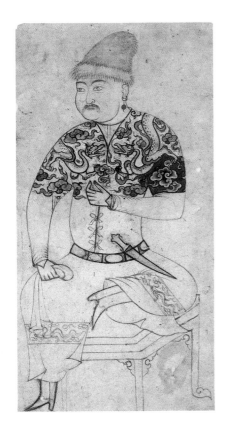

and of a third who was supported by the Uzbegs, as well as with assaults from the Chaghatai Khans in the east. Then, in 1467, he saw an opportunity to reconquer the Timurid lands in Iran. The Qara Qoyunlu were being challenged by a rival Turkmen confederation, the Aq Qoyunlu; Jahan Shah had been killed in a clash with the Aq Qoyunlu leader, Uzun Hasan. In February 1468 Abu Said launched a major expedition to Azarbaijan.

Initially, Abu Said found himself in a relatively strong position. Many Qara Qoyunlu amirs joined him, with, so it is alleged, up to 50,000 troops. He was also joined by Jahan Shah's son and the Shah of Shirwan. These advantages, however, were soon undermined by the problems of enduring a harsh winter in Azarbaijan and attenuated supply lines back into Khurasan which were regularly subject to Aq Qoyunlu raids. Timurid morale declined; allies melted away. The depleted remnant was crushed by the Aq Qoyunlu forces, and Abu Said surrendered. In Febru-

QARA QOYUNLU AND AQ QOYUNLU CONFEDERATIONS

Two tribal Turkmen confederations, the Qara Qoyunlu (Black Sheep) and the Aq Qoyunlu (White Sheep) had great influence over events at this time. The origins of the Qara Qoyunlu are obscure, but the confederation began to merge in the 1330s as the Il Khanid regime collapsed. Their lands were to the northeast of Lake Van in eastern Anatolia and for long they were allies of the Jalairids. In 1410, however, they overthrew the Jalairids and occupied large areas of Azarbaijan, Anatolia and Iraq. Jahan Shah, initially assisted by Shah Rukh, took them to the peak of their power, when momentarily they were able to reach into Khurasan. In 1467, however, he made the mistake of underestimating the Aq Qoyunlu, under Uzun Hasan, and was defeated and killed.

The Aq Qoyunlu confederation was initially based to the west of Lake Van with a focus at Diyarbakr. The expansion of their power began with the reign of Qara Uthman (1403–35). But the Qara Qoyunlu remained the stronger of the two Turkmen confederations, as they demonstrated when they defeated and killed Uthman in 1435. Their significant rise to

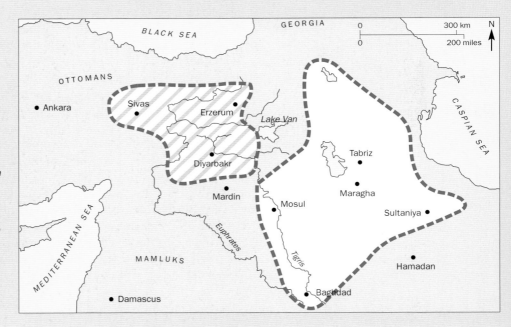

Map showing the approximate extent of the Qara Qoyunlu (right) and and Aq Qoyunlu (left) principalities.

Opposite 'The Demon in Chains', one of a group of 60 paintings, many of which are inscribed as 'the work of Siyah Qalam [Black Pen]'. Opinion is divided as to whether they come from the territories of the Golden Horde, a Mongol studio in Central Asia, early Timurid Samarqand and Herat, or eastern Anatolia, which might associate them with one of the Qoyunlu tribal federations.

ABU SAID	
Born	*Enthroned*
1424	1451 in Herat
Father	*Died*
Sultan Muhammad,	1469, after
son of Miranshah	surrendering to the
Mother	Aq Qoyunlu forces,
Shah Islam	he was handed over
Wives	to a great-grandson
Khanzade Begum,	of Shah Rukh to be
plus 34 others	killed in revenge for
Sons	his murder of
25, including Umar	Gawhar Shad
Shaikh, the father of	*Buried*
the Mughal Emperor	?
Babur	
Daughters	
34	

ary 1469 Uzun Hasan handed Abu Said over to Yadgar Muhammad, great-grandson of Shah Rukh, who killed him in revenge for his murder of Gawhar Shad.

Abu Said had been persuaded to undertake his expedition to the west by the Sufi shaikh, Khwaja Ubaid Allah Ahrar. The shaikh had much influence in Samarqand and Abu Said was his disciple. Indeed, there was a distinctly religious tone to Abu Said's rule; he reinstated the Islamic holy law and abolished the hated Mongol taxes on traders and craftsmen. Nevertheless, he also did what he could to associate himself with Timur, adopting the title *kuragan* and building a palace at Shahr-i Sabz named Aq Sarai as his great-grandfather had done. He was the most successful Timurid prince of his day. His downfall was a coup for Uzun Hasan and his son. They celebrated it by having the story, ending in the beheading of Abu Said, told in mural paintings decorating one of their palaces in Isfahan.

power came after Uzun Hasan seized the leadership in 1452. It was completed by his victory over Jahan Shah in 1467 and crowned by his defeat of Abu Said. Now he controlled the whole of Iran as far east as Kirman. In 1473 defeat at the hands of the Ottomans somewhat undermined his authority and by his death in 1478 he was facing several internal revolts. The confederation then broke into civil war, from which the Safavids emerged in the early 16th century as the rulers of Iran. The Safavid empire was the successor state to the Aq Qoyunlu confederation.

Sultan Husain
Baiqara
1469–1506

SULTAN HUSAIN BAIQARA	
Born	*Daughters*
1438	18
Father	*Enthroned*
Mansur, son of	Prayers said in his
Baiqara, son of	name from March
Umar Shaikh	1469 in Herat
Mother	*Died*
Firuza Begum	4 May 1506
Wives	*Buried*
Bike Sultan Begum,	Herat
plus 11 others	
Sons	
Badi al-Zaman, plus	
20 others	

Opposite Sultan Husain Baiqara, who was admired throughout the eastern Islamic world as a refined example of Timurid cultural prowess. According to the inscription on the painting, it is by Bihzad, but this would seem unlikely.

SULTAN HUSAIN BAIQARA

His eyes were slanted and he had the build of a lion, slender from the waist down. Even when he was old and had a white beard he favoured clothes of beautiful red and green silk.... His arthritis kept him from performing prayers; he did not fast either. He was talkative and good humoured. His character was a bit sharp, as were his words. In some of his dealings he maintained the religious law scrupulously.... He was abstinent for six or seven years when he came to the throne, but he later took to drink.... He was brave and courageous. Many times he took to the sword himself, and he often brandished it in battle. Of Timur Beg's progeny no one is known to have wielded the sword as Sultan Husain Mirza [Baiqara] did.

Babur

SUCH WAS THE ASSESSMENT of the Mughal emperor, Babur. In his youth, when he had been trying to carve out a kingdom for himself, Babur had known Sultan Husain personally, and respected him as the great ruler of his day. Born in 1438, Sultan Husain was descended from Timur on both

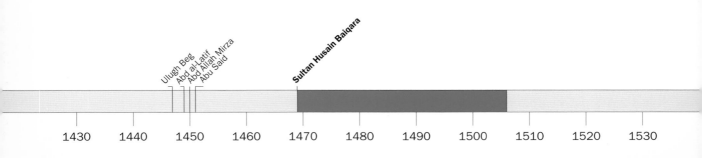

his father's and his mother's side – through Umar Shaikh and Miranshah respectively. In the 1450s, he served the Timurid princes who contested the succession with Abu Said. Then he struck out on his own. Basing himself in Khwarazm, he made frequent raids on Khurasan, earning the hostility of Abu Said. When, on 10 March 1469, the news of Abu Said's death in Azarbaijan reached Herat, he seized his opportunity and occupied the city, having Friday prayers read in his name. His succession, however, did not go uncontested. The Aq Qoyunlu leader, Uzun Hasan, declared Yadgar Muhammad, the executioner of Abu Said, the successor to the Timurid throne. On 15 September 1469, Sultan Husain had the better of Yadgar Muhammad's forces at Chinaram, but failed to secure his position because Uzun Hasan sent further reinforcements. Indeed, in July 1470, as Yadgar Muhammad's forces advanced once more, Sultan Husain found himself in such desperate straits that he was forced to withdraw from Herat. Within six weeks, however, he was able to gather reinforcements, defeat the sons of Abu Said who had entered the fray, and then defeat and execute Yadgar Muhammad. From now on Uzun Hasan and the Aq Qoyunlu played no part in the politics of Khurasan and its surrounding territories, which Sultan Husain ruled from Herat.

A last flowering of Timurid culture

Somewhat uncharacteristically for a Timurid prince, and particularly for one of such renown for his personal prowess in combat, from this moment Sultan Husain gave up warfare to preside over a brilliant last flowering of Timurid culture in Herat. His domestic policies helped to foster the conditions in which such a flowering could take place. He developed close alliances with the religious leadership, building shrines for popular Sufi saints and making sure that the ulama felt properly supported. He was particularly concerned to show his respect for Sufis. His forefathers might have placed their reliance on their armies, but he placed his, as he declared in his 'Apologia', on God. 'If some have been so magnificent and proud in their royal status that they disdained dervishes, He has made me humble and suppliant before that exalted group.' He also ensured that religious endowments, which had been plundered or destroyed in the disturbed times of the 1450s and 1460s, were restored. 'In former times,' he continued in his 'Apologia', because 'the foundations were in ruins, students were aggrieved and teachers deprived; but now, thank God, there are in the capital nearly one hundred educational institutions where religious learning and certain knowledge are to be found.' General prosperity was enhanced as Sultan Husain fostered trade by providing greater facilities and security for merchants, while the transfer of substantial quantities of land from the state to the Timurid elite, although it reduced state resources, gave that elite a stake in the peaceful pursuit of prosperity.

A key figure in Sultan Husain's success was his boyhood friend and foster brother, Mir Ali Shir, an Uighur Turk. They had made a pact when young that, whichever later in life did well, he would help the other. As

THE DEATH OF YADGAR MUHAMMAD

Husain Baiqara with a small detachment of crack troops rode hard for three days to Herat, which was held by Yadgar Muhammad. Hearing that Muhammad and his circle were carousing with women, he went straight to the garden where they were and broke in.

'By chance that night Prince Yadgar Muhammad Mirza was drunk and asleep in his mistress's arms. When the sounds of a commotion reached him, he jumped up and saw that the night had turned into the day of resurrection. Confused, he wanted to conceal himself in a corner of the garden, but a group of His Highness's bodyguards seized him and brought him before the Sultan. The prince's courage had probably failed him altogether, for he was so disconcerted that all he could do was stare at the ground, and, as was his old habit, remain taciturn. His Highness turned to him and said, "Knave! You have disgraced our family! Have you no shame? The Turcomans always obeyed the will of our ancestors. Are you not ashamed to be sat upon the throne of Shah Rukh Sultan by Turcomans...." At once he motioned to the swordsmen of execution to let the prince join his dead clansmen.'

Dawlatshah

MIR ALI SHIR NAWAI'I

Mir Ali Shir, who also bore the pen-name Nawai'i, was not only a major political figure but a multi-talented artist in his own right: he composed music, painted and was an immensely prolific poet. He was also a great patron. 'No one is known ever to have been such a patron and encourager of artists,' declared the emperor Babur, naming musicians and particularly the painters Bihzad and Shah Muzaffar as having been brought forward by him. Contemporaries left accounts of the assemblies he held of artists, poets and scholars in the palaces and gardens of Herat, which also figured in the paintings of Bihzad. Here there would be feasting, drinking of wine, music, singing, the recitation of poetry and the discussion of literary matters. Knowledge and quick wits were crucial to success on these occasions, if the brilliant and deeply learned host was to be impressed.

Mir Ali Shir wrote in both Persian and Turki. His work in the latter was of particular importance. He was responsible for a revival of the use of Turki at Sultan Husain's court, which some have come to regard as an assertion of the cultural and ethnic superiority of the Turks, who formed the military elite, over the Persians, who formed the majority of scholars and bureaucrats. 'It is well known,' Mir Ali Shir wrote in his treatise on the merits of the two languages, 'that Turkish is a more intelligent, more understandable, and more creative language than Persian, while Persian is more refined and profound than Turkish for the purpose of thought and science.' Sultan Husain had no doubt about Mir Ali Shir's achievement. 'He has infused life into the dead body of the Turkish language with his messianic breath,' he wrote in his *Apologia*.

Mir Ali Shir Nawai'i, in a portrait by Mahmud Muzahhib, c. 1500. Nawai'i was a most powerful man at Sultan Husain's court in Herat, a protagonist of the Turki language, and a great patron of musicians, painters and poets.

soon as Sultan Husain gained power, he called Mir Ali Shir to him and appointed him keeper of the Great Seal. In 1472 he was made a member of the Supreme Council. In 1487, after relations became strained with Sultan Husain, he was sent away from Herat to become Governor of Astarabad. Returning 15 months later, he gave up his positions in government, enabling him to develop a special relationship with his Sultan. Enormously wealthy, but without a family and frugal in his personal habits, he made large gifts of money to the Sultan and to high officials. He was a considerable patron of the building projects which improved conditions for the people of Khurasan. According to the chronicler Khwandamir he built 52 caravanserais, 19 cisterns, 20 mosques, 14 bridges, 9 baths, 7 khanqahs and 1 madrasa. This last, which he placed opposite Sultan Husain's madrasa, he called Ikhlasiyya, 'Sincerity'. He died in 1501 as he went out to greet the Sultan who was returning to Herat.

Like Mir Ali Shir, Sultan Husain was renowned for his patronage of the arts. 'Herat', declared the emperor Babur, 'had no equal in the world under Sultan Husain.' The royal library was the home of master painters and calligraphers, and royal patronage insisted on quality over quantity.

BIHZAD, THE MASTER PAINTER

Bihzad was arguably the greatest painter in the Perso-Islamic tradition. Born around 1460 in Herat, he was orphaned at an early age and was brought up by Amin Ruh Allah Mirak, the calligrapher who was head of the royal library. There, in an atmosphere of cultivation, surrounded by men of learning and of talent, and with the benefit of the patronage of great connoisseurs such as Mir Ali Shir and Sultan Husain Baiqara himself, Bihzad learned his skills. So great were those skills that a swiftly executed caricature of a courtier by Bihzad was said to be able to lift the Sultan out of a fit of depression.

Bihzad lived most of his life in Herat, where he stayed in the khanqah of the saint Abd Allah Ansari, living as a bachelor, frugally and only for his art. He stayed on after the Shaibanid occupation in 1506 and benefited from the return of patronage after the Safavid conquest in 1510. In 1514 the Safavid prince, Tahmasp (p. 185), became governor of Herat. Bihzad taught him painting and Tahmasp commissioned work. In 1522 Bihzad was made head of all the painters in the Safavid dominions. In 1529 he moved his studio to Tabriz, where Tahmasp now held court as Shah, and died in 1535.

Bihzad painted portraits, events drawn from life, historical scenes and book illustrations. His work is remarkable for its design, its natural sense of movement, its harmonious use of colour, the quality of its brushwork, its exquisite attention to detail, its humorous moments, and on occasion its spiritual quality – he was a practising Sufi. His illustrations for Sadi's *Bustan*, commissioned by Sultan Baiqara, have been described as 'the greatest achievement in book illustration of all time'. Others might grant this accolade to the *Shahnama* of Shah Tahmasp, the 258 paintings of which he oversaw. Bihzad had great influence, either through his works or through his pupils, on the development of miniature painting under the Shaibanid Uzbegs, the Ottomans, the Safavids and especially the Mughals. He was hugely esteemed by his contemporaries and by later generations. Only Babur sounded a discordant note: 'Bihzad … painted extremely delicately, but he made the faces of beardless people badly by drawing the double chin too big. He drew the faces of bearded people quite well.'

Right and opposite Celebration at the court of Sultan Husain Baiqara. The Sultan himself can be seen in the centre of the painting to the right, attributed to Bihzad.

Below Portrait of Bihzad, c. 1525, which may be by his pupil Mahmud Muzahhib. It is inscribed 'Portrait of Master Bihzad'. He is shown wearing a Safavid turban.

The supreme artist of the age, recognized in his time and by succeeding generations, was Bihzad. 'The late blessed Padishah [Sultan Husain]', recalled the chronicler Wasifi, 'chose Bihzad among the many practitioners of this … art; before him the painters of the seven climes [the whole world] bow their heads in supplication.' The court also supported many poets, including the great mystic Abd al-Rahman Jami. The emperor Babur recalled an exchange between Mir Ali Shir and the poet Bannai, when at a chess party he stretched out his leg and touched the poet's backside. '"What a sad state this is", Ali Shir Beg said in jest, "that in Herat one cannot stretch out a leg without poking a poet in the ass." "Yes", Banna'i retorted, "if you pull your leg back in you will poke another."' Sultan Husain himself wrote poems in both Persian and Turki under the pen name 'Husaini'. 'Many couplets in his diwan [collected work] are not bad,' declared Babur, 'it is however written in the same metre throughout.'

Towards the end of his reign Sultan Husain faced constant challenges from his sons as they competed for the succession. He defeated them all and was utterly ruthless in dealing with their supporters, who were all beheaded. There was, however, a much more serious threat. In 1501, the Uzbegs under Muhammad Shaibani captured Samarqand and began to consolidate their position in Transoxania. Eventually, Sultan Husain set out to address the threat, but died on 4 May 1506 while marching against them. His sons Badi al-Zaman and Muzaffar Husain proved hopeless at facing up to the prospect of an Uzbeg assault. In 1507 Muhammad Shaibani captured Herat and the Timurid regime came to an end. Both sons fled the city, Muzaffar Husain dying soon afterwards and Badi al-Zaman in 1517 in Istanbul.

The shrine of Khwaja Abd Allah Ansari at Gazar Gah, Herat. Abd Allah Ansari, a Sufi saint, died in 1098; his tomb became a major site of sunni Muslim pilgrimage. This building enclosing the tomb, which is decorated with fine tilework, was commissioned by Shah Rukh.

BABUR'S VIEWS ON SULTAN HUSAIN'S WOMEN

The Mughal, Babur, who was to found the Mughal empire, records happy visits to the court of Sultan Husain Baiqara in his youth. A man with high regard for women, to judge by the respect he showed those of his own family, he took a dim view of those in Sultan Husain's family:

'His first wife was Bika Sultan Begum, the daughter of Sanjan Mirza of Merv. Badi al-Zaman Mirza was born of her. Bika Sultan Begum was ill-tempered and Sultan Husain, who suffered greatly from her, came to such grief that in the end he put her away and was delivered. What was he to do? He had every right. An evil woman in a good man's house is hell on earth. May God not afflict any Muslim with this catastrophe. Oh God, may there be no more ill-tempered, irascible women in the world.'

Then, he noted of Khadija Begum, who had been his grandfather, Abu Said's concubine:

'After Sultan Abu Said Mirza's defeat in Iraq she came to Herat, where Sultan Husain fell in love with and married her. From the rank of concubine she advanced to the status of begum, after which she became completely dominant. Muhammad Mumin Mirza was killed through her machinations. It was mostly her doings that caused Sultan Husain Mirza's sons to rebel. She thought herself clever, but she was a brainless chatterbox female.'

THE FIRST 'SLAVE' SULTANS
1206–10

Qutb al-Din Aibak
1206–10

Aram Shah
1210

THE SHAMSIDS
1210–90

Shams al-Din Iltutmish
1210–36

Rukn al-Din Firuz Shah I
1236

Sultan Raziya
1236–40

Muizz al-Din Bahram Shah
1240–42

Ala al-Din
1242–46

Nasir al-Din
1246–66

THE GHIYATHIDS
1266–90

Ghiyath al-Din Balban
1266–87

Kaiqubad
1287–90

THE KHALJIS
1290–1320

Jalal al-Din Firuz
1290–96

Ala al-Din Muhammad
1296–1316

Qutb al-Din Mubarak Shah
1316–20

THE TUGHLUQIDS
1320–1414

Ghiyath al-Din Tughluq
1320–25

Muhammad bin Tughluq
1325–51

Firuz Shah Tughluq
1351–88

The Last Tughluqids
1388–1414

THE SAIYIDS
1414–51

Khidr Khan
1414–21

Mubarak Shah
1421–34

Muhammad bin Farid
1434–45

Ala al-Din
1445–51

THE LODIS
1451–1526

Bahlul Lodi
1451–89

Sikandar Lodi
1489–1517

Ibrahim Lodi
1517–26

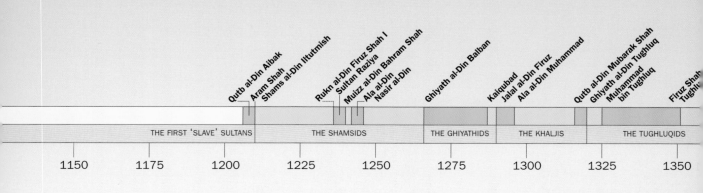

Qutb al-Din Aibak

The Sultans of Delhi
1206–1526

FROM THE EARLY DAYS OF THE ISLAMIC ERA, Muslims had led expeditions into India. Among the most significant were the first, that of Muhammad bin Qasim into Sind in 681, and the most famous, that of Mahmud of Ghazni in 1025/26, when he sacked many great cities and destroyed the great seaport of Somnath in Gujarat, carrying off the gold of its temples. From the 1170s a continuing series of raids and occupations of Indian territory was led by sultans from Ghur in Afghanistan. From 1206 this led to the establishment of the Delhi Sultanate by a man technically enslaved to the Ghurids. This Sultanate, after the first 'slave' rulers, was headed by six dynasties, the Shamsids, Ghiyathids, Khaljis, Tughluqids, Saiyids and Lodis, who steadily spread Muslim rule throughout India. By 1340, under Muhammad bin Tughluq, the Sultanate reached its greatest extent, controlling all but the southernmost part of the subcontinent. From this point, until the reign of the Mughal emperor Akbar, which began in 1556, Muslim political power fragmented. Nevertheless, the Muslim Sultans of Delhi created the framework in which a geopolitical development of enormous importance was to take place – the steady conversion of Indians to Islam, so that now South Asian Muslims represent over one-third of the Muslim peoples of the world.

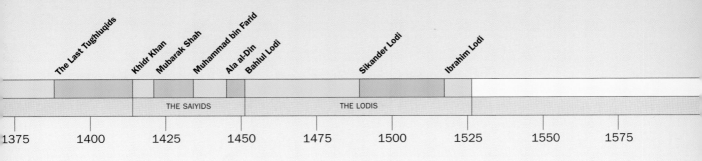

THE FIRST
'SLAVE' SULTANS
1206–10

Qutb al-Din
Aibak
1206–10

Aram Shah
1210

Previous page A coin of Qutb al-Din Aibak. A horseman is depicted on the reverse (right). The heavy cavalry was a major source of Turkish power, and so a horseman was a regular feature on the reverse of lesser value coins of the early Sultanate. On the obverse (left) are Qutb al-Din's titles 'The Supreme Sultan, Muhammad, son of Sam'.

QUTB AL-DIN AIBAK	
Born	*Enthroned*
Slave from Turkestan, raised in the family of the Qadi of Naishapur, Iran	27 June 1206
	Died
Master	1210, from a fall from his horse while playing polo
The Ghurid Sultan, Muizz al-Din	*Buried*
Wife	Anarkali Bazaar, Lahore; tomb restored by Pakistan Prime Minister Bhutto in 1970s
Name unknown (daughter of Taj al-Din Yildiz)	
Son	
Aram Shah	

QUTB AL-DIN AIBAK

Sultan Qutb al-Din was a brave and liberal king. The Almighty had bestowed on him such courage and generosity that in his time there was no king like him from the east to the west. When the Almighty God wishes to exhibit to his people an example of greatness and majesty he endows one of his slaves with the qualities of courage and generosity, and then friends and enemies are influenced by his bounteous generosity and warlike prowess. So this king was generous and brave, and all the regions of Hindustan were filled with friends and cleared of foes. His bounty was continuous and his slaughter was continuous.

Juzjani

IN 1192 THE VICTORY OF THE GHURID SULTAN, Muizz al-Din, over vastly superior Hindu forces at Tarain marked a decisive moment in the establishment of Muslim power in India. From now on Hindu chiefs of the Punjab paid tribute to the Ghurid sultan, and from now on Muslim forces were permanently stationed in India. At the time, Qutb al-Din (called Aibak because of a broken little finger) was a relatively junior officer in

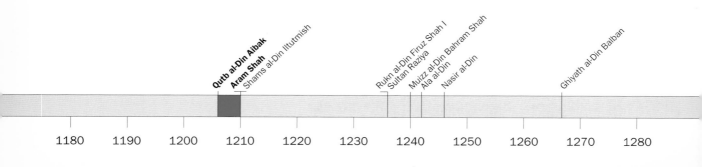

Qutb al-Din Aibak
Aram Shah
Shams al-Din Iltutmish
Rukn al-Din Firuz Shah I
Sultan Raziya
Muizz al-Din Bahram Shah
Ala al-Din
Nasir al-Din
Ghiyath al-Din Balban

1180 1190 1200 1210 1220 1230 1240 1250 1260 1270 1280

the Ghurid forces. He had been bought as a slave from Turkestan, raised in military pursuits by a distinguished family of Naishapur (Iran) and subsequently sold to Muizz al-Din. In India he proved to be one of the Sultan's most successful commanders, capturing Delhi and exercising authority from Gujarat through Rajasthan to northern India. Amongst the reasons for his success, and that of his fellow commanders, was the performance of the Turkish cavalry with its armoured horses (Turks from Central Asia, along with Iranians and Afghans, all served the Sultanate).

In 1206 Sultan Muizz al-Din made Qutb al-Din Viceroy of the Ghurid territories 'from the gates of Peshawar to the furthest parts of India'. A few weeks later in March, Qutb al-Din's opportunity came with the assassination of the Sultan by an Ismaili fanatic. Qutb al-Din went straight from Delhi to Lahore, the prime focus of Ghurid authority in the region, where in June he took up residence as ruler. Wisely, he strengthened his position by marriage alliances with rival leaders. He took as his wife the daughter of Taj al-Din Yildiz, the governor of Kirman (Iran). He married his sister to Nasir al-Din Qubacha, the governor of Sind, and his daughter to his leading slave commander, Shams al-Din Iltutmish. Soon Qutb al-Din came to adopt the title Sultan, becoming the first independent Muslim ruler of India. He did not enjoy his new position for long. In 1210 he died after falling from his horse playing polo. The horse fell on top of him, driving the pommel of his saddle through his chest.

ARAM SHAH

AS SOON AS QUTB AL-DIN DIED, a group of nobles of the court at Lahore raised Aram Shah, who seems to have been his son, to the throne. A second group of nobles offered their support to Iltutmish, Qutb al-Din's leading slave commander, inviting him to Delhi. Aram Shah's forces were defeated outside Delhi, where he is said to have been killed.

The Qutb Minar in the Quwwat al-Islam Mosque in Delhi (see plan p. 83). It was begun by Qutb al-Din Aibak in 1199 and is 73m (240 ft) high. It was both a lookout and a tower of victory 'to cast the shadow of God', as one of its inscriptions declares, 'over the East and over the West'.

THE SHAMSIDS
1210–90

Shams al-Din Iltutmish
1210–36

Rukn al-Din Firuz Shah I
1236

Sultan Raziya
1236–40

Muizz al-Din Bahram Shah
1240–42

Ala al-Din
1242–46

Nasir al-Din
1246–66

Obverse of a coin of Shams al-Din Iltutmish: 'The supreme Sultan, light (*shams*) of the world and the faith, father of the victorious, Sultan Iltutmish'. Reverse (not shown): 'In the time of the imam, the commander of the faithful, Caliph al-Mustansir'. This coin, probably issued *c.* 1232, celebrates the formal confirmation by the Caliph in Baghdad of Iltutmish's authority over the lands of the Delhi Sultanate. From now on the higher value coins of the Delhi sultans were to acknowledge the authority of the Abbasid Caliphate.

SHAMS AL-DIN ILTUTMISH

The future monarch was from his childhood remarkable for beauty, intelligence and grace...

Juzjani

It is firmly believed that no king so benevolent, so sympathizing, and so respectful to learned and to elders as he was, ever rose by his native energy to the cradle of empire.

Juzjani

SUCH WERE THE GIFTS OF ILTUTMISH when he was young that his brothers out of jealousy sold him in the slave market of Bukhara. In consequence he had the advantage of being brought up in a noble and learned family, spending part of his youth in Baghdad, seat of the Caliphate and at that time a great spiritual centre. Eventually, he was sold into the service of Qutb al-Din Aibak, becoming governor of Badaun, itself a notable centre of learned and holy men in north India.

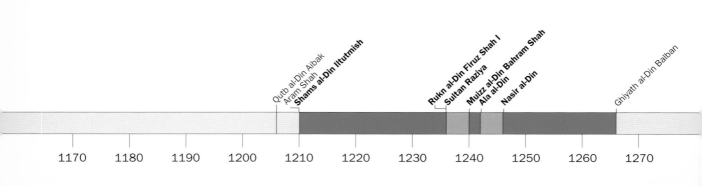

Qutb al-Din Aibak
Aram Shah
Shams al-Din Iltutmish

Rukn al-Din Firuz Shah I
Sultan Raziya
Muizz al-Din Bahram Shah
Ala al-Din
Nasir al-Din

Ghiyath al-Din Balban

1170 1180 1190 1200 1210 1220 1230 1240 1250 1260 1270

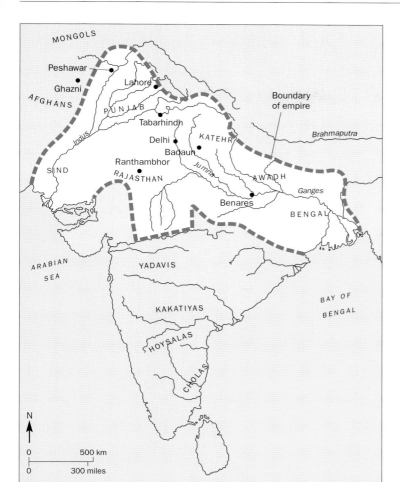

Map of India in 1236, showing the lands (in white) controlled by the Sultanate of Delhi under Iltutmish.

After Iltutmish overthrew Aram Shah, his position was by no means secure. Immediately, he had to assert himself over rivals in Badaun, Benares and Awadh. Further afield his authority was not recognized by the Muslim ruler of Bengal, while relatives by his marriage to the daughter of Qutb al-Din, Taj al-Din Yildiz and Nasir al-Din Qubacha, competed for territory in the west, from Lahore through to the Arabian Sea. In 1216 Iltutmish succeeded in destroying Yildiz, but this just created a vacuum which Qubacha was able to fill, increasing his pressure on Delhi. Arguably the nascent Delhi Sultanate was saved by two invasions from Central Asia. First came the Khwarazmian Shahs in 1221, fleeing the great westward campaign of Chingiz Khan. For three years the Khwarazmian forces ravaged Qubacha's territories, obliging him to submit to them. Then, in 1224, the Mongols swept through the eastern Punjab, but did not enter the territories of the Delhi Sultan. The outcome was that in the years up to 1228, Iltutmish was able to assert his authority from Sind through to Lahore: Qubacha eventually drowned himself in the river Jhelum to escape being taken alive by Iltutmish's forces. At the same time the Sultan and his son, Nasir al-Din Mahmud, were campaigning in Bengal, where by 1230/31 they had asserted the authority of Delhi.

Iltutmish was now the only Muslim ruler in India. A year earlier he had received the recognition that all Muslim rulers sought. The Caliph al-Mustansir had sent an embassy from Baghdad, which arrived in Delhi in February 1229 bearing robes of honour for Iltutmish and a formal confirmation of his authority over the lands he had conquered. This was a remarkable achievement for a man whose last contact with Baghdad had been as a slave in a noble household. Unusually, too, for the time, he died in his bed in Delhi on 29 April 1236.

Thus Iltutmish established the Delhi Sultanate as the prime focus of Muslim power in India. That he should succeed was no foregone conclusion. Most certainly he was fortunate in the invasions from the northwest which weakened his rival Qubacha. Also important in his success was his capacity both to accumulate treasure through warfare, which enabled him to fund larger armies than his rivals, and to attract to his service many gifted men from Western and Central Asia who wished to escape the Mongol onslaught.

SHAMS AL-DIN ILTUTMISH	
Born	Muizz al-Din
Slave from	Bahram, Nasir al-
Turkestan, raised in	Din, Qutb al-Din,
a learned family of	Jalal al-Din Masud
Baghdad	*Daughter*
Master	Raziya
Qutb al-Din Aibak	*Enthroned*
Wives	Seized power in
Name unknown	1210
(daughter of Qutb al-	*Died*
Din Aibak), chief	In his bed, 29 April
wife Shah Turkan	1236
(originally a servant)	*Buried*
Sons	Tomb in NW corner
Nasir al-Din	of the Quwwat
Mahmud, Rukn al-	al-Islam Mosque,
Din Firuz, Ghiyath al-	Mehrauli, Delhi
Din Muhammad,	

THE SHAMSIDS

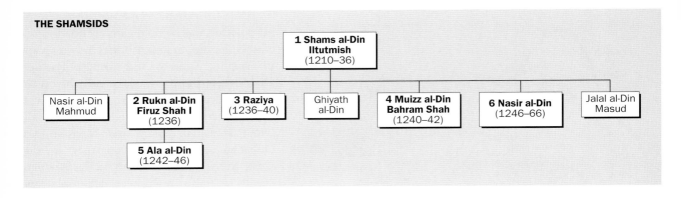

```
                          ┌─────────────────┐
                          │ 1 Shams al-Din  │
                          │    Iltutmish    │
                          │   (1210–36)     │
                          └─────────────────┘
```

| Nasir al-Din Mahmud | 2 Rukn al-Din Firuz Shah I (1236) | 3 Raziya (1236–40) | Ghiyath al-Din | 4 Muizz al-Din Bahram Shah (1240–42) | 6 Nasir al-Din (1246–66) | Jalal al-Din Masud |

5 Ala al-Din (1242–46)

Obverse of a coin of Rukn al-Din Firuz Shah I: 'The supreme Sultan, light of the world and the faith, the great Sultan, pillar (*rukn*) of the world and the faith, Firuz Shah.'

RUKN AL-DIN FIRUZ SHAH I

He was very generous; no king in any reign had ever scattered gifts, robes of honour and grants in the way he did.... He was so entirely devoted to riot and debauchery, that he often bestowed his honours and rewards on bands of singers, buffoons and catamites. He scattered his riches to such a heedless extent that he would ride out drunk upon an elephant through the streets and bazaars, throwing tankas of red gold around him for the people to pick up and rejoice over.

Juzjani

ILTUTMISH HAD INTENDED his daughter, Raziya, to be his successor, so well had she managed affairs while he had been away campaigning. In 1229 she was formally appointed his heir. However, when Iltutmish died, his son Rukn al-Din was with him. Rukn al-Din's mother, Shah Turkan, was Iltutmish's chief wife and a major patron of learned and holy men. This may explain why, on 30 April 1236, the nobles of the court placed Rukn al-Din on the throne.

Rukn al-Din quickly forsook the needs of state for the pursuit of pleasure. His mother seized the opportunity to kill harem rivals of the past and to blind and then execute Iltutmish's younger son, Qutb al-Din, a prince of great promise. Soon, nobles throughout northern India were in rebellion. Rukn al-Din led his army out of Delhi to meet them. In the meantime Raziya felt her life threatened by her mother, Shah Turkan. Dressed in red, as was the custom for the aggrieved, she appealed for the help of the people at Friday prayer, asking for a chance to prove herself and saying, according to one account, that, should she not prove better than the men, she should lose her head. The people attacked the royal palace, seizing Shah Turkan. As Rukn al-Din returned to Delhi to put matters right, his army deserted to Raziya and placed her on the throne. On 9 November 1236, Raziya's forces captured Rukn al-Din and he 'received the Almighty's mercy'.

RUKN AL-DIN FIRUZ SHAH I	
Born	*Son*
?	Ala al-Din
Father	*Enthroned*
Shams al-Din	30 April 1236
Iltutmish	*Died*
Mother	Killed by the
Shah Turkan	soldiers of his
Wife	sister, Raziya,
?	9 November 1236

Obverse of a coin of Sultan Raziya: 'The supreme Sultan, light of the world and the faith, the Sultan, the exalted praiseworthy one (raziyat) of the world and the faith.'

RAZIYA	
Born	*Enthroned*
?	c. November 1236
Father	*Died*
Shams al-Din	14 October 1240,
Iltutmish	after defeat in
Mother	battle
Shah Turkan	*Buried*
Husband	Bulbuli Khana, near
Malik Altuniya	the Turkman Gate,
Sons	Old Delhi
None	

Obverse of a coin of Muizz al-Din Bahram Shah: 'The supreme Sultan, strengthener (muizz) of the world and the faith, father of the victorious, Bahram Shah, son of the Sultan.'

MUIZZ AL-DIN BAHRAM SHAH	
Born	*Died*
?	1242, killed by his
Father	Turkish officers
Shams al-Din	*Buried*
Iltutmish	Tomb adjacent to
Mother	the Sultan Garhi,
?	District Malikpur,
Wife	Delhi
?	

SULTAN RAZIYA

Sultan Raziya was a great monarch. She was wise, just and generous, a benefactor to her kingdom, a dispenser of justice, the protector of her subjects and the leader of her armies. She was endowed with all the qualities befitting a king, but she was not born of the right sex, and so in the estimation of men all these qualities were worthless.

Juzjani

JUZJANI'S JUDGMENT SHOULD BE NOTED with care. He knew Raziya; indeed, he was appointed to two high-ranking positions by her. Raziya was finally established in power because a faction of Turkish nobles placed her there. Her reign was defined by her attempt to assert herself over them. First, she had to deal with a prolonged siege of Delhi by some of her nobles. Once she had established her authority outside her capital, her growing self-confidence was represented first by having coins struck in her own name, rather than in her name linked to that of her father, and then by donning the clothes of a man and riding her elephant fully visible to all around her. At the same time she tried to build up a cadre of non-Turkish officers, appointing, for instance, an Abyssinian, Jamal al-Din Yakut, as her personal attendant, and causing much 'jealousy among the Turkish generals and nobles'.

In 1239 and 1240 she had to confront two rebellions in the northwest. As she moved to deal with the second, led by Malik Altuniya, the commander of Tabarhindh, her Turkish troops turned against her, killed Yakut, and imprisoned her in Tabarhindh fort. When the news reached Delhi, the Turks placed her brother Muizz al-Din on the throne. Raziya's last throw was to marry Altuniya and head for Delhi to regain her throne. But the pair were defeated by her brother's forces and, fleeing alone from the battlefield, she was, according to Ibn Battuta, writing some hundred years later, killed by a peasant for the sake of her clothes.

MUIZZ AL-DIN BAHRAM SHAH

Sultan Muizz al-Din Bahram Shah ... had some virtues. He was shy and unceremonious, and had no tastes for the gorgeous attire which kings love to wear, nor for the belts, accoutrements, banners, and other insignia of royalty.

Juzjani

THE TURKISH NOBLES WHO PUT MUIZZ AL-DIN on the throne did so on condition that Malik Iktiyar al-Din Aitikin, one of their number, was appointed his deputy and all power was delegated to him. Aitikin quickly began to arrogate to himself the symbols of royalty, keeping an elephant and having music played outside his gate three times a day. Muizz al-Din had the man assassinated. A second malik (commander of 10,000 men) took control of the state and began to plot the overthrow of Muizz al-Din.

The plot was discovered and several of the plotters killed. Then, in 1241, the Mongols invaded, capturing Delhi and slaughtering the population. Muizz al-Din sent his army against them. But his Turkish commanders, after being tricked into believing that the Sultan wanted them killed, returned to Delhi, which was defended for three months by its citizens. Eventually, in May 1242, the city was captured by the Turkish commanders and Muizz al-Din killed.

ALA AL-DIN

In this army there was a party of good-for-nothing fellows who had gradually made their way into the society of the Sultan, and were the means of leading him into unworthy habits and practices. It was thus that he acquired the habit of seizing and killing his nobles. He became confirmed in his cruelty; all his excellent qualities were perverted, and he gave himself up to unbounded licentiousness, pleasure and hunting.

Juzjani

AFTER MUIZZ AL-DIN WAS KILLED, the nobles released three princes from their imprisonment in Delhi's White Palace. Two, Nasir al-Din and Jalal al-Din, were sons of Iltutmish, the third was his grandson, Ala al-Din, through Rukn al-Din Firuz Shah and it was he who became the next Sultan. The chronicler, Juzjani, who held high office under Ala al-Din, and met him from time to time, tells of how in the first two years of his reign the Sultan won many victories, and how in the third his armies were large enough to force the Mongols to retreat from India. But his cruelty and licentiousness turned his nobles against him. In June 1246 he was imprisoned and died.

Obverse of a coin of Ala al-Din: 'The supreme Sultan, glory (*ala*) of the world and the faith, father of the victorious, Shah Masud, son of the Sultan.'

ALA AL-DIN	
Born	Sons
?	?
Father	Died
Rukn al-Din Firuz Shah	In prison after 1246
Mother	Buried
?	?
Wife	
?	

NASIR AL-DIN

He was a mild, kind and devout king, and passed much of his time in making copies of the Holy Book. During the twenty years of his reign Balban was Deputy of the State, and bore the title of Ulugh Khan. He, keeping Nasir al-Din as a puppet [nomuna], carried on the government, and even while he was only a Khan used many of the insignia of royalty.

Barani

ALTHOUGH NASIR AL-DIN RULED for 20 years, little is recorded of his actions. We are told that he was particularly devout and showed great respect for descendants of the Prophet and for learned men. He spent much of his time making copies of the Quran, at the rate of two a year. These were then sold and he lived off the proceeds. Ibn Battuta, who saw one copy, praised its calligraphy. For the most part of Nasir al-Din's reign he was dominated by his able and enormously ambitious deputy, Ghiyath al-Din Balban, who hailed from Turkestan. Balban had been one of the 40 slaves originally attached to Iltutmish. Early on he showed his

Obverse of a coin of Nasir al-Din: 'The supreme Sultan, protector (*nasir*) of the world and the faith, father of the victorious, son of the Sultan.'

NASIR AL-DIN	
Born	Enthroned
?	12 June 1246
Father	Died
Iltutmish	1266, probably poisoned by Balban
Mother	Buried
?	?
Wife	
?	
Sons	
?	

great ambition. In 1242, as the nobles decided who of Iltutmish's descendants should succeed Muizz al-Din, he had seated himself on the throne and had his name proclaimed as king through Delhi.

Once Nasir al-Din was on the throne, Balban steadily drew all the strands of government into his own hands. After three years, he strengthened his position by giving his daughter in marriage to the Sultan, who in turn appointed him commander of the royal forces with the title Ulugh Khan-i Azam. Nasir al-Din made one bid to free himself from his over-mighty subject. In 1253 he dismissed Balban, banishing him to his estates, and put non-Turks in his administration in the place of Turks. Within a year the Turkish officers were besieging Delhi and Balban was negotiating his return to power. Soon afterwards he insultingly demanded the symbols of royalty from Nasir al-Din, including the white *chatr*, or parasol. An old noble, who commented sarcastically when Balban used the parasol at court the following day, was immediately dispatched. Ruthlessness was the mark of the man, and having robbed Nasir al-Din of all semblance of power or authority, there is persuasive evidence that he finished off the Sultan with one of his favourite weapons – poison.

Above Plan of the Quwwat al-Islam Mosque in Delhi, showing the original mosque and the Qutb Minar. Later sultans extended the complex greatly.

Below The Quwwat al-Islam (Power of Islam) Mosque was built by Qutb al-Din Aibak in 1195, with, according to an inscription, materials from 27 Hindu and Jain temples which had been demolished nearby.

THE GHIYATHIDS
1266–90

Ghiyath al-Din Balban
1266–87

Kaiqubad
1287–90

Obverse of a coin of Ghiyath al-Din Balban: 'The supreme Sultan, succour (*ghiyath*) of the world and the faith, the father of the victorious, Balban, the Sultan.'

GHIYATH AL-DIN BALBAN	
Born In Turkestan and sold as a slave to representatives of Shams al-Din Iltutmish	*Sons* Muhammad Khan-i Shahid (the Martyr Khan), Bughra Khan
Master Iltutmish	*Enthroned* 1266
Father ?	*Died* 1287, from grief at the death of his son, Muhammad
Mother ?	*Buried* Close to the Quwwat al-Islam Mosque, Mehrauli, Delhi
Wife ?	

GHIYATH AL-DIN BALBAN

Sultan Ghiyath al-Din Balban was a man of experience in matters of government. From being a malik he became a khan and from being a khan he became a king. When he attained the throne he imparted to it a new lustre, he brought the administration into order, and restored to efficiency institutions whose power had been shaken or destroyed. The dignity and authority of government were restored, and his stringent rules and resolute determination caused all men, high and low, throughout his dominion, to submit to his authority.

Barani

BALBAN HAD ENJOYED DRINKING AND GAMBLING, giving dinners two or three times a week, when he was a khan (the title given to slaves of Iltutmish, also a commander of 100,000 men). But after he came to the throne, Barani tells us, he allowed himself no prohibited indulgences. He worked hard at promoting the dignity and majesty of his position; he was not familiar with friends or strangers; he did not joke or permit others to do so; he did not laugh or allow others to laugh out loud; he was always severe, but fair. He maintained a network of spies throughout his territo-

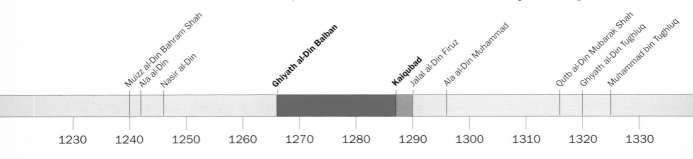

Muizz al-Din Bahram Shah
Ala al-Din
Nasir al-Din
Ghiyath al-Din Balban
Kaiqubad
Jalal al-Din Firuz
Ala al-Din Muhammad
Qutb al-Din Mubarak Shah
Ghiyath al-Din Tughluq
Muhammad bin Tughluq

1230   1240   1250   1260   1270   1280   1290   1300   1310   1320   1330

THE PRECEPTS OF BALBAN

THE PRECEPTS OF BALBAN

The first eight of 20 precepts Balban transmitted formally to his son, Prince Muhammad; they were derived from his personal experience:

1. Royal dignity should be maintained both in public and private. All etiquette and formalities should be meticulously followed under all circumstances.
2. You should understand that kingship is the viceregency of God.
3. Only noble, virtuous, wise and skilled people should be allowed to come near you. You should make huge grants in their favour so that your generosity and beneficence might earn a good name in this world and get a reward in the next. You will never be disappointed in either world if you support and patronize the noble and the virtuous people.
4. Under no circumstance should you allow the mean vulgar and the faithless people, and infidels to gather round you. If any person of humble birth and low origin is already in your service, you must be kind and generous towards him, but you should not make him your favourite or confidant. God will be displeased with you if you give high posts to mean, low-born and worthless people.
5. Do not incur the displeasure of God by indulging in luxuries.
6. Kingship and bravery are twins.
7. If a king lives in the same way as other people live and grants to people what others also can bestow, the glory of sovereignty vanishes. A king should live and behave in a way different from other people.
8. A king should be full of ambition, for kingship can never be successful without it.

Nizami

ries and steadily picked off all those who resisted his rule. He dealt most brutally with the Meos, a community claiming Rajput status, who lived to the south of Delhi and were driven by famine to conduct raids into the city. On two occasions he marched eastwards into the Gangetic plain to deal with vast bands of robbers who harried merchant caravans. 'Sixty years have passed since these events', declares the historian Barani, 'but the roads have ever since been free from robbers.' He moved with lightning speed to deal with a rebellion to the north in Katehr, ordering all males to be killed. 'The blood of the rioters,' declared Barani, 'ran in streams, heaps of slain were to be seen near every village and jungle, and the stench of the dead reached as far as the Ganges.' He was into the fifth year of his reign when his cousin, one Sher Khan, a distinguished soldier who had done much to hold back the raids of the Mongols, rejected Balban's command that he come to Delhi. Balban had him poisoned.

'When,' as Barani writes, 'Sultan Balban had secured himself in his dominion, and removed all his rivals and opponents ... he gave a royal canopy to his eldest son, proclaimed him his heir apparent, and made him governor of all Sind and the other dependent frontier districts.' This son, Muhammad by name, proved himself an able administrator, an effective warrior in confronting Mongol raids, a patron of poets and scholars, and a dependable son – every year he would come to see his father bearing treasure and presents. At their last meeting, the Sultan made a written will containing his formal counsel for governing.

One of the problems of ruling in all pre-modern states was maintaining the loyalty of those in charge of regions at a long distance from the capital. Bengal, in the far east, represented this problem for Balban. In the early 1280s, Tughril, one of his favourite slaves, whom he had made Viceroy, noting how preoccupied the court at Delhi was with Mongol incursions, seized the opportunity to set himself up as an independent sultan, having his name read in the Friday sermon and striking his own coins. Balban sent two armies against Tughril, both of which were defeated. Finally, Balban took command himself, defeated Tughril's army, killed the rebel and issued exemplary punishments for all those who had been involved in the revolt. In Lakhnawti, the main city of Bengal, all the male members of the family of Tughril, and all those who had served him in any way, were hung on gibbets placed along the two sides of the main bazaar.

In 1285 Balban suffered a great tragedy. His son Muhammad was killed in battle against the Mongols. 'The Sultan was more than 80 years old', writes Barani, 'and although he struggled hard against the effects of the bereavement, they day by day became more apparent. By day he held his court and entered into public business as if to show that his loss had not affected him; but at night he poured forth his cries of grief, tore his garments, and threw dust upon his head ... he gradually sank under his sorrow.' On his deathbed some months later he instructed his leading followers that they should make his grandson Kai Khusraw, the late Muhammad's son, his successor. After his death three days later, they

Obverse of a coin of Muizz al-Din Kaiqubad: 'The supreme Sultan, strengthener (*muizz*) of the world and the faith, father of the victorious, Kaiqubad, the Sultan.'

KAIQUBAD	
Born	*Son*
?	1
Father	*Died*
Bughra Khan	1290, kicked to
Mother	death by followers
?	of the Khaljis
Wife	*Buried*
?	?

chose to ignore his wishes. It seems that they had had differences with Muhammad and feared what his son might do. They chose instead, Kaiqubad, the son of Balban's younger and wayward son, Bughra Khan.

KAIQUBAD

He was ... a young man of excellent qualities ... he had been brought up under the eye of the Sultan, his grandfather. Such strict tutors had been placed over him that he never had the idea of indulging in any pleasure, or the opportunity of gratifying any lust.... When all at once, and without previous expectation, he was elevated to such a mighty throne ... all that he had read, and heard, and learned, he immediately forgot ... he plunged at once into pleasure and dissipation of every kind.

Barani

GIVING ALL HIS TIME TO THE PURSUIT of pleasure, Kaiqubad left government in the hands of Malik Nizam al-Din, his chief justice and deputy ruler. This able but unscrupulous man set out to become sultan himself. He had Kai Khusraw killed, and sidelined or killed many of the leading nobles of Balban's reign. Eventually Kaiqubad, fearing that it might be his turn next, arranged for Nizam al-Din to be poisoned. Two developments followed. First, the decimation of the old Turkish aristocracy by Nizam al-Din made it possible for non-Turks to come forward, such as the Khaljis, who were identified as Afghans primarily (having some Turkish blood). Secondly, the dissipation of Kaiqubad's life had such an impact on his health that he became paralysed and unable to attend to affairs. The old nobles of Balban's time, fearing for Turkish supremacy, reasserted themselves, deposed Kaiqubad and placed his infant son upon the throne.

The Khaljis then made a pre-emptive strike. They stormed the palace and seized the infant Sultan. Their leader, Jalal al-Din, then arranged for a malik whose father had been executed by Kaiqubad to deal with him. He entered the palace, Barani tells us, 'and found the Sultan lying at his last gasp in the room of mirrors. He despatched him with two or three kicks and threw his body in the Jumna [river] ... By the death of Sultan Kaiqubad ... the Turks lost the empire.'

The mausoleum of Balban close to the Quwwat al-Islam Mosque in Delhi. Although ruined, it is significant in India for offering the first example of a true Islamic arch.

THE KHALJIS

Jalal al-Din Firuz
1290–96

Ala al-Din Muhammad
1296–1316

Qutb al-Din Mubarak Shah
1316–20

Obverse of a coin of Jalal al-Din Firuz: 'The supreme Sultan, majesty (*jalal*) of the world and the faith, father of the victorious, Firuz Shah, the Sultan.'

JALAL AL-DIN FIRUZ	
Born An Afghan Khalji from the Helmand valley *Father* Yughrush *Mother* ? *Wife* Malika-yi Jahan *Sons* Khan-i Khanan, Arkali Khan, Rukn	al-Din, Hisam al-Din, Iktiyar al-Din, Qadr Khan *Enthroned* 13 June 1290 *Died* 1296, assassinated by his nephew and son-in-law, Ala al-Din *Buried* ?

JALAL AL-DIN FIRUZ

... he knew nothing about government.... Two things were required in Kings. 1. Princely expenditure and boundless liberality.... 2. Dignity, awe and severity, by which enemies are repulsed and rebels put down.... These qualities were wanting in him.

Barani

JALAL AL-DIN'S ARRIVAL ON THE THRONE brought about a revolution. For the previous 80 years northern India had been ruled by Turks. Now patronage shifted towards the Khaljis from Afghanistan. Even though they had Turkish blood in them, their contemporaries did not regard them as Turks. To begin with, the people of Delhi made Jalal al-Din unwelcome in the capital and he had to establish his court at Kilokhri on the banks of the Jumna outside the city. Then, in the second year of his reign, a Turkish rising, led by a nephew of Balban and strongly supported by the Hindus, was heavily defeated by the royal armies. 'The spiritless, rice-eating Hindustanis made a great noise,' declared Barani, 'but lost all their powers.' Jalal al-Din's treatment of the defeated leaders of the revolt, however, lost him the respect of his Khalji nobles. He refused to see them

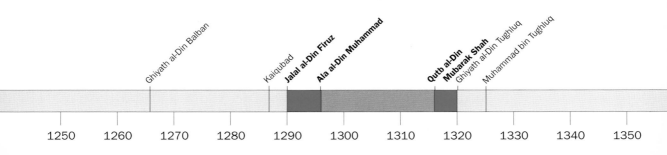

Ghiyath al-Din Balban
Kaiqubad
Jalal al-Din Firuz
Ala al-Din Muhammad
Qutb al-Din Mubarak Shah
Ghiyath al-Din Tughluq
Muhammad bin Tughluq

1250   1260   1270   1280   1290   1300   1310   1320   1330   1340   1350

THE KHALJIS

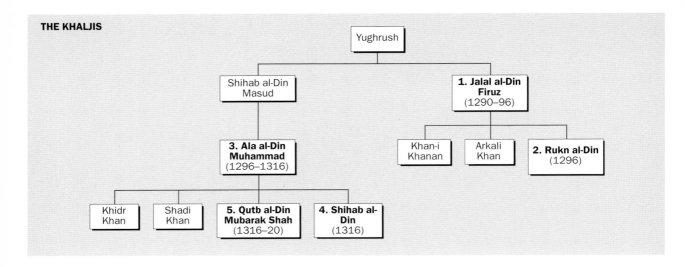

killed, or even humiliated, offering them considerate and luxurious treatment. When a leading counsellor complained, he replied: 'Oh Ahmad, I am aware of what you say ... but what can I do? I have grown old amongst Musulmans, and am not accustomed to spill their blood. My age exceeds seventy and I have never caused one to be killed; shall I now in my old days ... act against the principles of the law and bring Muhammadans to the block?' Indeed, a desire to preserve life where possible was the mark of the man. When he found he could not take the Rajput fortress of Ranthambhor without the loss of many Muslim lives, he raised the siege. And when, after defeating the Mongol invasion of 1292, he had many prisoners, including a grandson of Chingiz Khan, he did not slaughter them but had them converted to Islam and settled in a village outside Delhi, known to this day as Mughalpur.

But Jalal al-Din's humane and trusting approach eventually led to his death. He had made his nephew and son-in-law, Ala al-Din, the ruler of Kara, some 563 km (350 miles) east of Delhi. Ala al-Din used this as a base from which he campaigned southwards into the heart of the Deccan, where he sacked Deogiri, the capital of the Yadava kings. He collected much treasure, which he showed no intention of sharing, as was the custom, with his father-in-law. Jalal al-din, despite strong warnings from his advisers, believed the best of Ala al-Din and went with just a few attendants to meet him at the head of his forces. 'Ala al-Din advanced to receive him,' writes Barani who must have heard the story from eyewitnesses. 'When he reached the Sultan he fell at his feet, and the Sultan treating him as a son, kissed his eyes and cheeks, stroked his beard, gave him two loving taps upon the cheek, and said "I have brought thee up from infancy, why are thou afraid of me?"' Then, at a signal from Ala al-Din, his men fell on the Sultan and cut off his head, which was paraded on a spear. 'While the head of the murdered sovereign was yet dripping with blood,' Barani tells us, 'the ferocious conspirators brought the royal canopy and elevated it over the head of Ala al-Din.'

JALAL AL-DIN'S WIFE TRIES TO CONTROL THE SUCCESSION

Malika-yi Jahan, the wife of Jalal al-Din and the mother-in-law of Ala al-Din, had always been at odds with her son-in-law. When she heard that he had killed her husband, she immediately took action, but the wrong action, by placing her youngest son, Rukn al-Din, on the throne, and ignoring the claims of his elder brother, Arkali Khan, an able soldier and governor of Multan. As Ala al-Din slowly made his way through the rains to Delhi, and used his vast resources of treasure to bribe Malika-yi Jahan's supporters, she, whom the historian Barani describes as 'one of the silliest of the silly', begged Arkali Khan to come to Delhi thus: 'I committed a fault in raising my youngest son to the throne in spite of you. None of the maliks and amirs heed him, and most of them have joined Ala al-Din. The royal power has departed from our hands ... I am a woman and women are foolish.' The upshot was that Ala al-Din captured Delhi, Arkali Khan and Rukn al-Din were blinded and Malika-yi Jahan placed under house arrest.

Obverse of a coin of Ala al-Din Muhammad: 'The supreme Sultan, glory (ala) of the world and the faith, father of the victorious, Muhammad Shah, the Sultan [titles continue on the reverse, not shown], the second Alexander, the right hand of the Caliphate, helper of the commander of the faithful.'

ALA AL-DIN MUHAMMAD

'I have wealth and elephants, and forces beyond all calculation. My wish is to place Delhi in charge of a vice regent, and then I will go out myself into the world, like Alexander, in pursuit of conquest, and subdue the whole habitable world.' Over-elated with the success of a few projects, he caused himself to be entitled 'the second Alexander' in the khutba [Friday sermon] and on his coins.

Barani

RUTHLESSNESS, BLOODSHED and the pragmatic use of power were the features of Ala al-Din's reign, which, for the first time for over a thousand years, saw a ruler of northern India able to project his power far into the south of the subcontinent. Ala al-Din began his reign as he intended to proceed. His first task was to capture the sons of Jalal al-Din, who were then blinded. He then had all of Jalal al-Din's nobles whom he had bribed to come over to his side either blinded or killed and their property confiscated. Just the three nobles who had stayed loyal to his father-in-law remained untouched.

A powerful army lay at the heart of Ala al-Din's strategy. The overall size of his mounted force may have been at least 300,000 horsemen, and perhaps more. To support this vast number he first of all introduced measures to keep prices low, fixing those of grain and other key commodities. In the case of grain, hoarding was forbidden, and huge quantities were stored in government granaries in order to cope with times of famine. There were harsh penalties for breaking market regulations; merchants guilty of short weight would have the missing quantity cut from their own flesh. These measures, which were successful, kept the costs of maintaining his army down. Then, the resources available to him were increased by large-scale confiscations of property, by booty from successful campaigns and by taxation. All cultivated land was measured and one half of the gross produce was taken as a tax. Milk, like grain, was an essential food; all pasturage was taxed. The outcome was a substantial

The Alai Darwaza or 'Gate of Ala al-Din', built by the sultan in 1305 as a southern entrance to an enlarged Quwwat al-Islam Mosque. The Qutb Minar can be seen behind. Ala al-Din built a madrasa and his own tomb nearby.

shift of wealth from the countryside to the towns, and from the Hindu population to their Muslim rulers, thus providing the platform on which military forces of unusual size could be maintained. Such measures, of course, were not to be implemented without resistance. To deal with this Ala al-Din used spies, fear and force, remorselessly applied.

Ala al-Din certainly had need of his vast army. Within two years of his accession, the Mongols had begun to ravage the Punjab. In the following year he was leading his army against Mongol forces just 24 km (15 miles) north of Delhi. These raids stimulated Ala al-Din to pay serious attention to his military preparedness. The Mongols who had been settled outside Delhi and converted to Islam were slaughtered as a security measure. Increasingly, the Mongol raids

The Great Mosque of Dawlatabad, built by Qutb al-Din Mubarak Shah in 1318 inside the Hindu fort of Deogiri (Home of the Gods).

were met with striking victories for the Sultanate, so that 'the Mughals conceived such a fear and dread of the army of Islam', according to Barani, 'that all fancy for coming to Hindustan was washed clean out of their breasts.' Such was Ala al-Din's confidence that when the Il Khan Oljaitu (p. 30) sent an embassy in 1310–11, demanding his submission and a Khalji princess for a wife, he had no hesitation in having 18 of its members crushed by elephants. For the remainder of his reign his commander, Ghazi Malik, prevented the Mongols from penetrating much at all on to the plains of northern India.

Under Ala al-Din the might of the Sultanate came to be felt in central and southern India. In 1299 he sent his forces into Gujarat, where they defeated the Baghela Rajputs and collected vast booty in the rich port cities of the region. Subsequently, his forces defeated the Rajput kingdoms of Ranthambhor, Chitor and Malwa. These victories were followed by expeditions into southern India led by Malik Kafur, a Hindu slave with the sobriquet 'Hazardinari' or '1,000 dinars', the price for which he had been bought, and favourite of the Sultan. In 1307 he forced the Yadava ruler of Deogiri to pay regular tribute. In 1310 he did the same to the Kakatiya ruler of Warangal, and secured great wealth on the surrender of the Hoysala king. At the end of the year he made his final expedition against Ma'bar in the far south and, as Barani tells us, in the early part of 1311 the army returned to Delhi 'bringing with it six hundred and twelve elephants, ninety-six thousand mans [a measure of weight] of gold, several boxes of jewels and pearls, and twenty-thousand horses.'

The succession

In Ala al-Din's last years, such was Malik Kafur's ascendancy over the Sultan that he persuaded him to throw his chief wife out of the palace, kill her brother and imprison his son and heir, Khidr Khan. When in January 1316 Ala al-Din died of dropsy, an illness hastened to its end, it was said, by Kafur, the slave set about eliminating his princely rivals. Khidr Khan was blinded, as was his brother Shadi Khan, and a third brother, Qutb al-Din Mubarak Khan, was detained preparatory to blind-

ALA AL-DIN MUHAMMAD	
Born	Shihab al-Din, Farid
c. 1267–68	Khan, Abu Bakr
Father	Khan, Ali Khan,
Shihab al-Din	Baha Khan, Uthman
Masud (brother of	Khan
Jala al-Din Firuz)	*Enthroned*
Mother	12 October 1296
?	*Died*
Wives	2 January 1316, of
Name unknown	dropsy
(daughter of Jalal al-	*Buried*
Din Firuz), Mahru,	Before the Quwwat
Jhatiapali (daughter	al-Islam Mosque,
of Ramadeo of	Mehrauli, Delhi
Deogiri)	
Sons	
Khidr Khan, Shadi	
Khan, Qutb al-Din	
Mubarak Khan,	

ing. Ala al-Din's youngest son, Shihab al-Din, a mere boy, was placed on the throne as Kafur's puppet. But Kafur failed to realize how such actions might alienate the nobles. After 35 days they plucked up courage to kill Kafur and placed Qutb al-Din Mubarak Khan on the throne.

QUTB AL-DIN MUBARAK SHAH

QUTB AL-DIN MUBARAK SHAH	
Born	Khan)
c. 1299	*Sons*
Father	?
Ala al-Din	*Enthroned*
Mother	14 April 1316
Jhatiapali	*Died*
Wives	July 1320,
Name unknown	murdered by his
(daughter of Malik	slave Khusraw Khan
Dinar), Deval Devi	*Buried*
(former wife of Khidr	?

The Sultan from his good nature relieved the people of the heavy tribute and oppressive demands; and penalties, extortions, beating, chains, fetters and blows were set aside in revenue matters. Through his love of pleasure and extravagance, and ease, all the regulations and arrangements of the late reign fell into disuse; and through his laxity in business matters all men took their ease....

Barani

QUTB AL-DIN WAS YOUNG. His immaturity and the priority he gave to pleasure quickly had their effect. On coming to power he declared an amnesty and about 18,000 political prisoners were released. Soon afterwards, he abolished all the taxes and regulations which had brought huge resources to his father. Admittedly, he showed some of his father's imperial intent, tightening the Sultanate's hold over Gujarat and asserting its authority over Deogiri, the Raja being flayed alive for his rebellion. He also showed his father's ruthlessness, killing his three brothers. His position was weakened, however, by his appetite for pleasure. 'During [his reign of] four years and four months,' Barani writes, 'the Sultan attended to nothing but drinking, listening to music, debauchery and pleasure, scattering gifts and gratifying his lusts ... he cast aside all regard for decency, and presented himself decked out in the trinkets and apparel of a female before his assembled company.' His greatest and fatal weakness was, like his father, to place great trust in a youth with whom he was infatuated, a Hindu slave who had been brought up by his deputy chamberlain, Malik Shadi. Qutb al-Din gave the slave the title Khusraw Khan and made him Commander-in-Chief.

Soon, Khusraw Khan began to gather around him Parwaris from Gujarat whom he said were his kinfolk. Relying on the Sultan's infatuation with him, he succeeded in insinuating 300 Parwaris into the palace, who then killed the Sultan, throwing his headless body into the courtyard. Khusraw Khan assumed the throne under the title Sultan Nasir al-Din, ordered all personal attendants of the late Sultan to be killed, and their womenfolk to be given to Parwaris and Hindus. 'Horrid Parwaris', Barani declares, 'sported in the royal harem.... Copies of the Holy Book were used as seats, and idols were set up in the pulpits of the mosques.' But this did not last long. After a few months, Ghazi Malik, a loyal servant of the Khaljis, who had long protected the northwest from Mongol incursions, marched on Delhi. Khusraw Khan's army melted away. Parwaris and Hindus were cut down wherever they were found. Khusraw Khan was discovered hiding in Malik Shadi's garden and beheaded.

Obverse of a coin of Qutb al-Din Mubarak Shah: 'The supreme Sultan, pivot (*qutb*) of the world and the faith, father of the victorious, Mubarak Shah, the Sultan, son of the Sultan [titles continue on the reverse, not shown], Alexander of the age, right hand of the Caliph, helper of the commander of the faithful.'

THE TUGHLUQIDS
1320–1414

Ghiyath al-Din Tughluq
1320–25

Muhammad bin Tughluq
1325–51

Firuz Shah Tughluq
1351–88

Obverse of a coin of Ghiyath al-Din Tughluq: 'The Sultan, slayer of infidels, succour (*ghiyath*) of the world and the faith, father of the victorious [titles continue on the reverse, not shown], Tughluq Shah, the Sultan, helper of the commander of the faithful.'

GHIYATH AL-DIN TUGHLUQ	
Born Probably a Turco-Mongol Karawna	Nusrat Khan, Mubarak Khan, Masud Khan
Father Tughluq, a slave of Sultan Ghiyath al-Din Balban	*Enthroned* 26 August 1321
Mother ?	*Died* 1325, when the pavilion his son had built to welcome him collapsed
Wife Makhduma Jahan	*Buried* In the mausoleum he built at Tughluqabad, Delhi
Sons Muhammad Shah, Zafar Khan, Mahmud Khan,	

GHIYATH AL-DIN TUGHLUQ

Tughluq enjoyed undisturbed rule for four years, and he was just and upright.

Ibn Battuta

GHAZI MALIK, NOW KNOWN AS Ghiyath al-Din Tughluq, was of Turco-Mongol stock. He was proud of the service he had for many years performed for Ala al-Din Khalji in protecting the Sultanate's northwestern frontier. Ibn Battuta claimed to have seen an inscription in a mosque in Multan in which Tughluq announced 29 victories against the Mongols. On gaining power he sent his son, Muhammad, into the Deccan, where local leaders once conquered by Ala al-Din now rejected the Sultanate's authority. After two campaigns, they submitted. Tughluq in the meantime devoted his attention to the lands of Bengal and Bihar to the east. As he returned to Tughluqabad, the mighty fortress he had built himself near Delhi, he asked his son Muhammad to build him a temporary pavilion on the banks of the Jumna. According to Ibn Battuta, who reached Delhi nine years after the event, Muhammad arranged for the pavilion to collapse if a heavy weight was placed on one side of it. As the

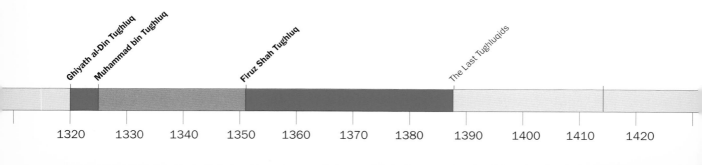

Ghiyath al-Din Tughluq — Muhammad bin Tughluq — Firuz Shah Tughluq — The Last Tughluqids

1320 1330 1340 1350 1360 1370 1380 1390 1400 1410 1420

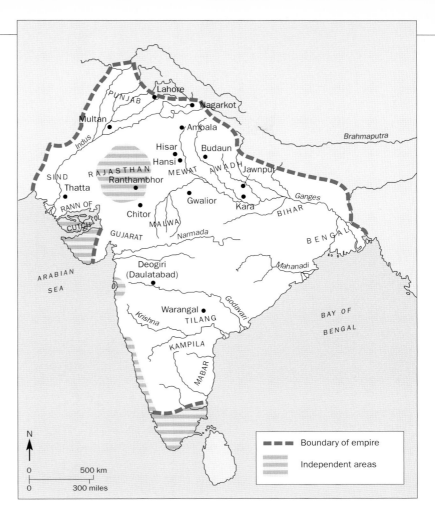

Map of India in 1335. Under Muhammad bin Tughluq sultanate power, based in northern India, reached its furthest extent. The Mughal conquests of the late 17th century recovered some, but not all of this territory.

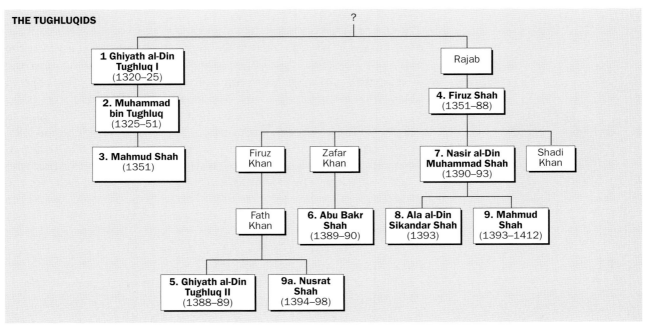

THE TUGHLUQIDS

?

1 Ghiyath al-Din Tughluq I (1320–25)

Rajab

2. Muhammad bin Tughluq (1325–51)

4. Firuz Shah (1351–88)

3. Mahmud Shah (1351)

Firuz Khan

Zafar Khan

7. Nasir al-Din Muhammad Shah (1390–93)

Shadi Khan

Fath Khan

6. Abu Bakr Shah (1389–90)

8. Ala al-Din Sikandar Shah (1393)

9. Mahmud Shah (1393–1412)

5. Ghiyath al-Din Tughluq II (1388–89)

9a. Nusrat Shah (1394–98)

The mausoleum of Ghiyath al-Din Tughluq, which, according to Ibn Battuta, he built himself. It stands in a small fortress, which was placed in a lake and connected by a causeway to the city of Tughluqabad. It is a worthy monument to a man who had spent his life defending the northwest frontier against the Mongols.

Sultan went into the pavilion with his favourite son, Mahmud, Muhammad asked permission to parade his elephants before him. He did so, and the pavilion collapsed. The Sultan's body was found bent in a protective position over that of his son. He was carried by night to the fine mausoleum he had built for himself outside Tughluqabad.

MUHAMMAD BIN TUGHLUQ

This king is of all men the most addicted to the making of gifts and to the shedding of blood. His gate is never without some poor man enriched or some living man executed ... for all that he is of all men the most humble and readiest to show equity and to acknowledge the right. The ceremonies of religion are strictly complied with at his court...

Ibn Battuta

Obverse of a coin of Muhammad bin Tughluq: 'The Sultan, the fortunate, the testifier, the slayer of infidels, succour of the world and the faith, father of the victorious [titles continue on the reverse, not shown], Tughluq Shah, the Sultan, may Allah illumine his proof.'

MUHAMMAD BIN TUGHLUQ'S REIGN saw the authority of the Delhi Sultanate in India acknowledged more widely than ever before. The Sultan's court itself was described by those who visited it as a place of majesty and magnificent ceremonies. Nevertheless, Muhammad's reign also saw the beginning of a decline in the Sultanate's fortunes from which it never recovered. We are fortunate to have two detailed descriptions of the reign: one from Zia al-Din Barani, an administrator who was for 17 years a close companion of the Sultan, and a second from the Moroccan traveller Ibn Battuta, who came to the court in 1333, was appointed qadi, or justice, and in 1341 moved on to China, where the Sultan had appointed him ambassador.

MUHAMMAD BIN TUGHLUQ	
Born c. 1300	*Enthroned* 1325
Father Ghiyath al-Din Tughluq	*Died* 20 March 1351 at Thatta, Sind, in his bed
Mother Makhduma Jahan	*Buried* In his father's mausoleum at Tughluqabad, Delhi
Wife ?	
Son Ghiyath al-Din Mahmud Shah	

Muhammad was an able and highly cultivated man, notable as a calligrapher and for his knowledge of Persian poetry, but also possessing a broad command of the learning of his time. 'No learned or scientific man, or scribe, or poet, or wit, or physician', writes Barani, 'could have had the presumption to argue with him about his own special pursuit, nor would he have been able to maintain his position, against the throttling arguments of the Sultan....' Arguably, he was much influenced in religious matters by the Syrian scholar Ibn Taimiya (d. 1325), whose pupil, Abd al-Aziz Ardabili, was welcomed to the court. Ibn Taimiya, whose ideas were to have a substantial impact on the Islamic revival of the 20th century, argued for a literal interpretation of the Quran and *Hadith* (the reported sayings and doings of the Prophet Muhammad) to save Islamic society from decay, and for the use of state power to put this interpretation into practice. By all accounts the Sultan was zealous in enforcing a strict interpretation of his faith.

Paradoxically, Muhammad was also interested in philosophy, a subject usually avoided by those of his puritan religious bent. Barani suggests that it was the 'dogmas of philosophers, which are productive of indifference and hardness of heart' that rendered him immune to the prospect of the day of judgment and enabled him to kill in cold blood large numbers of Muslims – learned and holy men, administrators, soldiers. Ibn Battuta lists a catalogue of executions of distinguished men; indeed, his pages give a real sense of the fear which stalked the Sultan's court. Yet, the Moroccan also records many acts of great generosity, in particular to foreigners. The overall picture is of a man who knew what was good for his people and did not feel it necessary to consult them. An intellectual bully of psychopathic tendencies, he became angry with his subjects as they increasingly resisted him. 'The mind of the Sultan lost its equilibrium,' declares Barani, 'in the extreme weakness and harshness of his temper he gave himself up to severity.'

Part of the Bijay Mandal (Wonderful Palace) built by Muhammad bin Tughluq in Delhi. It is thought that this formed part of the Sultan's Hall of 1,000 columns. 'The columns', Ibn Battuta writes, 'are of painted wood and support a wooden roof. The people sit under this, and it is in this hall that the Sultan sits for public audience....'

Raising revenues

On gaining power Muhammad's first concern was to address the consequences of the Sultanate's success in coming to rule the greater part of India. Past Sultans had always been able to restock their treasuries by making raids into enemy territory. Now this was no longer possible, he needed to organize an effective revenue system. Revenue records were developed for all provinces on the pattern of those operating in the Sultanate's heartland in the Ganges-Jumna plain. The accounts were all carefully audited at the centre. It was clear that Muhammad was concerned to exercise new levels of control over the provinces.

This desire, in all probability, contributed to the three revolts against him in the years 1326–28. Two, one in the Deccan and the other in Sind, were led by former officers of his father whom he had confirmed in their positions. The third was an attempt by a previously sovereign dynasty in Bengal to escape the Sultan's control. In each case the rising was suppressed and its leaders executed.

As Muhammad's grip on his dominions tightened, he began to develop the defining project of his first decade of rule – to invade the rich region of Khurasan in northeast Iran. Now that the Sultanate ruled most of India, the Sultan was arguably seeking to open up new sources of treasure in the rich cities of Khurasan and Transoxania. For this expedition the Sultan gathered a vast army in Delhi of at least 600,000 troops. Given problems of supply, an army of this size could not be assembled without reducing the populations of the city. Thus the elite, along with their families, with the exception of course of military officers, were instructed to move to Dawlatabad, the old Hindu city of Deogiri, in central India. The Sultanate bought the houses of these families in Delhi and gave them money and land around Dawlatabad.

The second problem caused by the mustering of such a vast force was how, given the other burdens which the Sultan's generosity and considerable programme of public works placed upon his treasury, to pay them. He thus introduced a copper and bronze coinage which was to represent the values of gold and silver coinage. The measure was an unmitigated disaster. 'The promulgation of this edict', declares Barani, 'turned the house of every Hindu into a mint ... with these [coins] they paid their tribute, and with these they purchased houses, arms, and fine things of all kinds.' After three years confidence in the token money evaporated and its value depreciated. The Sultan was forced to recall the coins and issue gold and silver specie in exchange. Given the outcome it was hardly surprising that, after the army of Khurasan had been mustered for a year, the Sultan had difficulty in paying for it and it melted away.

A copper coin introduced as token coinage by Muhammad bin Tughluq. The obverse (shown) reads: 'Sealed as a tanka in the reign of the slave hopeful (of grace) Muhammad Tughluq'; and the reverse (not shown): 'He who obeyed the Sultan obeyed the Merciful One.'

Growing resistance

From 1334 Muhammad was faced with a growing number of revolts, often leading to the loss of territory. The spur to these revolts, according to Barani, was the endemic unrest in the Ganges-Jumna plain, which followed the Sultan's attempts in the late 1320s substantially to increase the revenues received from this rich area. So severe and prolonged was the unrest that cultivation suffered and for several years Delhi was starved of grain. The rulers of more distant provinces took their cue. In Ma'bar in the far south of the subcontinent, the local governor rebelled. Muhammad set out at the head of an army, but before he could get to Ma'bar he and most of his army fell ill with the plague. Ma'bar was lost. This disaster, associated as it was with (false) rumours of Muhammad's death, encouraged others to rebel – in Konkan on the Indian Ocean coast, and in Lahore and Multan in the northwest. All these risings were suppressed; but others were not. In the mid-1330s the Sultanate lost Kampila

The entrance to the citadel of the city of Dawlatabad, which Muhammad bin Tughluq established on the site of the Hindu capital of Deogiri. It was deemed virtually impregnable, but still fell in 1347 to Hasan Gangu, the founder of the Bahmanid Sultanate.

in the south, which was to form the basis of the Hindu kingdom of Vijayanagar, Tilang, which Muhammad had conquered in the year before he became Sultan, and the rich province of Bengal. Such losses meant the loss also of revenue, which forced Muhammad to seek to raise more in his remaining territories, leading to rebellions in the Deccan and Awadh.

In the 1340s Muhammad took steps to strengthen his regime ideologically. For ten years he had been in correspondence with the puppet Abbasid Caliphs in Mamluk Cairo, where the Caliphate had been established after the destruction of Baghdad in 1258 by the Il Khan Hulagu (p. 18). In 1340/1 he symbolically acknowledged the Caliph, the successor of the Prophet Muhammad as the leader of the Muslim community, as his overlord, by replacing his own name on the coinage and in the Friday sermon with that of the Caliph. At the same time, he abolished taxes which had no basis in Islamic law and began to hear petitions in public twice a week for those complaining against oppression. In 1343 the Caliph's envoy, Hajji Sarsari, came from Egypt to Delhi bearing honours. 'The Sultan with all his nobles and Saiyids,' Barani tells us, 'went forth to meet the Hajji with great ceremony … and he walked before him barefoot for the distance of some long bowshots.' The symbolism of such public humility would not have been lost on those around him.

Rallying the religious forces to his side, however, was not enough to stop the continuing decline in the fortunes of his regime. In the mid-1340s, Muhammad came to the conclusion that the local military commanders in the Deccan and in Gujarat were holding back revenues due to the centre. He took over the management of the Deccan, and divided it into four sub-provinces ruled by men renowned for their ruthlessness. One began his rule by executing 80 local commanders. Immediately, local commanders elsewhere in the Deccan and in Gujarat were in revolt. Muhammad's attempts to suppress the risings in the Deccan led ultimately to one of the local commanders, Hasan Gangu, capturing Dawlatabad and being proclaimed in August 1347 the first sultan of the independent Bahmanid dynasty which was to rule the Deccan until the 16th century.

Muhammad was much cast down by the loss of Dawlatabad. 'One day', Barani tells us, 'while he was thus distressed, he sent for me … and addressing me, said: "My kingdom is diseased, and no treatment cures it … in my kingdom disorders have broken out, if I suppress them in one place they appear in another; if I allay them in one district another becomes disturbed."' Barani told him, so he says, of the various measures that rulers had adopted in such circumstances and of the supreme importance of building support and confidence amongst his subjects. The reply, which Barani puts into Muhammad's mouth, speaks loudly of the approach which had done so much damage to the Sultanate:

I am angry with my subjects, and they are aggrieved with me. The people are acquainted with my feelings and I am aware of their misery and wretchedness. No treatment that I employ is of any benefit. My remedy for rebels, insurgents, opponents, and disaffected people is the sword. I employ punishment and use the sword so that a cure may be effected by suffering. The more the people resist, the more I inflict chastisement.

Muhammad spent his last three years asserting his authority over that of his local commanders in Gujarat. While chasing one of them into Sind, he fell ill on the banks of the Indus close to Thatta after eating fish. On 20 March 1351, unusually for a Delhi Sultan, and somewhat unfairly for a man who spilled so much blood, he died in his bed.

FIRUZ SHAH TUGHLUQ

In the reigns of former kings the blood of many Musulmans had been shed and many varieties of torture employed. Amputation of hands and feet, ears and noses, tearing out the eyes, pouring molten lead into the throat, crushing the bones of the hands and feet with mallets, burning the body with fire, driving iron nails into the hands, feet and bosom, cutting the sinews, sawing men asunder; these and many similar tortures were practised. The great and merciful God made me, His servant, hope and seek for His mercy by devoting myself to prevent the unlawful killing of Musulmans, and the infliction of any kind of torture upon them or upon any man.

Inscription of Sultan Firuz Shah on the Friday Mosque, Firuzabad

Obverse of a coin of Firuz Shah Tughluq: 'Trusting in divine support, Firuz Shah Tughluq.'

FIRUZ SHAH, THE SECRET DRINKER

'... the wines which Firuz Shah used to drink were of different colours and different flavours; some were yellow as saffron, some red as the rose, some were white; and the taste of all was like sweet milk..... One morning after prayers the Sultan called for a glass to moisten his throat, and it so happened that Tatar Khan came to wait upon him just at the same time ... the Sultan was lying half naked on his couch; but before the Khan came in, he wrapped a garment around him, and, rising from his couch, sat down on a coverlet. The wine and cups he pushed under the bed, and covered all with a sheet. When Tatar Khan entered, he spied what was hidden under the bed, and his suspicions were aroused. He was so troubled by the sight that his lips failed to utter the usual salutation.'

Afif

AFTER THE REVOLTS AND TERRITORIAL LOSSES of Muhammad's reign, Firuz Shah's reign saw some stabilization of the position of the Sultanate. In his 37 years of rule there was only one revolt. Moreover, there were some small gains of territory and, according to the contemporary chronicler, Afif, 'favourable seasons and abundance of the necessaries of life prevailed ... not only in the capital, but throughout his dominions.' Certainly, as compared with the disasters that followed Firuz's death, it was a golden age.

Firuz was born in 1309, the son of Rajab, the brother of Sultan Ghiyath al-Din Tughluq. From early on he was trained to rule. Ghiyath al-Din, after he came to power, kept the young teenager constantly by him as he travelled through his dominions transacting business. When Muhammad bin Tughluq came to the throne, he made Firuz a commander of 12,000 horse and steadily exposed him to the responsibilities of government. By the time he reached the throne, Firuz was in his early 40s and deeply experienced.

When Muhammad died Firuz was with the army in Sind. The leaders present decided that Firuz should succeed, overruling a determined attempt by a daughter of Ghiyath al-Din Tughluq to place her son upon the throne. Firuz was unwilling to accept the burden, saying he would rather make a pilgrimage to Mecca. 'Writers of credit', so Afif tells us, 'report that Tatar Khan who was president of the meeting, then stood up, and taking the arm of Firuz Shah, forced him to sit upon the throne.'

Firuz's succession was in fact disputed, but only, it would appear, as the result of a mistake. While Muhammad's armies had been engaged in Sind, he had appointed an old and trusty official, Khwaja-yi Jahan, to take charge in Delhi. He then received news from Sind that the Sultan had died, that the army was being harried by Mongol forces and that Firuz Shah, for whom he had great affection, was among the leading nobles killed or missing. He mourned his monarch and his friend, and proceeded to place one Mahmud Shah, a son of Muhammad bin Tughluq, upon the throne. Subsequently hearing of the accession of Firuz he realized his mistake. As Firuz's army approached Delhi, 'The Khwaja went into his presence with a chain around his neck, his turban off ... and a naked sword fastened to his throat.' Firuz was most unwilling that any harm should be done to the Khwaja, but his advisers insisted that his political offence was too grave for him to live. Firuz resisted them for several days, but eventually, 'his heart rent with sorrow', he gave way. The Khwaja was instructed to go to his estates and devote his days to religion. On the road he was overtaken by a courtier whose purpose was clear. The Khwaja 'looked at the executioner', Afif tells us, 'and asked if he had a sharp sword, and the executioner, who was a friend of Khwaja, showed his weapon. The old man then told him to make his ablutions, say his prayers and use his sword. When the man had completed his devotions, the Khwaja bowed his head to his prayer carpet, and while the name of God was on his lips his friend severed his head from his body.'

Nobles and slaves

Firuz Shah built up a sizeable group of nobles around his throne. Some he inherited from the previous regime – indeed, by this time it is possible to identify families who had served several sultans. The most significant aspect of his reign, however, was the way in which slaves came to be a substantial part of the aristocracy. Firuz rewarded his provincial governors and nobles for providing him with them; the value of each slave was deducted from the taxes they owed. Slaves performed tasks from administration and military duties through to reading the Quran and artisan work. Forty thousand slaves were ready at any time to attend the Sultan and their number, according to Afif, amounted to 180,000. So important were they to the Sultanate that Firuz created a special department to manage them. Subsequently, their presence was to undermine the regime.

One reason why Firuz's nobility was so content with his rule was that he made it worth their while, and their position was substantially improved as compared with Muhammad bin Tughluq's time. Firuz transferred a large proportion of the Sultanate's territory from crown land to revenue assignments, which nobles were responsible for collecting. The payment of these revenues to the centre was not as carefully audited as under his predecessor; some nobles became very wealthy. Firuz also paid larger salaries to his officers and permitted revenue assignments to

FIRUZ SHAH TUGHLUQ	
Born 1309	*Sons* Firuz Khan, Zafar Khan, Nasir al-Din Muhammad Shah, Shadi Khan
Father Rajab, brother of Ghiyath al-Din Tughluq	*Enthroned* 23 March 1351
Mother Bibi Naila (daughter of Rana Mall Bhatti, Rais of Dipalpur)	*Died* 26 September 1388, in his bed
Wife ?	*Buried* Hauz Khas, Delhi

become hereditary, an action of which he was particularly proud, but which would have horrified his predecessor. Thus Firuz bought the peace which marked his time. The price was the strengthening of the provinces against the centre, and ultimately the break up of the Sultanate.

One appointment which became hereditary to dire effect was that of chief minister. The process began with a Hindu named Kannu from southern India, who, on coming to Muhammad bin Tughluq's court, had converted to Islam and then risen to be deputy chief minister. 'Although he had no knowledge of reading or writing', Afif tells us, 'he was a man of great common sense, acumen and intelligence, and was an ornament to the Court.' Firuz made him his chief minister with the title Khan-i Jahan (Commander of the World), and greatly valued the authority he had over the machinery of government. When in 1368 this chief minister died, Firuz appointed his son in his place with the same title and the same revenue assignment.

A believer and a builder

Like his predecessor, Firuz maintained relations with the Abbasid Caliphs in Egypt and received embassies from them acknowledging his authority in India. But there the resemblance stops. He was much more orthodox than Muhammad bin Tughluq. He showed respect for learned men, as opposed to killing them, and made a point of visiting the shrines of holy men. He abolished taxes which were against Islamic law, and extended the jizya, or poll tax, to all Hindus, delighting in the way it persuaded many to convert to Islam. He suppressed heretical or sectarian views amongst Muslims, and destroyed Hindu temples, in particular when their presence seemed likely to draw Muslims from the straight path. Indeed, he was particularly concerned to enforce lawful behaviour amongst Muslims, forbidding women to attend saints' shrines on holy days (frequently the occasion of misconduct), ordering all pictures of individuals to be removed from houses and furniture, and requiring men to avoid sumptuous clothes and follow instead the Prophet's modest sartorial example. This said, Firuz gave himself a royal dispensation when it came to alcohol.

Firuz Shah was a great builder. He constructed canals which brought new tracts of land under cultivation and enabled more than one crop a year to be taken from others. In the vicinity of Delhi, according to Afif, he laid out 1,200 gardens, and restored others. He founded several cities, including Hisar to the west of Delhi, Jawnpur, some 560 km (350 miles) to the east, and Firuzabad, his own city of Delhi, positioned on the Jumna some 8 km (5 miles) north of the old Delhi of Qutb al-Din Aibak and Iltutmish. Afif tells how people used to travel for pleasure between the two cities so that every mile between them 'swarmed with people, as with ants or locusts … the fare of a carriage was four silver jitals for each person.' Most unusually for a Sultan, Firuz restored, and endowed as necessary, the tombs, tanks, mosques and madrasas built over the previous two centuries by his predecessors. He also built monasteries, inns, a

The Hawa Mahal (Palace of the Winds) in the Firuz Shah Kotla, close to the Jumna river, Firuzabad, Delhi. This vast fortified palace had halls of public and private audience, gardens, water features, barracks and armouries. A *baoli*, or stepped well, still survives, surrounded by underground rooms to provide refuge from the summer heat, as does the Hawa Mahal in the form of a stepped pyramid, where it is thought Firuz Shah's concubines lived. The Ashokan pillar is to be compared to the similar pillar erected in the Quwwat al-Islam Mosque by Qutb al-Din Aibak (see p. 83). It is regarded as the model for later Mughal palaces.

hospital and a great palace enclosure some 366 x 732 m (1,200 x 2,400 ft) by the Jumna, which is regarded as a model for later Mughal palaces. In this Firuz Shah Kotla, as it was known, he arranged to erect one of Ashoka's pillars (r. 273–232 BC, the greatest of the Mauryan emperors, who inscribed his edicts on pillars), which had been transported by ingenious means from Ambala, some 210 km (130 miles) away.

Firuz, however, was not the complete Sultan; he was a rotten general. Although painfully aware of how much territory his cousin had lost, he did not venture into the Deccan. In two campaigns into Bengal in 1353 and 1359 he failed to show the necessary ruthlessness, when he had the military advantage, to finish off the enemy. In 1364 he did have some success in conquering the princedom of Nagarkot in the Himalayas. In the following year his expedition into Sind was an unmitigated disaster; he failed to take its capital, his supplies ran out, his horses died from epidemic disease and the army got so lost in the Rann of Cutch that nothing was heard of it in Delhi for six months. After the death of the brilliant Khan-i Jahan in the 1360s, he gave up campaigning altogether, and it is arguable that his neglect of military matters helped to undermine the capacity of the Sultanate to resist Timur's invasion at the end of the century. In 1384, now in his late 70s, Firuz Shah fell ill; he died in 1388.

THE LAST TUGHLUQIDS 1388–1414

FIRUZ SHAH'S DECLINING YEARS had seen growing rivalry between his chief minister, Khan-i Jahan II, and his son, Nasir al-Din Muhammad. This was brought to a head in 1387 when the chief minister tried to turn the ailing Sultan against his son, and was killed for his pains. The struggle for power now became one between Muhammad and his father's slaves. On Firuz Shah's death his great-grandson, **Ghiyath al-Din Tughluq (II)**, was with the help of the slaves made Sultan; Muhammad was forced to flee the capital. After Ghiyath al-Din was killed in a rising, a grandson of

THE SACK OF DELHI 1398

'On the 16th of the month a number of soldiers collected at the gate of Delhi and derided the inhabitants. When Timur heard of this he directed some of the amirs to put a stop to it. But it was the divine pleasure to ruin the city and to punish the inhabitants.... On the 17th of the month the whole place was pillaged, and several palaces in Jahan-panah and Siri were destroyed. On the 18th the like plundering went on. Every soldier obtained more than 20 persons as slaves, and some brought as many as 50 or 100 men, women and children as slaves of the city. The other plunder and spoils were immense, gems and jewels of all sorts, rubies, diamonds, stuffs and fabrics of all kinds, vases and vessels of gold and silver, sums of money in 'ala'i tankas [coins], and other coins beyond all computation. Most of the women who were made prisoners wore bracelets of gold or silver on their wrists and legs and valuable rings upon their toes. Medicines and perfumes and unguents, and the like, of these no one took any notice.'

Yazdi

Obverse of a coin of Mahmud Shah ibn Muhammad (1393–1413): 'Supreme Sultan, father of the victorious, Mahmud Shah, Muhammad Shah, Firuz Shah, the Sultan.'

Obverse of a coin of Nusrat Shah (1395–99): 'Confiding in divine support, Nusrat Shah, may his kingdom endure.'

Firuz Shah, **Abu Bakr**, was made Sultan. By 1389, Abu Bakr controlled Delhi and the war elephants, and had the support of his great-grandfather's slaves, while Muhammad controlled much of the countryside with the support of the military commanders and their troops. In September 1389, Muhammad ordered his followers to kill all his father's slaves they could find. In 1390 the slaves supporting Abu Bakr split, one faction choosing to invite Muhammad into Delhi. Abu Bakr fled, dying soon afterwards. Once in control of the all-important elephants, **Muhammad** had all the slaves either slaughtered or expelled. During these years of struggle for power at the centre, local leaders, both Hindu and Muslim, asserted their independence. After Muhammad's death in 1393, power at the centre was further diluted as factions of court nobles supported two puppets, one being **Mahmud Shah**, the son of Muhammad, and the other **Nusrat Shah**. The former controlled old Delhi and the latter Firuzabad. For three years there was almost daily fighting between the two sides.

In this situation, it was hardly surprising that Timur, ever on the look out for booty and for personnel to enrich Samarqand, should have turned his attention to Delhi (p. 44). The size of the army with which Mahmud Shah confronted the Mongols is witness to how far the Sultanate had been weakened. According to Timurid sources, which had no reason to minimize the armies Timur defeated, Mahmud had just 12,000 horsemen, 40,000 foot and 120 elephants, which was but a tithe of the armies Firuz Shah, Muhammad bin Tughluq and Ala al-Din Muhammad had been able to field. There were several reasons for this, among them were the reduction in the supply both of elephants as a consequence of the formation of independent sultanates in eastern India, and of warhorses because of increased demand in Central Asia. Central revenues also had fallen, despite increasing agrarian prosperity, because of the abolition of uncanonical taxes. Furthermore, expenditure on the military had been reduced because of increasing spending on building works and on learned and holy men. Another factor was the increasing alienation of central revenues as assignment in return for which military provision was required, but increasingly not made available.

On 16 December 1398, Mahmud met the Mongol army on the plain outside Delhi. 'The soldiers of India fought bravely for their lives', declared the chronicler Sharaf al-Din Yazdi, 'but the frail insect cannot contend with the raging wind, nor the feeble deer against the fierce lion, so they were compelled to take flight.' Delhi was captured and sacked, its people scattered to other parts of northern India, and its wealth transported to Central Asia. The event represented the end of the Sultanate as a major force in the politics of India. Mahmud continued as Sultan, but was constantly at the mercy of rival sultans and overmighty subjects.

After his death in 1412, which brought the Tughluqid dynasty to an end, the throne was offered in 1413 to one such subject, the Afghan Dawlat Khan Lodi. In 1414, however, he was ousted by Khidr Khan, who had been appointed ruler of Multan in the Punjab by Firuz Shah.

THE SAIYIDS
1414–51

Khidr Khan
1414–21

Mubarak Shah
1421–34

Muhammad bin Farid
1434–45

Ala al-Din
1445–51

Obverse of a coin of Mubarak Shah: 'In the time of the Sultan, the slayer of infidels, the truster in God, the glory of the gracious, Mubarak Shah, Sultan.'

Mubarak Shah began by issuing coins in the name of Firuz Tughluq and his son Muhammad, but towards the end of his reign he issued coins under his own name.

KHIDR KHAN	
Born Claimed to be a Saiyid by ancestry, i.e. a descendant of the Prophet Muhammad *Father* Malik Sulaiman, adopted son of Nasir al-Mulk Mardan Dawlat, amir of Firuz Shah Tughluq *Mother* ?	*Wife* Makhduma-yi Jahan *Son* Mubarak Shah *Enthroned* 6 June 1414 *Died* 20 May 1421 *Buried* Tomb on the banks of the Jumna close to District Okhla, Delhi

THE SAIYIDS

While he [Khidr Khan] distributed his favours among his own officers, he refrained from assuming royal titles, and gave out that he held the government for Timur in whose name he caused the coin to be struck and the khutba to be read. After the death of Timur, the khutba was read in the name of his successor, Shah Rukh Mirza, to whom he some-times even sent tribute to his capital of Samarqand.

Ferishta

THE CHRONICLER, SIRHINDI, refers to **Khidr Khan** as a Saiyid, a descendant of the Prophet Muhammad, and so he and his three successors have come to be known as the Saiyids. It should be clear by now that the Saiyids did not rule very much territory and faced constant threats from rival sultanates and assertive Hindu rulers. It should also be clear that Timurid influence was strong in northern India. Khidr Khan acknowledged the suzerainty of Timur, and, after his death, Shah Rukh, and in return received a robe of honour and a banner. On Khidr's death in 1421, he was succeeded by his son **Mubarak**, who also paid tribute to Shah Rukh and received a robe of honour and a ceremonial parasol in return.

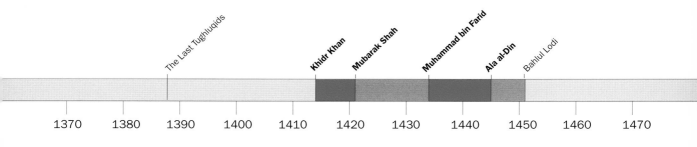

The Last Tughluqids   Khidr Khan   Mubarak Shah   Muhammad bin Farid   Ala al-Din   Bahlul Lodi

1370   1380   1390   1400   1410   1420   1430   1440   1450   1460   1470

MUBARAK SHAH	
Born ? *Father* Khidr Khan *Mother* Makhduma-yi Jahan *Wife* ? *Son* Adopted son, Muhammad, his nephew	*Enthroned* 22 May 1421 *Died* Assassinated 19 February 1434 *Buried* Tomb on the banks of the Jumna, District Mubarakpur, Delhi

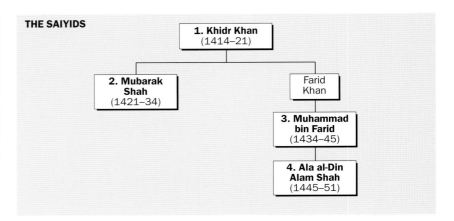

THE SAIYIDS

1. Khidr Khan (1414–21)

2. Mubarak Shah (1421–34)

Farid Khan

3. Muhammad bin Farid (1434–45)

4. Ala al-Din Alam Shah (1445–51)

Obverse of a coin of Muhammad bin Farid (1434–45): 'The supreme Sultan, father of virtues, Muhammad Shah, son of Farid Shah, ruler at the capital (*hadrat shah*), Sultan.'

Obverse of a coin of Ala al-Din (1445–51): 'Alam Shah, son of Muhammad Shah, at the capital Delhi.'

MUHAMMAD BIN FARID	
Born ? *Father* Farid, but adopted by his uncle, Mubarak Shah *Mother* ? *Wife* ?	*Sons* Ala al-Din Alam, addressed Bahlul Lodi as his son *Died* 1445 *Buried* Tomb in District Kharpur, opposite Safdar Jung's tomb, Delhi

Mubarak's reign was consumed in dealing with threats to Delhi from Hindu tribesmen from the Punjab, more Timurid invasions, the sultanate of Jawnpur and the rulers of Mewat. In 1434 his thankless task came to an end when he was assassinated at the instigation of his chief minister, while he was preparing to say his prayers. He was succeeded by his nephew and adopted son, **Muhammad bin Farid**. Within four months the conspirators who had murdered his father were caught and killed, and the nobles pledged their allegiance to him. Sultan Muhammad, however, turned out to be more interested in self-indulgence than in pursuing matters of state. Some nobles took matters into their own hands, inviting the sultan of Malwa to take over Delhi. Sultan Muhammad responded by asking his Afghan nobles under Bahlul Lodi, who had become an increasingly powerful presence at court, to meet the threat. The outcome was an indecisive battle, a treaty with the sultan of Malwa which further reduced the reputation of Delhi, and a substantial increase in the power of Lodi and his Afghan supporters.

When Muhammad died in 1445, he was succeeded by his son, **Ala al-Din**, whom the chronicler Harawi tells us was 'more negligent and incompetent than his father in the duties of government'. He retired to the town of Budaun to the east of Delhi, leaving the capital in the hands of his chief minister. When order broke down, Bahlul Lodi seized his opportunity, capturing Delhi and deposing the chief minister. Having won the Delhi nobility to his side, he wrote to Ala al-Din in Budaun offering to rule the Sultanate in his name. 'Since my father addressed you as a son', Ala al-Din replied, 'I consider you as my elder brother. I have therefore made over the government to you and have contented myself with the pargana of Budaun. Would to God that the Sultanate of Delhi might prosper under you.' On 19 April 1451, Lodi ascended the throne of Delhi. Ala al-Din was to live a further 27 years and, unusually for a sultan who had been deposed, died in peace.

THE LODIS
1451–1526

Bahlul Lodi
1451–89

Sikandar Lodi
1489–1517

Ibrahim Lodi
1517–26

Obverse of a coin of Bahlul Lodi:
'The truster in God, the glory of
the gracious, Bahlul Shah, Sultan.'

BAHLUL LODI	
Born In a family related to the Ghilzai Pathans of Afghanistan *Father* Malik Kala *Mother* Name unknown (daughter of Malik Shah Sultan Lodi of Sirhind) *Wives* Shams Khatun (daughter of Malik Shah Sultan Lodi of Sirhind), Zeba (a goldsmith's daughter)	*Sons* Barbak, Nizam Shah (Sikandar Lodi), Alam Khan, Azam Humayun, Khan Jahan *Enthroned* 19 April 1451 *Died* July 1488, at Malawali, near Aligarh *Buried* By the Dargah of Nizam al-Din Awliya, Delhi

BAHLUL LODI

Bahlul Lodi was esteemed a virtuous and mild prince, executing justice to the utmost of his knowledge, and treating his countries [sic] rather as companions than subjects. When he obtained the crown, he divided the public treasure amongst his friends, and could be seldom prevailed to ascend the throne: saying that it was enough for him that the world knew that he was king, without his making a display of royalty.

Ferishta

BAHLUL LODI BEGAN THE RESTORATION of the power of the Delhi Sultanate. An orphan, he was brought up by an uncle, Islam Khan, who was governor of Sirhind in the Punjab under the Saiyid Khidr Khan. As a young man Bahlul Lodi showed himself to be such an effective soldier that his uncle made him his successor above the claims of his own sons. Thus, when in May 1431 Islam Khan was killed fighting the Mongols, Bahlul became governor of Sirhind in his place. By the time the Saiyid Ala al-Din came to the throne he was master of all the Punjab. In consequence, when Bahlul came to the throne of Delhi, the Sultanate immediately became a more substantial force. To secure his regime he gave all leading administrative

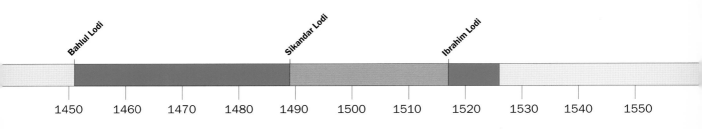

The mausoleum of Bahlul Lodi, close to the shrine of the Chishti Sufi saint, Chiragh-i Delhi, from Saiyid Ahmad Khan's (see box p. 178) survey of the archeological ruins of Delhi, *Athar al-Sanadid* (Traces of the Great).

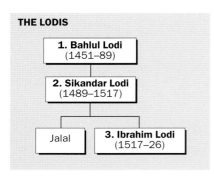

THE LODIS

- **1. Bahlul Lodi** (1451–89)
  - **2. Sikandar Lodi** (1489–1517)
    - Jalal
    - **3. Ibrahim Lodi** (1517–26)

posts to Afghans, whom he also placed in key fiefdoms and military positions. Unsurprisingly, there was much resentment amongst the old Delhi nobility; Afghans at the time being seen as little more than good soldiers.

Some nobles then invited the sultan of Jawnpur, some 640 km (400 miles) east of Delhi, to supplant the Afghans. The sultanate of Jawnpur had emerged thus: in 1394 Mahmud Shah had appointed a powerful slave, known as Khwaja Jahan, to be Sultan al-Sharq or 'King of the East', with his headquarters at Jawnpur; after Timur sacked Delhi, he set up as an independent monarch, and the Sharqi or Eastern dynasty came to rule a prosperous sultanate. Sultan Mahmud Sharqi was pleased to receive the invitation to intervene in Delhi, in part because the more powerful Delhi Sultanate under Bahlul Lodi needed to be curbed before it became too much of a threat to Jawnpur, and in part because his wife, a feisty Saiyid princess, urged him to reclaim her patrimony, threatening to lead the campaign herself if he procrastinated. Thus began a 27-year war between Delhi and Jawnpur, which was the dominant feature of Bahlul's reign. It was not until 1479 that Bahlul was finally able to conquer Jawnpur and incorporate it, making his son Barbak governor. Bahlul's victory was a remarkable achievement, as in almost every battle of the long-fought war his armies faced superior numbers. Among the reasons for his success were his cautious and intelligent leadership, the large number of Afghans – many excellent at archery – who flocked to his standard and the arrogance of the Jawnpuris.

In July 1489 Bahlul's long life, largely consumed by warfare, came to an end as he returned to Delhi from yet another campaign. He had been able to wage war in other areas, such as Multan, Rajasthan, Sind, Gwalior, but the price of his obsession with Jawnpur was the loss of firm control over the Punjab region to the west of Delhi. Here, as in other things, the strength derived from one course of action had led to weakness in another area. In the same way, as his regime gained strength from his Afghan supporters, it also incurred weakness from the Turks, Indian Muslims and Hindus who felt excluded. Equally, his egalitarianism, which meant that in his court he would sit on the same carpet as his courtiers and address them with the highest compliments, had the disadvantage of raising the power of the nobles at the expense of that of the Sultan.

SIKANDAR LODI	
Born	*Enthroned*
c. 1457–58	17 July 1489
Father	*Died*
Bahlul Lodi	21/2 December
Mother	1517
Zeba	*Buried*
Wife	Lodi Gardens, Delhi
Buwa	
Sons	
Ibrahim, Jalal	

SIKANDAR LODI

… his person … was remarkable for its beauty and comeliness, as was his mind for the store of learning and good sense which it contained. During his reign, all the articles of life were cheap and abundant, and peace pervaded his dominions. He never omitted to devote a certain time to hear complaints in public, and he has been frequently known to sit at business the whole day long, even after his appointed time for meals and for rest. He was in the habit of praying regularly five times daily.

Ferishta

BAHLUL'S DEATH, as was usually the case after the demise of a sultan, was followed by a power struggle. Several of his nine sons threw their hats into the ring, as did a nephew. Bahlul had nominated his son Nizam Khan, the governor of Delhi, as his successor. As the nobles discussed who should succeed, Nizam Khan's mother, Zeba, the daughter of a goldsmith, made a dramatic intervention on his behalf from behind a curtain, drawing the retort from Nizam Khan's cousin: 'What business have goldsmiths' sons with the reins of government, since it is proverbial that "monkeys make but bad carpenters".' Nizam Khan resolved matters by taking charge of the situation, disarming his opponents, and on 17 July 1489 ascended the throne in the palace of Firuz Shah, with the support of most of the nobles and bearing the title Sikandar Shah.

Sikandar's first task was to deal with those rivals who still did not recognize his authority: his younger brother Alam Khan, governor of Rapri, his elder brother Barbak, ruler of Jawnpur, and his cousin Azam Humayun, governor of Kalpi. In each case his method was to avoid war if possible, and to show magnanimity in victory. Within a few months, and aged just over 30, he was the undisputed ruler of Delhi. In the years

Obverse of a coin of Sikandar Lodi: 'The Truster in God, the glory of the gracious, Sikandar Shah, Bahlul Shah, Sultan.'

The mausoleum of Sikandar Lodi, an octagonal tomb, placed in a large walled garden with octagonal turrets at the corners and a monumental gateway. Sikandar Lodi was the most successful of the Lodi sultans.

SIX REGIONAL SULTANATES

In the vacuum created by the gradual collapse of the Delhi Sultanate, between the reign of Muhammad bin Tughluq and the invasion of Timur, a series of independent sultanates emerged from the former territories of Delhi. These would make appearances of varying degrees of significance in the stories of both the Delhi Sultans and the Mughal emperors.

The Bahmani Sultanate 1347–1518

In 1347 Hasan Gangu rebelled against Muhammad bin Tughluq, seized Dawlatabad, and founded the Bahmanid dynasty as Sultan Ala al-Din I, assuming the name of Bahman because he claimed descent from the Persian king of that name, usually known as Artaxerxes. For most of the dynasty's duration its dominions reached across the Deccan from the Pen Ganga river in the north to the Krishna river in the south, and from the town of Bonagir in the east to the Arabian Sea in the west. Bahmanid sultans constantly waged war against the Hindu kingdom of Warangal to the east and the great Vijayanagar empire to the south. The sultanate's territories reached their greatest extent under Muhammad Shah III (1463–82), but by 1518 had shrunk to a small area around the then capital of Bidar.

The sultans do not appear to have been attractive men. Between 1347 and 1518 there were 14 of them. Several drank hard enough to die of the effects; these and others debauched themselves with women. All, bar Muhammad II (1378–97), were notably bloodthirsty in their ways. Four were murdered, and two deposed and blinded. The sultanate is notable for its architecture, however. The sultans devoted themselves to building a large number of fortresses, the greatest ever built in India. They had, it seems, the advice of Christian architects from Palestine and Syria who, after the failure of the Crusades, had been sold in India as slaves. These fortresses are extraordinary for their strength and ingenuity. There is also much civilian architecture, in the form of mosques, mausoleums, madrasas and palaces, especially in the two capital cities, first

Gulbarga and then Bidar. Given the significance of 'foreigners' under the Bahmanids, it was not surprising that, for instance in the reign of Ala al-Din II (1436–58), tensions developed between Deccani Muslims and Abyssinian settlers on the one hand, who were largely Sunni, and outsiders, Arabs, Turks, Persians and Mughals, on the other, who were usually Shia. In 1518 the sultanate divided into five separate sultanates, which were to be features of the Mughal era.

The Sultanate of Bengal 1336–1576

The rich province of Bengal, through which the Ganges and the Brahmaputra rivers run to meet the Indian Ocean, always presented difficulties of control to powers based hundreds of miles to the west on the plains of Delhi. In 1342 a powerful noble, Shams al-Din Ilyas (r. 1342–57) asserted Bengal's independence from the rule of Muhammad bin Tughluq. Several times the Tughluqids tried to reconquer it, but from 1359 onwards the young sultanate was left alone. The Bengal sultans proclaimed a strong sense of their independent power and authority. Shams al-Din Ilyas was described on his coins as 'the second Alexander, the right hand of the caliphate'. His son Sikandar (r. 1357–89) built the Adina mosque in his capital of Pandua. Measuring 172 x 97 m (565 x 317 ft), this remains one of the largest mosques on the Indian subcontinent to this day. His successor, Ghiyath al-Din Azam Shah (1389–1410) paid for the building of madrasas in Mecca and Medina. Throughout the 14th century these sultans proclaimed their authority in Perso-Islamic terms, promoting both Persian and Islamic symbols of authority, elaborate court ceremony, a hierarchical bureaucracy and Islam as the state religion. Ghiyath al-Din Azam Shah even tried to persuade the great poet Hafiz (p. 40) to move from Shiraz to his court in Bengal.

The early 15th century saw increasingly strong demands from Hindu nobles to be admitted to the governance of the sultanate. Indeed, sultan Jalal al-Din Muhammad (r. 1415–37) was himself the son of a Hindu. The outcome was the beginning of a steady

indigenization of the sultanate. On the one hand, Jalal al-Din Muhammad continued the Islamic claims of the sultanate, referring to himself as 'the caliph of Allah', but on the other, Bengali came to be used widely at court, Brahmin scholars were patronized and architecture came to reflect indigenous as opposed to foreign inspiration. The sultanate reached what is widely regarded as its high point under Ala al-Din Husain Shah (r. 1493–1519), a Meccan Arab, who rose to chief minister under the patronage of an Abyssinian slave, and his son, Nasir al-Din Nusrat Shah (r. 1519–32). During this period the administration was substantially indigenized, the court patronized literature in Bengali and Sanskrit, the sultanate's lands reached their furthest extent, and visitors were impressed by its power and wealth. After the assassination of Nusrat Shah in 1532, the sultanate was ruled first by the Afghan Suri rivals of the Mughals and then by the Afghani Kararani family until 1576, when it was incorporated into the Mughal empire.

The Sultanate of Jawnpur 1394–1479

This sultanate was founded in 1394 by Khwaja Jahan, the slave minister of Mahmud Shah II of Delhi, with the title Sultan al-Sharq or 'King of the East'. His adopted son, Mubarak Shah (r. 1399–1402), used the weakness of Delhi after the invasion of Timur to assert the sultanate's independence. Under his brother, Shams al-Din Ibrahim (r. 1402–40), the greatest of the Sharqi line, Jawnpur became a notable centre of scholarship, attracting eastwards those who had lost patronage due to the decline of the Delhi Sultanate (it was known as the 'Shiraz of the East') and developing a distinctive regional style of architecture, notably magnificent entrances to mosques. The latter half of the sultanate was marked by a 27-year war with Delhi, in which the Jawnpur sultans failed to make effective use of their greater command of resources. The sultanate was brought to an end in 1479 when Sikandar Lodi finally succeeded in capturing Jawnpur and in driving the last sultan, Husain Shah (r. 1458–79), into Bengal.

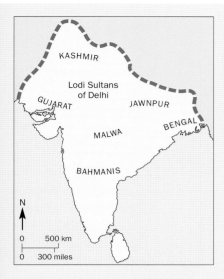

Map of the six regional sultanates of the 15th century.

defeated by the Mughal emperor Humayun, but was saved by Humayun's retreat from Gujarat to face his Afghan rival, Sher Shah Suri. It was, however, only a temporary relief. Seeking help from the Portuguese to fight the Mughals, he was killed while negotiating with the Portuguese governor of Diu. The remaining history of the sultanate was one of anarchy until, in 1572, it was annexed by the Mughal emperor Akbar. The architecture of the sultanate offers the richest of India's regional styles, and is notable for the way in which some of the most skilled craftsmen of India translated Islamic requirements into their own idiom.

The Sultanate of Malwa 1401–1531

Malwa covered a major area in central India, with the sultanates of Delhi and Jawnpur to the north, Gujarat to the west and of the Bahmanids to the south. Around 1310 this area was annexed by the Delhi Sultanate, and in 1401 the governor, Dilawar Khan Ghuri, set up as an independent sultan, establishing a dynasty which lasted until 1436. Its most notable ruler was Hushang Shah (1405–35) who created its great capital city of Mandu on the summit of a hill in the Vindhya range, surrounded by 40 km (25 miles) of wall. The second dynasty began when the chief minister, Mahmud Khan, a Khalji Turk, poisoned the last Ghurid sultan. Mahmud Shah (r. 1436–69) devoted his life to fighting his neighbours. His successor, Ghiyath al-Din (1469–1500) ended his peaceful regime by voluntarily giving up his throne to his son, who then poisoned him. The sultanate came to an end in 1531 when it was conquered by Bahadur Shah of Gujarat. Like Gujarat it was remarkable for the architecture left behind, in particular in the cities of Mandu and Chanderi.

The base of the carved stone minaret of the Friday Mosque in Ahmadabad built by Ahmad Shah in 1423. The most magnificent of the city's mosques, the intricate carving of its stonework reflects the decorative traditions of the region's Hindu temples.

The Sultanate of Kashmir 1346–1586

In the late medieval period the name Kashmir referred to the valley of Kashmir, some 128 km (80 miles) long and 40 km (25 miles) wide, in the southern reaches of the Himalayas north of Delhi. The first sultan was an Afghan adventurer, Shah Mirza, who became a minister of Kashmir's Hindu ruler and in 1346 usurped the throne, taking the title Shams al-Din. The sultanate had two notable rulers. First, Sikandar, the sixth sultan (1393–1413), whose generous patronage attracted scholars from West Asia to his mountain kingdom, but whose eagerness to promote Islam and to destroy Hindu temples and idols led to his sobriquet 'idol-breaker'. The second was his younger son, Zain al-Abidin (1420–70), who presided over a golden age in the valley. He promoted policies of tolerance towards Hindus, repealing the poll tax on them, permitting new temples to be built and forbidding the slaughter of cows. He established Persian as the court language, patronized the arts and sciences and had many works in Sanskrit, Arabic and other languages translated into Persian. After his death the sultanate was weakened by civil war and invasion. From 1540 to 1551 it was ruled by Mirza Haidar Dughlat, a relative of the Mughal emperor Humayun. In 1586, Akbar annexed the sultanate to the Mughal empire.

The Sultanate of Gujarat 1407–1573

Gujarat covered the fertile lands between the Rann of Cutch and the Western Ghats. Blessed with many seaports, it had long enjoyed a vigorous commerce. Annexed by the Delhi Sultanate in 1297, it was ruled by governors until in 1401 the governor Muzaffar Khan withdrew his allegiance from Delhi and in 1407 established the sultanate of Gujarat. Two great rulers dominate the history of the sultanate. The first was Ahmad Shah (r. 1411–41). He extended the sultanate's territories, spread Islam, improved administration and was never defeated in battle. Among his achievements was the building of the city of Ahmadabad between 1410 and 1417, widely admired by contemporaries for its beauty and splendour. The second great ruler was Ahmad's grandson, Mahmud 'Bigarha', meaning 'two cities', after the great fortresses of Champanir and Junagarh which he conquered.

Mahmud (r. 1459–1511) was a most successful ruler who focused most of his energy on internal governance. In the last years of his reign he became caught up in battles with the Portuguese for the control of Indian Ocean trade. Allied with Egypt, he won and lost naval battles before deciding that the best way to deal with the Portuguese was to offer them a site for a factory at Diu and make peace. The last sultan of any note was Mahmud's grandson, Bahadur Shah (r. 1526–37). In 1535 he was badly

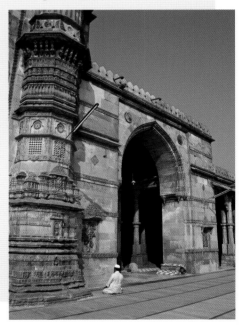

which followed he concentrated on crushing all opposition to the east of Delhi, so that by 1499 he had not only confirmed his authority over Jawnpur but annexed Bihar. Sikandar then turned his attention to the south of Delhi, to the state of Gwalior, which was ruled by the great liberal-minded Hindu raja, Man Singh (1486–1517). Amongst Sikandar's concerns was that Gwalior was frequently a place of refuge for chieftains fleeing from the imposition of Lodi authority in the Punjab. Sikandar's first five years of campaigns were unsuccessful. Matters began to change when in 1505 he accepted the recommendation of his officers that he should move his capital southwards to Agra so that he could move more quickly to deal with military affairs in the Gwalior region. By 1509 he had succeeded in encircling Gwalior with a chain of Lodi-controlled fortresses. Then, from 1509 to 1516, he was in the position to make inroads yet further south into the sultanate of Malwa. There was a price to pay, however, for 16 years spent driving the Sultanate's influence southwards. Sikandar's neglect of his northwest frontier encouraged greater independence amongst the chieftains of the Punjab and suggested to the Mughal leader, Babur, that Hindustan was an area which most certainly could be raided and perhaps even conquered.

Sikandar was the most successful Lodi sultan. He kept close watch on the workings of justice, raised the educational standards of the Afghans who served him and tightly supervised his administration. The consequence of his efficient governance was stability, increasing trade and falling prices of foodstuffs. As an individual he was cultivated, being both a practising poet in Persian under the pseudonym 'Gulrukhi' ('Rose-cheeked') and a lover of music. He is said both to have kept the company of learned and holy men and, to an unusual extent, to have rewarded them with land and gifts. He vigorously opposed the following of non-Islamic customs by Muslims, but was not without his share of human weakness; though clearly devout, he drank wine secretly 'to keep himself in health'. This said, there is one issue which has worried the historians: his harshness towards Hindus, involving iconoclasm and the replacing of temples with mosques. It is worth noting that these actions were restricted to areas where he was engaged in campaigns of political subjugation, but they also stand out because the 15th century was a time of fruitful interaction between the Muslim and Hindu traditions.

IBRAHIM LODI

Ibrahim ... at a very early period, contrary to the custom of his father and grandfather ... made no distinction among his officers, whether of his own tribe or otherwise, and said publicly, that kings should have no relations or clansmen, but that all should be considered as subjects and servants of the state; and the Afghan chiefs who had hitherto been allowed to sit in the presence, were constrained to stand in front of the throne with their hands crossed before them.

Ferishta

Obverse of a coin of Ibrahim Shah Lodi: 'The truster in God, the glory of the gracious, Ibrahim Shah, Sikandar Shah, Sultan.' The legends on his coins are often difficult to read.

KABIR

One feature of the 15th century was the emergence of socio-religious thinkers in northern India influenced both by Islam, in particular Sufism, and by a spiritual revival amongst Hindus in southern India. The most important figure in this movement was a Muslim weaver of Benares called Kabir (?1398–1448). A mystic poet and illiterate, Kabir opposed superstition, idol worship, pilgrimages, ritual and blind belief in scripture. He aimed to unite Hindus and Muslims, removing all distinctions of caste and creed. For him the essence of Hinduism and Islam was the same. There was only one God, though he might be known by different names. He preached a faith of universal brotherhood and set out to show in Hindi verse – which had enormous influence at the time in north India, from the Punjab to the Deccan, and has continued to have influence ever since – how man might come to merge his soul with God. The verse of Kabir set out below indicates why Sikandar Lodi's religious intolerance was so out of harmony with his time.

O Servant where does thou see Me?
Lo, I am beside thee.
I am neither in temple nor in mosque;
I am neither in Kaaba nor in Kailash.
Neither am I in rites and ceremonies,
Nor in Yoga and renunciation.
If you art a true seeker, thou shalt at once
See Me, thou shalt meet Me in a moment of time.
Kabir says, 'O Sadhu! God is the breath of all breath.'

IBRAHIM LODI	
Born	Enthroned
?	1st: 22 November
Father	1517; 2nd: 30
Sikandar Lodi	December 1517
Mother	Died
Buwa	21 April 1526 in the
Wife	battle of Panipat
?	Buried
Sons	By the roadside at
?	Panipat

ON SIKANDAR'S DEATH, the nobles decreed that the Sultanate should be divided between his two ablest sons, Ibrahim and Jalal, the former, and elder, ruling from Agra, and the latter from Jawnpur. Thus, on 22 November, the day after Sikandar's death, Ibrahim was crowned at Agra. 'So splendid a coronation had never been witnessed', declared the chronicler Ahmad Yadgar, 'and the people long remembered the day....' At the same time, Jalal made his way to Jawnpur.

Ibrahim quickly realized that the division of the Sultanate was, in effect, a plot by the nobility to divide and rule. He immediately set about imposing his will on the whole kingdom. He began by trying to use persuasion: Jalal was invited to Agra and the nobles of the districts around Jawnpur were instructed not to pay allegiance to him; all his remaining brothers were imprisoned. Jalal refused to come to terms. So on 30 December 1517, Ibrahim had himself crowned again, this time as ruler of the whole Sultanate, and set about using force to bring Jalal to heel. In 1518, by dint of skilful negotiations, Jalal was persuaded to surrender the symbols of royalty, his parasol and kettledrum, to Ibrahim, on condition that he kept his lands around Kalpi. Ibrahim did not honour these terms, wishing only to destroy Jalal completely. Jalal fled to seek shelter with the Raja of Gwalior. Ibrahim immediately went to war against Gwalior and succeeded, where his father had failed, in capturing the Rajput capital. But, by this time, Jalal had moved on to seek shelter in central India, where the Gond king, Sangram Shah, keen to win the goodwill of Ibrahim, captured the Lodi prince and sent him to the Sultan. Jalal entered the royal court with his hands bound behind him. Quickly, Ibrahim had him poisoned.

Ibrahim had eliminated his main rival, but it did not make him feel more secure. He had killed, imprisoned or otherwise offended, many of his father's nobles. In 1519 the nobles rebelled in the east of the Sultanate. Ibrahim crushed the rebellion in one of the bloodiest battles for many years, with 10,000 dying on each side. Despite this success, however, he still felt vulnerable; he continued to pick off nobles he suspected of disloyalty, and found himself faced once more by a major rising in the east. Ibrahim sent for Dawlat Khan Lodi, the governor of the Punjab, to come to his aid. Such was the lack of trust that Ibrahim by now inspired, that Dawlat Khan thought better of the journey to Agra, and instead, in 1523, invited the Mughal, Babur, to come from Kabul to destroy the power of Ibrahim Lodi. Other rulers, including the Hindu ruler of Mewar, also issued invitations. In November 1525 Babur, after a series of expeditions into India which had begun in 1505, launched his invasion of the land. On 21 April 1526, Ibrahim Lodi, with an army of at least 100,000 effective soldiers and 1,000 elephants, faced Babur's army of no more than 12,000 on the plain of Panipat northwest of Delhi. Ibrahim was defeated, bettered by Babur's tactics and command of gunpowder. Ibrahim died on the battlefield, the only one of the Sultans of Delhi to do so. Afghan rule in India was broken, and the Sultanate now passed into the hands of the Mughals.

THE GREAT MUGHALS
1526–1707

Zahir al-Din Muhammad Babur
1526–30

Humayun
1530–40, 1555–56

Akbar
1556–1605

Jahangir
1605–27

Shah Jahan
1627–58

Awrangzeb
(Alamgir I)
1658–1707

THE LATER MUGHALS
1707–1858

Bahadur Shah I
1707–12

Jahandar Shah
1712–13

Farrukhsiyar
1713–19

Muhammad Shah
1719–48

Ahmad Shah
1748–54

Alamgir II
1754–59

Shah Alam
1759–1806

Akbar II
1806–37

Bahadur Shah II
1837–58

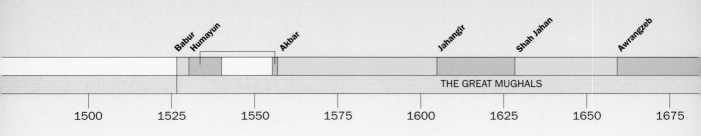

Babur

Shah Jahan

Awrangzeb

Bahadur Shah

THE MUGHALS
1526–1858

THE MUGHALS, WHO RULED IN INDIA from 1526 to 1858, are one of history's more remarkable dynasties. Their rule embraced a population of between 100 and 150 million, and was, along with Ming China, the richest of the pre-modern empires. Ruling a highly centralized empire, the early Mughals continued the Mongol/Timurid tradition of running the central administration along the lines of one vast military camp. Their authority came to embrace most of the subcontinent, which they controlled for longer and to greater effect than the Delhi Sultanate. At the heart of the empire was an effective partnership between the Muslim Mughals and the warrior nobles of India, most of whom were Hindu.

On this platform a great cosmopolitan court was created, which drew on the Timurid inheritance of persianate culture, but was no less able to achieve a creative interaction with the Hindu cultures which it ruled, while also being open to new cultural possibilities from the Christian West. The outcome was to bring to a peak the developing traditions of Muslim statemaking and to see the consequent wealth and power and patronage expressed in a stream of works of art and architecture of the highest quality. Such was their image of power that the British both initially derived legitimacy for their own rule from them and used Mughal forms to express aspects of their own authority: it is not by chance that to this day Mughal, usually spelled as Mogul, remains a metaphor for a powerful man.

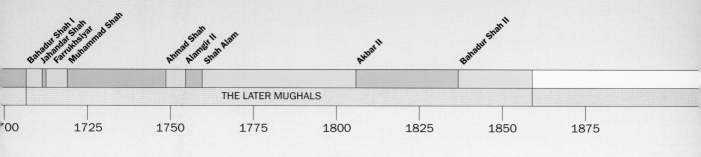

Bahadur Shah I
Jahandar Shah
Farrukhsiyar
Muhammad Shah

Ahmad Shah
Alamgir II
Shah Alam

Akbar II

Bahadur Shah II

THE LATER MUGHALS

'00   1725   1750   1775   1800   1825   1850   1875

THE GREAT MUGHALS
1526–1707

Zahir al-Din Muhammad Babur
1526–30

Humayun
1530–40, 1555–56

The Great Mughal Babur, founder of the dynasty, who strove for over twenty years to win an empire which would match the achievements of his ancestors, Timur and Chingiz Khan. His memoirs reveal a life of extraordinary endurance and a mind of unusual sophistication.

BABUR	
Born 1483	Begum, and three others
Father Umar Shaikh, son of Abu Said, descendant of Timur	*Sons* Humayun, Kamran, Askari, Hindal
Mother Qutlugh Nigar Khanum, descendant of Chingiz Khan	*Daughters* Gulbadan Begum, Gulran, Gulchihra, Gulazar Begum, Masuma Sultan
Wives *Aisha, *Masuma, *Zainab (*divorced before 1509), Gulrukh Begum, Maham, Bibi Mubarika, Dildar	*Enthroned* 1526
	Died 26 December 1530
	Buried First in a garden in Agra, second in a garden tomb in Kabul

ZAHIR AL-DIN MUHAMMAD BABUR

He was a prince of great humanity, and carried his liberality to such excess, that it bordered on prodigality. With respect to the first, he so often pardoned ingratitude and treason that he seemed to make a principle of rendering good for evil: he thus disarmed malice, and made his enemies the admirers of his virtues. He … never omitted his daily prayers. He had few equals in the arts of poetry, prose composition and music. He wrote his own life in the Turki language, with such elegance and truth, that the performance is universally admired.

Ferishta

THIS REMARKABLE MAN WAS DESCENDED on his father's side from Timur through Abu Said of Herat (p. 63), while his grandfather on his mother's side was Yunus Khan of Tashkent, Great Khan of the Mongols, and 13th in line of descent from Chingiz Khan. Babur, whose name means 'Tiger', never forgot his glittering ancestry. After his father died in 1494, when he was but 12, Babur found himself catapulted into the competition for power in Transoxania, in part with his own relatives, but increasingly with the Uzbeg Turks. Babur's aim was to recapture his patrimony, Samarqand, which he said 'for nearly 140 years … had been in our

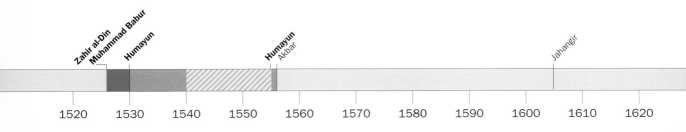

1520	1530	1540	1550	1560	1570	1580	1590	1600	1610	1620	

Zahir al-Din Muhammad Babur • Humayun • Humayun • Akbar • Jahangir family'. He besieged it three times and conquered it twice, the first time when he was 15, but often his army was no more than a ragged band in desperate straits. But then, in 1504, he captured Kabul and managed to turn it into a permanent base. From Kabul he was constantly engaged in campaigns, for the most part against the Uzbegs to the north, and at one point, just for a moment, he succeeded in recapturing Transoxania.

From his capture of Kabul, however, Babur, as he himself put it 'had craved Hindustan'. For many years he was held back by the opposition of his officers. But, in 1519, he succeeded in overcoming the opposition and began the first of four probing expeditions into India. Then, in 1523, he received a formal invitation to make a full-scale invasion from Dawlat Khan, the governor of the Punjab (p. 111). It was evident that there was substantial opposition to the Afghan Lodi regime and that this would be a good time to strike. Babur had prepared for the invasion, both by training his men thoroughly and by acquiring the latest gunpowder technology. Then, as he wrote, 'we placed our feet in the stirrup of resolve, grabbed

Map illustrating the expansion of Mughal rule over the subcontinent down to the beginning of the 18th century, when it reached its greatest extent and when the power of the Hindu Marathas was beginning to be felt in western India. The map should be compared with that on page 93 which illustrates the furthest extent of the power of the Delhi Sultanate from its base in north India.

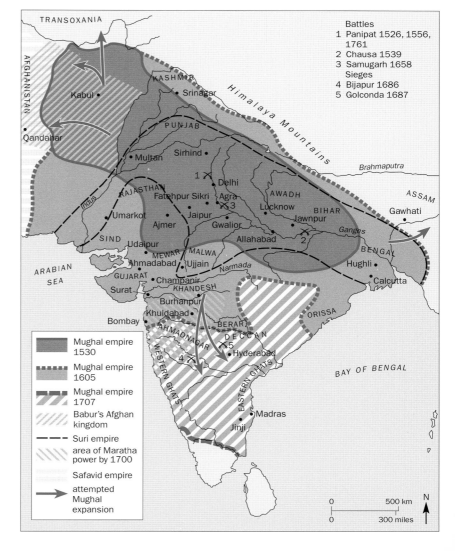

BABUR AND GUNPOWDER

Gunpowder weaponry was crucial to Babur's victories at Panipat and Kanua. Arguably, this more than anything else created the opportunity for the establishment of Mughal power. Gunpowder devices had been used in siege warfare from the 14th century. But Babur was the first to use gunpowder weapons on the battlefield, and in doing so his tactics were very similar to those used by the Ottomans against the Safavids at Chaldiran in 1514, and by the Safavids against the Uzbegs at Jam in 1528. The three main weapons were the *kazan*, a form of mortar on a four-wheeled cart; the *zarbzan*, a light cannon on a two-wheeled cart; and matchlocks. The matchlockmen provided covering fire for the artillery. In his memoirs Babur gives regular reports on the experiments, activities and achievements of his two artillery men, Ali Quli and Mustafa Rumi, who it seems did not get along too well. Over a few decades the new weapons were to spread throughout India and revolutionize warfare.

The zarbzans *or light cannon which Babur used to devastating effect in the battle of Panipat, 1526.*

the reins of trust in God, and directed ourselves against Sultan Ibrahim….'

The fate of India was decided in two great battles. On 21 April 1526 on the plain of Panipat, north of Delhi, Babur's army of 12,000 faced Ibrahim Lodi's 100,000 men supported by 1,000 elephants. By clever tactics Babur forced the Afghan centre into a bottleneck against his defences, rolled up the Afghan wings with his cavalry, and then pounded the seething mass with his guns. By midday, around 16,000 Afghans lay dead: Ibrahim Lodi's head was brought to Babur, who treated it with respect. In the second battle, in March 1527 at Kanua, just west of Agra, Babur faced Rana Sanga of Mewar, the leader of a confederacy of Hindu Rajput princes, and Mahmud Lodi, the brother of Ibrahim. On this occasion the opposition fielded 200,000 men. Babur used the same tactics, and once more his command of gunpowder weaponry was decisive. Babur ordered a tower of heads to be built in honour of his victory.

In the years between Kanua and his death Babur explored his dominions and took life more easily. He was marvellously curious, noting rivers and mountain ranges, Rajput forts and Hindu temples, and particularly flora and fauna. He was distinctly underwhelmed by some of what he found: 'Hindustan is a place of little charm', he wrote, 'there is no beauty in its people, no etiquette, nobility or manliness. The arts and crafts have no harmony or symmetry … the one nice aspect of Hindustan is that it is a large country with lots of gold and money.' Afghan resistance still bubbled; he had to put down an attempted military campaign by Mahmud Lodi, who had made himself sultan of the eastern province of Bihar. At last, he had time to give himself over to pleasures. He made gardens, wrote books and poetry, caroused with companions, and enjoyed in particular the attention of two Caucasian slave girls, Gulnar and Nar-gul, presents from Shah Tahmasp of Iran (p. 185). In his attitude to governance, however, he showed himself a man who understood war better than peace. He divided up the Lodi treasury and dominions amongst his nobles, but made no arrangements for regular revenue collection.

Babur the man

We are extremely fortunate to have two works which shed intimate light on Babur and his world: his own memoirs and those of his son, Humayun, written by his daughter, Gulbadan. Of course, Babur was a man of action. 'When one has pretensions to rule and a desire for conquest', he wrote of the setbacks of his early life, 'one cannot sit back and watch if events don't go right once or twice.' He gives, moreover, stirring vignettes of hand-to-hand fighting: 'Mirza Quli Kulkaldash took down a foot soldier with his flail. After Mirza Quli crossed [the road] an older foot soldier took aim at Ibrahim Beg, but just as Ibrahim Beg crossed yelling "Hey, hey!" the soldier shot me in the side from a short distance away. Two plates of my Qalmaqi armour were pierced and broken. I shot at his back as he fled.'

Babur's Gardens

In his memoirs Babur records the magnificent gardens which his ancestors and relations had created at Samarqand and Herat. It is no surprise, therefore, that, as soon as he conquered Kabul, he should lay out gardens. In all there were 10, in addition to the one destined for his tomb. They reflected for the most part the Iranian *chahar bagh* design in which waterways and pathways at right angles create four flowerbeds. Babur's favourite garden was the Bagh-i Wafa, or Garden of Fidelity, to which he sent banana and sugarcane plants from India and whose beauty 'when the oranges turn yellow', he remembers with delight. Babur's gardens, however, were not just for pleasure, they also had a practical purpose. His court was an encampment constantly on the move; it was so much better to be able to pitch tents in a garden. As soon as he conquered India, he set about creating gardens in and around Agra and ordered that *chahar bagh* gardens should be made in all large cities. He took a dim view of the prospects of creating gardens in India because of the lack of running water, but this was overcome by the digging of step wells and the use of water wheels. And eventually 'in unpleasant and inharmonious India', as he wrote, 'marvellously regular and geometric gardens were introduced. In every corner were beautiful plots and in every plot were regularly laid out arrangements of roses and narcissus.'

Babur created gardens wherever he went. Here we see him in the process of laying out his favourite garden, the Bagh-i Wafa (Garden of Fidelity), which he created outside Kabul in 1508–09 on rising ground facing south. The chahar bagh *design and the use of water are evident.*

Babur's strong sense of history, and the place of his family and himself in it, was never far away. On capturing Samarqand he writes a full, historically informed description of the glories of the city created by his family. After taking Delhi he made a point of touring the tombs of the Delhi Sultans. Moreover, he had a clear picture of his achievement in conquering India. From the time of the Prophet, he wrote, only two others had achieved this, Mahmud of Ghazni and Shihab al-Din Ghuri. 'My accomplishment, however, is beyond comparison with theirs ....'

Literature was a major pleasure for Babur. Poetry was never far from the pages of his memoirs, both his and those of others. At one point he realized that the game he had developed with his companions of versifying whatever came to mind, however obscene or improper, was not appropriate at a time when he was also putting a treatise on Islamic law into verse for the benefit of his second son. He regarded a fever he caught, which caused him to cough up blood, as a consequential punishment from God. Books were a passion. His first act after one conquest was immediately to go to the library of the vanquished and seize what was best. He had, moreover, very strong views on literary style. 'As I asked, you have written your letters', he wrote to Humayun, 'but you didn't read them over, for if you had had a mind to read them you would have found that you could not. After reading them you certainly would have changed them. Although your writing can be read with difficulty, it is excessively obscure. Who has ever heard of prose designed to be an enigma? ... Probably your laziness in writing letters is due to the fact that you try to make it too fancy. From now on write with uncomplicated, clear, and plain words. This will cause less difficulty both for you and for your reader.'

Babur delighted in the humanity of those who peopled his world. Listen to his description of his father: 'he was short in stature, had a round beard and a fleshy face, and was fat. He wore his tunic so tight that to fasten the ties, he had to hold in his stomach; if he let himself go, it often happened that the ties broke.... He was a good-natured, talkative and well-spoken man.... He was fun to be with in a gathering and good at reciting poetry to his companions.' Then Babur tells us with paternal pride of Humayun's success in his first taste of action in the skirmishing with the Afghans before the battle of Panipat and declares: 'In this camp on that same day, Humayun first put the razor and scissors to his face.'

THE GREAT MUGHALS

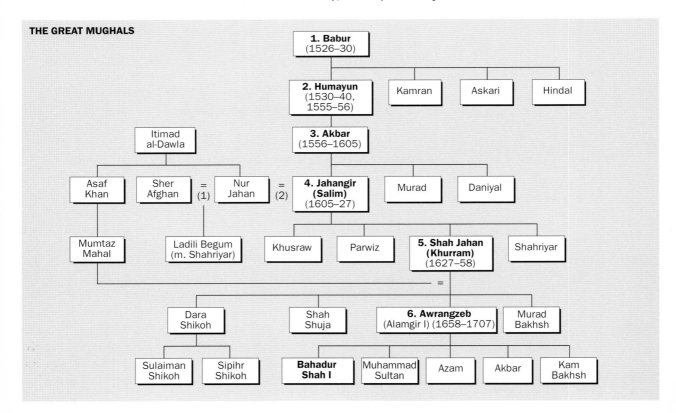

Magnanimity is a feature of the best of princes, and that of Babur was renowned. On one occasion it nearly led to his death. After his victory at Panipat he made generous provision for the mother of Ibrahim Lodi, one Buwa, and her dependents. This she repaid a few months later by attempting to poison him. Ever keen to experiment, Babur tried Indian food, employing some of Ibrahim Lodi's cooks. Buwa arranged for Babur's taster to be bribed to persuade the cooks to poison his food. Babur was lucky to avoid most of the poison and escape with severe vomiting. Two days later those involved confessed. 'I ordered the taster to be hacked to pieces and the cook to be skinned alive. One of the two women I had thrown under the elephants' feet, and the other I had shot. I had Buwa put under arrest', he wrote, 'she will pay for what she has done.'

Babur's respect for women and love of drink

Women, and respect for women, figure prominently in Babur's memoirs. His mother's mother was a key adviser in his early years and he quotes political guidance on the politics of Transoxania from his mother. He reminds us of how his mother shared some of the hardships of his early desperate campaigns; he records her death. His older wives, Aisha, Masuma and Maham are all given due place; indeed, he tells us that it was Masuma who took the initiative in their marriage. During his last years in India, he records the comings and goings of his aunts; in Agra he would go every Friday afternoon to see them. His daughter, Gulbadan, records the arrival from Kabul of Babur's sister and other women of his household. Considerable provision was made for their comfort. She also records her own arrival from Kabul with her adoptive mother, Maham, Babur's favourite wife, how he came a long way from Agra to greet them, and how she was forced to wait for her meeting with her father while he and Maham had some time alone.

Until his early 20s Babur did not drink and tells of how he was a wet blanket at parties when in Herat. But, by his mid-20s he was drinking regularly, and his memoirs are filled with tales of drinking parties, and the stupid things said and done under the influence of alcohol. In 1527, as he faced the armies of Rana Sanga and Mahmud Lodi, he made a formal vow to God to give up drink. 'The thought of giving up drinking had long been on my mind', he wrote, 'and my heart had continually been clouded by committing this illegal act.' He had all his gold and silver goblets smashed, the pieces distributed to the poor, and all the wine in his camp destroyed. His soldiers were forced to follow suit. Within a year or so he had regretted his action:

> *I am distraught to have given up wine.*
> *I do not know what to do and I am perplexed.*
> *Everybody regrets drinking and then takes the oath;*
> *But I have taken the oath and now regret it.*

He was soon back to his old ways.

BABUR'S MEMOIRS

Babur's memoirs, the *Baburnama*, are arguably the most remarkable autobiography of medieval Islamic civilization and rank with the finest produced anywhere. No one knows why he chose to write the memoirs. He himself declares: 'I have not written all this to complain; I have simply written the truth. I do not intend what I have written to compliment myself: I have simply set down exactly what happened … May the reader excuse me; may the listener take me not to task.' The memoirs were highly valued by the Mughals, and not least for the contribution they made to their imperial ideology. To make sure they had their effect Akbar had them translated from the Chaghatai Turki, in which Babur wrote, into Persian, the language of the Mughal court. Many copies were reproduced, some handsomely illustrated in the imperial Mughal workshops. A large chunk is missing and the memoirs break off in mid-sentence in 1529, the last section having the feel of a first draft just copied from a diary. Nevertheless, the memoirs enable us to listen to the unique voice of a brilliant Timurid prince, a highly cultivated man of action, courageous, frank, intellectually curious and deeply humane.

Babur describes in the Baburnama *how he spent a day with friends on a boat in 1519, drinking spirits and chewing* majun, *a mild narcotic. Here in an illustration by Farrukh Beg we see him returning to camp where the party continued: 'It was no time before the drunks began to talk all sorts of nonsense' he recalled, 'no matter how we tried to get the party under control, nothing worked.'*

Babur's strange end

During his last years, from time to time, Babur was ill. But his end came in a most extraordinary manner. Gulbadan tells us that Humayun fell ill and his mother, Maham, went to fetch him and 'the two, mother and son, like Jesus and Mary, set out for Agra'. She records the following exchange when Babur saw how ill his son was: 'My lady said: "Do not be troubled about my son. You are a king; what griefs have you? You have other sons. I sorrow because I have only this one." His Majesty rejoined: "Maham! Although I have other sons, I love none as I love your Humayun … I desire the kingdom for him and not for the others, because he has not his equal in distinction."' Babur sought advice as to what should be done and favoured counsel which said that Humayun, to be saved, must give up the most valuable thing he possessed. Babur said 'I am the most valuable thing that Humayun possesses … I myself will be his sacrifice. He is in extremity and I have lost the power to behold his powerlessness, but I can endure all his pain.' Babur then said his prayers and walked three times around Humayun's bed. 'When his prayer had been heard by God', Abul Fadl tells us, 'he felt a strange effect upon himself and cried out, "We have borne it away. We have borne it away."' From that moment Babur became ill, and Humayun recovered. He died on 21 December 1530. In the 1540s he was finally laid to rest in his favourite garden in Kabul.

Opposite The Mughals were concerned to emphasize their dynastic legitimacy and the tradition of wielding power in their bloodline back to Chingiz Khan, and then further, as Abul Fadl made clear in the *Akbarnama*, to the mythical Mongol queen, Alanqoa (see also pp. 7, 49). Here, Timur hands on his crown to Babur, with Humayun looking on. Their viziers, Mirza Rustam, Mirza Shah Rukh and Bairam Khan observe the scene.

Humayun, Babur's gifted eldest son, lost his empire to the Suri Afghans; he had to fight both his three brothers and the Afghans before regaining it in 1555. His stay in Iran at the court of the Safavid Shah Tahmasp (see p. 185) enabled him to introduce Persian cultural influences, particularly in painting, to India.

HUMAYUN	
Born	*Daughters*
1508	Aqiqa Begum,
Father	Bakhshibanu
Babur	Begum, Bakht al-
Mother	Nisa Begum, Fakhr
Maham	al-Nisa Begum
Wives	*Enthroned*
Hamida (Mariam	1st: 30 December
Makani),	1530; 2nd: 23 July
Mahchukak, Bega,	1555
Gunwar Bibi, Bigah	*Died*
Begum	24 January 1556,
Sons	falling down the
Akbar, Muhammad,	stairs of his library
Hakim	*Buried*
	Humayun's Tomb,
	Delhi

HUMAYUN

… he was glorious for right-mindedness and lofty courage in every enterprise that he engaged in and every service that he undertook. In the whole of his auspicious life, he adorned the world by joining knowledge with power, and power with compassion and clemency. In many sciences and especially in mathematics, he had no rival or colleague. His noble nature was marked by the combination of the energy of Alexander and the learning of Aristotle.… But superiority in spiritual perfections (which is real sovereignty), that was his own by God's grace; none of his brothers shared in the dainties of that table of inheritance.

Abul Fadl

ABUL FADL'S ENCOMIUM OF HUMAYUN is endorsed, for the most part, by other chroniclers of his reign. But what Abul Fadl does not say is that this most gifted prince was also too inclined to put off much-needed action in favour of parties and pleasure, the latter including opium taken as a pellet with rosewater. On coming to power he found an unstable situation. His own effective dominion was limited in northern India from Jawnpur in the east through Delhi to the Punjab. To the east of Jawnpur in Bihar, the Afghans under the leadership of Mahmud, the brother of Ibrahim Lodi, were eager to regain their patrimony in Delhi. To the south there was Bahadur Shah, Sultan of Gujarat, who was advancing steadily towards Agra after victories over the Rajputs. To the northwest there was his brother, Kamran, whom his father had made ruler of Kabul. Kamran, and his younger brothers, Askari and Hindal, overtly expressed their loyalty to Humayun, but like all young Mughal princes were ready to advance their cause against their brother.

The Afghan threat

Humayun turned first to deal with the Afghan threat, and in 1531 defeated Mahmud outside Lucknow, putting an end to any thought of a Lodi revival. This left one significant Afghan leader still in play, Sher Khan. He had risen from a minor position to be prime minister under the Lohani Afghans, who called themselves sultans of Bihar. Humayun made, in hindsight, the mistake of not finishing him off, being content to receive his submission. Humayun now turned to deal with the threat from Gujarat. In 1535 he conquered both Gujarat and Malwa, doubling the size of his kingdom, and in the process showing personal gallantry as the 41st Mughal soldier in the escalade which enabled the great fortress of Champanir to be taken by storm. But he failed to impose an effective system of control on his new dominions, preferring to spend his time in pleasure. This meant that, when he was forced to face the Afghan threat in the east once more, the Sultan of Gujarat just marched back into his former territories.

In 1537 Humayun marched eastwards to confront Sher Khan, now a much more substantial threat. While he was in the east his younger brother Hindal showed his hand, having himself proclaimed sultan in Delhi, an action which was stamped on by Humayun's loyal nobles. But, at the same time, as Gulbadan tells us, there arose in Kamran 'a desire for sovereignty'. Humayun's campaign in the east turned out to be a disaster, exacerbated by a further period of indolent merrymaking in Bengal. In 1539, after being cleverly deceived by Sher Khan, Humayun only just escaped with his life in his defeat at Chawsa. The following year his army was defeated again at Kanauj on the Ganges, and he and his brothers, with Sher Khan hard on their heels, were forced to flee, Kamran and Askari to Kabul, and Hindal and Humayun into the deserts of Sind and Rajputana.

Exile and return

Humayun spent three years in this arid region trying to raise support for his cause. The one notable event was his marriage to the 14-year-old

THE SURI SULTANS OF DELHI

Sher Khan was the grandson of an Afghan who came to India to seek service under Bahlul Lodi. After the defeat of Mahmud Lodi he was the most powerful Afghan leader to remain and he set about building a powerful set of alliances from Jawnpur and Benares through to Bengal, which formed the platform from which he finally defeated Humayun in 1540. In military matters his reign was taken up with warfare against the Rajputs. He died on 22 May 1545 from wounds received when a pile of grenades exploded next to him outside the walls of Kalinjar.

In his short reign, Sher Shah, as he was known, proved himself one of India's most effective rulers; he worked extraordinarily hard in the process, beginning his day at 3 a.m. He created a system of local government which prevented the concentration of power in the hands of one person; he developed a method of land revenue assessment based on the measurement of land; and he prevented provincial officers from identifying with particular localities by

rotating them every two years. Villages were made responsible for crimes within their limits; justice was swift and administered without fear or favour. Corrupt practice in the military was addressed, and his armies on the march were said to be scrupulous about paying for any damage their movement might cause. Four great roads were built across northern India, planted with fruit trees and 1,700 caravanserais were built at regular intervals along their length. A sound coinage was introduced based on the silver rupee and the copper paisa; trade flourished. A believing Muslim, the Shah was even-handed between Hindu and Muslim.

His administrative innovations created the basis on which Akbar and his ministers were able to build the wealth and power of the Mughal state. A son, Islam Shah, who succeeded Sher Shah, maintained his father's administrative innovations but was unloved; he forced his nobles to respect his authority by bloody and systematic purges, rather than by winning their loyalty. After his death in 1554 his nobles placed his 12-year-old son Firuz on the throne. Within a month Islam Shah's nephew had killed Firuz and seized the throne, and the struggle for power amongst rival Afghan princes began which gave Humayun his opportunity to return.

The mausoleum of Sher Shah Suri at Sasaram in Bihar, which was completed just after his death in 1545. It was placed on an island in the middle of a small lake surrounded by small hills covered with flowering trees. A fit resting place for a ruler of unusual effectiveness.

HAMIDA BEGUM

Both Humayun's valet, Jawhar, and his half-sister, Gulbadan, describe in their memoirs the coming together of the 14-year-old Hamida with Humayun. Humayun caught sight of the girl at an entertainment given by Dildar Begum, the mother of Hindal and Gulbadan. He said straightaway: 'I will marry her.' But Hindal and Hamida put up strong opposition to the proposal for 40 days. Humayun pressed his case. Hamida was notably assertive, even cheeky. On one occasion when Humayun called her to him, she refused to come saying: 'If it is to pay my respects, I was exalted by paying my respects the other day. Why should I come again?' On another occasion she said: 'To see kings once is lawful; a second time is forbidden. I shall not come.' Dildar Begum then intervened, advising Hamida that she would marry one day so why not marry a king. 'Oh yes I shall marry someone', Hamida replied, 'but he shall be a man whose collar my hand can touch, and not one whose skirt it does not reach', and then as Gulbadan tells us, 'my mother gave her much advice'. Towards the end of September 1541, Humayun and Hamida were married. On 15 October 1542, in the words of Abul Fadl, 'the pains of travail came upon her majesty Mariam Makani [Mary of the Place, the title given to Hamida], and awoke her and in that auspicious moment the unique pearl of the viceregency of God [Akbar] came forth in his glory'. Hamida was to become the great matriarch of Akbar's household.

The inscribed stone at Umarkot, Sind, marking the spot where Hamida, wife of Humayun, gave birth to Akbar on 15 October 1542.

Hamida, the daughter of Hindal's spiritual adviser, an act which alienated Hindal, who had his eyes on the girl himself. Hindal left Humayun to try to set up his own regime in Qandahar. On 15 October 1542 at Umarkot in Rajasthan, Hamida gave birth to Akbar, the greatest of the Mughals. In 1543, seeing no immediate future for himself in India, Humayun and Hamida, with a very small entourage of just 44 men and two women fled Sind to seek the aid of Shah Tahmasp, the Safavid ruler of Iran (p. 185).

Humayun's party was well-received by the Shah, who sent his three brothers to meet the Mughals. After the two sovereigns met and embraced, Gulbadan tells us, 'the friendship and concord of those two high-placed pashas was as close as two nut-kernels in one shell. Great unanimity and good feeling ensued, so that during his Majesty's stay in that country, the Shah often went to his quarters, and on days when he did not, the Emperor went to his.' Not all went easily; there was a difficult passage when the Shah strove to convert Humayun and his party to Shia Islam. But Humayun was able to spend a most pleasant year, sightseeing the great buildings of his ancestors at Herat, hunting and partying, most memorably with the Shah amidst the ruins of Persepolis, before moving back towards India at the head of an army consisting mainly of Persians.

In 1545 Humayun seized Qandahar from his brother, Askari, and then ejected Kamran from Kabul. For the next nine years Humayun struggled with Askari and Kamran for the ascendancy in eastern Afghanistan. It was a schizophrenic affair. When the brothers met, there were festivities, displays of affection, tears, and then they would return to the struggle for power out of which only one might survive. Hindal was killed in a night raid by Kamran on Humayun's camp; Askari was captured by Humayun and ordered, as was the usual pattern for those being dismissed from worldly affairs, to go on a pilgrimage to Mecca; Kamran, after a final dinner with his brother, was blinded.

In 1554, Humayun's opportunity to regain his kingdom came as three members of Sher Khan's family competed for the throne. He invaded India, his army under the able generalship of Bairam Khan, who had served him and Babur with great distinction, and defeated the Afghans. On 23 July Humayun remounted his father's throne. But he was not to enjoy it for long. On Friday 24 January 1556, he was on the roof of his library, discussing with his astrologers when Venus was expected to rise. Going downstairs, he heard the muezzin make the call to prayer from the nearby mosque. Sitting to wait until the call had finished he caught his foot in his robe and fell, hitting his head on the stone steps. He died two days later. Like his father, he both lost a kingdom, and gained one, and came from Kabul to do so.

Akbar
1556–1605

Akbar was the greatest of the talented line of Great Mughal rulers. In a reign of 49 years he secured Mughal rule throughout north India, entrenched his dynasty for a further 100 years and left a memory of good government which has been cherished to the present.

AKBAR	
Born Umarkot (Sind), 15 October 1542	Mal Rai of Bikanir), name unknown (daughter of Rawal Har Rai of Jaisalmir); there were said to be 300 women in all
Father Humayun	
Mother Hamida (Mariam Makani)	*Sons* Salim (Jahangir), Murad, Daniyal
Wives Ruqaiya, name unknown (daughter of Kamran), Harkha (daughter of Raja Bihari Mall of Amber), Salima (widow of Bairam Khan), name unknown (daughter of Miran Mubarak Shah of Khandesh), name unknown (niece of Rai Kalyan	*Daughters* Shakar al-Nisa Begum, Aram Banu Begum, Shahzada Khanum
	Enthroned 14 February 1566
	Died 25 October 1605
	Buried Mausoleum at Sikandra

AKBAR

In his august appearance he was of middle height, but inclining to be tall; he was of the hue of wheat; his eyes and eyebrows were black, and his complexion rather dark than fair; he was lion-bodied, with a broad chest, and his arms long. On the left side of his nose he had a fleshy mole, very agreeable in appearance, of the size of half a pea.... His august voice was very loud, and in speaking and explaining had a particular richness. In his actions and movements he was not like the people of the world, and the Glory of God manifested itself in him.

Jahangir (Salim) on his father, Tuzuk-i Jahangiri

ALONG WITH THE EMPEROR ASHOKA of the 3rd century BC, Akbar is remembered as the greatest ruler India has seen. In the 49 years of his reign he secured Mughal rule through all of northern India and built the basis of his dynasty's power for a century or more. He created a system of government in which all peoples could have a stake. He matched this with an approach to religion which was inclusive of all faiths, and designed ultimately to subordinate religious matters to the progress of the Mughal

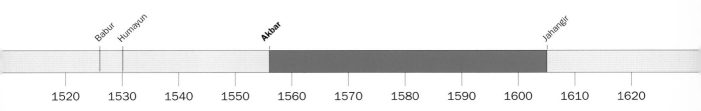

As a boy Akbar was strong, energetic and hyperactive. Here in Kabul he had been quarrelling with an older cousin, Ibrahim, over a painted drum. His uncle Kamran made the boys wrestle for the drum, a contest which Akbar won.

state. Building on the work of his Afghan predecessors, he fashioned a system of revenue collection which both encouraged the peasant to increase his productivity while permitting the state to build vast reserves of treasure at the centre. He then used these reserves to take patronage of all the arts, but in particular painting and architecture, towards the peak of achievement they would reach under his successors. In doing so he left a memory of potent magnificence and of good government which is treasured to the present.

Akbar was 13 when he came to power. Long before, when aged just under three in Kabul, he had shown evidence of his will and unusual strength. He had been quarrelling with his older cousin, Ibrahim, his uncle Kamran's son, over the possession of a painted drum. Kamran made the boys wrestle for it, at which Akbar 'grappled with Ibrahim Mirza according to the canons of the skilful and so lifted him up and flung him on the ground that a cry burst forth from the assemblage.' And so the boy turned out a strong, energetic, indeed a hyperactive child. The despair of those appointed to give him formal schooling – he wore out four teachers – Akbar infinitely preferred to be hunting with dogs, flying pigeons, and racing camels and horses. He particularly enjoyed the martial arts, being a crack shot with bow and gun. He was, moreover, without fear. Time after time as a young man he was to take the lead in facing danger when others held back, slaying a tigress who was defending her young, controlling an enraged elephant on heat, and against all odds in battle carrying everything before him by the zest and ferocity of his attack. But, aged 13, he was not yet ready for power.

Akbar takes control of government

On Humayun's death effective power was assumed by Bairam Khan, whom Humayun had made Akbar's guardian. At the time the two were campaigning in the Punjab. Bairam immediately had Akbar formally enthroned at Gurdaspur and set about consolidating the Mughal position. Matters were by no means secure. Three Suri princes (see box, p. 123) were still at large and hoping to reassert Afghan power. But the real danger came from a Hindu, Hemu, a vegetable seller, who by dint of genius rose to become the chief arbiter of power under Adil Shah Suri. On Humayun's death Hemu led the Afghan army to the capture of both Agra and Delhi, had himself proclaimed Raja Vikramaditya and coinage struck in his name. On 5 November 1556, Bairam Khan faced Hemu's greatly superior forces on the historic field of Panipat. As both the Mughal wings were rolled back defeat seemed certain, until Hemu, directing the battle from his elephant, was hit in the eye by an arrow and rendered senseless. His army melted away. Bairam personally decapitated him, sending the head to Kabul and torso to Delhi. Many captives were slaughtered and a tower, Mongol-style, was made of their heads. Seeing that matters were now more stable, Akbar's mother Hamida, and other women of the Mughal royal family, set out from Kabul to join their menfolk. As they approached the Punjab, Akbar went out to meet his mother, a day's ride from his camp.

Predictably, as the young monarch became increasingly aware of his status and responsibilities, tensions grew between him and Bairam. There were difficult interchanges over Akbar's household expenses and his plan, after the Begums arrived, to marry not just Ruqaiya, the daughter of Hindal, but also a relative of Kamran. Bairam's power and self-confidence began to grate. The presence of the Begums made matters worse; with his mother and his able foster-mother, Maham Anaga, to advise him, he was less dependent on Bairam. It seems likely, moreover, that Maham Anaga was actively working to bring about the downfall of the man Akbar called 'Baba Khan', father Khan. Bairam, according to Abul Fadl, because 'the wind of arrogance was in his brain', failed to see the danger, on one occasion wantonly killing an elephant driver of Akbar's who had offended him. There was a showdown. In 1560 Akbar thanked Bairam for his services to his family. 'Now that we have applied our own mind to the business of government...', he said, Bairam 'should for a time gather up his skirts from business and turn his attention to the bliss of pilgrimage ....' Sightseeing in Gujarat on his way to Mecca, Bairam was assassinated by a group of Afghans who had a vendetta against him.

Even at this stage Akbar was not completely his own man. The effective management of government lay in the hands of Maham Anaga, who operated through one Bahadur Khan as chief minister. 'For this noble work, wisdom and courage were necessary, and in truth Maham Anaga possessed these two qualities in perfection', declares Abul Fadl. But Maham Anaga failed to control her son, Adham Khan, who made the grave mistake on conquering Malwa of not observing the custom of sending his ruler all the spoils. Akbar immediately asserted himself. Adham Khan followed this error in May 1562 by killing Atga Khan, whom Akbar had made chief minister instead of Maham Anaga's place-

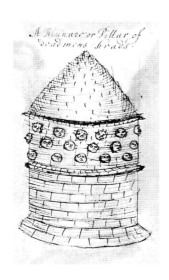

The Mughals, like their Mongol and Timurid ancestors, built towers of the heads of those whom they defeated. The Englishman, Peter Mundy, who travelled in Mughal lands in the early 17th century, found them still being built. Here is his drawing of one such tower, with 'heads mortered and plaistered in, leaveinge out nothing but their very face.'

FATEHPUR SIKRI

'Over the course of fourteen or fifteen years', declared Prince Salim, 'that hill, full of wild beasts, became a city containing every type of structure and garden, noble, elegant buildings and delightful places.' It seems Akbar moved his capital to this hill, named Sikri, a short distance from Agra, in part for strategic reasons, in part because building a city appealed to his outsized Timurid creative instincts, and in part because through it he was able to add to the legitimacy of his regime. Renamed Fatehpur ('City of Victory') Sikri after Akbar's conquest of Gujarat, it formed a rectangle some 3 x 5 km (1.86 x 3.11 miles), which was fortified on three sides by a wall and on the fourth by a large reservoir. At the heart of the city on a rock ridge stood the royal enclave. In the southwest of this enclave stood the Friday Mosque, at the time the largest mosque in the Mughal empire, much admired by contemporaries and described over its gateway as being in elegance 'second only to the mosque at Mecca'. At the heart of the mosque stood the shrine of the Chishti saint, Shaikh Salim (d. 1572), who had prophesied the birth of Akbar's longed-for heir, Prince Salim, and in whose house Salim had been born in 1569. Thus, the Mughals aligned themselves with India's most popular Sufi order. Arguably, the architecture, a good deal of which survives, reflected the inclusiveness of Akbar's regime. Much of it was in the trabeated style favoured by Hindu architects and its decoration drew on a shared Hindu-Muslim vocabulary developed under the Delhi Sultanate. It was in this remarkable environment that much of the work of creating the Mughal state was done by Akbar and his advisers.

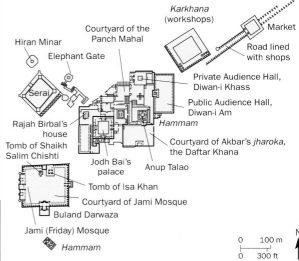

Top *The Buland Darwaza (Magnificent Gate) of the Friday Mosque, which was rebuilt in 1573 to celebrate Akbar's victory over Gujarat. Facing south towards Gujarat, on its stepped plinth, it rises over 53 m (174 ft) high. An inscription on its north side states in Persian: 'Said Jesus Christ, blessing upon him, the world is a bridge so pass over it and do not build on it....'*

Above *Plan of the royal enclave at the heart of Fatehpur Sikri. It was surrounded by an artificial lake, bazaars and so much building that Ralph Fitch, who visited in 1610, claimed that it was larger than London or Rome.*

Left *The wrongly named Diwan-i Khass (Hall of Private Audience). Scholars are divided as to its purpose, but note the likely Gujarati inspiration for its internal arrangements and carved stonework. It may have had a religio-symbolic purpose.*

man. Akbar, who had been awoken by the disturbance, found Adham Khan at the door of the harem demanding to be let in. Akbar immediately knocked Adham unconscious and ordered him to be thrown down from the harem terrace so that his brains were spilled. Maham Anaga never recovered from the shock. In this way Akbar took full control of his government.

Akbar expands the empire

Akbar was almost continually in the field. War kept the treasury full, the army fit and the people reminded of his power. Akbar had no fixed capital, but during his reign his armies set out from first Agra, then Fatehpur Sikri, then Lahore, and then again Agra. The Mughal court was thus, for much of the time, in Akbar's highly organized camp. The use of different bases at different times followed, for the most part, the changing strategic emphases in the expansion of Mughal power.

Down to 1571 Agra was the base. In this period Akbar fashioned his special alliance with the Hindu Rajput princes, which was to be a key pillar on which the empire rested. As early as 1562 he had shown his sensitivity to Rajput concerns by agreeing to marry the daughter of the Raja of Amber. Then, a revolt in 1564 led by his Uzbeg nobles showed him that he needed to expand his nobility. The Uzbegs, though servants of the Mughal house, had also been its nemesis; it was they who had driven Babur from Samarqand. The Uzbegs invited Akbar's half-brother, Hakim, the ruler of Kabul, to invade India. Akbar moved quickly, first to confront his brother in the Punjab and then to defeat and kill all those Uzbegs who had opposed him. It was clear to Akbar that he should not depend on foreign nobility, at this point almost equally divided between Uzbegs and Persians. He set out to recruit nobles of Indian background. Some were from Muslim families long-established in India, but the most important were the heads of the great Rajput clans, who gave their daughters as wives to the Mughal emperor in return for their inclusion in the nobility. By 1580 there were 47 Persian nobles, 48 Uzbegs and 43 Rajputs. The Rajputs surrendered all control over their territories, the revenues from them being collected by the Mughal administration and adjusted against their salaries, but they benefited from the honour and authority they gained through their association with the Mughals. Not all the Rajputs gave in without a fight. In 1568 Akbar had to besiege the Rana of Mewar in the great fortress of Chitor, and in 1569 it was the turn of Rai Surjan in Ranthambhor, which with Chitor controlled the trade route to the sea. The fall of these great fortresses underlined the folly of resistance.

In 1571 Akbar moved his capital 42 km (26 miles) westward to Fatehpur Sikri, a city he designed to reflect both the cultural inclusiveness and the Islamic legitimacy of his regime. From here he drove the empire's boundaries southwest into Gujarat and to the Arabian Sea. He saw great advantages in linking the rich maritime region, with its busy ports, to the agrarian wealth of the Indo-Gangetic plain. By 1573 he had asserted his control over the region. He then turned his focus eastwards. Todar Mal,

---

THE IMPERIAL CAMP

'The ancient custom is that the royal pavilion ... should be placed in a pleasant open space, if such can be found. On the right are the tents of the King's eldest son and his attendant nobles; these are placed next to the royal pavilion. On the left are those of the second son and his attendants. ... the most important nobles ... have their quarters to the right and left in the second line, next to the king's pavilion. Behind these come the rest of the troops in tents clustered as closely as possible round their own officers. To avoid crowding and confusion they are divided into messes, each with its own location. A separate bazaar is established for the King and each of the princes and the great nobles, ... Those established for the King and the princes are very large and very well-stocked, not only with stores of grain and other provision, but also with all sorts of merchandise, so that these bazaars seem to belong to some wealthy city instead of to a camp. They are always made on one plan, so that anyone who has spent a few days in camp knows his way about the bazaars as well as he does the streets of his own city .... During the advance for a campaign the artillery is grouped together in front of the camp, opposite the entrance to the royal quarters, in the broadest part of the open ground.'

Monserrate

The Mughal empire was built on the close relationship between the Mughals and the Rajput princes. Several Rajput families supplied wives for Akbar, and here Rajput princes queue up to pay homage to him.

his gifted Hindu minister, conducted a campaign against the Afghan rulers of Bihar and Bengal, and also Orissa, which enabled him in 1576 formally to annex these regions. This said, Hindu and Afghan resistance was not finally suppressed until the late 1580s.

In 1585 Hakim died, which increased the threat to Kabul from Abd Allah Khan, the leader of the Shaibanid Uzbegs of Bukhara. He was subsidizing the Afghan tribes and had just occupied Badakshan. Akbar moved his capital to Lahore, brought Kabul under direct imperial administration and negotiated a treaty with Abd Allah Khan. He then set about pacifying the Afghan tribes, in particular the great Yusufzai confederation, an action which was crucial to enabling India's rich caravan trade to flow through the Khyber Pass to Central and West Asia. Eventually Akbar succeeded in bringing the tribes under central control, but not without – as has been the fate of other empires in the Hindu Kush – the Mughals suffering their worst defeat in the mountain passes of Bunar in February 1586. At the same time Akbar turned his attention northwards to Kashmir, which by 1589 he had brought fully under control, and then southwards to Sind, whose ruler by 1593 had travelled to Lahore to pay homage. Now the lower Indus valley, like the Himalayan fastness of Kashmir, became a Mughal province.

In 1598 Abd Allah Khan died. With the threat of Uzbeg invasion reduced and the northwest of his empire largely secure, Akbar was free to return to Agra. He could now move south to face the five Muslim sultanates of the Deccan: Khandesh, Ahmadnagar, Berar, Bijapur and Golconda. He had already tried to soften them up. In 1591 he had sent embassies to each sultan demanding their submission. Four rejected the demand, and just the Sultan of Khandesh sent his daughter to be married to Akbar's eldest son, Salim, though he later withdrew his fealty. In 1595 Akbar ordered the invasion of the Ahmadnagar sultanate, a campaign which ended in the annexation of Berar. Subsequent operations in the Deccan, under Akbar's second son Prince Murad, made little progress. Then Akbar himself took command and in his last campaign of 1599 and 1600 annexed Ahmadnagar and Khandesh. In just over 40 years he had conquered an empire which reached from the Helmand river in the west to the Brahmaputra in the east, and from the Godavari river in the south to the Himalayan mountain barrier.

Akbar's interest in religion

A key feature of Akbar's empire was that the vast majority of its inhabitants were non-Muslims, mostly Hindus, and that government policies needed to take account of this fact. A key feature of Akbar himself was his profound interest in religion; he was attracted to mystical and ecstatic beliefs and progressed much in religious understanding as he grew older. In the early stages of his rule he showed a statesmanlike inclusiveness. In 1563 he abolished the Muslim privilege of being able to make slaves of prisoners captured in war. The following year he repealed the tax levied on Hindu pilgrims. Yet, at the same time, he was of orthodox temperament. He performed his prayers regularly, supported the pilgrimage to Mecca and made a point of visiting saints' shrines, of whom the two Chishti saints, Muin al-Din of Ajmer and Salim of Fatehpur Sikri, were particularly important. He offered special prayers before conducting every enterprise.

A second phase in Akbar's religious interests began in the mid-1570s, growing to such a pitch that he spent nights and days in meditation. He began a systematic study of theology and comparative religion, and built a special hall at Fatehpur Sikri to house debates. Initially, these were confined to Islamic issues, and Akbar was greatly disappointed by the contributions of the ulama (religious scholars). Subsequently, contributions were encouraged from Jains, Hindus and Parsis, and finally, in 1580, Christians – Jesuits from Goa. Over this period Akbar became disenchanted with Islam, began to tolerate non-Muslim ideas and practices, and to develop his own eclectic faith. As a ruler he increasingly came to see the ulama as a danger to his empire of many faiths. In consequence, he reviewed the grants which supported ulama, resumed those which could not be justified and began to make grants to support the priests and learned men of other faiths. Next, in 1579, he first abolished the *jizya*, a discriminatory tax levied annually on the property of all non-Muslims, and then by edict arrogated to himself supreme power in all matters of religious doctrine. Those ulama who objected were told to go on a pilgrimage to Mecca and stay there. A Muslim ruler, he had made it clear that people of all faiths in his empire should be treated equally.

Akbar was enormously interested in religion, and in a most open-minded way constantly sought to advance his knowledge and understanding. Here he presides at a debate in his House of Worship at Fatehpur Sikri. Two Jesuits, whose custom was to launch vehement attacks on Islam, are taking part. Akbar's free-thinking brought him strong opposition from the ulama, but his liberal approach made good sense in a multi-faith empire.

AKBAR'S LADIES ON
PILGRIMAGE TO MECCA

The conquest of Gujarat and the
development of better relations with
the European powers in the Indian
Ocean eased the pilgrimage to
Mecca. In 1575, Akbar's aunt,
Gulbadan, led a group of 10 ladies
from the royal household in making
the pilgrimage, an act not just of
devotion but also of courage. Prince
Salim saw the party off and, when
they returned in 1582, went out to
meet them at Ajmer some 60 km (37
miles) from Fatehpur Sikri. Akbar then
arrived and Abul Fadl describes the
family gathering, the enquiries after
health, the joy at being together
again, the gifts brought from Mecca.
'There were hospitalities', he says,
'and that night they remained awake
and in pleasing discourses.'

In the 1580s Akbar entered the third phase of his spiritual development, in which his own personal quest seems to have become united
with state purpose. In 1582 he closed the hall for religious debates and
announced the foundation of the *Din-i Ilahi*, the Religion of God. He had
already begun openly to worship the sun and to engage in a range of
Hindu practices, for instance adopting a vegetarian diet and abstaining
from sex. Now on Sundays, and before a sacred fire, he would initiate
groups of followers, largely from the nobility. They would swear to sacrifice their life, property, religion and honour for him. After they had
prostrated themselves, Akbar would raise them up, place a turban on
their heads with a medallion representing the sun, and hand them a portrait of himself to wear upon the turban. Initiates were required to greet
each other saying *Allahu Akbar* (God is Great), to which the reply was
Jalla Jalaluhu (Glorious is God). Historians have struggled to interpret
Akbar's purpose in creating this fraternity, which moved so far from
orthodox Islam. It is worth noting, however, that the cult was restricted
to the court, and followers were largely from the nobility. Arguably, in
this personal cult Akbar was aiming to strengthen the unity of the elite
which ran the empire by requiring its members to suppress individual
loyalties in favour of an overriding loyalty to him.

Improvements to government and finance

Akbar's genius was not just restricted to warfare and religion. He and his
advisers created a centralized administration which was able to expand
as new provinces were added and which endured for well over a century.
The emperor was at the head of the machine. Beneath him there were
four ministers responsible for revenue and finance; army and intelligence; the judiciary and religious patronage; and the royal household and
public works. This pattern was replicated in the provinces under a
provincial governor who reported directly to the emperor. The Mughal
nobility filled all the top positions at the centre and in the provinces, and
in doing so ran lavish households which emulated the style and manners
of the imperial model. All nobles held *mansabs*, that is the right to
collect the revenues of a particular territory in return for which they held
imperial offices and supplied men and material for war. There was also a
class of lesser holders of *mansabs*, imperial civil servants who had not
gained the rank of noble. The emperor personally reviewed the rank,
titles and postings of all but the lowest officials, who were not only
moved regularly to posts all over the empire but also had the lands from
which they were entitled to collect revenue changed at frequent intervals, in order to prevent the development of local attachments.

The imperial finances were managed by brilliant administrators: Fadl
Allah Shirazi, Khwaja Shah Mansur and Raja Todar Mal. Officials were
salaried down to town and district levels. There was strict accountabil-
ity, with treasuries reporting their balances in writing every 15 days. The
empire enjoyed substantial budget surpluses. Effective revenue collection was central to the health of the Mughal regime. Here Akbar built on

the innovations of the Afghan Suris, and improved upon them. The aim was to maximize the return to the state while encouraging cultivators to increase their productivity.

Raja Todar Mal was the key figure in implementing change, with a drive for accurate production statistics backed up by newly standardized weights and measures. All cultivated lands were measured field by field. Data was collected for a 10-year period on yields and harvests, by cultivator and by village, as well as on market prices for all crops. Out of this was produced a standard assessment for each area and each crop. The state levied between one-third and one-fifth of the value as tax, depending on the nature of the crop. This had to be paid in coin so the cultivator was forced to enter the market. Every 20 or 30 years all the information on production and sales would be gathered again to produce a fresh assessment. The Mughals were much more successful than their predecessors, both in expropriating rural surpluses for the benefit of the state and in stimulating rural productivity.

Akbar's wide-ranging interests

Akbar was as remarkable as an individual as he was a ruler. His interests ranged widely and he pursued anything he did, from cutting wood to conquering territory, with enormous intensity. He was illiterate, some now say dyslexic, yet became a learned man. He had a huge thirst for knowledge. He had books read to him regularly from his library of 24,000 volumes, and made good use of his retentive memory. He was a lover of the art of the book and commissioned a series of masterpieces for his library, among them an illustrated translation of the Hindu epic, the *Mahabharata*, and the great history of his reign, the *Akbarnama*. A considerable patron of music, he drew leading musicians to his court, including Tansen, from whom most north Indian musicians today trace their musical descent. Akbar himself was a singer and a drummer. Poetry was the attribute of any cultivated man of the time; Akbar composed in Hindi as well as Persian. He had great interest in crafts and machinery,

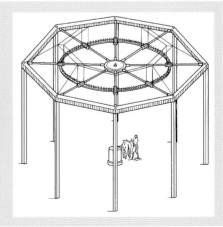

AKBAR AND MUGHAL PAINTING

Akbar's powerful and attentive patronage presided over the elaboration of the distinctive traditions of Mughal painting. On coming to power Akbar set up his own library workshop. At the head of it he put the two Safavid painters, Abd al-Samad and Mir Saiyid Ali, whom his father had brought with him from the court of Shah Tahmasp. Akbar paid close attention to the progress of his painters. 'The works of all painters are weekly laid before his Majesty by the … clerks', Abul Fadl tells us, 'he then confers rewards according to the excellence of the workmanship, or increases the monthly salaries.' Because Akbar was concerned that artists should get credit for their achievement, officials were asked to note the contributions of each artist to each picture. As a result we not only know the names of 18 painters whom Abul Fadl tells us were the leading artists of the time, but of over 100 who contributed to the library workshop's output. There are many Hindu as well as

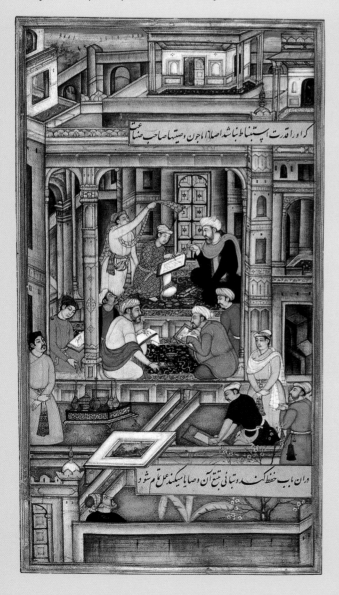

Muslim names, which underscores the distinctive achievement of the Safavid masters in India in leading a fusion of Safavid refinement with Indian vitality and realism.

The first output of the library workshop reflected Akbar's interest in tales and fables from the Indian and Islamic traditions. One notable early work was an illustrated edition of the *Tutinama* (Tales of a Parrot'), and a second was the *Hamzanama* (The Story of Hamza, or the mythical adventures of the uncle of the Prophet Muhammad). The latter contained 1,400 paintings divided equally into 14 volumes. From *c.* 1580 Akbar was concerned increasingly that art should serve the purposes of the Mughal regime. One manifestation was the Razmnama, the translation into Persian from Sanskrit of the great Hindu epic, the *Mahabharata*. When it was finished in 1586, Akbar instructed his nobles to have copies made for their libraries so that knowledge of this central Hindu text would spread through his dominions. Another manifestation was a series of commissions designed to celebrate the achievement of the Mughal line – to project the imperial ideology. There was the *Tarikh-i Alfi*, the 'History of the Millennium', glorifying Muslim rulers; the *Chingiznama* and the *Timurnama*, which set out the achievements of Chingiz Khan and Timur, and their descendants; and then there was the record of his grandfather's achievements, the *Baburnama*,

Opposite left *For rulers in the Mongol and Timurid tradition, illustrated books were a major source of artistic patronage and a major way of disseminating dynastic propaganda. Here painters and calligraphers work in Akbar's library workshop – a place of great productivity.*

Opposite right *Akbar receiving his sons at Fatehpur Sikri on his return in 1573 from his triumphant Gujarat campaign. This is an illustration from the Akbarnama, the official history of his reign, which Akbar commissioned Abul Fadl to write.*

Right *A further illustration from the Akbarnama shows Akbar (top right) directing the attack on the Rajput fortress of Ranthambhor in 1569. As throughout the illustrations to the history of his reign, Akbar is depicted at the centre of the action, the figure around whom all events revolve. The capture of the Rajput fortresses of Chitor and Ranthambhor in 1568 and 1569 helped pave the way for the Mughal conquest of Gujarat.*

which Akbar had asked the son of Bairam Khan, his assassinated guardian, to translate from Chaghtai Turki into Persian, and finally there was the *Akbarnama*, the vast record of Akbar's reign which on 4 March 1589 he had ordered his friend, the polymath Abul Fadl, to write. The illustrations to the *Akbarnama*, as also to the *Baburnama* and the *Timurnama*, show these great Timurid rulers at the centre of events, shaping the world in which they move.

commissioned much architecture, but was not, unlike others in his family, particularly interested in gardens. He enjoyed all sports, especially wrestling and polo, in which he had the skill to hit the ball in mid-air. Elephants were his favourite animals. He flew pigeons, hunted with cheetahs, and, to the horror of the orthodox, kept dogs. Hunting was a passion until an extraordinary incident in 1578. Over 10 days beaters had driven animals into a *c.* 80-km (50-mile) circle of forest at Bhera in the Punjab for the hunt when, according to the contemporary historian Badauni, 'suddenly, all at once, a strange state and strong frenzy came upon the Emperor'. Akbar ordered the hunt abandoned, not a bird or an animal was to be harmed.

It was observed that, while on one level Akbar was open and frank, on another he was quite unknowable; part of himself was kept well concealed. There was no doubt he was a great king 'for he knew', according to the Jesuit Du Jarric, 'that the good ruler is he who can command, simultaneously, the obedience, the respect, the love and the fear of his subjects'. He treated all men, high or low, neighbour or stranger, the same. He worked hard and slept little. As a young man he had huge appetites, whether it was for food or for sex; he had seven wives and his harem may have numbered as many as 300 women. But with age he became restrained, even austere; he virtually gave up eating meat and recommended monogamy. Akbar had three sons: Salim, who was born in 1569 to the daughter of the Raja of Amber; Murad, who was born in 1570 to Salima Begum, the widow of Bairam Khan; and Daniyal, who was born in 1572, probably to a relative of his Amber wife.

AKBAR AND HIS MOTHER

Akbar was devoted to his mother, Hamida, or Mariam Makani, 'Mary of the Place', to give her Mughal title. He went out of his way to show her respect, and usually listened to her advice. His affection for her, indeed a need for her company, was strong. Feeling such a need he wrote thus in verse in 1589: 'This pilgrim may go to the Kaaba [Hamida] to perform the Haj. O God! May the Kaaba come towards us.' Her affection for him was no less strong. On hearing of his trance on the hunting field at Bhera, she rushed from Fatehpur Sikri to care for him. In the summer of 1604, desperate to prevent a clash between Akbar and Salim, she begged him not to set out with his army for Salim's headquarters at Allahabad. En route Akbar heard that she was mortally ill; he sped back to be at her bedside. On 29 August she died. 'Who shall describe the grief of H.M.', declared Muhibb Ali. 'He shaved his hair, moustaches etc … and cast off his turban and donned the garb of woe.' She was buried by the side of her husband, Humayun, in his mausoleum at Delhi.

In his last years Akbar was beset by personal grief, the death of his beloved mother and his poor relations with his son, Salim. The wear and tear seems to show in this drawing of him, probably in the last year of his life, aged 63.

The gateway to Akbar's mausoleum at Sikandra, close to Agra. Completing this was his son Salim's (Jahangir's) most important architectural project and was so huge in conception that it was not finished until 1613. The mausoleum lies at the centre of a vast enclosed garden of *chahar bagh* design. The room in which the sarcophagus was placed was decorated with paintings, including Christian subjects according to a European traveller. Many of the mausoleum's fine inscriptions were executed by Amanat Khan of Shiraz, who was also responsible for those of the Taj Mahal (see p. 153). Amongst the lines on the south façade of the gateway are:

The pen of the mason of the Divine Decree has written on its court; These are the gardens of Eden, enter them and live forever.

It cannot have been easy being the son of such a mighty father. Both Murad and Daniyal died from drink before him; Salim's health was compromised by his own addiction to drink and opium, which may have led him to defy his father. In 1600 he took the field against Akbar, but retreated to his base at Allahabad after receiving a stiff letter. In 1602 he had the gall to have his name read in Friday prayers and coins struck in his name as emperor. When Akbar sent Abul Fadl, his close friend of many years, to intercede, Salim had him killed. Then the women of the royal family, in particular Akbar's wife Salima and his mother Hamida, intervened, but only with temporary effect. Finally, in 1604, Salim, who was now threatened by his own son, Khusraw, was persuaded to come to court, where Akbar slapped his face, put him in the charge of a doctor, and imprisoned his followers. Relations improved. Then Akbar's health suddenly gave way. On 21 October, Akbar, unable to speak, invested Salim as his successor. On 25 October, aged 63, he died. The following morning he was placed in the mausoleum he had prepared for himself at Sikandra, some 8 km (5 miles) west of Agra.

Jahangir
1605–27

Jahangir, a man of intelligence, intellectual curiosity and great connoisseurship, was amongst the most interesting of the Great Mughals. Here, in a painting by Bichitr, he is depicted holding the orb of power and wearing a halo, a feature which, once encountered in European painting, was quickly brought into Mughal iconography as indicating divine nature.

JAHANGIR	
Born	Gosain (daughter of
House of Shaikh	Mota Raja), name
Salim Chishti, Sikri,	unknown
later Fatehpur Sikri,	(granddaughter of
30 August 1569	Raja Man Singh),
Father	name unknown
Akbar	(daughter of Ram
Mother	Chand Bandilah),
Harkha (daughter of	Malika Jahan
Raja Bihari Mall of	(daughter of Rawal
Amber)	Bhim), plus 10
Wives	others
Nur Jahan, name	*Sons*
unknown (sister of	Khusraw, Parwiz,
Raja Man Singh),	Khurram (Shah
Sahib-Jamal	Jahan), Shahriyar
(daughter of Khwaja	*Daughters*
Hasan), name	Sultan al-Nisa
unknown (daughter	Begum, Bihar Banu
of Raja Baghwan	Begum
Das of Amber), Jodh	*Enthroned*
Bai (daughter of	24 October 1605
Mota Rai Udai Singh	*Died*
of Jodhpur),	28 October 1627
Karamsi (daughter	*Buried*
of Raja Keshu Das	Mausoleum, Lahore
Rathor), Jagat	

JAHANGIR

He is very affable and of a cheerefull countenance ... and not proud in nature, ... full of gentle conversation ... the wisdome and goodness of the king appeares above the malice of others ....

Sir Thomas Roe

IN AGRA A FEW DAYS AFTER AKBAR'S DEATH, and 'having seated myself on the throne of my expectations and wishes', Salim writes in his memoirs, 'I caused also the imperial crown, which my father had caused to be made after the manner of that which was worn by the great kings of Persia, to be brought before me, and then in the presence of the whole assembled Ameirs [sic], having placed it on my brows, as an omen auspicious to the stability and happiness of my reign, kept it there for the space of a full astronomical hour.' Soon afterwards, noting that his name was the same as that of the Ottoman sultan, he changed it 'in as much as the business of kings is controlling the world', calling himself Jahangir ('World-Seizer'). His first order on his accession was to have a 'Chain of Justice' with 60 bells attached slung from the battlements of Agra fort to the banks of the Jumna, which anyone who felt oppressed by his officials could ring to attract his attention: he wished to be known as a just ruler.

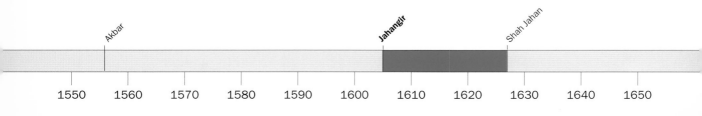

Akbar	Jahangir	Shah Jahan

1550   1560   1570   1580   1590   1600   1610   1620   1630   1640   1650

Jahangir was already 36 when he came to the throne, which was old for a man of his family, and indeed of his time. In part at least this may explain his rebellion against his father from 1600. This said, it was the fate of Mughal princes, like Jahangir, his own son, Shah Jahan, and his grandson, Awrangzeb, to fight for power with their fathers, as well as with their siblings. As a boy Jahangir seems to have been a harem favourite, being made much of by his stepmother, Salima, and his grandmother, Hamida. He was educated under the close personal supervision of his father and proved himself both an able scholar and skilled at martial arts. Aged 12 he was introduced to the realities of military command and administration. But, as a teenager, he seems to have fallen out with his father.

The Jesuit, Fr. Anthony Monserrate, noted that although Akbar loved his children dearly, as they grew up he could only talk to them in gruff words often accompanied by blows. On one occasion, after being berated by Akbar for being laggardly in bringing the harem into camp, he 'shut himself in his tent', Abul Fadl tells us, 'and abstained from food and sleep'. Some even suspected a sexual jealousy between them. Akbar was said to have immured alive a favourite concubine, Anarkali ('Pomegranate Blossom') for smiling at Jahangir. Whatever the causes, this powerful relationship continued even after Akbar's death; the shadow of his father, for whom he professes the greatest respect, is ever present in Jahangir's memoirs.

In this light it is not surprising that the first serious matter Jahangir had to deal with was the rebellion of his eldest son, Khusraw, aged 18. Six months after the accession, Khusraw slipped out of Agra at night and rode towards Kabul, picking up supporters on the way. Jahangir, hearing that he might be aiming to link up with Persian and Uzbeg enemies of the Mughals, immediately set out in pursuit. Within three weeks the young prince was brought into Jahangir's presence in chains, where he stood 'trembling and weeping'. Jahangir had Khusraw imprisoned and he was forced to watch 300 of his followers being impaled. Moreover, the fifth Sikh Guru, Arjun, who had offered Khusraw his support as he made his way northwest, was killed. A little later Khusraw was caught plotting his father's assassination from jail. Jahangir knew that his son's action deserved death 'yet paternal affection did not allow me to take his life'. He had his son blinded.

Great men rarely make easy fathers, and from his adolescence onwards Jahangir's relationship with his father was stormy. His memoirs, however, reiterate his great respect for Akbar, which is also shown in this miniature of *c.* 1614.

Jahangir's intellectual curiosity and aestheticism

Jahangir's reign was a time of growing power and magnificence for the Mughal empire. This is not because of any particular skills of governance possessed by Jahangir, but because he continued and consolidated his father's policies. And, while he did so, most of his dominions enjoyed peace. We know much about Jahangir, in part because of the records left by Europeans who visited his court, but also because of the engaging memoirs he himself left of his reign. These reveal an observant and reflective man, but also a playful one; while giving a wine party to friends in a garden in Kabul, 'I ... on account of hilarity and excitement ordered those who were of equal age to myself ... to jump over the stream that flowed through the middle of the garden.' Jahangir made the jump successfully, but many of his courtiers got wet. Most particularly, he reveals himself as a man of great personal warmth towards members of his family, especially women, and those who had served him well; many an affectionate tribute figures in his pages.

Sensation was important to Jahangir. Like his father, he loved fruit – the mangoes of northern India and the cherries of Kashmir. He was particular about the food he ate, preferring, for instance, the flesh of the *rohu* above other fish, and the milk of the camel above that of other beasts. The sensation, however, he seemed to like best was intoxication. He took opium every day, and at one stage his consumption of liquor rose to 20 cups of double distilled spirits a day. 'Matters went to such a length', he wrote, 'that in the crapulous state from the excessive trembling of my

SIR THOMAS ROE

Roe was the first English ambassador to be attached to the Mughal court. He presented himself to Jahangir at Ajmer in January 1616 and travelled with the court to Mandu in Malwa and Ahmadabad in Gujarat, setting off to return to England in February 1619. Roe would appear to have had somewhat greater success than his predecessors at the Mughal court because, after English victories over the Portuguese in 1612 and 1615, it was clear that they were a force to be reckoned with in the Indian Ocean. Nevertheless, Roe regarded his embassy to Jahangir as a failure: he did not return with a treaty governing trade between England and Mughal India. He saw Asaf Khan, whom he thought was closely connected to the Portuguese, as a particular obstacle.

From the point of view of posterity, however, there was a considerable benefit in his embassy because Roe left a diary which gives a lively picture of everyday life at the Mughal court: the magnificence of the imperial camp; the fixed times at which the emperor appeared in public 'as regular as a clock that stricks at sett howers'; the great dignity of the emperor's appearance in court on a high throne, with courtiers and officials at precisely measured distances from him.

Roe also records his success at avoiding having to prostrate himself before the emperor and his acceptance, by his own account as there is no corroboration in Jahangir's memoirs, as one of the emperor's drinking companions. He was himself an object of fascination for the harem whose 'curiositie made them breake little holes in a grate of Reed that hung before [the Durbar hall] to gaze at mee'. He also confirms the influence of Nur Jahan, who, he told the future Charles I, 'governs him, and wynds him up at her pleasure'.

Sir Thomas Roe (1581–1644) made his reputation through his mission to the Mughal court. He was subsequently ambassador to the Ottoman empire and prominent in negotiations during the Thirty Years War.

One innovation of Jahangir was to break the Islamic prohibition on the representation of human images in a particularly public way by placing images of himself on coins. Akbar had raised the standard of minted coins by putting the artist Abd al-Samad in charge of his mint. Jahangir began the move away from pure calligraphy by using signs of the zodiac for the name of the month. He then moved to images of himself, and then a portrait of himself with a cup, as in this gold coin.

hand I could not drink from my own cup, but others had to give it me ....' Not surprisingly, as the English ambassador Sir Thomas Roe tells us, he would doze off while entertaining friends. He suffered, moreover, from an uncertain temper, and this essentially genial man could become savage. When a groom and some bearers allowed a nilgai (a type of deer) to escape on a hunt, he had the groom killed and the bearers hamstrung.

Intellectual curiosity was also a feature. In 1610, for instance, he worked out just how many birds and beasts he had killed since he began the hunting he loved so much aged 11 – the total was 17,167 beasts, of which 86 were tigers, and 13,964 birds, of which 10,348 were pigeons. He was constantly observing nature, whether it was the mating and nesting habits of cranes or how elephants were born feet first, or by cutting open animals either to see what they had been eating or to learn something of their physiology. On visiting Kashmir he noted the flowers, trees and fruits to be found, as well as listing the birds which were not to be found.

Jahangir was a connoisseur of beauty in life and art. His women, and there were said to be 20 wives and 300 concubines in his harem, were chosen not for their political connections but for their looks. Kashmir fed his love of beauty in nature: 'it is a garden of eternal spring ... its pleasant meads and enchanting cascades are beyond all description.' But it was in painting that his aesthetic response, and his creativity, was most fully revealed (see box pp. 142–43). He was fascinated by what could be learned from the achievements of European art and keen to take the work of the imperial library away from the recording of human activities and events to more reflective work revelatory of human personality. 'As regards myself, my liking for painting and my practice in judging it', he declares in his memoirs, 'have arrived at such a point that when any work is brought before me, either of deceased artists or those of the present day, I say on the spur of the moment that it is the work of such and such a man.' Unlike his father and his eldest son, Jahangir was not a great builder. He did, however, ensure that his father's mausoleum was completed according to its original design, put up structures in the forts of Agra and Lahore, and built a number of pavilions and hunting lodges. Gardens were his great pleasure.

There was no significant expansion of Mughal territory under Jahangir; the emphasis was rather on consolidation. The Rajputs of Mewar to the south were finally subdued, a fact which signalled to many local leaders that it might be better to submit to the Mughals than just hope that their officials would go away. In the northeast the Mughals were almost every year engaged in fighting the Ahom peoples of Burma who were spreading down the Brahmaputra valley. In the north they made sure that their authority was well understood by the Rajput kingdoms of the Himalayan foothills. And throughout they kept a wary eye on the Safavids and Shaibanid Uzbegs to the northwest. This did not prevent, however, the Safavid Shah Abbas from recapturing in 1622 the strategically important city of Qandahar.

JAHANGIR AND PAINTING

Jahangir was fascinated by painting. His highly knowledgeable and involved patronage took Mughal painting to its peak. Long before he came to power he was commissioning and collecting works of art, first when the court was at Lahore from 1585 to 1598, and then after he set up his own court at Allahabad from 1600. He continued the process, initiated by his father, of exposing his artists to European paintings and engravings. In 1595 Jesuits noted his great hunger for examples of European religious painting, although their hope that it was for spiritual reasons was quickly disabused. Indeed, Jahangir was known to intercept consignments of European paintings intended for his father. From the 1580s through to the 1620s, driven by imperial patronage, Mughal artists interacted with European models, a process leading to experiments with light and shade and the use of perspective. This was interwoven with a transition in style from busy records of events to simpler compositions focusing on the interplay of individuals and the revelation of personality. Side by side with this was a move from the great illustrated state documents of Akbar's day to individual pictures and portraits, which might be brought together in an album. The arrival of Sir Thomas Roe, a cousin of the leading English miniaturist Isaac Oliver, at the court in 1616 brought this development to its zenith. Roe brought paintings with him which fascinated the emperor, and it is from this time that Mughal portraiture uses striking symbolic imagery.

Bichitr's portrait of Jahangir paying attention to a Sufi shaikh rather than to kings is a masterpiece of the genre. Jahangir sits on an hourglass denoting the passing of time, while the angels at its foot write 'O Shah may your reign last a thousand years'. The Sufi is probably Shaikh Husain Chishti, the contemporary representative of the shrine of Muin al-Din at Ajmer. Kingly power is represented by King James I of England and the Ottoman Sultan, Selim. The bottom left-hand figure is the artist himself. Jahangir's interest in the natural world was also reflected in his commissions; he ordered birds and animals to be painted, many of them by the richly talented Mansur, named 'wonder of the Age' by his sovereign.

Left The Jesuit, Jerome Xavier, recalled that he saw Jahangir directing painters to trace out two Christian paintings, one of which was a Deposition. It is tempting to suggest that this Deposition from the Cross of c. 1598 is that very painting.

Below Jahangir was fascinated by nature and this was reflected in the work he commissioned. This is a 17th-century copy of a painting of a pair of cranes by Mansur. Jahangir describes the mating ritual of these cranes in his memoirs.

Opposite Bichitr's great allegorical picture of Jahangir preferring a Sufi shaikh to kings.

Jahangir and religion

Jahangir's approach to religion, like that of his father, was a mixture of the political and the personal. Politics dictated a tolerant approach. Early on in his reign he introduced measures respecting Hindu sensibilities, such as banning cow slaughter. And when a distinguished learned Muslim, Shaikh Ahmad Sirhindi, claiming that he was the present-day manifestation of the companions of the Prophet and the renewer of the second millennium of Islam, called for a reversal of policies favouring Hindus, and gained a popular following, Jahangir had him locked up. But, we should also note, this generally tolerant approach was marred by apparently random acts of violence against non-Muslims, as when he demolished the temples of the Jains in Gujarat. When it came to Jahangir's personal beliefs, on the other hand, many wondered if he had any at all: 'his religion is his owne invention', declared Sir Thomas Roe. This said, he does seem to have had considerable respect for Hindu and Muslim mystics. From 1616 to 1620, for instance, he made several visits to the Hindu ascetic Gosain Jadrup of Ujjain. 'I heard sublime words', he wrote after one visit, 'of religious duties and divine things'.

Jahangir maintained the personal leadership of the elite of his realm which his father had pioneered in the *Din-i Ilahi*. He continued to use Akbar's imagery of sun and light, adopting the title Nur al-Din, 'Light of the Faith'. Discipleship was highly valued. We have a record in an autobiography of how a Persian nobleman, who was fighting the Ahoms on the northeast frontier, believed that Jahangir had cured him of a serious fever, and of how he then petitioned to be made a royal disciple. Sir Thomas Roe, a favoured drinking companion of Jahangir, was well aware of the honour when he was made a disciple and given a picture of Jahangir on a gold medal to wear. Then, as his father had done, at least in the early part of his reign, Jahangir acknowledged his own discipleship of the Chishti saint, Muin al-Din, whose holy line presided over his own birth and whose spiritual benison added to the authority of Mughal power.

Like his father, Jahangir showed respect for both Hindu and Muslim holy men. Between 1616 and 1620 he made several visits to a Hindu ascetic who lived naked the year round in a cave. In this painting he is shown with the ascetic, Gosain Jadrup, on one of his visits, which he records in his memoirs.

The ascendancy of Nur Jahan

The most striking feature of Jahangir's reign, both for contemporaries and for posterity, was the ascendancy of his leading wife, Nur Jahan. In 1611, when he was 42 and she was 34, Jahangir fell in love with the lady-in-waiting of one of Akbar's widows. Named Mihr al-Nisa, 'Sun among Women', she was the widow of a Persian noble. A great beauty, highly intelligent and a strong personality, she quickly came to dominate the harem and

NUR JAHAN

Jahangir's queen was a woman of many gifts, and not just in politics. She designed lace, brocades and carpets, wrote poetry, brought new recipes into Mughalai cuisine, and invented the perfume Attar of Roses. Her charity was such that she enabled, so it was said, 500 orphan girls to marry by giving them a dowry. She was, moreover, a crack shot, on one occasion killing four tigers with six shots. 'Until now', her proud husband wrote, 'such shooting was never seen, that from the top of an elephant and inside of a howdah … six shots should be made and not one miss.' She was a considerable patron of architecture. She built several gardens, including the Bagh-i Nur Afshan at Agra, now known as Ram Bagh, on the site of Babur's Bagh-i Gul Afshan. She also built caravanserais on the main trade arteries of the empire. That at Agra could house over 2,000 people and 500 horses and, placed at the end of the key imperial road from Patna, enabled the queen to control the tariffs on the rich trade from eastern India. Her masterpiece, however, was the mausoleum she built for her father on the banks of the Jumna at Agra. Enclosed within a walled garden some 165 m (540 ft) long on each side, built of white marble inlaid with semiprecious stones, it remains as a shimmering testament to the taste of this remarkable woman. Her tomb in Lahore bears the following epitaph: 'On the grave of this poor stranger, let there be neither lamp nor rose. Let neither butterfly's wing burn nor nightingale sing' (trans. Wheeler Thackston).

Right *Jahangir embraces the love of his life, Nur Jahan. Painting by Govardhan, c. 1620.*

Below *Nur Jahan was a crack shot, as Jahangir records in his memoirs. Here she is painted loading her musket.*

Above right *The mausoleum which Nur Jahan built for her father, Itimad al-Dawlah. Substantially her taste, its white marble is decorated with semiprecious stones – cornelian, topaz, onyx, jasper and lapis lazuli.*

As Jahangir's reign progressed Nur Jahan became increasingly involved in government, her name appearing on imperial edicts, and on coins such as this one, above.

Opposite above One senses that this drawing by Hashim of Jahangir in old age reveals on his visage the traces of a life spent consuming much alcohol and opium.

Opposite below The mausoleum of Jahangir at Shadera near Lahore, the construction of which Nur Jahan occupied herself with after his death. It stands in a square garden each side of which is 400 m (1,300 ft) long. The garden is divided into 16 equal sections; at each intersection there is a fountain and a pool. At the centre is the mausoleum which owes its style to the tomb Nur Jahan built for her father (see p. 145). Unfortunately, the marble pavilion on the roof, which relieved the long horizontal line of the building, was dismantled in the 19th century. Jahangir's marble cenotaph within the mausoleum is inlaid with semiprecious stones representing cyclamen and tulips. Nearby are the tombs of Nur Jahan and her brother, Asaf Khan.

her husband. Initially, she was renamed Nur Mahal, 'Light of the Palace', but soon became Nur Jahan, 'Light of the World'. Jahangir makes clear in his memoirs how much he depended on her support. On one occasion, when sick, he confided the fact just in her, 'than whom I did not think anyone was fonder of me'. And on another, when seriously ill, he placed his faith in Nur Jahan 'whose skill and experience were greater than those of the physicians … I relied on her kindness. She, by degrees, lessened my wine, and kept me from things that did not suit me …'. Jahangir also made clear how much he came to value maintaining a high profile with Nur Jahan in affairs of state: her name went alongside his on imperial edicts and he had coin struck in her name with this inscription: 'By order of King Jahangir, gold has a hundred splendours added to it by receiving the impression of the name of Nur Jahan, the Queen Begum.'

Nur Jahan's father was a distant relative of the Safavid royal family. He had sought his fortune at Akbar's court and rose to become superintendent of the royal household. Jahangir appointed him chief minister with the title Itimad al-Dawla, 'Pillar of the State'; he was a formidable administrator. The year after Nur Jahan married Jahangir, Itimad al-Dawla's granddaughter by his son Asaf Khan, later to be known as Mumtaz Mahal, 'Paragon of the Palace', married the emperor's son, Khurram, an able general. This group of four, Nur, Asaf, Khurram and Itimad al-Dawla, became a clique which exercised great influence over Jahangir. That the relationship was also one of great respect and affection, at least on Jahangir's side, is clear from his comment in 1621, as first the chief minister's wife dies, and then the man himself: 'I could not bear the agitation of Nur Jahan'.

Even before the chief minister's death, Jahangir's increasing bouts of illness had enabled Nur Jahan more and more to act as sovereign. Inevitably tensions arose over the succession. All four sons of the emperor were candidates: the blind Khusraw, Parwiz, who lived in an alcoholic stupor, Khurram, the able but arrogant general, and Shahriyar, a somewhat foolish son had with a concubine. Other key players, apart from Jahangir himself and Nur Jahan, were Mahabat Khan, the leading soldier of the empire, and Asaf Khan, Nur Jahan's brother. In 1619 Nur Jahan made an early move by marrying her daughter by her first husband to Shahriyar; this gave this powerful woman a major card. Khurram immediately saw his route to the succession threatened, and when ordered to crush a major rising in the Deccan said that he would not go unless Khusraw was handed over to him. In 1621 Khurram fought a most successful campaign in the Deccan and took the opportunity to do away with Khusraw.

Then, in 1622, he was given a major cause for alarm when the command of an expedition to recapture Qandahar was given to Shahriyar, along with the rents of some of his lands. He rebelled. After being defeated by Mahabat Khan, and harried by the armies of Jahangir and Nur Jahan, he accepted terms dictated by the Queen, which forced him to remain in the Deccan and to send two of his sons as hostages to court. At

this point, Mahabat Khan, who had already protested to the Emperor about the influence of Nur Jahan, telling him that 'the whole world is surprised that such an eminent and sensible emperor as Jahangir should permit a woman to have so great an influence over him', entered the lists as the backer of Parwiz. In 1626, a complete failure of ruthlessness on his part when he had both Jahangir and Nur Jahan at his mercy, left him no alternative but to flee to join Khurram. In October 1626 Parwiz died, leaving Khurram and Shahriyar as the remaining contenders.

On 28 October 1627, Jahangir died on the way from Kashmir to Lahore. At this point, Asaf Khan revealed himself to be his son-in-law's backer. He put his sister in confinement, retrieved Khurram's hostage sons, put Khusraw's son, Dawar Baksh, on the throne as a temporary puppet, and defeated the army of Shahriyar. When, after 20 days, news of what had happened reached Khurram in the Deccan, the prince immediately started for the north and ordered Asaf Khan to kill Shahriyar, the puppet emperor and the remaining mature male Timurid cousins. On 24 January 1628, Khurram, now bearing the title Shah Jahan, 'Emperor of the World', entered Agra. Nur Jahan went into retirement, receiving a pension of 200,000 rupees a year. She died in December 1645.

Shah Jahan
1627–58

Shah Jahan, in whose reign Mughal power and magnificence reached its zenith.

SHAH JAHAN	

Born
  5 January 1592
Father
  Jahangir
Mother
  Jagat Gosain, but
  brought up by
  Ruqaiya, Akbar's
  wife
Wives
  Mumtaz Mahal
  (Arjumand Banu),
  Akbarabadi Begum,
  Fatehpuri Begum,
  Sirhindi Begum
Sons
  Darah Shikoh, Shah
  Shuja, Awrangzeb,
  Murad Bakhsh
	Daughters
	  Jahanara,
	  Rawshanara,
	  Gawharara
	Enthroned
	  14 February 1628
	Died
	  1 February 1666,
	  from the effect of
	  medicines to revive
	  his flagging sexual
	  powers
	Buried
	  Taj Mahal, Agra

SHAH JAHAN

I never saw so settled a countenance nor any man keepe so constant a gravity, never smiling, or in face showing any respect of difference of men, but mingled with extreme pride and contempt of all....'

Sir Thomas Roe on the young Shah Jahan

ON 14 FEBRUARY 1628 SHAH JAHAN was crowned in Agra. In the same month the two princes, Dara Shikoh and Awrangzeb, who had been held hostage by Nur Jahan, were returned to the court in the care of Asaf Khan. Thus began the reign which saw Mughal power, wealth and magnificence reach its apogee. The reign, however, also saw the beginnings of a break with the inclusive approach to other religions which had been the hallmark of Mughal rule. In part reflecting a growing revivalist movement amongst Indian Muslims, Shah Jahan adopted an approach to religion more in harmony with the holy law. He celebrated Muslim festivals with vigour, supported the pilgrimage to Mecca, and sent nine missions to Mecca and Medina with Indian goods to be sold for the benefit of the poor. He also imposed restrictions on the repair and construction of Hindu temples and Christian churches. In telling us of the fate of 400 Christian prisoners captured after the destruction in 1632 of the Portuguese trading settlement at Hughli, the court librarian, Inayat

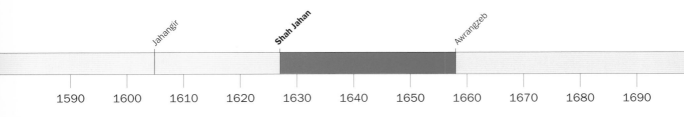

Jahangir   **Shah Jahan**   Awrangzeb

1590   1600   1610   1620   1630   1640   1650   1660   1670   1680   1690

Khan, makes the change of emphasis clear: 'the faith-enlightening, infidel-consuming monarch immediately directed the learned divines to explain to them the tenets of Islam, and to put to death whoever refused to be converted.'

In the year following his accession, Shah Jahan faced a potentially serious rebellion from one of his leading nobles, an Afghan, who raised the prospect of a general rising of the Afghan nobility. Khan Jahan Lodi had been a favourite of Jahangir; after an inglorious military career, he had been made governor of the Deccan. Here, his first mistake was to conclude a duplicitous arrangement with the Nizam Shahi ruler of Ahmadnagar, which led to the loss of Mughal territory, and his second was to refuse to support Shah Jahan's campaign for the succession. After Shah Jahan came to power, Khan Jahan Lodi was laggardly in coming to court, and under deep suspicion when he did so. Eventually, he fled the court first for the Deccan, where he was made commander of the Nizam Shahi army, and then to the Punjab. It was a tribute to Shah Jahan's authority that not one noble supported Lodi. After Lodi was caught, his head and that of his son were sent to the Emperor.

Expanding the empire

Shah Jahan put considerable effort into expanding Mughal power both internally and externally. Areas not fully under control felt the weight of Mughal authority. Thus, he developed systems for policing the peoples of Sind in the lower Indus valley and for taxing their pastoral farmers, while the minor Rajput lineage of the Bundelas, which had a record of defiance, was brought sharply into line.

Beyond the borders of the empire, in 1646–47 Shah Jahan tried to achieve the dream of his forefathers, that of reasserting Mughal authority over Samarqand. He failed, doing no more than to extend the Mughal frontier a few miles north of Kabul. Despite several attempts between 1649 and 1656, and the manufacture of especially large siege guns for the purpose, he was unable to dislodge the Safavids from the frontier city of Qandahar. The empire had reached the limits of its power in the northwest.

In the Himalayas immediately to the north, Shah Jahan did succeed in imposing Mughal authority in Garhwal and Baltistan. In the northeast, several campaigns led to Mughal control of the lower Brahmaputra valley, while they recognized the independence of the Ahom kingdom in Assam. In the Deccan, Shah Jahan persuaded the two remaining sultanates of Bijapur and Golconda to recognize Mughal supremacy; they were required to strike coins in the emperor's name and have it read out as that of the ruler in Friday prayers. When the sultan of Bijapur was slow to submit, Shah Jahan sent three armies to ravage his territories. His ultimate submission to the emperor was abject.

The nobility remained at the heart of the working of the empire. By the 1640s the numbers of senior nobles had doubled since Akbar's time to 443, reflecting the expansion of territory. Power, however, remained highly concentrated. The 73 most senior nobles controlled some 37 per

On Shah Jahan's succession, Khan Jahan Lodi, a favourite of Jahangir, threatened to lead the Afghan nobility in a rebellion against the new emperor. This illustration from the *Padshahnama*, the magnificent record of Shah Jahan's reign, shows the brutal end of Lodi and his supporters.

cent of the imperial revenues; Shah Jahan's four sons alone controlled 8.2 per cent. Some 90 nobles, or 20 per cent of the imperial elite, were Hindus, of whom 73 were Rajputs and 10 were Marathas. The inclusion of the latter was symptomatic of the empire's recent expansion in the Deccan. As far as the relationship between the emperor and his nobles was concerned, Shah Jahan, respecting orthodox opinion, put an end to the idea of imperial discipleship. In its place there grew up the idea of the 'sons of the Emperor's household'. Great nobles, for instance, came to see themselves as hereditary servants of the Mughals. All supported the values of loyalty to the emperor, of aristocratic military honour, of the forms of persianate etiquette to be expressed in public and in private, and of the knowledge of the arts appropriate to a cultivated man. The relationship between noble and emperor was symbolized by the way in which, on the birth of a son, the noble sent the emperor a gift and asked him to name the son.

Shah Jahan and his nobles ruled a vast empire which stretched from northern Afghanistan in the west to Assam in the east, and from the edge of the Tibetan plateau in the north to the centre of the Deccan plateau in the south. Since Akbar's time the annual revenues of the empire had doubled, in part through the acquisition of extra territory, but in part also through greater productivity. Thirty million rupees, or one-seventh of the annual revenues of the empire, went directly to the imperial treasury. In the late 1640s, even though Shah Jahan had spent vast sums on military campaigns and on buildings, he had accumulated since the beginning of his reign reserves amounting to 95 million rupees, half in coin and half in jewels.

Shah Jahan, patron of the arts and architecture

Right from the beginning of his reign, Shah Jahan used the great resources of his realm to express in buildings and works of art the greatness of his state. At his coronation he ordered the construction of the Peacock Throne, which was to set the tone of his era of magnificent display. He ordered 8.6 million rupees worth of jewels and 1.4 million rupees worth of gold to be used in its construction, which took seven years. When, on 20 March 1635, Shah Jahan mounted it for the first time, every surface was decorated with diamonds, rubies, emeralds and pearls. Above the canopy there was a peacock with a raised tail covered with blue sapphires and other stones. In the centre of its breast was a ruby of great value, which had been given by Shah Abbas, the Safavid emperor, to Jahangir. 'And on this ruby', Inayat Khan tells us, 'were inscribed the names of the great Emperor Timur ... Mirza Shahrukh, Mirza Ulugh Beg and Shah Abbas – as well as the names of the Emperors, Akbar, Jahangir, and that of His Majesty himself.' In the same year, 1635, Shah Jahan commissioned the *Padshahnama*, an illustrated history of his reign. One volume of this magnificent work survives in the Royal Library, Windsor Castle. It has none of the vibrant energy of the *Akbarnama*; we learn nothing from it of the interests or enthusiasm of the emperor. The paintings record military

victories and court ceremonials. In doing so they convey the majesty and stateliness of the court and the power of the regime.

Above all, Shah Jahan expressed his power, and his sense of art, in buildings, and in doing so fashioned the quintessential Mughal style of white marble structures inlaid with semiprecious stones. As a young prince he had commissioned works in Ahmadabad, Udaipur and Burhanpur; Jahangir was particularly impressed by work he commissioned when but a teenager in Kabul fort. On coming to power he made much of Ajmer, the site of the shrine of Muin al-Din, whose Chishti Sufi line was so closely linked to Mughal power, constructing gardens, pavilions and a Friday Mosque in the shrine itself. In the first ten years of his reign he made major renovations to the forts at Gwalior, Lahore and Agra. In Lahore he added to the structures of Akbar and Jahangir's time, very much with an eye to effective court ceremonial. In Agra he replaced most of the buildings put up by Akbar and Jahangir with buildings of white marble or stucco. As in his other palaces, all buildings of white marble which overlooked the river were for his personal use. And, as at Lahore, the main purpose of the renovation was to project imperial majesty, through ceremony, to best possible effect. Indeed, it was the failure to achieve a satisfactory outcome here which led him to move his capital to Delhi and build a new city, Shahjahanabad, with a palace at its heart designed to create the ideal ceremonial environment. In addition, Shah Jahan built several hunting lodges and gardens in Sirhind, Lahore and Srinagar. But his finest achievement was his wondrous mausoleum for his wife, Mumtaz Mahal, the Taj Mahal.

SHAHJAHANABAD DELHI

On 29 April 1639, work began on a new capital city, Shahjahanabad, alongside the other cities of Delhi. On 19 April 1648, Shah Jahan made a state entry to inaugurate the city. It has been well described as a 'carefully designed courtly city'. At the eastern end overlooking the Jumna and at the crossing of its two main roads stood a great palace fortress, now known as the Red Fort. Its walls were more than 3 km (1.8 miles) in circumference; it has been estimated that about 57,000 people lived within them, catering to every aspect of the emperor's needs.

Entering by the Lahore gate the visitor passed through a shopping arcade, which still exists, to the hall of public audience, and thence to the hall of private audience where stood the Peacock Throne, and where Shah Jahan had inscribed on the walls: 'If there be a paradise on earth, it is this, it is this, it is this'. Beyond lay the private quarters of the emperor, his harem and household. Outside the fort was

a walled city of some 2,590 ha (6,400 acres) supporting 400,000 people. On a hillock opposite the Fort stood the Friday Mosque, the largest in India at the time. Major developments in and around the city were the outcome of the patronage of royal women: two of the emperor's wives, Akbarabad and Fatehpur, built important mosques, while his daughter Rawshanara laid out a large garden, the Shalimar, outside the city, and another daughter, Jahanara, built a serai for the wealthier merchants in the heart of the city, which was much admired by the European visitors Manucci and Bernier.

The Red Fort seen from the wall overlooking the Jumna river. Immediately behind the wall are the Diwan-i Khass (Hall of Private Audience) to the right, the Khass Mahal in the centre, and the Rang Mahal to the left. In the centre of the picture is the Zar Jharoka (Golden Balcony), on which the emperor displayed himself to the people.

THE TAJ MAHAL

In Mughal documents of the time the Taj Mahal was referred to as 'the illumined tomb'; it was only in the writings of contemporary foreigners that it was referred to under its present name, perhaps reflecting what was already popular parlance. This masterwork of Mughal civilization was intended by Shah Jahan as a mausoleum for his beloved Mumtaz Mahal. But it was also a statement of the emperor's profound Islamic belief and of the central place which Islam had in his empire.

The mausoleum, which took 17 years to build, is the focal point of a large complex of gateways, courtyards and tombs. It stands overlooking the river Jumna at the end of a walled garden, divided into four by waterways in the classic Persian *chahar bagh* fashion. The mausoleum complex, we are told, 'was conceived as a vast allegory of the Day of Resurrection, when the dead shall rise to be judged beneath the Divine Throne.' Every aspect of it was designed to represent paradise. The garden is entered through a magnificent sandstone gateway. The four water channels of the gardens were the four Rivers of Paradise. The raised marble tank at the intersection of the channels was the celestial tank of abundance. The mausoleum was the throne from which God would dispense judgment on the Day of Resurrection, its four minarets the four supports of the throne of God of medieval cosmology. The allegory is underscored by inscriptions from the Quran which appear as calligraphy on the main gateway and the arches of the mausoleum. Sura (chapter) 89 on the gateway reminds the

Left *The Taj Mahal, showing the* chahar bagh *design of the garden, with the four water channels representing the four rivers of paradise and, at the intersection, the celestial tank of abundance. This allegory of the Day of Resurrection was the conception of Shah Jahan, and was wonderfully described by Rabindranath Tagore as 'a teardrop on the cheek of time'.*

Opposite above *The Taj Mahal is placed on a plinth overlooking the Jumna river. Recent excavations have revealed a garden on the opposite bank with water features designed to capture the reflection of the mausoleum in moonlight.*

Opposite centre *Here we see white marble inlaid with precious stones, a feature of Shah Jahan's architecture.*

Opposite below *Calligraphy from the south arch of the mausoleum. The arches, one on each side of the tomb, are surrounded by calligraphy representing Sura 36: Ya sin, which proclaims what will happen on the Day of Judgement. The calligrapher was Amanat Khan of Shiraz (see also p. 137).*

believer of the inevitability of judgment, but also of God's mercy, ending: 'Enter thou among my servants. And enter thou my paradise'. Sura 36 on the mausoleum itself proclaims what will happen at judgment, how men and women will be measured according to their deeds, and go either to heaven or to hell.

Skilled men from all over the eastern Islamic world contributed to the Taj. The architect was Ustad Ahmad of Lahore, who also had an important role in the planning of Shahjahanabad; the calligrapher was Amanat Khan of Shiraz. It is likely that Shah Jahan himself was much involved. Each year, moreover, he would visit the mausoleum on the date of Mumtaz Mahal's death for the purpose of remembrance.

Shah Jahan and Mumtaz Mahal

Shah Jahan was born to rule. The son of a Rajput princess, Jagat Gosain, he was taken away from his mother at birth and given to Ruqaiya Begum, Akbar's childless wife, to bring up. He became Akbar's favourite grandson and reciprocated the affection, refusing to leave the emperor's bedside as he lay dying. As a young prince he quickly proved himself a gifted soldier and administrator. Then, as he developed, everything about him became magnificent – his black-bearded face, his bearing, his courtly Persian manners. He had a strong sense of power. When a favourite, a junior noble, deceitfully disobeyed an instruction, he immediately had him beaten to death. Unlike most of his family, he drank little wine, and then only at the insistence of his father. Amongst his pleasures were hunting, dancing girls, music, singing – he was said to have a pleasing voice – and jewels.

Although he had several wives, like his father he was passionately in love with one woman, Mumtaz Mahal, the niece of his father's favourite queen, Nur Jahan: '... his whole delight was centered in his illustrious lady', Inayat Khan tells us, 'to such an extent that he did not feel towards the others one-thousandth part of the affection he did for Her Late Majesty ....' They were married in 1612, when he was 20 and she was 19, and were to be inseparable; Mumtaz, like her aunt, became increasingly involved in her husband's affairs. It was a good thing that she was fertile because, fearing rivals to her sons, she insisted that the children of her husband's other women should be aborted. Mumtaz had 14 children, of whom seven survived: four princes – Dara Shikoh, Shah Shuja, Awrangzeb and Murad Bakhsh – and three princesses, Jahanara, Rawshanara and Gawharara. When on 17 June 1631, Mumtaz Mahal died in childbirth, Shah Jahan was in despair. 'For a whole week', Inayat Khan reports, 'His Majesty from excess of grief did not appear in public nor transact any affairs of state.... After this calamity he refrained from the practice of listening to music, singing and wearing fine linen. From constant weeping he was forced to use spectacles: and his August beard and moustache, which had only a few white hairs in them before, became in a few days from intense sorrow more than one-third white.'

After his release from this almost monogamous relationship, Shah Jahan by all accounts gave himself over to venery. He accumulated concubines, had liaisons with the wives of his nobles and held an annual eight-day fair for women at which he chose those he fancied. European visitors towards the end of his reign picked up a great deal of palace gossip, including the rumour that Jahanara, his gifted and beautiful eldest daughter, whom Manucci tells us 'he loved to an extraordinary degree', was also his partner in an incestuous relationship. Eventually, his desire for sex was his downfall. In September 1657 he made himself ill by taking an astringent aphrodisiac: 'for already being an old man of sixty-one, Manucci records, 'he wanted still to enjoy himself like a youth....' When, for a moment, this illness seemed mortal, it triggered an almighty battle amongst his sons for the succession.

SHAH JAHAN AND THE WIVES OF NOBLES

The intimacy of Shah Jahan with the wives of Jafar Khan and Khalil Allah Khan (two of his nobles) was so notorious that when they went into court, Manucci records, the mendicants called out in loud voices to Jafar Khan's wife: '"O breakfast of Shah Jahan! Remember us!" And when the wife of Khalil Alah Khan went by they shouted: "O Luncheon of Shah Jahan! succour us!" The women heard, and without taking it as an insult, ordered alms to be given.'

Dara Shikoh (1615–59), whose name means 'The possessor of glory', was both the eldest son of Shah Jahan and Mumtaz Mahal and the emperor's favourite, whom he designated as his heir. He was a Sufi intellectual, a follower of Lahore's Qadiri Sufi saint, Mian Mir. The focus of his thought was to find a common mystical language between Hinduism and Islam. Amongst the works he produced in this pursuit were: a translation of the Hindu *Upanishads* from Sanskrit into Persian, and his *Majma al-Bahrain* (The Mingling of the Two Oceans), which was an attempt to find common theological and spiritual ground between Hindus and Muslims. He also patronized painting, music and dancing. His younger brother, Awrangzeb, disliked all he represented.

The struggle for the succession

The following was the line-up in the competition for Shah Jahan's crown. There was Dara Shikoh, aged 42, whom the emperor had designated his heir and whom, out of love of his company, he kept close to him. Dara was highly cultivated and a serious scholar. Among other things he had the *Upanishads*, key Hindu scriptures, translated into Persian, and himself argued in one of his six books that Hinduism was in its essence the same as Islam. He loved talking to Sufis, Jesuits and Hindu mystics, and left the impression amongst his contemporaries, probably wrongly, that he was not a Muslim. In his open-mindedness and wide-ranging religious interests he took after his great-grandfather, Akbar. His difficulty was that Islamic revivalist sentiment was now more strongly embedded in Mughal society. Moreover, a warm heart and graciousness could not compensate for the fact that he was proud and would not listen to advice, would not stoop to cultivate the great nobles of the court and was a bad general.

Awrangzeb, aged 39 and governor of the Deccan, was his main opponent. He was secretive and most energetic in pursuing his aims. Anxious that the world should recognize his gifts and his wisdom, he was also puritan in his way of life and deeply pious, much interested in the formal knowledge of Islam, and greatly supportive of Islamic orthodoxy. Naturally, he regarded Dara Shikoh as a threat to the existence of Islam in India. He had proved himself a successful commander and administrator in campaigns in the northwest and the Deccan. His psyche, however, was seared by the fact, as Manucci tells us, that he knew his father did not love him.

Then, there were lesser players. Shah Shuja, Shah Jahan's second son, aged 41, was governor of Bengal. He had proved himself to be a man of parts, but he also had his father's weakness for song, dance and women, spending whole days and nights at his pleasures. Murad Bakhsh, the fourth son, aged 33, was the governor of Gujarat. He was a great soldier, known for his valour, but of little judgment and constantly in search of the next amusement. Two princesses also entered the fray: Jahanara, the head of Shah Jahan's household, on the side of Dara, and Rawshanara, plain but highly intelligent, on the side of Awrangzeb. Dara was also assisted by his own sons, Sulaiman and Sipihr.

The struggle was desperate. All knew that by the end of the affair only one of the male contenders was likely to be alive. Shah Shuja was the first to move. Believing his father to be dying, he had himself crowned, his name read in Friday prayers and coins struck, and then he set out for Delhi. In February 1658 he was defeated, though not killed, by an army sent by Dara from Delhi. In Gujarat, Murad Bakhsh crowned himself, captured the fort of Surat, and, bolstered by the treasure he found there, he also set out for Delhi. By this time Shah Jahan had recovered. But it was too late: the princes were set on their bloody course.

Awrangzeb was more cautious than his brothers. He was not going to crown himself until his predominance was sure. On hearing of his

Above Shah Jahan receives his elder sons, Dara Shikoh, Shah Shuja and Awrangzeb at his accession ceremonies in 1628. Thirty years later, the three brothers, along with the fourth, Murad Bakhsh, would be fighting to the death for Shah Jahan's throne.

father's illness, he immediately engaged in secret correspondence with his brothers, and ultimately developed an alliance with Murad, promising him the Punjab, Afghanistan, Kashmir and Sind if they were successful. He also engaged in an intense correspondence designed to win the nobles of the Deccan to his side. In February, he and Murad defeated one imperial army sent against them. Then, on 8 June, on a plain at Samugarh by the Jumna river close to Agra, they confronted Dara and his army of 50,000 men. In the early stages of the battle Dara had the advantage as a result of charges led on one wing by Sipihr and on the other by the Rajputs. But then Dara hesitated and Awrangzeb was able to steady his men. The end came when, his howdah (the canopied seat) having been hit by a rocket, Dara got down from his elephant to fight on horseback. His troops saw the empty howdah as a sign that all was lost, and retreated. Dara fled north to Lahore. Awrangzeb went straight to Agra, made his father prisoner and took control of the fort's vast magazine and treasure. On 12 June, he outwitted Murad, made him captive and took command of his brother's troops. Then, on 31 July, in the Shalimar garden in Delhi, he crowned himself with the title Alamgir 'World-Seizer', although Awrangzeb is the name by which he is generally known.

This drawing illustrates the key moment in the battle of Samugarh in 1658 when Dara Shikoh, after his howdah was hit by a rocket, got down from his elephant to continue fighting on horseback. His troops, seeing the empty howdah, thought Dara Shikoh had fallen, and retreated. On the right of the picture Awrangzeb can be seen in his howdah, and bottom right Murad Bakhsh fleeing the field.

Awrangzeb (Alamgir I)

1658–1707

Awrangzeb, the last of the Great Mughals, who gave himself heart and soul to the business of ruling the empire. A devout man, he is shown here on his knees. Ascetic, he strove to live on selling caps he made for his nobles, Qurans he calligraphed for sale and the proceeds of a small farm he bought near Delhi.

AWRANGZEB	
Born 3 November 1618	(Bahadur Shah I), Muhammad Kam Baksh
Father Shah Jahan	
Mother Mumtaz Mahal	*Daughters* Zeb al-Nisa, Zinat al-Nisa, Zubdat al-Nisa, Badr al-Nisa, Mihr al-Nisa
Wives Dilras Banu Begum (daughter of Shah Nawaz Khan), Rahmat al-Nisa, named Nawab Bai (daughter of Raja Raju of Kashmir), Awrangabadi Mahal, Udepuri Mahal (former wife of Dara Shikoh)	*Enthroned* 31 July 1658; gave himself the title Alamgir, 'World Seizer'
	Died 3 March 1707 of old age
Sons Muhammad Azam, Muhammad Akbar, Muhammad Sultan, Muhammad Muazzam, named Shah Alam	*Buried* In a grave of earth open to the sky at the Mausoleum of Shaikh Zain al-Haqq at Khuldabad, Deccan

AWRANGZEB

I wish you to recollect that the greatest conquerors are not always the greatest Kings.... He is the truly great King who makes it the chief business of his life to govern his subjects with equity.

Awrangzeb to Shah Jahan

AWRANGZEB'S FIRST TASK ON BECOMING EMPEROR was to wipe out those members of his family who might still challenge him for the crown. In the summer of 1658 the most pressing problem seemed to be Dara, who had fled to Lahore, where he was raising an army. Awrangzeb followed him; Dara retreated south to Multan. Then, Awrangzeb heard that Shah Shuja was advancing from Bengal and was preparing to march on Agra. In November 1658 he left the pursuit of Dara to his generals and sped back to defend Agra. In January he found Shah Shuja's army at Kara, close to Allahabad. Although he had great superiority in men and guns, he nearly lost the battle. According to Khafi Khan, Awrangzeb's courage, calm and resolution – he had the legs of his elephant tied together so that his men knew he could not flee – were crucial to rallying his forces and winning the day. For the following 16 months, Awrangzeb's forces so harried Shuja across the lands of Bengal that eventually he was

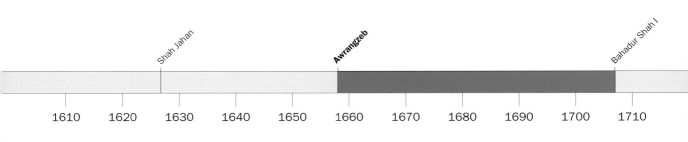

Shah Jahan   **Awrangzeb**   Bahadur Shah I

| 1610 | 1620 | 1630 | 1640 | 1650 | 1660 | 1670 | 1680 | 1690 | 1700 | 1710 |

compelled to flee to the pirate kingdom of Arakan in the east, where in 1661 he was killed after plotting the overthrow of the ruler.

Awrangzeb now turned to deal again with Dara, who was advancing on Agra from Gujarat. In mid-March he defeated his brother in a hard-fought battle over three days in the hills outside Ajmer. Dara fled once more, dogged by imperial armies, through Gujarat and Sind, until he was a few miles from the Bolan Pass, which would take him into Afghanistan, and then perhaps Iran. Here he placed himself in the hands of an Afghan chieftain whose life he had once saved. But the Afghan showed no gratitude, handing Dara and his son Sipihr over to Awrangzeb's men. Forty days later the two were paraded through Delhi in an open howdah on a mangy elephant, a soldier with a drawn sword behind to despatch them in case of a rescue attempt. Dirty and dejected they were forced to wait for two hours in the midday sun before the Red Fort. It was a 'melancholy spectacle', Manucci tells us, 'creating compassion in all those who saw him. For in such a brief space was this prince, so mighty, so rich, so famous, so powerful, reduced to the last stage of misery.' Awrangzeb debated with his nobles what should be done. Most, his sister Rawshanara foremost amongst them, demanded death for Dara because of his apostasy from Islam. The following day he was killed, his headless body paraded through Delhi, before he was buried in Humayun's mausoleum. Sipihr was imprisoned in Gwalior Fort, from which he did not emerge.

There were still further relations to be dealt with. Dara's eldest son Sulaiman had taken refuge with the Raja of Srinagar. Awrangzeb forced the Raja to hand him over, and he too was imprisoned in Gwalior Fort and made to drink opium water until he died. Dara's wives were told that they must marry Awrangzeb. Udepuri, of Georgian extraction, did so, eventually bearing him his fifth son, Kam Bakhsh. But Ranadil, a former dancing girl who had been the love of Dara's life, refused, slashing her face to ribbons to destroy her charms. Murad Bakhsh, his one living brother, remained locked up in Gwalior Fort. In 1661, a rescue attempt underlined the need for action. Typically, rather than just have him put to death, Awrangzeb arranged for the son of a man whom Murad had killed to demand justice under the holy law, saying he would only be satisfied with the execution of Murad as retribution.

There remained his father, whom Awrangzeb had imprisoned in Agra Fort, where the old emperor would sit at a window gazing over the river Jumna at his wife's mausoleum. Awrangzeb never went to see his father, indeed he had not seen him since 1652, but he did correspond, writing in a hectoring tone and complaining that his father had loved Dara and not him. Awrangzeb had his psychological revenge when he sent him Dara's head in a meat dish. On lifting the lid, Manucci tells us, Shah Jahan 'uttered one cry and fell on his hands and face upon the table, and, striking against the golden vessels, broke some of his teeth and lay there apparently lifeless.' Various meannesses were visited upon the old emperor: Awrangzeb pursued him for his personal jewels, and it was made difficult for him to get proper slippers and to have his violins repaired. But, he was able to live out his life in the royal apartments, in the company of his women, and in particular that of Jahanara, who gave him loving care. On 1 February 1666, he died, aged 74, from the same illness that had led to the succession struggle in 1657: retention of urine brought on by medicines designed to revive his flagging sexual powers. As was customary, the palace wall was breached, the body carried through and then taken by boat to the Taj Mahal, where it was laid to rest beside that of Mumtaz Mahal. As Shah Jahan lay dying, Jahanara had persuaded him to sign a letter pardoning Awrangzeb.

Awrangzeb the ruler

Awrangzeb's bloody ascent to power, united to the poor reputation history has awarded him amongst most Hindus and many Muslims, has given him a bad press. But he was not quite the monster that many have wished to make him. He was a man of great personal courage, as he demonstrated aged 14 when he confronted an enraged elephant. Just once, moreover, he showed his susceptibility to passion. In his early 30s he became infatuated by a Hindu dancing girl and gave himself over to music and hedonism, from which he was only saved by her death. But once in power, all his passion was expressed through the business of ruling, which he embraced with an implacable and joyless sense of duty. Ascetic, he wore cheap clothes and few jewels, and strove in his personal life to live on the proceeds of caps he made for his nobles, Qurans he calligraphed for sale and the proceeds of a small farm he bought near Delhi. Having secured his position, he showed himself to be humane, mild and

---

JAHANARA BEGUM

The eldest daughter of Shah Jahan and Mumtaz Mahal, Jahanara, was yet another Mughal woman of great ability. Beautiful, learned and statesmanlike, on the death of her mother she became head of Shah Jahan's household and his companion for the rest of his life. An indication of her status was her inheritance of half her mother's movable property – the remainder being shared amongst her six siblings – the raising of her annual stipend from 600,000 to 1 million rupees, and her custody of the royal seal. An indication of her father's affection was his personal care for her, to the extent of changing dressings himself, during the nine months it took her to recover from being badly burned after her dress caught alight.

Jahanara's wealth enabled her to be a major patron of architecture. She built mosques, serais and gardens in Agra, Delhi, Lahore and Kashmir. Her political wisdom kept her close to power for much of her life. A key figure in the succession struggle, she favoured Dara. 'I love my brother Dara Shikoh extremely both in form and spirit', she is said to have declared. 'We are, in fact, like one soul in two bodies and one spirit in two physical forms.' Her favour of the hated Dara did not prevent Awrangzeb from admiring her too. After her father's death, he made her first lady of the empire with the title Padshah Begum, raised her stipend to 1.7 million rupees and assigned her a magnificent house in Delhi where he would often visit her. In 1681, aged 67, she died. A deeply religious woman, who supported both the Chishti and the Qadiri Sufi orders, she was buried in the compound of Shaikh Nizam al-Din in Delhi.

Tomb of Jahanara in Nizam al-Din, Delhi. Inscribed by her wish on the tombstone are these words: 'Let no rich canopy surmount my resting place. This grass is the best covering for a grave of a lowly heart.'

Awrangzeb was noted for his personal courage. In June of 1633 Shah Jahan and his sons were watching a fight between two enormous imperial elephants, Sudhakar and Surat Sundar. At one stage Sudhakar ran in the direction of Awrangzeb. Here the *Padshahnama* records the moment at which the young prince drove his spear into the elephant's forehead. The elephant then gored Awrangzeb's horse and he was forced to face the beast on the ground; courtiers came to the rescue. The *Padshahnama* closed the episode saying: 'the Emperor first drew Prince Muhammad Awrangzeb to the bosom of affection and kissed him with emotion, awarding him all sorts of favours and the title Bahadur [Champion].'

moderate, and especially considerate towards the lowly. Genuinely humble, he was hard on himself but tolerant of weakness in others. His letters to his sons reveal many sides of the man: his pleasure in good horses; his command of Persian poetry; his love of fruit; and in particular his overwhelming desire to transmit the principles and practice of good government. In 1704 he wrote to Prince Azam in Gujarat thus:

Exalted son, the artillery and palace superintendent has been appointed [by you] the police officer of Navah of Ahmadabad. He appoints his vulture-like [i.e. bribe-receiving] relatives and friends to 'patelships'. The complainants against the power of the above-mentioned superintendent do not get admittance into your court. Robbers and vagabonds have become the companions of his son-in-law who afflicts God's people [our subjects]. I wonder what answer we shall give on the day of judgment. The Holy and High God is just …. It is we who allow oppression by giving power to tyrants and withholding justice from the oppressed.

Awrangzeb's religious policies

The dominant theme, however, running through Awrangzeb's correspondence was fear of God. And so, too, religious orthodoxy was the dominant theme of his reign. Indeed, he completed the transition, begun by his father, from Akbar's inclusive approach in ideology and governance to one which increasingly operated as a Muslim state, following the holy law, governing for the benefit of Muslims and with the aim of converting infidels. Thus, Awrangzeb abandoned the practice, begun by Akbar, of showing himself to the people at dawn so that they could worship him. He ended the great tradition of Mughal illustrated chronicles, disbanding the teams of artists he had inherited from his father. His building programme was largely confined to religious structures. Un-Islamic celebrations were banned from court, as were wine and opium, while imperial patronage, which had done so much for the development of Hindustani music, was stopped. Regulators of public morals were appointed for major towns and cities. The ulama, who had been stripped of lands and influence under Akbar, now found these restored, much to the disapproval of senior nobles. Moreover, with the aim of producing a clear guide to correct behaviour for orthodox Muslims, Awrangzeb ordered a codification of legal judgments, the *Fatawa-i Alamgiri*.

Given that for 500 years inclusiveness had been the wise policy for the Muslim rulers of India, Awrangzeb's actions against non-Muslims, the vast majority of the population, were striking: temples recently built or repaired were demolished; Hindu pilgrims to shrines and festivals were taxed; Hindus paid twice the internal custom duties paid by Muslims; provincial governors were instructed to replace Hindu officers with Muslims; and then, most controversially, the *jizya*, the poll tax on non-Muslims which Akbar had abolished, was restored. This last action brought popular protest in Delhi to the very walls of the Red Fort. But it also persuaded some to convert to Islam. Awrangzeb went out of his way to congratulate and reward those who did so.

Awrangzeb's religious policies led to strains in relations with non-Muslim communities. In the 1660s a young Sikh Guru, Tegh Bahadur, began a vigorous missionary campaign across northern India from the Punjab to Assam. Large numbers of Jats, the largest cultivating group of the region, were converted, as were some Muslims. Awrangzeb did not approve. In 1675 Tegh Bahadur was arrested and executed; the Sikhs became enemies of the Mughal regime. Awrangzeb's attitudes also incited serious trouble from a senior Rajput clan. In 1679 imperial disrespect towards the Rathors, plus the requirement that a Rathor prince become a Muslim in order to be a noble, led to rebellion. The Mughal war machine quickly dealt with this, destroying many temples in the process. The Rathors resorted to guerrilla warfare. At this point Prince

One of the few areas in which Awrangzeb patronized artistic activity was architecture. This said, he avoided Shah Jahan's use of luxury materials, such as marble and red sandstone, in favour of brick and rough stone. Fittingly, his greatest building was a mosque, the Badshahi Mosque at Lahore, which is one of the largest in South Asia. The three great domes, seen here from the courtyard, are regarded as a particular success.

Akbar, Awrangzeb's favourite son, who had been secretly in contact with the Rathors, in alliance with his sister, Zeb al-Nisa, rebelled against his father. Agreeing with the Rajput view that Awrangzeb's bigotry would lead to the destruction of the Mughal empire, on 1 January 1681 Akbar crowned himself emperor. But, as a military leader, Awrangzeb easily outwitted his son, who was forced to flee to Maratha lands and thence to Iran, where he died. His sister, a woman of great learning, was imprisoned, losing both her property and her allowance. The Rathors kept up a guerrilla opposition for the rest of the reign.

The empire becomes richer

It is important to note that, despite the occasional rebellion, under Awrangzeb the empire continued to grow in wealth. State revenue demand more than doubled, from under 6 million dams in Akbar's time to over 13 million dams at the end of Awrangzeb's reign. The increase was met by raising the revenue demand and conquering new lands. It was also assisted by a steady growth in the amount of land under cultivation and a movement towards high-value cash crops – indigo, cotton, sugar, opium, tobacco, maize. The rapidly growing cash economy meant that local landlords and village elites were able to accumulate resources. One sign of the new wealth was the emergence of hundreds of small towns known as qasbas in northern India, which were centres for markets, money-lending and the grain trade, but also the favoured home of retired officials, military officers and ulama – a Muslim gentry. Another sign was the increasing engagement of particular areas of India in international trade, led by the English, French and Dutch, and encouraged by the Mughals. Thriving trades in agrarian commodities and Indian manufactured goods, in particular textiles, developed. By Awrangzeb's time coastal areas and their hinterlands were being transformed by these trades: Surat in Gujarat, Madras on the Coromandel coast, the area between Krishna and Godavari rivers on the north Coromandel coast, and the port of Hughli with its Bengal hinterland. In the century after 1660, the English and the Dutch shipped on average each year 34 tons of silver and half a ton of gold to pay for their purchases.

Awrangzeb's wars

Awrangzeb needed an empire growing in wealth – it had to support almost constant warfare. In the north he was unable to spread his authority much beyond that of his predecessor. In the northeast in the early 1660s he succeeded in pushing up the Brahmaputra valley against the Ahoms as far as Gawhati, but only held the position for 20 years. On the Bengal coast, however, he was able to drive Mughal authority eastwards into the kingdom of Arakan. In the northwest, the Mughal governor of Kabul strove hard to keep trade routes open into Iran and Central Asia, and to maintain peace amongst the tribes of the frontier region. In the 1660s and 1670s, the Mughals had to deal with a number of tribal revolts and several armies were lost or badly mauled. It required Awrangzeb's

SHIVAJI'S LETTER TO AWRANGZEB

Shivaji wrote in sarcastic protest against the re-imposition of the *jizya* tax, saying that he wrote as a well-wisher of the emperor and reminding him that success had met the efforts of Akbar, Jahangir and Shah Jahan, who had not imposed the tax:

'But in your Majesty's reign many of the forts and provinces have gone out of your possession, and the rest will soon do so, too, because there will be no slackness on my part in ruining and devastating them. Your peasants are down-trodden; the yield of every village has declined, in the place of one lakh [100,000 rupees] only one thousand and in the place of a thousand only ten are collected, and that too with difficulty. When poverty and beggary have made their home in the palaces of the Emperor and the princes, the condition of the grandees and officers can be easily imagined. It is a reign in which the army is in ferment, the merchants complain; the Muslims cry, the Hindus are grilled; most men lack bread at night, and in the day-time inflame their own cheeks by slapping them [in anguish]. How can the royal spirit permit you to add the hardship of the *jizya* to this grievous state of things? The infamy will quickly spread from west to east and become recorded in books of history that the Emperor of Hindustan, coveting the beggars' bowls, takes *jizya* from Brahmans and Jains, yogis, sanyasis, bairagis, paupers, mendicants, ruined wretches, and the famine-stricken – that his valour is shown by attacks on the wallets of beggars – that he dashed down the name and honour of the Timurids!'

personal attention and the use of frequent bribes to keep the trade routes open. Further expansion in the northeast was out of the question.

The real opportunities for expansion, however, lay in the Deccan. At the beginning of his reign Awrangzeb was confronted by a Hindu leader of genius, Shivaji, a Maratha, who had carved out a kingdom in the Western Ghats and the Konkan coast, based on a network of easily defended fortresses. A series of daring raids on Mughal territories, including the sacking of the most important port in western India, Surat – a city of 200,000 – which netted him 10 million rupees worth of loot, meant action had to be taken. In 1665, faced with overwhelming Mughal force, Shivaji surrendered and became a Mughal vassal. After a brief stay at the Mughal court, Shivaji regretted his decision and fled back to his lands. Two years later Awrangzeb pardoned him, making him a high-ranking noble. But it was not long before Shivaji was raiding the sultanate of Bijapur and Mughal lands, including a second sacking of Surat, which this time yielded 6.5 million rupees of treasure. Shivaji asserted his independence from Mughal authority in 1674 by having himself crowned as a Hindu ruler with appropriate Hindu ceremonies and hosts of Brahmins in attendance. Shivaji then did a deal with the sultan of Golconda by which the sultanate subsidized his military campaigns against the Mughals. In 1680 Shivaji died, leaving a compact Maratha state and a tradition of raiding Mughal territories; in 1681 he was succeeded by his elder son, Shambhaji.

It was at this point that Awrangzeb turned his attention towards expanding Mughal power in the Deccan, which was to occupy him for the rest of his life. He shifted the capital of the empire from Delhi to the Deccan, and for a long time it was wherever he was in camp. He was drawn south by the need in part to counter the threat represented by Prince Akbar, who was then sheltering at Shambhaji's court, but also to discourage Maratha raids into Mughal territory. Over four years, Awrangzeb made little progress against the Marathas and so turned his attention to the remaining Deccan sultanates. In 1685 he conquered Bijapur; in 1687, Golconda. In 1688, he turned once more to deal with the Marathas. By dint of decisive action he caught Shambhaji and his chief minister alive. Condemned to die for having killed Muslims, the two were hacked to death and their remains fed to dogs. By 1689 Awrangzeb had thus increased Mughal territories by a quarter – over 570,000 sq. km (220,000 sq. miles). Muslim authority now reached as far south as it had in the time of Muhammad bin Tughluq.

After his victory, Awrangzeb set about imposing Mughal systems of administration on his newly conquered territories. This was relatively easy in Golconda, but harder in Bijapur, where the Marathas were a continuing nuisance. Matters were worse on the southeast coast of India, where for eight years the Mughals disputed control with the Marathas, until in 1698 they finally captured the great fort of Jinji. But in the western Deccan the Marathas remained a serious problem. Awrangzeb declared holy war, and year by year invested the great Maratha strongholds; this remarkable man in his 80s often personally supervised the

Shivaji (1630–80), the Maratha hero, led a series of daring raids on Mughal territories in the Deccan. He was a constant thorn in Awrangzeb's side, the Great Mughal being unable either to co-opt him into the empire or to defeat him. On his death, Shivaji left a compact Maratha state which continued his practice of raiding Mughal territories.

Opposite Awrangzeb in old age reading a Quran. At the end of his life he was haunted by the thought that he had failed.

sieges. Fortress after fortress fell to a combination of bribery and the sheer weight of Mughal force. But, while Awrangzeb focused on strongpoints, the Marathas were raiding far and wide across the Deccan. Such was the disruption that the long-distance caravan trade route from Hyderabad to Gujarat and northern India was shut down between 1702 and 1704. In the western Deccan, Marathas levied protection money on a regular basis. Increasingly, local leaders began to transfer their allegiance from the Mughals to the Marathas, who then raided further and further north into Gujarat and Malwa.

The Deccan wars weaken the empire

Awrangzeb never returned north. The fact that the last 26 of his 49 years of rule were spent away from the imperial heartland left its mark on the workings of the empire. Mughal nobles were divided between those who worked in the Deccan and those who worked in the north. Those in the north rarely attended court, and were less and less subjected to the rituals which made them part of the imperial family. Some Mughal nobles went native, avoiding their duty as soldiers, and found it easier to deal with Maratha leaders, whom they had often come to know well. Large numbers of Deccanis were enrolled in the nobility, 64 from the elites of Bijapur and Golconda, and 96 Hindu Marathas, that is over 16 per cent of the total nobility. None of these Marathas had the heavy exposure to court and persianate high culture which their Rajput co-religionists in the north had had. The numbers of new nobles, combined with the predatory warfare of the Marathas, led to a serious decline of revenue assignments to support them.

Awrangzeb's obsession with it led the centre of gravity of the empire to swing towards the Deccan and meant that he had difficulty in asserting imperial authority elsewhere. Towards the end of the 17th century, the Dutch, French and English East India companies became increasingly assertive in their footholds around the coast. In the 1690s, Awrangzeb was unable to prevent the English at Bombay minting rupees with the head of the English monarch on the coin, and in 1702 his men failed to assert the empire's authority over the English settlement in Madras. In the 1690s there was a serious uprising in Bengal, which led to the substantial surpluses of that province no longer arriving in the Deccan. Awrangzeb sent his grandson, Azim al-Shan, to reimpose order, and a brilliant Brahman convert to Islam, with the title Murshid Quli Khan, to restore the revenues. In the long run, the latter proved a more effective ruler than the prince, who was pushed aside with Awrangzeb's assent. Before the emperor died, Murshid Quli Khan had built a strongly independent position for himself.

Some years earlier, in the 1680s, the Jats around Agra had begun to plunder the great caravans of nobles and traders which travelled the royal road from Delhi to the Deccan. When in 1687 Awrangzeb sent his grandson to restore order, the Jats outmanoeuvred the Mughal forces and, fired by resentment at the revenue demands made of them by the regime,

MANUCCI DESCRIBES AWRANGZEB LEADING HIS ARMY IN OLD AGE

'The old king … still shows his eagerness for war by the gestures he used on the march. While seated in his palanquin, he unsheathes his sword, makes cuts in the air, first one way, then the other, and smiling all the while, polishes it with a cloth, then returns it to its scabbard. He does the same with his bow, to show that he can still let fly an arrow. But most of the time he sits doubled up, his head drooping so much that his beard lies on his chest, and it looks to you as if it grew out of his throat. When his officers submit any petition, or make report to him of any occurrence, he gently raises his head and straightens his back. He gives them such an answer as to leave no opening for reply, and still looks after his army in the minutest particulars.'

'marched to the mausoleum of that great conqueror Akbar', Manucci tells us. 'Against him living they could effect nothing; they therefore wreaked vengeance of his sepulchre. They began their pillage by breaking in the great gates of bronze which it had, robbing the valuable precious stones and plates … of gold and silver, and destroying what they were not able to carry away. Dragging out the bones of Akbar, they threw them angrily into the fire and burnt them.' Awrangzeb was outraged. Although it did not seem so at the time, this act symbolized in a most powerful way the collapse of Mughal authority which was to come.

Tragic final years

It is hard not to see the last years of Awrangzeb as tragic, but tragic in a different way from those of his father. Increasingly he felt that he had failed and was dogged by fear of the succession struggle which would break out on his death. His mid- to late 80s were consumed by campaigning, until, in May 1705, he broke down with severe pains in his limbs and did not appear for public audience for 12 days. Amazingly, he recovered and set out for Delhi. But, in January 1706, he pitched camp at Ahmadnagar and decided to stay. Clearly fading he was cared for by his daughter Zinat al-Nisa and his wife Udepuri. But he remained in charge of his faculties. Two weeks before the end he sent two of his sons, Azam and Kam Bakhsh, to different parts of the empire because he could not take the risk of leaving 'two unchained lions' together, and when the court astrologer recommended that he give away an elephant and a diamond to counteract the evil influences of the stars, he rejected the advice as following a Hindu custom, sending 4,000 rupees to charity instead. In his final testaments he advised the partitioning of the empire amongst his sons and requested the humblest of burials, to be paid for by the money he had earned by making caps and copying the Quran. On 3 March 1707, he died, and was buried the following day by the tomb of the Sufi saint, Zain al-Haqq, at Khuldabad, in a grave of earth, open to the sky, and surrounded by stone. The contrast between this humble orthodox burial and the great mausoleums of his immediate forefathers underscores how he differed from them. In a letter written to Prince Azam a few days before he died, Awrangzeb's words bear a bitter sense of failure:

May peace be upon you and those who are near you. Old age arrived and … strength departed from the limbs. I came alone [in this world] and I go as a stranger [to the next world] …. I was devoid of administrative [tact] and care for the welfare of the people. [My] dear life has been spent in vain. God is present in this world but I do not see Him…. The whole [royal] army is confused and confounded…. Though I have strong hope in the favours and mercy [of God], my actions do not allow me to think over [i.e. I am afraid on account of my actions]…. Though outwardly the Begum [Zinat al-Nisa] is grieved, God is her protector. The short-sightedness of women has no fruit except disappointment. Good-bye; good-bye; good-bye.

THE LATER MUGHALS
1707–1858

Bahadur Shah I
1707–12

Muhammad Shah
1719–48

Jahandar Shah
1712–13

Ahmad Shah
1748–54

Farrukhsiyar
1713–19

BAHADUR SHAH I	
Born 29 October 1643 *Father* Awrangzeb *Mother* Name unknown (daughter of Shah Nawaz Begum) *Wife* ? *Sons* Azim al-Shan, Jahandar Shah, Rafi al-Shan, Jahan Shah	*Daughters* Mihr al-Nisa, Aziz al- Nisa, Nur al-Begum *Died* 18 February 1712; Lahore *Buried* In the Munhajjar Shah Alam Bahadur Shah, near the dargah of Bakhtiar Kaki, behind the Qutb Minar, Delhi

JAHANDAR SHAH	
Born 1664 *Father* Bahadur Shah I *Mother* ? *Wife* Chief wife, Lal Kunwar (daughter of a musician) *Son* Aziz al-Din Khan (Alamgir II)	*Enthroned* 29 March 1712 *Died* 11 February 1713, strangled on the orders of Farrukhsiyar *Buried* Humayun's Tomb, Delhi

BAHADUR SHAH I

For generosity, munificence, boundless good nature, extenuation of faults and forgiveness of offences, very few monarchs have been found equal to Bahadur Shah in the histories of past times, and especially in the race of Timur. But though he had no vice in his character, such complacency and such negligence were exhibited in the protection of the state and in the government and management of the country, that witty sarcastic people found the date of his accession in the words Shah-i be-khabr 'Heedless King'.

Khafi Khan

As AWRANGZEB FEARED, his death was followed by a succession struggle. His eldest son, Muazzam, moved at speed from Afghanistan to Agra, where he took charge of the treasury. In June 1707 he defeated and killed his brother, Azam, along with his two sons, and then in 1708 at Hyderabad (Deccan) he defeated Kam Bakhsh, who died of his wounds. Muazzam ascended the throne with the title Bahadur Shah. Elements of a political crisis became evident in his reign: the Turkish and Iranian nobles resented his appointment of large numbers of Indians to the nobil-

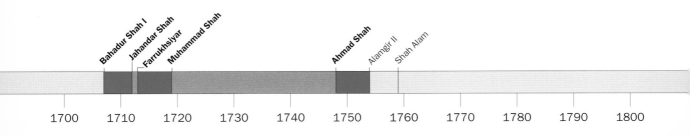

Awrangzeb's eldest son Muazzam succeeded him as Bahadur Shah I. To do so he had to kill two of his brothers and two nephews.

ity and began to put their interests before those of the crown. Moreover, many rebellions broke out: the Jats around Delhi and Agra; the Rajputs to take control of their states; the Sikhs in the Punjab; followed from 1713 by a Maratha uprising in the Deccan. The wars of succession and those of rebellion were a huge drain on the imperial treasury. 'The income of the Empire', declared Khafi Khan, 'was insufficient to meet the expenses ....' In his late 60s, after five years of rule, Bahadur Shah died in his bed.

JAHANDAR SHAH

When Farrukhsiyar drew near to Agra, and his forces were compared with Jahandar's, most men anticipated a victory for the latter. But the Emperor's partiality for low women, his liking for low company, and his patronage of base-born nameless men, had disgusted all the nobles of Iran and Turan. ... The victory of Farrukhsiyar became the hope of every man in the army, great and small.

Khafi Khan

BAHADUR SHAH WAS STILL ON HIS DEATHBED when his four sons launched a war of succession. Azim, the ruler of Bengal, with substantial treasure and a large army, seemed to have the best chance. But, after three months of warfare, it was Jahandar Shah who eliminated his three brothers and came out on top. Under this dissolute man imperial institutions were weakened further: for the first time nobles who had supported losers in the succession struggle were punished, some by loss of property and some by loss of life; the emperor ceded full control of the reins of power to his *wazir* (finance minister), and then began to plot against him; then he shocked the nobility by making the daughter of a minstrel his chief wife. In this situation Farrukhsiyar, the son of the late Prince Azim, raised an army in

JAHANDAR KEEPS LOW COMPANY

'Another story about him was spoken of in society, and has become notorious from city to city. He used to go out sometimes in a cart with a mistress and some companions to enjoy himself in the market and drinking shops. One night he and his favourite went out this way, and both drank so much that they became drunk and senseless. On arriving at the door of the palace, Lal Kunwar was so drunk that when she got out she took no notice whatever of the Emperor, but went to bed and slept heavily. The Emperor, who was perfectly helpless, remained fast asleep in the cart, and the driver drove home and put the cart away. [In the morning] Lal Kunwar recovered sufficient sense to see that the Emperor was not by her side, and fell a-crying. People went running about in all directions till the Emperor was found in the cart.'

Khafi Khan

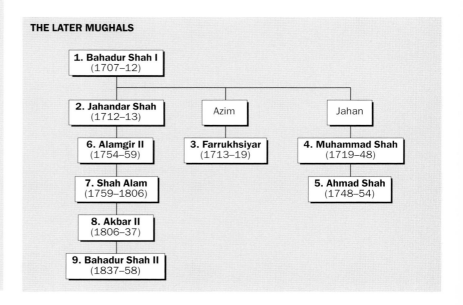

THE LATER MUGHALS

- 1. **Bahadur Shah I** (1707–12)
  - 2. **Jahandar Shah** (1712–13)
    - 6. **Alamgir II** (1754–59)
      - 7. **Shah Alam** (1759–1806)
        - 8. **Akbar II** (1806–37)
          - 9. **Bahadur Shah II** (1837–58)
  - Azim
    - 3. **Farrukhsiyar** (1713–19)
  - Jahan
    - 4. **Muhammad Shah** (1719–48)
      - 5. **Ahmad Shah** (1748–54)

Above Farrukhsiyar, a great-grandson of Awrangzeb, was a weak ruler in the hands of the powerful Barha Saiyids. Under his rule the authority and revenues of the Mughal empire declined substantially.

Opposite Muhammad Shah, who ruled for 30 years, was dedicated to his pleasures, in particular those of the harem, as this picture suggests. In his reign, the Mughal provinces of Hyderabad, Awadh and Bengal became independent states, Delhi was sacked by Nadir Shah – with vast quantities of treasure, including the Peacock Throne, being carried off to Iran – and the prestige of the Mughal empire greatly damaged.

Bengal and had himself crowned in Patna. He allied himself with the governors of Bihar and Allahabad, Husain Ali Khan and Abd Allah Khan, both from the Indian Muslim family of Barha Saiyids, and marched on Delhi. Farrukhsiyar faced a much larger army led by Jahandar Shah, but it was divided and morale was poor. After defeating Jahandar Shah, Farrukhsiyar had him strangled and his body left to rot outside the gate to the Red Fort. All the Mughal princes who might have had a claim to the throne were blinded.

FARRUKHSIYAR

Farrukhsiyar had no will of his own. He was young, inexperienced in business, and inattentive to affairs of State. He had grown up in Bengal, far away from his grandfather and father. He was entirely dependent on the opinions of others, for he had no resolution or discretion. By the help of fortune he had seized the crown. The timidity of his character contrasted with the vigour of the race of Timur, and he was not cautious in listening to the words of artful men.

Khafi Khan

FARRUKHSIYAR BEGAN HIS REIGN by rewarding his Barha Saiyid allies. Abd Allah Khan was made *wazir* and Husain Ali Khan, *mir bakhshi* – chief paymaster. In this was he made a great mistake at the outset, Khafi Khan tells us, because the office of *wazir* was 'such a high and important trust that former kings always bestowed it on wise, great and high-minded men, remarkable for patience, experience, clemency and affability, whose qualities had been tested by long experience ….' The Saiyids then participated in the next great error of the reign – the slaughter of the nobles who had opposed Farrukhsiyar's succession. An atmosphere of terror pervaded the court. As time went on, Farrukhsiyar came increasingly to rely on advisers who were concerned to undermine his relations with the Saiyids. All the while, rebellions from Sikhs, Rajputs, Jats and Marathas forced him to make major concessions to buy off the rebels. Widespread famine broke out. Revenues declined disastrously and the regime could not pay its way.

Eventually, in 1719, Farrukhsiyar commanded Husain Ali Khan, who had campaigned long in the Deccan for the empire, to attend court. Fearing for his life, Husain Ali Khan came with his army and camped outside Delhi. 'There', Khafi Khan records, 'he showed his rebellious

FARRUKHSIYAR	
Born 1683	*Son* ?
Father Azim al-Shan, son of Bahadur Shah I	*Enthroned* 10 January 1713
Mother ?	*Died* Strangled in 1719
Wife Indira Kunwar (a Rajput princess of Jodhpur)	*Buried* Humayun's Tomb, Delhi

designs by ordering his drums to be beaten loudly in defiance; for it is contrary to all rule for [a subject's] drums to be beaten near the residence of the emperor. Complaining of the Emperor, he entered his tents, and repeatedly said that he reckoned himself no longer among the servants of the monarch.' With his brother he secured control of the gates of the Red Fort, and marched in to see the emperor. 'In return for all our service to you', Abd Allah Khan told him, 'we have received nothing from you ungrateful King, but evil thoughts and suspicions and treacherous designs.' The two Saiyids demanded control of all the great offices of state. Farrukhsiyar fled into his women's quarters. The Saiyids followed him there, finding him hidden in a corner of the roof. He was dragged out, blinded and imprisoned. After being caught planning to escape, he was put to death and buried in Humayun's tomb.

MUHAMMAD SHAH

He was a good-looking young man, with many good qualities, and of excellent intelligence.... His mother was well-acquainted with state business and was a woman of much intelligence and tact.

Khafi Khan

AFTER THE DEPOSITION OF FARRUKHSIYAR, the Saiyids put up several puppet rulers from amongst the descendants of Awrangzeb, who all died quickly, until they hit upon Muhammad Shah, the grandson of Bahadur Shah through his youngest son, Jahan Shah. The beginning of the reign was dated from the deposition of Farrukhsiyar. At the beginning, Muhammad Shah was no more than a puppet of the Saiyids; all his servants were their men, and he could not move without their permission. His salvation lay in the fear among the nobles of Iranian and Turkish extraction – with whom he and his mother had opened up lines of communication – that the Indian Muslim Barha Saiyids wished to marginalize them completely and overthrow the Mughals. The Iranian and Turkish nobles then assassinated Husain Ali Khan in his camp close to Fatehpur Sikri, sending his head to Muhammad Shah. The emperor now placed himself at the head of Husain Ali Khan's army and marched against Abd Allah Khan. In a battle lasting a night and two days, Abd Allah's army was

THE PARLEY BETWEEN MUHAMMAD SHAH AND NADIR SHAH

'The next day Muhammad Shah repaired in person to the Persian camp.... When they drew near, the Shah himself came forth, and the etiquette usual between the Persian and Mughal courts was faithfully observed. The two monarchs, holding one another by the hand, entered the audience-tents, and seated themselves side by side on a *masnad*. It was as if two suns had risen in the East, or as if two bright moons shed their light at one time! ... Nothing that courtesy and friendship require was omitted during the whole conference, which lasted a quarter of the day.... These proceedings restored tranquility to the minds of the soldiery; all looked forward with joy to renewed plenty, to a return to their beloved Shahjahanabad and the society of friends; but fate smiled at these fond hopes, for more suffering, more bloodshed awaited them.

Mukhlis

MUHAMMAD SHAH	
Born	Udham Bai
17 August 1702	*Son*
Father	Ahmad Shah
Jahan Shah, son of	*Enthroned*
Bahadur Shah I	September 1719
Mother	*Died*
Qudsiya Begum	26 April 1748
Wife	*Buried*
Malika-yi Zamani	In the Muhajjar
(daughter of	Muhammad Shah in
Farrukhsiyar),	the dargah of Nizam
Sahiba Mahal,	al-Din Awliya, Delhi

defeated, he was captured, and subsequently, it seems, poisoned: the pretensions of the Barha Saiyids were finished. Now, in principle, Muhammad Shah was in a position to take over the reins of power, but he preferred to devote himself to the pleasures of the harem and the diversions of animal fights. The leadership of the empire fell to his *wazirs*, of whom Qamr al-Din, who held office from 1724 to 1748, was both indolent and a drunkard.

In these circumstances the Mughal empire disintegrated. Control over the Punjab was steadily ceded to the Sikhs and local Hindu leaders, and the province was increasingly exposed to invasion from the north-west. In western India Muhammad Shah made an alliance with the Marathas, permitting them to take 35 per cent of the revenue. The conditions were created in which the hereditary Maratha prime ministers, the *peshwas*, were able to fashion a kingdom which steadily grew in size, while their raids penetrated as far as Delhi and Calcutta. In Hyderabad in the eastern Deccan, Nizam al-Mulk, who had been Muhammad Shah's leading Turkish ally amongst the nobles in his struggle against the Saiyids, established in 1724 the dynasty of the Nizams, which was to last until 1948. In the rich province of Bengal, Murshid Quli Khan dutifully sent revenue to Delhi. But, from 1727, his successor refused to do so, and the governorship became a hereditary dynasty. Much the same took place in Awadh, where the Iranian noble Burhan al-Mulk was made governor in 1722, establishing a dynasty which was to last until 1858.

How far the empire was weakened by these losses was soon apparent. In 1737 the Marathas raided for the first time as far as the suburbs of Delhi. In 1739, Nadir Shah (p. 208), who had overthrown the Safavid dynasty of Iran in 1736, invaded India and defeated the imperial army some 160 km (100 miles) from Delhi. Muhammad Shah, seeing that further resistance was hopeless, parleyed with Nadir Shah, and the two monarchs made separate state entries into Delhi. Then disaster fell. The citizens of Delhi rose against the Iranians. Nadir Shah ordered a massacre. 'For a long time', declared an eyewitness, 'the streets remained strewn with corpses, as the walks of a garden with dead flowers and leaves. The town was reduced to ashes, and had the appearance of a plain consumed with fire.' The royal treasury was emptied, the Peacock Throne carried off to be broken up, and a ransom levied on all the surviving households in the city. Nadir Shah returned to Iran with fabulous treasure. He left the Mughal emperor as an impotent reminder of once great power.

Others noted the weakness of the Mughals. In 1748 the Afghans under Ahmad Abdali, the former captain of Nadir Shah's guard, made the first of more than 10 invasions of northwest India in the period up to 1760. The Mughals, with the help of the Nawab of Awadh, defeated them, and the threat passed for the moment. At this point Muhammad Shah died; his son, Ahmad Shah, was still with the army chasing the Afghan forces. To conceal the emperor's death until Ahmad arrived, the corpse was shrouded in a tablecloth purloined from the royal kitchens, placed in the case of a European grandfather clock and buried in the garden.

AHMAD SHAH

AHMAD SHAH	
Born 24 December 1725	*Enthroned* 15 April 1748; deposed in 1754 by his *wazir* and blinded
Father Muhammad Shah	
Mother Udham Bai	*Died* 1 January 1775
Wife ?	*Buried* In the mausoleum of Mariam Makani (Akbar's mother) before Qadam Sharif Mosque, Delhi
Son No male heirs	

Ahmad Shah was not a man of great intellect; all the period of his youth till manhood had been spent in the harem, and he had absolutely no experience whatever of the affairs of a kingdom or of the cares of government.

Anon, Tarikh-i Ahmad Shah

ON COMING TO POWER AHMAD SHAH made Ghazi al-Din, the son of the Nizam of Hyderabad, his *mir bakhshi*, and Safdar Jang, the ruler of Awadh, his *wazir*. These were able nobles. But the initiative in government fell to Nawab Jawed Khan, head eunuch and manager of the harem of the late Muhammad Shah. The Nawab, an illiterate but intelligent man, impressed the emperor, who, as the chronicle of his reign declared, 'gave of the entire management of the country to him'. Moreover, as he had long had a liaison with Ahmad Shah's mother, Udham Bai, a former dancing girl, he governed the country together with her. And, as the chronicler also states, 'the Emperor considered it to be most agreeable to him to spend all his time in ease and leisure, and he made his zenana [harem] so large that it extended for a mile. For a week together he would remain without seeing the face of any male being....'

Ahmad Shah, like his father Muhammad Shah, was devoted to the affairs of the harem, and heedless of events in the world beyond. The Afghan, Ahmad Abdali, raided his territories regularly. By the end of his reign the Mughal emperors had become puppets in the hands of powers great and small.

While Ahmad Shah remained heedless of events in the real world, Ahmad Abdali continued his invasions. After the third invasion of 1751–52, the Mughal ruler of the Punjab transferred his allegiance to the Afghan king. The provinces of Kashmir and Multan also fell into Afghan hands, and Ahmad Abdali ruled peoples from Herat to Lahore. Meanwhile, the centre of the dwindling Mughal empire was in the throes of a vicious power struggle. First, the lines were drawn between Safdar Jang, *wazir* and ruler of Awadh, supported by nobles of Iranian background, and Nawab Jawed Khan, Udham Bai and the emperor, supported by nobles of Turkish origin. In August 1752, Safdar Jang had the Nawab murdered, but was not able to prevail against the Turkish nobles and place his nominee on the throne. He lost his office as *wazir* and retreated to Awadh. A second struggle ensued between Safdar Jang's successor as *wazir* and Ghazi al-Din, who allied himself with the Marathas. On 5 June 1754 Ghazi al-Din instructed Ahmad Shah to give him the office of *wazir*, then placed Aziz al-Din, an elderly son of Jahandar Shah, on the throne with the title Alamgir II. He then blinded Ahmad Shah and his mother. From now on the Mughals, although always a source of authority, were no more than puppets in the hands of powers great and small in northern India.

Alamgir II
1754–59

Shah Alam
1759–1806

ALAMGIR II (AZIZ AL-DIN)	
Born	*Enthroned*
c. 1699	2 June 1754
Father	*Died*
Jahandar Shah	29 November 1759,
Mother	killed at the behest
Lal Kunwar	of his *wazir*
Wives	*Buried*
Zinat Mahal, plus	Humayun's Tomb,
several others	Delhi
Sons	
Shah Alam, plus 4	
others	

ALAMGIR II

The new Emperor was fifty-six years of age.... He used to come out of his apartments into the stone mosque or into the public hall to say his prayers at the five appointed times in the congregation; he applied himself to reading books of history, and took no pleasure in seeing dancing or hearing singing....

Anon, *Tarikh-i Alamgir-sani*

IN FULL CONTROL OF THE EMPEROR, Ghazi al-Din was now, in theory, poised to impose his will on the situation. But in his five years or so as *wazir* he was unable to do so. At the heart of the matter was his inability to raise the resources to pay the troops who would enable him to ensure a revenue stream. He also could not pay the Marathas, who had assisted his rise to power, so they plundered the suburbs of Delhi. In addition, he was unable either to prevent the Jats from expanding their influence at the expense of the empire around Agra, or the Rohilla Afghans from taking control of large tracts to the east and north of Delhi. The situation in Delhi grew more and more grim. Measures to raise funds from its citizens to pay the Marathas led to anarchy. The imperial family lived a thread-

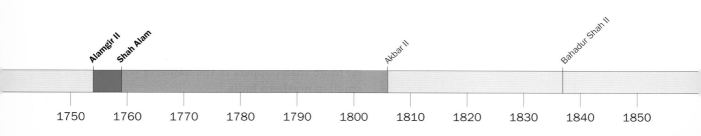

Shah Alam was the eldest and ablest of the sons of Alamgir II, but this did not prevent him from being a major loser in the fluid politics of the north India of his day. His reign saw his personal humiliation and that of his family at the hands of a former retainer, the establishment of the British bridgehead in the East when in 1765 he granted them revenue control of Bengal, Bihar and Orissa, and the establishment of British control over north India in 1803 when they defeated the Marathas outside Delhi.

bare existence. At one point Ghazi al-Din's special forces, Turkish soldiers from Badakshan, mutinied because they had not been paid, tore the clothes off Ghazi al-Din, dragged him half-naked through the streets, gave him a pummelling, and forced him to sit and listen as they shouted at him for their pay.

Then, in 1756, Ghazi al-Din made a bid to improve his situation by recovering Lahore from the Afghans. At the same time, Najib Khan, leader of the Rohilla Afghans, opened up communications with Ahmad Abdali. Ghazi al-Din's action was clear provocation. Ahmad Abdali responded by taking Delhi, having the Friday sermon read in his name and then graciously handing the empire back to Alamgir. Delhi was systematically looted of treasure and beautiful women. Many were slain. Ghazi al-Din was ousted from his position, then restored, but Najib Khan became the effective power in Delhi. Ahmad Abdali went on to loot and kill in Agra and the Hindu holy cities of Mathura and Brindaban. He returned to Afghanistan with his loot, loaded on 28,000 animals, as well as about 20 Mughal princesses, including the daughter of Muhammad Shah whom he intended as a wife. Alamgir II now was no more than a pawn whom ambitious competitors for power aimed to control in order to legitimize their rule. On 29 November 1759, Ghazi al-Din, fearing that his pawn might fall into the hands of Ahmad Abdali, had him killed while on a visit to the Firuz Shah Kotla, hoping to meet a Sufi. The emperor's corpse was thrown on to the riverbank below. It was buried in Humayun's tomb.

SHAH ALAM

Through the perfidiousness of the nobility and vassals this anarchy has arisen, and everyone proclaims himself a sovereign in his own place, and they are at variance with one another, the strong prevailing over the weak …. In this age of delusion and deceit His Majesty places no dependence on the service or professions of loyalty of anyone but the English chiefs.

Letter from Shah Alam to the East India Company, 1768

SHAH ALAM WAS THE ELDEST SON of Alamgir II and had always been destined to succeed him. Aged 30 when his father died, he was able, knowledgeable about religion, familiar with Arabic, Persian, Turkish and Urdu, studious in his habits and of an inquiring mind. While still a prince he was targeted by Ghazi al-Din, who saw him as an obstacle to his power. The prince's house in Delhi was besieged by Ghazi al-Din's men, and he only escaped by cutting his way through the *wazir*'s troops. For

SHAH ALAM

Born	*Enthroned*
15 June 1728	25 December 1759
Father	*Died*
Alamgir II	10 November 1806
Mother	*Buried*
Zinat Mahal	In the Mahajjar
Wives	Shah Alam Bahadur
Several	Shah, near the
Sons	dargah of Bakhtiar
Many, including	Kaki, behind the
Jawan Bakht, Akbar,	Qutb Minar, Delhi
Sulaiman Shukoh,	
Ahsan Bakht	

the following 14 years he was, like his ancestors Babur and Humayun, a prince struggling to regain his patrimony.

In the years 1759–61 Shah Alam led three campaigns designed to establish his authority in Bihar and Bengal (see box p. 176). After the first, hearing of his father's murder, he proclaimed himself emperor on 24 December 1759. An attempt by Ghazi al-Din to establish a puppet emperor fizzled out after nine months. In 1761, British power put an end for the moment to his attempts to establish his authority over territory, and he was given an allowance of 1,800 rupees a day in return for recognizing British claims in Bihar and Bengal. The years 1761–62 saw him allied with the Nawab of Awadh, now his *wazir*, in a failed advance on Delhi; 1764 saw the destruction of the Nawab's forces at Buxar, as they made yet another invasion of Bihar. This was followed on 16 August 1765 by the Treaty of Allahabad, by which the British bestowed on Shah Alam the Awadh districts of Kara and Allahabad, worth 2.8 million rupees per annum, giving him a further 2.6 million rupees per annum in return for his bestowing on them the Diwani, i.e. revenue control, of the huge area of Bihar, Bengal and Orissa. From this point he was an English pensioner.

From 1765 to 1771 Shah Alam lived a relatively comfortable life in the royal fort at Allahabad, though all the while he was concerned to return to Delhi. The British never fulfilled their oft-made promise to help him return there. The matter became urgent in 1768 when the declining health of Najib Khan, the Afghan strongman who guarded the royal palace in Delhi for Shah Alam, led to him being forced out. The emperor became concerned for the security of his womenfolk, a concern sharpened by frequent letters of distress from the queen mother. As the British would not help him, Shah Alam made an agreement with the Marathas by which, in return for large payments of rupees, they would secure the imperial capital for him. On 3 January 1772, the queen mother and several princes came to meet him some 6 km (4 miles) southeast of Delhi. On 6 January, with them at his side, he rode back into the city.

Mughal affairs in Delhi from 1772 to 1782 were increasingly dominated by a soldier-statesman of noble Iranian descent, Mirza Najaf Khan. He secured imperial authority in Delhi and made a point of both keeping up-to-date with the latest military technology and employing able European military officers. Thus, he was able to defeat the Sikhs, crush the Jats, deal decisively with Rohilla Afghan aspirations and defend Delhi against Maratha depredations. When he died in 1782 the authority of Delhi had been restored from the river Sutlej in the Punjab to the jungle south of Agra, and from the river Ganges to Jaipur.

The years 1782 to 1789 descended from anarchy to tragedy. First, the four lieutenants of Mirza Najaf Khan competed to succeed to his role. Then, in 1784, order was restored when the Maratha chieftain, Mahadji Sindhia, in support of Shah Alam, first crushed the competing factions and, in exchange for handsome tribute, took on the roles of regent of the empire and commander-in-chief. It was a very successful arrangement until Sindhia's power was much reduced by the failure of his campaign in

1787 against the Rajputs at Lalsot. A host of enemies gathered against him, in particular Muslims who resented a Hindu regency of the empire.

Ghulam Qadir's revenge

The temporary eclipse of Sindhia's power made it possible for Ghulam Qadir, Rohilla Afghan chief and grandson of Najib Khan, to occupy Delhi from 18 July to 2 October 1788. Revenge was the order of the day. Ghulam Qadir was paid 1.2 million rupees by Malika-yi Zamani, widow of the emperor Muhammad Shah, who sought vengeance from Shah Alam for the way in which his father had blinded her stepson, Ahmad Shah. Shah Alam was to be replaced by Ahmad Shah's son, Bidar Bakht. Ghulam Qadir sought vengeance for himself from Shah Alam for the way in which a decade before Mirza Najaf Khan had sacked his family fortresses. Moreover, he believed himself to be the 'scourge of God', who, with his manly Afghan followers, would purge the Mughals of weakness.

On entering Delhi Ghulam Qadir took control of the Red Fort, posting 4,000 men in and about it. Marching into Shah Alam's private apartments, he disarmed the emperor and the princes, and put Bidar Bakht on the throne. The Afghans began to plunder the palace. In the search for treasure eunuchs were beaten to death, maidservants tortured, and the emperor and princes left out in the hot sun. When the emperor complained, he was flung to the ground and blinded. When, on the following day, the emperor abused Ghulam Qadir, the Afghan and another tore his eyes out with their bare hands, and blinded three princes. And on the next day, as the emperor lay on the ground, his eyes running with blood, Ghulam Qadir seized him by the beard and said: 'I have inflicted all this severity on you for your faults, but I spare your life for God's sake, otherwise I would have no scruple in tearing you limb from limb.' By this time, members of the royal family, who had been without food and water for three days, were beginning to die. Ghulam Qadir ordered that they should be buried where they died. Then, on pain of having their noses cut off, the Mughal princes were made to dance and sing for his pleasure – a great insult.

Ghulam Qadir broke all the normal codes of decency by physically abusing the royal women. Some were taken into his harem. Others he said, 'he would give to his Afghans, so that they might have a chance of bringing forth men of courage.' No one, including his allies Bidar Bakht and Malika-yi Zamani, was spared his attentions in his search for treasure. The former was forced to hand over his jewels. When the latter said she had no more money for him, he sent his men into the harem, an act no other invader had dared to commit, stripped the ladies, dug up the floors and probed the walls, until there was nothing precious left to be found. It is said that he realized goods to the value of 250 million rupees.

After two months, for want of food, Ghulam Qadir was forced to withdraw from Delhi. The following day Sindhia's forces entered the city. Ghulam Qadir's partisans were hunted down, any loot discovered returned to the royal family and the Friday sermon was read once more in

---

THE SAVAGERY OF GHULAM QADIR

'Ghulam Qadir sprang up and threw himself on the Emperor's bosom, Qandahari Khan and Purdil Khan seized his hands, two of their companions held his feet; Qandahari Khan tore out one of his eyes, and that bloodthirsty reckless ruffian tore out the other with his own hands, amid the wailings of the Emperor. Ghulam Qadir then gave orders that the needle should be passed into the eyes of Prince Akbar, Sulaiman Shukoh and Ahsan Bakht. The ladies came out from behind their curtains, and threw themselves at the feet of Ghulam Qadir, to pray for mercy; but he kicked them on their breasts, and sent them away.... Then he called for a painter, and said, "Paint my likeness at once, sitting, knife in hand, upon the breast of Shah Alam, digging out his eyes." He then forbad his attendants to bring any food or water either to Shah Alam or his sons.'

Khair al-Din

the name of Shah Alam. Five months later, Ghulam Qadir was caught and killed, his eyeballs, nose and ears being sent by request to the emperor. Down to 1803 the Marathas supplied the umbrella of power under which the Mughals were able to eke out an existence. In 1803, the British under Lord Lake defeated the Marathas beneath the walls of Delhi, and Shah Alam passed under British protection. The sight which met Lake's eyes as he attended his first audience with the emperor showed how far the dynasty had fallen. 'The descendant of the great Akbar and Awrangzeb', a companion wrote, 'was found blinded and aged, stripped of authority and reduced to poverty, seated under a small tattered canopy, the fragment of royal state and the mockery of human pride.' In 1806, Shah Alam died.

THE BATTLE OF PANIPAT, 1761

While Shah Alam was trying to resurrect his fortunes in Bihar and Bengal a great battle was fought at Panipat north of Delhi – where in 1526 Babur had defeated Ibrahim Lodi and in 1556 Bairam Khan had defeated Hemu – which had a major bearing on the future both of the Mughal empire and of India. On 14 January 1761 a large Maratha army was comprehensively defeated by Ahmad Abdali at the head of a Muslim coalition which included Najib Khan and Shuja al-Dawla, the ruler of Awadh. Up to mid-day the Maratha force had the advantage, but then a charge by Ahmad Abdali's forces carried all before it. Nearly 30,000 Marathas were killed, including most of the main chiefs; every tent in the Afghan king's camp had a pile of heads outside it. Ahmad Abdali was not able to take advantage of his victory; mutinous troops forced him to return home. He had, however, substantially reduced Maratha prestige, as well as their capacity to intervene in northern India. He thus helped to create the power vacuum in the region which enabled the British to expand from Bengal northwestwards and become the protectors of the last Mughal rulers.

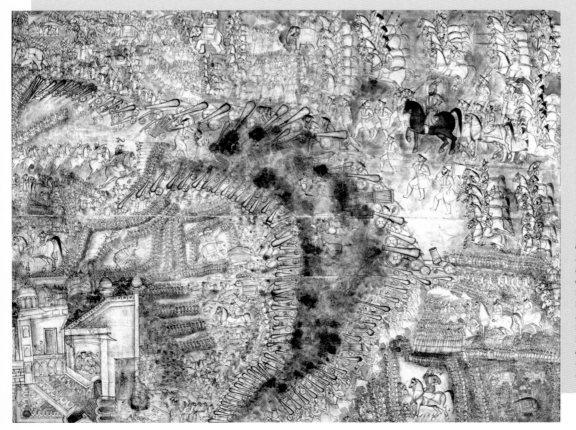

This picture of the battle of Panipat, 1761, shows the Maratha forces entrenched with their backs to the town of Panipat. During a long stay they suffered badly from starvation. Ahmad Abdali is shown on the right, leading his forces.

Akbar II
1806–37

Bahadur Shah II
1837–58

Akbar II, attended by courtiers. By the time of his reign, the Mughal emperors were no more than pensioners of the British, devoting their energies to ceremonies and processions, and trying to keep up appearances in their vast Red Fort palace.

AKBAR II	
Born	*Died*
23 April 1760	28 September 1837
Father	*Buried*
Shah Alam	In the Mahajjar Shah Alam Bahadur Shah, near the dargah of Bakhtiar Kaki, behind the Qutb Minar, Delhi
Mother	
?	
Wife	
Lal Bai	
Son	
Bahadur Shah Zafar	
Enthroned	
19 November 1806	

AKBAR II

A mild and Benevolent Prince, but more fitted to reign under the protection of the British Government than in the troublesome times of his unfortunate Father and his immediate Predecessor.

Sir Thomas Metcalfe

AKBAR II, THE SON OF SHAH ALAM, inherited an impotent Mughal throne. Under a treaty with the British of 1805 the imperial family were assigned the revenues of a small area near the city and 90,000 rupees a month. In Delhi itself the emperor's jurisdiction was limited to the Red Fort and the confirmation of death sentences passed by British courts. As was to be expected, there were some difficult and humbling encounters with British officials. Much energy was given to court ceremonies and striking public processions at the great festivals, when the emperor, his ministers and the princes on elephants, with assorted soldiers and musicians on foot, would parade through the streets in colourful cacophony. Bishop Heber, on being presented to the emperor on 31 December 1824, reflected on how dirty and tattered every thing was, on the gulf between the high-flown rhetoric of the court officials and 'the poor old descendant of

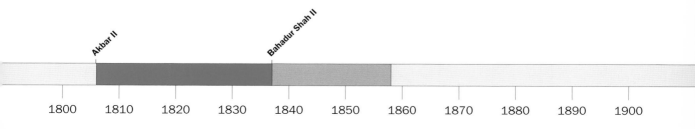

Akbar II | Bahadur Shah II

1800 1810 1820 1830 1840 1850 1860 1870 1880 1890 1900

AKBAR SHAH'S GRACIOUS BEHAVIOUR

'The young Saiyid Ahmad Khan, who was to be the leader of the Muslims of north India later in the century, tells of the Emperor's gracious behaviour when, a child, he overslept and arrived late in court: "As soon as His Majesty caught sight of me, he turned to my father, who was standing nearby, and enquired if I was his son. My father respectfully replied that I was. His Majesty remained silent, and all the courtiers waited for him to go into the palace. When he came to the *Tasbih Khana*, he stopped and taking his place on the raised platform where the court was sometimes held, he commanded his attendant to fetch the tray of jewels. I had also arrived there by this time. The Emperor beckoned to me and graciously asked me the reason for my late arrival. The assembled guests told me to apologize and beg His Majesty's pardon. But I remained silent. When the Emperor repeated his question, I merely answered that I had overslept. His Majesty smiled and told me to get up earlier in future. He then let go of my hands. The people told me to pay my respects, which I did. The Emperor invested me with the robes in the customary manner, and I presented my gift to him. He then rose and made his way back to the palace. The whole court congratulated my father on the grace which His Majesty had shown to me."'

Hali

Tamerlane' he saw before him. The great hall of public audience 'when we saw it, was full of lumber of all descriptions, broken palanqueens and empty boxes, and the throne so covered with pigeon's dung that its ornaments were hardly discernible. How little did Shahjehan ... foresee what would be the fate of his descendants ....' While the fortunes of the imperial family might have become run down under the British peace, those of the imperial city flourished. It became an important trading entrepot; the population grew towards 150,000; its citizens, confident of the new security, began to build bungalows outside the city walls; and it hosted a flowering of learning, which has come to be called the Delhi renaissance. In September 1837, aged 81, Akbar II died.

Portrait of Bahadur Shah II from the *Delhie Book* of Sir Thomas Metcalfe, the British Resident. By his reign, Mughal authority was restricted to the Red Fort, and even then there were constraints; Bahadur Shah could not, for instance, give jewels from his own crown jewels to members of his family without asking the Resident's permission.

BAHADUR SHAH II

... the Ceremony of [installation was] performed by the Agent to the Governor General in the Tusbeeh Khana or Oratory adjoining the great Hall of audience. The Prince on his accession assumed the Style and Title of Bahadur Shah. He is mild and talented but lamentably weak and Vacillating [sic] and impressed with very erroneous notions of his importance, productive of great mortification to himself and occasionally of much trouble to the Local Authorities.

Sir Thomas Metcalfe

BAHADUR SHAH II ENGAGED HIMSELF, as his father Akbar II had, in court ceremonies and processions. Amongst his serious enthusiasms were kite-flying and poetry. In the latter his pen-name was 'Zafar', or victory. The leading poet of the age, Ghalib, was present at court from 1847, and from 1854 was the emperor's poetry teacher. We are fortunate that Ghalib left much poetry and many letters which, amongst other things, reveal the humorous relationship between the two. After

The last Mughal, Bahadur Shah II. This photograph is usually assumed to have been taken during his exile in Rangoon. In fact, it was probably taken after his trial in Delhi in 1858. What a distance has been travelled from the vitality of Babur and the force of Akbar!

Ghalib ended one of his poems thus: 'Ghalib, you write so well upon these mystic themes of Love Divine. We would have counted you a saint, but that we knew your love of wine', the emperor responded 'No, my friend; even so we should never have counted you a saint.' To which Ghalib replied: 'Your Majesty counts me one even now, and only one speaks like this lest my sainthood should go to my head.' This said, Ghalib, perhaps a little unfairly, had a low opinion of the emperor's abilities as a poet – his style was too easy to reproduce.

In 1854, the British decided that after Bahadur Shah died, his successor should be downgraded to a prince, the royal family should be moved out of Delhi and its allowance reduced. But, before this could happen, the Mutiny Uprising broke out. A mutiny in the Company's sepoy (Indian soldier) army set alight the many disaffections created by the rapid rate of change the British had imposed upon northern India in the previous 20 years. In May 1857, the sepoys took over Delhi and proclaimed the Mughal Empire restored. Bahadur Shah was now their puppet and had little choice but to go along with them. Through the British siege of the city he did his best to ensure that Hindus and Muslims co-operated. The British recapture of the city in September 1857 was accompanied by appalling and indiscriminate slaughter, looting and destruction. All the citizens were driven out; Hindus were not allowed to return till January 1858, and Muslims till January 1859. As the British forced their way into Delhi, the royal family fled to Humayun's tomb, some 8 km (5 miles) outside the walls. An irregular officer, William Hodson, took it upon himself to capture them. He is said to have promised the Queen, Zinat Mahal, who negotiated with him, that the lives of the family would be spared if they surrendered. He then put them into a farmer's cart and drove them to Chandni Chawk in the middle of the city. There, according to Harriet Tytler, who was in Delhi at the time, 'Hodson called out in a stentorian voice, "Come out you rascals to be shot", upon which the men put up their hands in supplication and said, "Sahib, you promised us our lives". Hodson replied to them "I never did. I only promised Zinat Mahal, her son and your father their lives."' The Mughal princes were shot. Bahadur Shah was tried in the Red Fort for treason and rebellion. He was exiled to Rangoon where he died in 1862 aged 87. So came to an end one of the greatest dynasties of rulers the world has seen. The pathos is reflected in these lines of verse the old emperor wrote in exile:

I am the light of no one's eye
The balm of no one's heart
I am no use to anyone
A handful of dust, that's all.

AN ENGLISHWOMAN'S VIEW OF DELHI

'In short, Delhi is a very suggestive and moralizing place – such stupendous remains of power and wealth passed and passing away – and somehow I feel that we horrid English have just "gone and done it," merchandised it, revenued it, and spoiled it all.'

Emily Eden

BAHADUR SHAH II	
Born	Sultan, Mirza Fath
24 October 1775	al-Mulk, Jawan
Father	Bakht, plus a
Akbar II	further 11 sons and
Mother	31 daughters
Lal Bai	*Enthroned*
Wives	1837
Taj Mahal Begum,	*Died*
Zinat Mahal, plus	7 November 1862
four further wives	*Buried*
and several	Near the Shwe
concubines	Dragon Pagoda at 6
Sons	Ziwaka Road,
Mirza Mughal, Khidr	Yangon (Rangoon),
Sultan, Khwaja	Myanmar

THE SAFAVIDS
1501–1773

Shah Ismail I
1501–24

Shah Tahmasp
1524–76

Shah Ismail II
1576–77

Muhammad Khudabanda
1577–88

Shah Abbas I
1588–1629

Shah Safi I
1629–42

Shah Abbas II
1642–66

Shah Sulaiman
1666–94

Shah Sultan Husain
1694–1722

The Ghilzais and Remaining
Safavids
1722–73

THE AFSHARIDS
1736–96

Nadir Shah
1736–47

Shah Rukh
1748–50, 1750–96

THE ZANDS
1751–94

Karim Khan Zand
1751–79

The Remaining Zands
1779–94

THE QAJARS
1796–1925

Aqa Muhammad Qajar
1796–97

Fath Ali Shah
1797–1834

Muhammad Shah
1834–48

Nasir al-Din Shah
1848–96

Muzaffar al-Din Shah
1896–1907

Muhammad Shah
1907–09

Ahmad Shah
1909–25

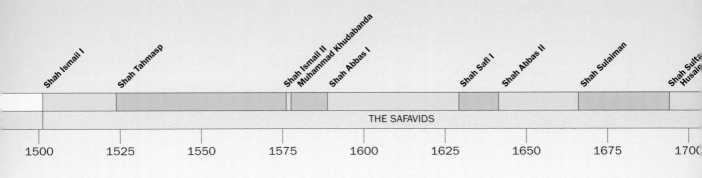

Shah Abbas I

Nadir Shah

Karim Khan Zand

Ahmad Shah

THE SAFAVIDS, AFSHARIDS, ZANDS AND QAJARS 1501–1925

THE PERIOD COVERED BY THE REIGNS OF THE SAFAVIDS and their successors from 1501, when the head of the militant Safavi order took power, to 1925, when Riza Khan Pahlavi deposed the last Qajar shah, saw the entrance of Iran into the modern world. The Safavids laid the foundations of the modern Iranian state, establishing for the most part its geographical boundaries, fashioning an effective standing army and creating a centralized administration; at the same time they imposed the Shia form of Islam upon their peoples. Under the Safavids considerable wealth was generated through trade, and as a consequence the court and many citizens were able to patronize an extraordinary flowering of the arts.

In the 18th century the Safavids were overthrown and were replaced by two short-lived dynasties: first, the Afsharids and then the Zands. A period of anarchy followed, out of which rose the Qajars, a new dynasty, which rebuilt strong central government but found itself increasingly forced to do so in forms of collaboration with outside commercial and political forces. Throughout the 19th and early 20th centuries the Russians pressed into Iran from the northwest and the British from the southeast. Iranians found their world increasingly engaged with, and influenced by, outside powers.

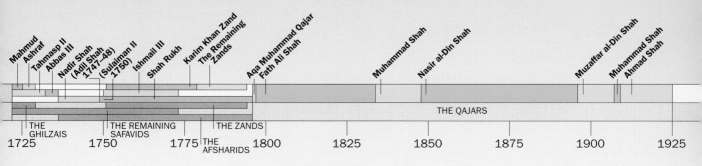

Mahmud
Ashraf
Tahmasp II
Abbas III
Nadir Shah
(Adil Shah 1747–48)
(Sulaiman II 1750)
Ishmail III
Shah Rukh
Karim Khan Zand
The Remaining Zands
Aqa Muhammad Qajar
Fath Ali Shah
Muhammad Shah
Nasir al-Din Shah
Muzaffar al-Din Shah
Muhammad Shah
Ahmad Shah

THE QAJARS

THE GHILZAIS
THE REMAINING SAFAVIDS
THE ZANDS
THE AFSHARIDS

1725   1750   1775   1800   1825   1850   1875   1900   1925

THE SAFAVIDS
1501–1722

Shah Ismail I
1501–24

Shah Tahmasp
1524–76

Shah Ismail II
1576–77

Muhammad Khudabanda
1577–88

Shah Ismail, the founder of the Safavid dynasty, kills an Ottoman cavalryman at the battle of Chaldiran. Although the Shah seems to be doing well in this mural from Isfahan's Chihil Sutun, the battle was a disaster for the Safavids.

SHAH ISMAIL I	
Born 12 July 1487 *Father* Shaikh Haidar *Mother* Alam Shao, daughter of Uzun Hasan, the Aq Qoyunlu leader, by his Christian wife Despina *Wives* Tajlu Khanum (a Mawsilla woman from the Qizilbash), name unknown (Georgian wife), name unknown (daughter of Sultan Khalil Shirvanshah), plus other wives	*Sons* Tahmasp, Sam Mirza, Bahram Mirza, Alqas Mirza *Daughters* Khanish Khanum, Pari Khan Khanum I, Pari Khan Khanum II, Shahzade Sultanum, plus 1 other *Enthroned* Summer 1501 *Died* 23 August 1524 *Buried* Family shrine at Ardabil

SHAH ISMAIL I

Shaikh Ismail is a man of about thirty years, large and of medium build, rounded face, clean shaven … a jovial and cheerful man, very handsome. Having been a very rich man with much revenue, he is now very poor, gives of his wealth very liberally, and his expenses cannot be reckoned. There can be no revenue in the entire world to satisfy him. He had a great treasure, the Turk came against him, and defeated him, and took away all his possessions ….

Comment of the Portuguese ambassadors to the Court of Shah Ismail, *Documentos Elucidativos*, 1515

SHAH ISMAIL CAME FROM A LINE of hereditary shaikhs of the Safavid Sufi order. This had been founded by (and named after) Safi al-Din (d. 1334), whose ancestors had gained a reputation for piety in the town of Ardabil in Azarbaijan. Shaikh Safi's achievement was to transform a pious tradition of only local importance into one with disciples throughout eastern Anatolia, Syria, Iran, the Caucasus and even amongst the Mongol nobility. In time, his shrine in the town of Ardabil became a focus for pilgrimage and was made wealthy through the endowments of followers. In the mid-15th century one of Safi's successors, Junaid, was forced into

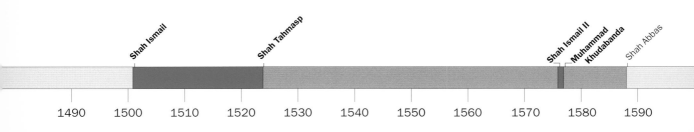

Shah Ismail   Shah Tahmasp   Shah Ismail II   Muhammad Khudabanda   Shah Abbas

1490   1500   1510   1520   1530   1540   1550   1560   1570   1580   1590

THE SAFAVIDS

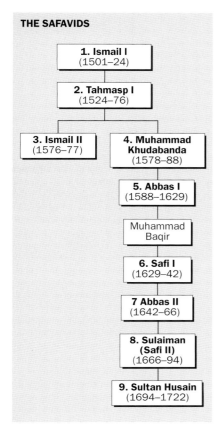

```
┌─────────────────────┐
│   1. Ismail I        │
│    (1501–24)         │
└─────────────────────┘
          │
┌─────────────────────┐
│   2. Tahmasp I       │
│    (1524–76)         │
└─────────────────────┘
       │        │
┌──────────┐ ┌──────────────────┐
│3. Ismail │ │ 4. Muhammad      │
│   II     │ │    Khudabanda    │
│(1576–77) │ │    (1578–88)     │
└──────────┘ └──────────────────┘
                      │
             ┌──────────────────┐
             │   5. Abbas I     │
             │   (1588–1629)    │
             └──────────────────┘
                      │
             ┌──────────────────┐
             │   Muhammad       │
             │   Baqir          │
             └──────────────────┘
                      │
             ┌──────────────────┐
             │   6. Safi I      │
             │   (1629–42)      │
             └──────────────────┘
                      │
             ┌──────────────────┐
             │   7 Abbas II     │
             │   (1642–66)      │
             └──────────────────┘
                      │
             ┌──────────────────┐
             │   8. Sulaiman    │
             │   (Safi II)      │
             │   (1666–94)      │
             └──────────────────┘
                      │
             ┌──────────────────┐
             │ 9. Sultan Husain │
             │   (1694–1722)    │
             └──────────────────┘
```

exile, which he spent recruiting followers amongst the Turkmen of Syria and Anatolia. These followers adopted radical beliefs of a Shia nature, and regarded both Ali, the first Shia Imam, and Junaid as divine. On returning from exile, Junaid made the political move of marrying a sister of Uzun Hasan, the Aq Qoyunlu Turkmen leader (see box pp. 64–65), who ruled most of Iran from Tabriz, while his son, Haidar, married Uzun Hasan's daughter. It was Haidar who invented the distinctive Safavid hat with 12 red sections, which, it was said, represented the 12 Shia Imams. This in turn led the Turkman confederation of tribes who were followers of the Safavids to be called, Qizilbash, 'red heads'.

In the 1490s the Aq Qoyunlu began to see the Safavids as serious rivals, and turned against them. Haidar was killed in battle and the Aq Qoyunlu murdered his successor, Sultan Ali, in prison. Ismail, Ali's seven-year-old brother, became head of the order and fled into hiding in Gilan on the Caspian shore. In 1499, aged 12, Ismail, ignoring those advisers who tried to dissuade him on account of his extreme youth, marched out of Gilan to confront the Aq Qoyunlu. He spent 18 months assembling his Turkman following, who came from as far as Syria and Anatolia. In 1501 his army of just 7,000 men destroyed an Aq Qoyunlu army of 30,000. He then captured Tabriz, was crowned Shah in the summer of 1501, and announced that 'Twelver' Shiism was to be the official religion of the Safavid state.

In 1501 Shah Ismail ruled just Azarbaijan. By 1510 he had extended his rule to eastern Anatolia, the Shia shrine cities of Iraq and all of Iran except Khurasan. At this point he came to face the major powers which were to trouble the Safavids for the rest of the century. In the northeast there was the rising power of the Shaibanid Uzbegs who were raiding far into Iran. In 1510 Shah Ismail defeated their forces at Merv, killing their leader Muhammad Shaibani in the process; Shaibani's head was made the mould for a golden drinking cup which, by way of choice insult, Ismail sent to the Ottoman sultan. An attempt to help the Mughal, Babur, recapture Samarqand failed, but Ismail did succeed in fixing the frontier between the Safavids and the Uzbegs along the Amu Darya (Oxus) river, which meant that Herat and the province of Khurasan were part of Iran.

In the northwest, the Ottomans were provoked by Qizilbash revolts against their rule in central Anatolia and by the Safavid presence in eastern Anatolia. They sent an ultimatum to Ismail, brutally oppressed the Qizilbash by either killing or deporting them, and marched into eastern Anatolia to confront Shah Ismail. On 23 August 1514, at the battle of Chaldiran, just north of Lake Van, the

Map of the Safavid Empire.

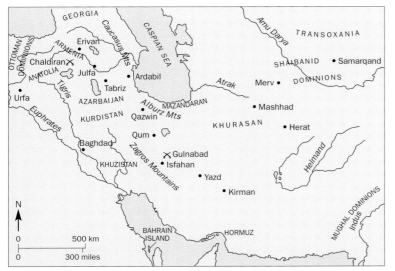

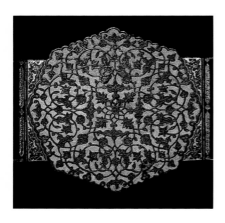

Above Plaque from an armband which appears to go together with a belt bearing the name Shah Ismail and dated 1507–08. Steel inlaid with gold, it was part of the booty carried back to Istanbul by the Ottomans after the battle of Chaldiran.

Right The shrine of Safi al-Din, in Ardabil, eastern Azarbaijan, the founder of the Safavid Sufi order from whose descendants Shah Ismail emerged to found the Safavid empire. A place of pilgrimage and wealth, it lay at the heart of the Safavid mystique. These buildings were erected by Shah Tahmasp.

Ottomans destroyed the Safavid army, Shah Ismail escaping with a few hundred men. The Ottomans won in part because they outnumbered the Safavids 2:1, in part because of an arrogant Safavid belief in Ismail's invincibility, which led them to carouse until dawn on the day of the battle, and in part because the Ottomans made clever use of field artillery. Like Babur at the battle of Panipat 12 years later, the Ottomans had field guns and their opponents did not. Moreover, they lined them together to form a barrier which the Safavid army of horse archers could not penetrate. This signalled the end of the dominance of the old steppe forms of warfare.

The Ottomans occupied Tabriz, capturing much booty, including books and paintings, which they sent back to Istanbul. But the Safavids were soon back in their capital: the Ottoman soldiers refused to winter so far from home. Nevertheless, the defeat was a major shock for Ismail. He went into mourning, wearing black and dyeing his military standards the same colour. He abandoned public affairs: the governance of the country fell into the hands of Iranian officials, in particular his *vakil* or viceroy, and he never again led his armies on the field of battle. 'Most of his time', as one chronicler put it, 'was spent in hunting, or in the company of rosy-cheeked youths, quaffing goblets of purple wine, and listening to the strains of music and song.' One further outcome was that his authority over his Qizilbash disciples was undermined – he no longer seemed to be semi-divine and invincible.

On 23 August 1524, Shah Ismail died and was buried in the family shrine at Ardabil. His achievement was considerable. He had established the boundaries of modern Iran (but for some losses of territory in the 19th century) and he had gone a long way towards establishing the three pillars on which the Safavid state was to rest. One was the Qizilbash, the Turkman tribesmen who supplied the armies of the state and whose leaders held offices as provincial governors or at court. They were for long a powerful force in the land, but never an easy one to control. The second pillar was the bureaucracy. Iran's deeply rooted administrative

traditions meant that continuity was achieved between the Safavid regime and the Turkman which had preceded it, supported by the host of civil servants of which the cities of central Iran had a ready supply. Of course, as at the Mughal court, there was rivalry between Turk and Iranian, between soldier and bureaucrat. The third pillar was Shiism. Most Iranians were Sunnis. Shah Ismail imposed Shiism at the point of the sword; death was the price of resistance. Shia ulama were imported from Bahrain, Iraq and the Lebanon to provide guidance in theology and law. They were to become the nucleus of a religious establishment of great power in Iranian affairs, caring for the people at large and resisting foreign intervention. Relations were not always easy between the ulama, as guardians of orthodoxy, and the Safavid shahs, who claimed absolute authority, being the reincarnation of the Hidden Imam (see box p. 191) and the shadow of God on earth.

SHAH TAHMASP

Shah Tahmasp was extremely avaricious in regard to the accumulation of money, property and treasure. Of the rulers of Iran and Turan since the invasions of Chingiz Khan – or even since the advent of Islam – no king at any period expended so much effort as Shah Tahmasp to accumulate treasure....

Sharaf al-Din Bitlisi

SHAH TAHMASP, THE FIRST SON of Shah Ismail and his favourite queen Tajlu Khanum, was born on 22 February 1514. He spent his early years as the ward of a Qizilbash governor in the sophisticated environment of Herat. In 1522 he returned to Tabriz, where, amongst other things, he studied painting under Sultan Muhammad, the head of the Tabriz library workshop, and where he was noted by the Portuguese, Antonio Tenreiro, drinking hard at the Nawruz (Iranian new year) festivities of 1524. After his father's death, rival Qizilbash leaders fought to control the regency. Then, in 1533, Tahmasp took control of the situation: he appointed an Iranian as his viceroy, made his brother, Bahram Mirza, army commander, and executed the Qizilbash chief Shamlu, his cousin and guardian of his child. Now the Qizilbash tribal chiefs knew where they stood.

The major issues of the first 20 years of Tahmasp's reign, as in the time of his father, were the threats from the Uzbegs in the northeast and the Ottomans in the northwest. In the 1520s and 1530s there were five Uzbeg invasions of Khurasan, all of which were beaten back. Near defeat in one battle, that of Jam in 1528, was turned into victory by Tahmasp's bravery and leadership. The Safavids also began to use field artillery to good effect on the Uzbegs who did not have it; their threat weakened.

The Ottomans, on the other hand, under the leadership of Sulaiman the Magnificent, were a major threat. In the two decades from 1534, the Safavids endured four invasions and Tabriz was occupied twice. Tahmasp, faced with overwhelming forces – in 1534 he had 7,000 men

Shah Tahmasp is shown at the right of this detail from a mural in Isfahan's Chihil Sutun entertaining the Mughal refugee, Humayun, who sits on the left. In the first part of his reign Shah Tahmasp was a great patron of the arts.

Opposite Patterned silk textiles were of major importance in the life of the Safavid court. The trade in them was to be a major aspect of the economic strategy of Shah Abbas. This silk textile fragment shows a horseman, his boy or page, and a prisoner. It is a Lampas weave of the mid-16th century woven on a drawloom.

SHAH TAHMASP	
Born	*Daughters*
22 February 1514	Gawhar Sultan
Father	Khanum, Pari Khan
Shah Ismail	Khanum, Khadija
Mother	Begum, Maryam
Tajlu Khanum	Begum, Zaynab
Wives	Begum, plus 9
Sultana Begum (a	others
Mawsilla woman	*Enthroned*
from the Qizilbash),	1524
4 Georgian wives, 1	*Died*
Circassian, 1	14 May 1576
Daghestani, plus 4	*Buried*
concubines	Mashhad, but
Sons	moved by Shah
Ismail, Muhammad	Abbas to Isfahan
Khudabanda,	
Haidar, plus 10	
others	

Rock crystal seal of Shah Tahmasp dated 963, i.e. 1555–56, showing the writing in mirror reverse. The text emphasizes the association of Shah Tahmasp with Imam Ali and thus stresses the central role of Shiism for Safavid rule. Seals were essential tools of administration for the Safavids and their contemporaries.

against the 90,000 of the Ottomans – managed his campaigns brilliantly. He avoided battles with the enemy, adopted a scorched-earth policy and harried the Ottomans as a lack of provisions and the strain on their long lines of communication invariably forced them to retreat. In 1555 he completed the Treaty of Amasya with Sulaiman which, at the cost of losing the Shia shrine cities of Iraq, gave him peace in the west for the rest of his reign.

In 1540, Shah Tahmasp led the first of four campaigns into Christian Georgia to the north. One objective was certainly booty; the Georgian churches were rich repositories of gold and silver objects and this was followed by revenue from the newly acquired territories. One outcome – it is not known if it was an objective – was the acquisition of large numbers of Georgian, Circassian and Armenian prisoners who were to become the basis of a 'third force' in Safavid society between the rival Turks and Iranians. The prisoners were required to convert to Islam and went into the royal household in civil or military positions. The Georgian and Circassian women, much prized for their beauty, were recruited to the royal harem, where they were to become significant players in court politics.

Art and religion

The first part of Shah Tahmasp's reign marks a high point in the art of Iran, flowing particularly from his interest and patronage. The Shah was fascinated by illustrated books, a passion he had pursued during his stay at Herat and which he continued on his return to Tabriz. He brought with him the great Bihzad (see box pp. 70–71), who became head of the royal library workshop, and a number of Bihzad's pupils. In 1524 the Shah commissioned the masterpiece of the age, a *Shahnama* with 258 pictures of outstanding quality. So close was the Shah's attention to the work of book production that while he was on the march, which he was for most of the first 20 years of his reign, the tent which housed his painters was pitched close to his sleeping quarters. Shah Tahmasp's brother, Bahram Mirza, and half-brother, Sam Mirza, were also important patrons. When in the 1540s Tahmasp's interest in the arts began to wane, they and other royal relatives maintained the tradition of princely patronage.

The tone of the second half of Shah Tahmasp's reign was very different from the first. Military campaigning came to an end. He moved his capital away from Ottoman danger to Qazwin on the great trade route from India and Khurasan in the east to Azarbaijan and Anatolia in the west. Here he stayed most of the time. Simultaneously, he imposed a religious policy of an increasingly orthodox nature. In the 1530s he had shown his preferences by banning wine-drinking and homosexuality. In 1555 he required all his great nobles to renounce all acts forbidden by Islamic law and issued a Decree of Sincere Repentance. In line with his growing puritanism, artists, musicians and poets were released from court service. Shah Tahmasp appears to have neglected the work of government, spending years at a time shut away in his palace. One major interest was money. He hoarded coin and materiel. On his death his trea-

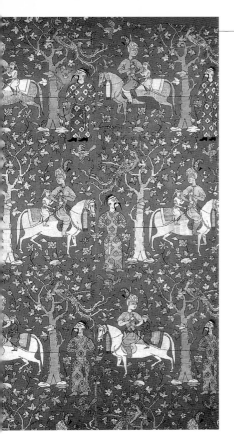

sury was found to have 380,000 tomans (the basic unit of Iranian coinage) of gold and silver, plus arms and armour for 30,000 men. The second was women, mostly Georgian and Circassian slaves, with whom he discussed affairs of state and who came to acquire influence over him.

In general, historians have not been kind to Shah Tahmasp, accusing him of being a miser, a bigot and treacherous; he handed the Ottoman Prince Bayazid and his sons, who had sought sanctuary with him, back to Sulaiman the Magnificent and certain death. But he gained the upper hand over the Qizilbash, passed on his kingdom intact and presided over the production of one of the greatest works of Iranian art – in sum, not a bad record. He died on 14 May 1576.

SHAH ISMAIL II

IN SHAH TAHMASP'S LAST YEARS two factions formed at court, aiming to control the succession. Both were made up of Qizilbash tribes, but one contained the Georgians at court and aimed to elevate a prince with a Georgian mother, while the other contained Circassians, with a similar objective. In the outcome both the Georgian and Circassian princes were killed and the factions had to make do with a Turkman prince, Ismail. Ismail immediately set about blinding or killing all the other royal princes he could find, and executing Qizilbash whom he thought were opposed to him. In November 1577 he was poisoned by his sister, Pari Khan Khanum.

MUHAMMAD KHUDABANDA

MUHAMMAD KHUDABANDA, one of the other royal princes, was already virtually blind, which may explain why Shah Ismail had not yet got round to eliminating him and his three sons. The Qizilbash had no alternative but to place him on the throne. A power struggle immediately broke out between Pari Khan Khanum, who had been ruling through a council of Qizilbash chiefs, and Khudabanda's wife, Mahd-i Ulya. The latter, realizing that there was not room for two women at the head of affairs, had Pari Khan Khanum strangled. Mahd-i Ulya now had complete control over the government. She promoted Iranians in the administration and humiliated the Qizilbash. Eventually, the latter submitted a formal complaint to the Shah, who tried to appease them. Mahd-i Ulya refused to change her style or policies. A group of Qizilbash took matters into their own hands, burst into the harem and strangled her.

The Ottomans and Uzbegs took advantage of the weakness at the heart of the Safavid state. In 1578 the Ottomans invaded and began a war in northwest Iran which was not finished until 1590. In the northeast the Uzbegs invaded Khurasan. All the while Qizilbash nobles manoeuvred for power. Eventually one, Murshid Quli Khan, who had gained possession of the Shah's son, Abbas, marched on Qazwin, and deposed Muhammad Khudabanda. On 1 October 1588 Abbas was crowned.

SHAH ISMAIL II	
Born 1533/34	*Sons* ?
Father Shah Tahmasp	*Enthroned* 22 August 1576
Mother Sultana Begum	*Died* 24 November 1577
Wife Name unknown (niece of Shah Tahmasp)	*Buried* Mashhad

MUHAMMAD KHUDABANDA	
Born 1532	*Sons* Hamza, Abu Talib, Abbas
Father Shah Tahmasp	*Enthroned* November 1577
Mother Sultana Begum	*Died* 1595
Wife Name unknown (daughter of a Gilani notable), Khair al-Nisa (Mahd-i Ulya)	*Buried* ?

EARLY SAFAVID PAINTING

Illustrated books, as Babur's memoirs remind us, were the prized possession of rulers in the Timurid tradition. Easily portable, they travelled with their owners in their endlessly peripatetic existence around their dominions and on campaign. They were, of course, also highly valued booty, which is how, after the Ottoman occupation of Tabriz in 1514, many items from the old Turkman library came to enter that of the Topkapi palace in Istanbul. In the time of Shah Tahmasp, artists, who included painters, calligraphers, illuminators, margin rulers, gold sprinklers etc, travelled with the Shah, enabling him to keep a close eye on projects. Moreover, the artists also performed the functions of a design studio, whose work might be used by other craftsmen – metalworkers, saddle makers, jewellers, weavers – thus helping to create a coherence of design across different media.

Above *A prince and his page, from an album compiled by the calligrapher Dust Muhammad at the request of Shah Tahmasp for his brother, Bahram Mirza. The representation of the two figures makes clear who is the prince and who the page. This said, it should be noted that the children of nobles served in the Safavid household and were chosen more for their beauty than their skills.*

Left *Shah Tahmasp's* Shahnama *was the major project of his library workshop in the 1520s and 1530s. Here, in one of its 258 illustrations, Siyawus, the son of Shah Kay Kawus, enthroned in his palace at Balkh, discusses the terms of a treaty with the son of the ruler of Turan, while Rustam looks on from the left. At the same time the Turanians, under the firm control of a major domo, parade their gifts before Siyawus.*

Opposite *The story of Laila and Majnun is one of the tales in the* Khamsa *of Nizami. Qais had fallen in love with Laila at school, in consequence of which he was called Majnun, 'madman', by his schoolmates. Laila was withdrawn from school. Here Majnun, who had teamed up with an old woman, is approaching the tent of Laila in her family encampment. This painting by Mir Saiyid Ali offers a host of information and incident: women wash clothes and cook meals, the tents of Laila's family are differentiated from those of their servants even down to the guy ropes, while boys throw stones at the pair as they approach Laila's tent and a dog with hennaed legs barks.*

A particular delight of illustrated books is that, with little remaining of the visual environment of the Safavid world, their illustrations enable us to see it as Safavids wished it to be seen. 'The stuff of royal Safavid daily life', Sheila Canby tells us, 'from clothes to wine cups, carpets to thrones, appears in miniature paintings ....' Shah Ismail had the good fortune to take over the royal Turkman library in Tabriz, one of the great libraries of its time, and heir to the traditions of the Il Khanids and Jalairids. Shah Tahmasp, by bringing Bihzad and his disciples from Herat to Tabriz, enabled the master painter, as head of the royal library, to preside over a fusion of the Timurid and Turkman styles, which, in the 1530s, was to emerge as a distinctive Safavid style.

The developing expression of the style can be seen in Shah Tahmasp's magnificent *Shahnama* for which 258 illustrations were produced between 1522 and the late 1530s. Three artists in succession directed the project and 15 altogether worked on the illustrations. This was followed by a *Khamsa* of Nizami, commissioned by Shah Tahmasp and produced between 1539 and 1543; its 14 illustrations are regarded as the apogee of Safavid painting. In the 1540s a younger generation of Safavid painters began to work on portraits for albums. As Shah Tahmasp's interest in painting waned, some leading artists moved to both the Mughal and the Ottoman courts, where they were to have great influence on the development of painting.

Shah Abbas I

1588–1629

Shah Abbas I was the greatest of the Safavid Shahs. He secured the frontiers, asserted royal power over that of the tribes, built a vibrant economy and presided over one of the finest flowerings of Iranian art. 'When this great prince ceased to live', declared a European traveller some 80 years after his death, 'Persia ceased to prosper.' Here, he is painted by Bishn Das whom the Mughal emperor, Jahangir, sent with an embassy to the Safavid court for this very purpose.

SHAH ABBAS I	
Born	Khudabanda,
27 January 1571	Ismail, Imam Quli
Father	*Daughters*
Muhammad	6
Khudabanda	*Enthroned*
Mother	1 October 1588
Khair al-Nisa (Mahd-i Ulya)	*Died*
	19 January 1629
Wife	*Buried*
Yakhan Begum	In the Imamzada of
Sons	a descendant of the
Muhammad Baqir,	6th Imam, Jafar al-
Hasan,	Sadiq, in Kashan

Opposite In 1612 Shah Abbas I endowed the family shrine at Ardabil with 1,205 pieces of Chinese porcelain and six of jade. All the Ardabil gifts were engraved with this personal seal of Shah Abbas recording the endowment. It says: 'Abbas, slave of the King of Holiness [i.e. Ali], made endowment of the shrine of Shah Safi'.

SHAH ABBAS I

Now that I am king we are going to forget about the practice of Sultan Muhammad Shah [Khudabanda]; the king is going to make the decisions now.

Shah Abbas quoted by Iskander Munshi Beg

ON COMING TO POWER AGED 17, the position of Shah Abbas was not good. The Ottomans occupied many of his dominions in the northwest; the Uzbegs were once more raiding Khurasan. Central government had been impotent for some years. His father had been unable to bring to justice those Qizilbash who had murdered his queen; he himself was a puppet, or so his Qizilbash guardian, Murshid Quli Khan, hoped. His kingdom was rent by rivalry between Turk and Iranian, and by Qizilbash factionalism. Abbas had three main tasks: to drive the Uzbegs out of the northeast; to drive the Ottomans out of the northwest; and to assert royal authority over all others within his dominion. His response to a crisis in the first year of his reign revealed his kingly qualities. Murshid Quli Khan had given himself the title of *vakil*, or representative of the Shah. When a group of heavily armed Qizilbash broke into the palace with the aim of

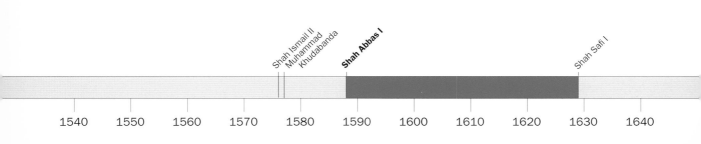

Shah Ismail II
Muhammad Khudabanda
Shah Abbas I
Shah Safi I

1540 1550 1560 1570 1580 1590 1600 1610 1620 1630 1640

assassinating Murshid Quli Khan and seizing power, Abbas took charge of the situation. He saved the life of his *vakil*. He asked those Qizilbash who loved the Shah to come to his side and to remove the remainder from the palace – they were then executed. A little later he had Murshid Quli Khan assassinated. He had signalled with cool judgment and with ruthlessness his will and his capacity to take control.

Measures to confront external threats

Soon after this he began to address the external threats. Well aware that he did not have the resources to deal with enemies in the northeast and the northwest at the same time, in 1590 he took the pragmatic step of concluding a humiliating treaty with the Ottomans. Much of northwest Iran was lost, including Tabriz, the old Safavid capital. There was just one saving grace: he retained control of Ardabil and the Safavid shrine.

Thus freed, Abbas turned his attention to the northeast. But, although he took his army to Khurasan in 1590, he was careful to avoid committing his forces to pitched battle. In 1598 this changed when the death of the Uzbeg leader led to a succession struggle. Abbas now had his opportunity. The Uzbegs retreated from city after city, knowing that they could always return when the Iranian forces left the province. Abbas, on the other hand, now sought a battle. Eventually, by dint of apparently retreating and then doubling back and making a remarkable forced march, he caught the Uzbegs in the open. The battle hung in the balance until he led his bodyguard of 200 in a charge against the Uzbeg leader's bodyguard of 1,000. The Uzbeg ranks were broken, a lucky thrust wounded the Uzbeg leader, and the day was Abbas's. By 1600, through alliances with local Uzbeg chiefs, he had stabilized the northeast frontier.

In 1603 Abbas turned his attention to the northwest. He quickly recaptured the old royal capital, though Tabriz was a desolate sight after 20 years of Ottoman occupation. By 1605 he had subjected Ottoman forces to a crushing defeat at Sufyan outside Tabriz, and by 1607 he had reconquered all the territories recognized by the Ottomans as belonging to the Safavids in the treaty of Amasya (1555). It was not until 1618, however, that the Ottomans acknowledged Safavid control of these territories. The Ottomans had to accept further losses when in 1623 Abbas captured Baghdad. He then conducted a subtle and brilliant defence of the city, which led in 1626 to the Ottomans retreating in disorder and with much loss of life.

Shah Abbas builds up central power

Central to the success of Abbas, and to the capacity of the regime to survive for a century after his death, was his creation of a 'third force' in the state to balance against the Qizilbash tribes and the Iranians of the cities. He continued, and considerably developed, the process begun under Shah Tahmasp of making Circassian, Georgian and Armenian slaves central to the working of his household, his administration and the army. An early priority was the creation of a standing army of about

40,000 men, consisting largely of slave regiments of cavalry and infantry armed with muskets, an artillery corps, and a royal bodyguard exclusively of slaves. The emergence of the predominantly slave force meant a reduction of Qizilbash influence in the state; no longer were they to be able to march into the palace and dictate terms. Indeed, the great generals of the reign of Shah Abbas were both slaves – Allahwardi Khan, a Georgian, and Qarachaqai Khan, an Armenian.

The decline of Qizilbash influence was manifest in some of the measures taken to pay for the new army. Lands which had previously formed revenue assignments out of which the Qizilbash maintained their forces and their government functions were transferred into crown lands under slave control. The changeover was gradual enough to stave off rebellion, but eventually large areas of Iran became crown lands. By the end of the reign of Shah Abbas half of the provincial governorships were in the hands of slaves.

Shah Abbas encourages trade to increase revenue

Abbas, however, was determined not to be dependent purely on land revenue for the health of his regime. He aimed to boost trade by all possible means: he encouraged the production of goods for the market, in particular carpets and textiles; he built caravanserais along all the main trade routes; he welcomed foreigners of all kinds – English, Dutch, Portuguese, French, Russians, Indians, Jews, Armenians – to encourage trade; and sought thus to take full advantage of the great shift which took place in the 16th century in the positioning of the Eurasian trade route from the old land-based Silk Route to the Indian Ocean.

Key to the international trade policies of Shah Abbas were the Armenians. In 1604 he transported several thousand Armenian families from their town of Julfa on the river Aras in Azarbaijan to a suburb of Isfahan south of the Zayanda river, known as New Julfa. His aim was to put their commercial expertise to the service of the Safavid state. He granted them special privileges: they were enabled to practice their Christian faith without hindrance, the Shah even contributing funds to the decoration of their new cathedral; they were permitted to operate for the most part as a self-governing community; and they were made substantial interest-free loans to boost their capacity to contribute to national and royal prosperity. Armenians traded throughout Europe, some becoming very rich. Their most important trade was the royal monopoly in silk, which they handled, and which was the largest single source of cash for the royal treasury.

Shah Abbas was keen to boost trade and so welcomed foreigners of all kinds to his territories. This painting has inscribed upon it in the top right-hand corner: 'portrait of the Russian ambassador done according to the wish of the noble, most holy, superior Shah Abbas.' This portrait is of either Grigorii Vasilchikov, ambassador 1588–89, or Andrei Zvenigorodsky, ambassador 1594–95.

RIZA ABBASI: ARTIST

Shah Abbas revived the royal library, which his grandfather had closed as he entered his religious phase. Among his leading artists was Riza Abbasi (*c.* 1565–1635), who became head of the library when it was transferred to Isfahan. Riza was responsible for the calligraphy on the Lutf Allah and Royal Mosques in the *Maidan-i Naqsh-i Jahan*. But his prime fame lay in developing, along with his contemporaries, the style which was to dominate Safavid painting through the 17th century. He produced single-page paintings depicting young courtiers of either sex, or older men such as labourers or Sufis. Connoisseurs note a greater naturalism entering painting from this moment; it is also the time when European influences, which were to increase steadily, began to be felt.

Above *A portrait of a young man in European clothes feeding wine to a dog; it indicates the increasing European presence in Isfahan.*

Right *A portrait of a youth reading, by Riza Abbasi, painted in the 1620s.*

Europeans of all kinds were a permanent presence in Safavid Iran and the Shah was a welcoming host. When in 1602 three Augustinian fathers arrived from Goa, Abbas gave them permission to build a convent in Isfahan, as well as a church, offering, as with the Armenians, to contribute to its decoration. The Augustinians represented the King of Spain. Four years earlier, when Abbas had returned to Qazwin after defeating the Uzbegs, he found a group of 26 Europeans waiting for him, headed by two Englishmen, Sir Anthony and Sir Robert Sherley. Sir Anthony was despatched to Europe with letters of friendship for the Pope, the Holy Roman Emperor, the kings of France, Spain, Scotland and Poland, the Queen of England, the Seigneur of Venice and the Grand Duke of Tuscany. He was to enlist the support of all these rulers against their common enemy, the Ottoman Sultan, while Sir Robert remained in Iran as surety. In the outcome, Sir Anthony failed utterly, not even returning to Iran. Sir Robert, however, remained an important link between the court of Shah Abbas and Europe until his death in Isfahan in 1627. By this time the English in general and the East India Company in particular had come to develop a significant profile. Throughout the 16th century, the

Portuguese had exercised a powerful influence over the Iranian coastline and its trade, in particular from their base at Hormuz. In 1616, however, the Shah gave the East India Company the right to trade freely throughout Iran. It was understood that the English would work with the Shah to drive the Portuguese out of Hormuz, which they did in 1622. From now on the English were to share the customs dues levied at Hormuz 50:50 with the Shah. The Portuguese ascendancy was at an end. Throughout the 17th century the English competed with the Dutch, until in the 18th century they gained the upper hand in the Indian Ocean.

Shiism, the third pillar of the Safavid state

If slaves and Armenian traders were two key elements in Shah Abbas's remoulding of the pillars of the Safavid state, Shiism, and the ulama who helped shape it into a broad-based imperial ideology, was the third. Shah Abbas put renewed effort into the work of his predecessors to make Iran a Shia society. He encouraged a fresh migration of scholars from the great centres of Shia learning in Iraq, who worked to spread an orthodox understanding of the faith which embraced the details of law and ritual. Major attempts were made to make this knowledge available to society at large through the writing of accessible works in Persian, the most important of which was a popular legal compendium, the *Jami-yi Abbasi*. The law was to help integrate both the disparate elements amongst the peoples of the shah's dominions, and state and society. The crucial position of law in the ideology of the Safavid state meant that those who transmitted it to society at large, the ulama, and in particular the *mujtahids* who used their reasoning skills to apply the law to new situations, came to have a position of growing power. While Shah Abbas was alive he was able to keep their claims to authority in check.

Isfahan, symbol of the reign of Shah Abbas

One achievement more than any other symbolizes the reign of Shah Abbas – the establishment of his capital of Isfahan, creating what was arguably the most beautiful early modern city. No one knows precisely why he decided to make the move from Qazwin. In 50 years as capital, Qazwin had not become a great city while Isfahan, the former Seljuk capital, was this already. Moreover, it was well-placed, 1,500 m (4,900 ft) high on the plateau in the centre of Iran, in a rich oasis with plentiful supplies of water from the Zagros mountains. The latest scholarship suggests that he made the decision to move as early as 1590, and from 1602 had resolved to develop the new capital around a great maidan (piazza) well to the south of the old city centre.

The city was a formidable trading centre with Chinese, Central Asian and Turkish merchants, as well as communities of Europeans, Indians, Jews and Armenians in addition to the Iranians. It was also a great religious centre; this was where the leading families of Shia scholars came to live. And increasingly, as the court became less peripatetic, it was the established seat of government. The French traveller Sir John Chardin

ISFAHAN

The Isfahan of Shah Abbas was, like Fatehpur Sikri and Shahjahanabad of the Mughal emperors, virtually a new city. This was not the Shah's original intention. His first thought was to refurbish the areas surrounding the Maidan-i Harun Wilayat by the city's Friday Mosque (Jami Masjid). But, such was the opposition of the city's merchants, who feared losing their properties, that the Shah chose instead to build a new city to the south of the old one. He was assisted in his planning by a veritable Leonardo da Vinci of Iran, Shaikh Baha al-Din Amili, theologian, philosopher, Quran-commentator, lawyer, astronomer, teacher, poet and engineer.

The plan for the new city had two main features. The first was the Maidan-i Naqsh-i Jahan, 'The Maidan of the Exemplar of the World', the northern outlet of which led to the main thoroughfare of the royal bazaar which stretched over 2.4 km (1.5 miles) to the Maidan-i Harun Wilayat. And the second was the Chahar Bagh Avenue, which ran from the city's Dawlat Gate over some 4 km (2.5 miles) to the foot of the mountains to the south. The royal palace lay between the Avenue and the Maidan. Four parallel rows of plane trees stretched the length of the Avenue, water flowed down a channel in its centre, and there were separate pathways for pedestrians and horsemen. On either side of the Avenue were gardens with houses for courtiers, foreign diplomats and members of the harem, as well as pavilions of public resort.

Eventually, the Avenue passed over the Zayanda river on a great bridge built by the Shah's Commander-in-Chief, Allahwardi Khan. Leaving the Armenian quarter of Julfa to the right, it culminated in the Abbasabad garden. The Avenue was much favoured by the nobility and citizens of Isfahan as a place to take the evening air.

Below The Allahwardi Khan Bridge which carries the Chahar Bagh over the Zayanda river. It was built by the Georgian slave of that name who became Commander-in-Chief of the Safavid army in 1598, and remained so until his death in 1613.

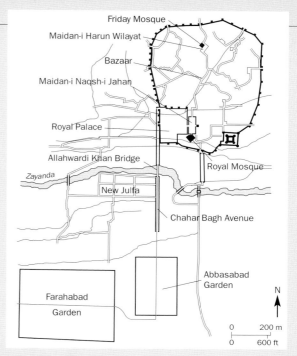

Above *Map of Isfahan.*

Below *The Chahar Bagh Avenue, lined by trees.*

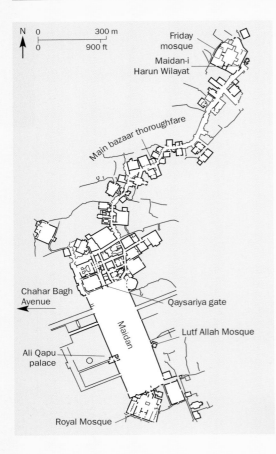

THE MAIDAN

The Maidan was the centre of the Safavid city of Isfahan. This was where the religious, economic and political aspects of life came together. The Maidan-i Naqsh-i Jahan was a magnificent piazza 507 x 158 m (1,663 x 518 ft). A watercourse ran all the way around the edge, and by it was a row of plane trees to offer shade. At one end stood the Royal Mosque, one of the triumphs of Iranian architecture, and at the other was the gateway to the bazaar. Along one side was the royal palace with the Ali Qapu, the High Gate, from which the Shah would watch events in the Maidan. Opposite was the Lutf Allah Mosque, the Shah's private mosque, another triumph of Iranian architecture. The Maidan was a market by day – the warehouses of the merchants filled its surrounding walls. At night it throbbed with activity as players, storytellers, acrobats, prostitutes, and hucksters of all kinds plied their trades. It was also the place for religious processions, during Muharram for instance, and for imperial spectacle – polo (the Shah's marble polo posts still stand), horseracing, military parades, fireworks, mock battles and the reception of foreign ambassadors.

Above Plan of the Maidan-i Naqsh-i Jahan and the bazaar. Note how the Royal Mosque (now Masjid-i Imam) at the bottom of the plan is at an angle to the maidan to accommodate its orientation to Mecca. At the opposite end of the maidan is the entrance to the bazaar which winds its way for 2 ½ km until it reaches the Maidan-i Harun Wilayat by the city's Friday Mosque.

Above right The Maidan was a market by day but might also be used for royal ceremonies and for sport. Its marble goal posts for polo erected by Shah Abbas still stand.

Right The Lutf Allah Mosque, the Shah's private mosque, which stands opposite the Ali Qapu on one side of the maidan.

Above *The Royal Mosque seen from the Ali Qapu. Very large and richly clothed in tiles, it took 35 years to complete. With the Lutf Allah Mosque it is regarded as a pinnacle of Iranian architecture.*

Right *The Ali Qapu, which was both a palace, an administrative centre and a gateway into the palace grounds. The terrace on top of the second floor operated as a grandstand for watching events in the Maidan. The opinionated travel writer, Robert Byron, dismissed it as 'that brick boot-box'. Many of its rooms, however, are exquisitely decorated.*

reckoned the circumference of the city was 24 miles, with 12 gates, 162 mosques, 48 madrasas, 1,802 caravanserais, 273 public baths, and a population of 600,000. It was, with its water courses and many gardens – which from afar made the city seem like a wood – above all a place where people could live well. As the Persian jingle went *Isfahan-i nisf-i Jahan*, 'Isfahan is half the world'.

The achievement of Shah Abbas

Starting from a virtually hopeless position in 1588 Shah Abbas had by his death in 1629 brought Iran to a position of power in the world which it has not held since. He secured the state borders and he stimulated the economy, in particular through the encouragement of trade, creating the conditions for one of the great periods of patronage of the arts in Iran. At the heart both of trade and the arts was his beautiful capital city of Isfahan. Moreover, he remoulded the pillars of the Safavid state, creating a strong centralized government, with an ideology to match, which was able to sustain the state through nearly one hundred years of the weaker rule of his successors.

'His person is such as well-understanding nature would fit for the end proposed for his being', wrote Sir Robert Sherley of Shah Abbas, 'excellently well-shaped, of most well-proportioned stature, strong and active; his colour somewhat inclined to man-like blackness, is also more black by sun-burning; the furniture of his mind infinitely royal, wise, valiant, liberal, temperate, merciful; and an exceeding lover of justice, embracing royally other virtues as far from pride and vanity as from all unprincely sins or acts.' To this should be added other qualities: great intellectual curiosity, which led him to discourse with many who came his way, from Muslim and Christian theologians to Western merchants and diplomats; leadership qualities, which inspired his followers to give their utmost for him; a common touch – he would go in disguise through the streets of Isfahan – which made his people love him; connoisseurship in the arts, which left his personal mark on his buildings; immense energy, which galvanized those around him; and ruthlessness in dealing with disloyalty.

Indeed, it was his fear of rebellion which led to the one notable failure of his regime – his treatment of his sons. He began by following the practice of the day and appointed them as governors of provinces. While minors, however, they would be in the care of a Qizilbash chief. But, after the rebellion of one, he had them immured in the harem, where their sole company consisted of eunuchs and women, and they remained ignorant of worldly affairs. They left the harem only to accompany Abbas on campaigns – a security measure. This became Safavid practice for the rest of the dynasty, leading to a poor quality of leadership. As it happened, not one of Shah Abbas's sons was able to succeed him. In 1615, imagining that his eldest son, Muhammad Baqir, was plotting against him, he had him stabbed to death as he returned from his bath. Two other sons he found plotting against him were blinded. The remaining two predeceased him. He died on 19 January 1629 in his summer palace in Mazandaran.

Shah Safi I
1629–42

Shah Abbas II
1642–66

Shah Sulaiman
1666–94

Shah Safi I was a murderous and weak ruler. Nevertheless, the able administrators he inherited from Shah Abbas meant that Safavid Iran continued to prosper.

SHAH SAFI I	
Born	*Son*
c. 1610	Sultan Muhammad
Father	(Shah Abbas II)
Muhammad Baqir,	*Daughter*
son of Shah Abbas I	Maryam Begum
Mother	*Enthroned*
Dilaram Khanum	17 February 1629
Wife	*Died*
Anna Khanum, a	12 May 1642
Circassian	*Buried*
	Qum

SHAH SAFI I

Tis certain there has not been in Persia a more cruel and bloody reign than his.

Fr. Krusinski, *Chronicle of the Carmelites*

SHAH SAFI WAS THE SON of the assassinated Muhammad Baqir and therefore a grandson of Shah Abbas. Sources differ as to his nature. Some, in particular Christians who were dependent on his favour, found him generous, charming and pleasant to deal with. But others regarded him as ruthless and cruel, even while acknowledging that in some cases *raison d'état* might explain his actions. This said, within five years of his accession he had all the remaining princes of the dynasty assassinated, including the two uncles blinded by his grandfather. A similar fate overtook a good number of the senior officials he inherited. Most striking was his execution, on unconvincing grounds of conspiracy with junior officials in Georgia and northwest Iran, of Imam Quli Khan, who ruled most of southern Iran, and his sons. Imam Quli Khan was the son of his grandfather's commander-in-chief, Allahwardi Khan; his death permitted the considerable revenues of his province of Fars to be transferred to the royal treasury.

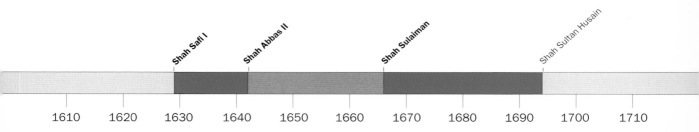

Shah Safi I   Shah Abbas II   Shah Sulaiman   Shah Sultan Husain

1610   1620   1630   1640   1650   1660   1670   1680   1690   1700   1710

On the constructive side, Shah Safi maintained the royal library workshops, which his grandfather had re-established as a source of designs for much of the Safavid production of luxury goods, though not carpets and textiles. Moreover, he permitted the valuable royal monopoly on silk to become an Armenian monopoly, recouping the loss of income through taxes on exports.

His weakness as a leader was soon apparent to Iran's traditional foreign enemies, however. In 1633 the Ottomans captured Erivan in Armenia and devastated Tabriz. In 1639 they captured Baghdad, reconquering all of Iraq and its Shia shrine cities, all of which was to remain in Ottoman hands till the end of the First World War. In Khurasan and the northeast the Safavids had to endure 11 raiding expeditions from the Janid Khans of Bukhara. In the east, Qandahar, which Shah Abbas had conquered some 14 years earlier, was in 1638 lost to the Mughals.

Despite these losses, central revenues reached unprecedented levels. Key to this success was the excellent administration provided by those officials who were inherited from the time of Shah Abbas and who survived Shah Safi's murderous moods. Most important of these was Mirza Muhammad Taqi, known as Saru Taqi ('Taqi of the fair hair'). He had administered great schemes of public works in Mazandaran under Shah Abbas and Shah Safi made him chief vizier in 1634. Renowned as selfless and incorrruptible, his efficient administration – which did not make him liked – meant that, when in 1642 Shah Safi died from the effects of the large amount of alcohol he drank to counter his opium addiction, although Safavid Iran may have become rather smaller than in the time of Shah Abbas, what remained was prosperous and relatively well governed.

A young man entertained outdoors, from a *Diwan* of Baqi dated 1636. It is thought that this *Diwan* may have been made for Shah Safi.

SHAH ABBAS II

...the king is so much intent on sensuality that he does not think any-thing about his kingdom ... an inflammation of the throat coming from excessive 'drinking' was the proximate cause of Abbas II's death ... for the rest ... he was a just, liberal and magnanimous monarch, lover of the Franks, 'who let the missionaries alone'.

Chronicle of the Carmelites

SHAH ABBAS II	
Born	*Enthroned*
c. 1633	12 May 1642
Father	*Died*
Shah Safi	25/26 October
Mother	1666
Anna Khanum	*Buried*
Wife	Next to his father in
Nakihat Khanum	Qum
Sons	
Safi (Sulaiman)	
Mirza, Hamza Mirza	

Shah Abbas II, a man with a passion for justice, but also for alcohol. 'His manner was affable but nevertheless majestic,' declared Father Sanson. 'He had a masculine and agreeable voice, a gentle way of speaking and was so very engaging that, when you had bowed to him, he had seemed in some measure to return it by a courteous inclination of the head, and this he always did smiling.'

ON 12 MAY 1642, AGED EIGHT AND A HALF, Abbas II succeeded his father. The succession was managed by the young Shah's grandmother and Saru Taqi, who, being a eunuch, had access to the royal harem. In one sense his early accession was a blessing because it enabled him to escape from the harem and receive an education suited to his task. He developed a passion for horsemanship, hunting and polo. He learned to read and write to the point that he was able to comprehend religious texts, laying the foundation of what was to be a lifelong interest in Shia theology. He had, moreover, lessons in painting from European as well as Iranian artists.

He also acquired an interest in architecture, perhaps from Saru Taqi, himself a great patron.

Shah Abbas had a brutal introduction to public life. In 1645, when he was 12, Saru Taqi was assassinated by a group of Qizilbash chiefs. A few days later he had the assassins executed. From now on he was increasingly drawn into government. One feature of his rule was a steady consolidation of royal power achieved by increasing the proportions of crown lands and therefore of royal revenues. A second feature was the passion for justice he shared with his great-grandfather, Shah Abbas I. He devoted three days a week to presiding over a judicial tribunal which dealt with military and civilian cases, and a further two in hearing grievances from all parts of the empire. One outcome was that he frequently intervened to protect peasants and other subjects from unjust treatment by his officials. European observers noted that in Iran the condition of the rural population was much better than in the West. He was in general tolerant in religious matters, giving Christians in particular considerable freedom. The one exception were the Jews, who were required to convert to Islam.

In foreign affairs, Shah Abbas II adopted a largely passive policy. He made no attempt to regain the lands which had been lost to the Ottomans, and the one territorial gain of his reign was the recapture in 1648 of Qandahar, the key strategic point on the land trade route into India. There was a downside to this policy, which was that Safavid military forces, in particular the artillery, began to decline. On the other hand, the Western trading companies, especially the English, the French and the Dutch, became an increasingly strong presence in Iran, which now began to open up to the West. Iranian traders travelled to Europe; Europeans stayed in Iran, in particular in Isfahan, where their presence was both recorded in painting and influenced its execution.

Patronage of the arts and architecture

In one of the two great buildings Shah Abbas II bequeathed to Isfahan, the European presence is strikingly manifest. This was the Chihil Sutun (meaning 40 pillars, although it only had 20, the remaining 20 being found in their reflection in the long rectangular pool in front of the building), which was an elegant and imposing audience hall built in the Ali Qapu palace complex. Among the many murals decorating the hall and its associated chambers were representations of the magnanimity of the Safavids towards their neighbours and of literary themes, and paintings of Europeans.

The second of Abbas II's buildings in Isfahan was the pleasing Khwaju weir and bridge over the Zayanda river, with an octagonal pavilion in the centre and two half-octagonal pavilions at either end. Beyond these, Abbas helped to repair the Friday mosques in Isfahan, Kashan, Qazwin and Qum, and made architectural contributions to the Shia shrines at Mashhad and Qum and to the family shrine at Ardabil.

The painting of the period reflects the changing nature of Safavid society and its openness to new influences from outside. In matters of technique and style there is a range of European features, whether felt directly or through exposure to developments in Mughal painting, which

The Chihil Sutun, Isfahan, completed by Shah Abbas II in 1647. The palace is decorated with six large murals in the audience hall (for elements of two of them see pp. 182, 185). The remaining rooms all contain decoration similar to that in the Ali Qapu. Some of the spaces are decorated with men and women in European dress.

This painting by Mir Afzal Tuna, Isfahan, *c.* 1640, of a lady watching her dog drink wine from a bowl and in a distinctly deshabillé state, is strongly suggestive of a strand of sensuality and eroticism present in Isfahanian society at the time.

in turn was under European influence. There are experiments with chiaroscuro, European buildings appear in the background, and flowers and plants reflect the careful depiction of European botanical drawings. This said, the work of Riza Abbasi remained the starting point for most artists. Themes are no longer the tales of heroes or the great works of Iranian literature, favoured by the royal workshops, but representations of real life, dandies, picnics, lovers, Europeans, a cloth merchant or an old man scratching his head. These were single album sheets collected by connoisseurs, nobility and merchants. Some expressed an unabashed eroticism, reflecting perhaps a new interest in individual feeling, but perhaps, too, the lascivious example set by the monarch.

Unsurprisingly, the ulama took exception to the dissolute example set by the court. There were attempts to ban alcohol and the visual representation of individuals, but with no success. The ulama were also displeased by the concessions shown to Christians and by the willingness of the Shah to intervene on their side in judicial proceedings with Muslims. One of the ulama was reported by the French traveller Chardin as saying that kings were unjust and impious, and that it was their task to act only at the behest of the most learned among the ulama – a warning for the future.

Shah Abbas II died, aged 32, on the night of 25–26 October 1666, from the effects of over-indulgence in alcohol. He was buried in Qum close to his father. In his reign Safavid Iran reached the height of its prosperity.

THE EUROPEAN INFLUENCE ON PAINTING

Painting under Shah Sulaiman continued the Europeanizing trends which had begun under Shah Abbas. Court painters were clearly well-acquainted with European prints and were encouraged to learn from them. Among the leaders of this trend were Ali Quli Jabbadar, who both copied European prints and individualized the portraits of nobles in group scenes, and Muhammad Zaman, who displayed techniques such as cast shadows, well-defined drapery folds and rows of birds in the sky.

The commercial side of the market also followed the Europeanizing trends. There were paintings following European prints of Christian themes, probably commissioned by Armenians. One painter signed his works 'Jani who works in the European style, son of Bahram who works in the European style'.

SHAH SULAIMAN

In the beginning of his Reign, like another Nero, he gave good Specimens of his Inclinations, not unworthy of the Heroes that were his Ancestors, but when he began to Hearken to Flatterers, and give himself over to Idleness, he left off to Govern, and lifted himself in the service of Cruelty, Drunkenness, Gluttony, Lasciviousness and abominable Extortion…

John Fryer

SULAIMAN WAS 19 WHEN, on 1 November 1666, he came to the throne. The son of a Circassian slave woman, he knew nothing of the world; the company of women and eunuchs was his preparation for the throne. He turned out to have all his father's weaknesses – addiction to drink, drugs and licentiousness – plus a few of his own – irascibility, indolence and superstition. On the other hand, he was noted for his love of peace and his personal charm. He began by taking the ruling name Shah Safi II.

The first years of the reign were a disaster, with a succession of famine, disease, a major earthquake, a rise in prices, Cossack raids in the Caspian provinces, and he himself was ill. It was decided that the

SHAH SAFI II/SHAH SULAIMAN	
Born	*Daughter*
1647	Shahr Banu
Father	*Enthroned*
Shah Abbas II	1st: 1 November
Mother	1666; 2nd: 20
Nakihat Khanum	March 1668
Wife	*Died*
?	24 July 1694
Sons	*Buried*
Abbas, Husain, plus	Qum
5 others	

astrologers must have miscalculated the date on which his reign should begin. A new date was set, and on 20 March 1668 he was crowned a second time, taking the name of Sulaiman.

Sulaiman soon revealed that he had little appetite for the work of government and retired to the harem; his viziers were expected to manage affairs. But, as time went on, the custom of the morning audience fell into desuetude and access to the Shah became more and more difficult to achieve. Sulaiman came to discuss affairs of state with his women and eunuchs, increasingly establishing a private administration within the harem. The officials of the state became merely the executive of the harem body, and the state's business the plaything of eunuchs, concubines and princesses. In consequence, grave abuses of power flourished. There were no sanctions against oppression or corruption. Administrative decisions increasingly ignored the state's best interests; the army became useless.

On 24 July 1694, Shah Sulaiman died in Isfahan – according to one source from gout, to another from a stroke while deep in his cups, and to a third from the accumulated effects of debauchery. There is no doubt that he presided over the squandering of the magnificent legacy of his predecessors. Yet, he was a popular ruler, keeping his country out of war and maintaining a magnificent royal household. He was also a considerable connoisseur of painting, presiding over a further Europeanization of Iranian art.

Shah Sulaiman, who, over 28 years of rule, squandered the legacy of his predecessors. Here he is with his courtiers in a painting by Ali Quli Jabbardar, Isfahan, *c*. 1670.

Shah Sultan Husain
1694–1722

Under Shah Sultan Husain, an indolent, uxorious, pious and eventually drunken man, the Safavid state crumbled so much that it was overcome in 1722 by a relatively small force of Ghilzai Afghans. Here, Sultan Husain distributes New Year (Nawruz) presents in 1721. Painting by Muhammad Ali, son of Muhammad Zaman, Isfahan, 1721.

SHAH SULTAN HUSAIN	
Born	*Enthroned*
?	6 August 1694
Father	*Died*
Shah Safi II	Executed in 1726
Mother	on the orders of
?	Ashraf Ghilzai
Wives	*Buried*
Numerous	?
Sons	
Tahmasp, Mahmud, Safi	

SHAH SULTAN HUSAIN

Shah Sulaiman left by different mothers, two sons capable of succeeding him, the elder named Abbas Mirza, the younger, Husain, who had to his detriment a bodily deformity – legs that were monstrously crooked and withal he was splay-footed; he was born without ambition and liked solitude and had been wrapped up in reading the Quran, so that they gave him the nickname 'Darwish'.

Chronicle of the Carmelites

SHAH SULAIMAN DID NOT APPOINT A SUCCESSOR. However, he told his courtiers that if they wished to expand the empire they should choose Abbas, but, if they wanted an easy time, they should opt for Husain. Sulaiman's death was discovered by his aunt, Princess Mariam Begum. This forceful woman was soon able to persuade the eunuchs that their best interests lay with the placid and pliable Husain. Thus it was that the claims of Abbas, a warlike, manly, sober and able man, were passed over in favour of Husain, an indolent, uxorious, pious, and eventually a drunken man. On 6 August 1694 he was formally enthroned. Once more the monarch was to be at the mercy of the powerful personalities around him.

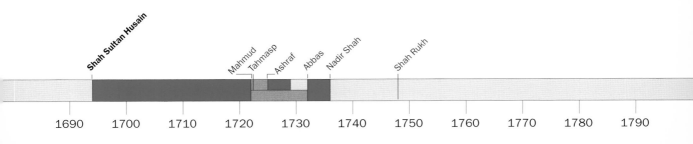

Shah Sultan Husain | Mahmud | Tahmasp | Ashraf | Abbas | Nadir Shah | Shah Rukh

1690   1700   1710   1720   1730   1740   1750   1760   1770   1780   1790

The man who presided over Husain's enthronement, girding the young monarch with his sword, was Muhammad Baqir Majlisi, Shaikh al-Islam and most learned theologian of the time. Majlisi exerted much influence over Husain, reflecting in part the growing authority of the ulama in Safavid society. He persuaded Husain to enforce a strict understanding of Islam, with laws against alcohol, and, despite the Safavid patrimony, against Sufis, as their practices were now deemed unorthodox. Policy became increasingly intolerant of those who did not follow orthodox Shiism. Philosophy, one of the triumphs of Iranian scholarship, was discouraged; life became difficult for Christians and Jews; and Sunni communities felt pressure to conform.

The harem got its revenge on Majlisi by introducing Husain to wine, thus exploiting the family weakness, a process in which Princess Mariam Begum, a serious drinker herself, took the lead. This subversion of Majlisi's policy, achieved by deploying the concept associated with the office of Shah – that he could do no wrong – did not lessen the pressure on the Sunnis, most of whom lived in the border regions of the empire. There were revolts by the Abdali Afghans in Herat, and by the Ghilzai Afghans in Qandahar. By 1720 there was unrest in the Caucasus, Kurdistan and Khuzistan, while the rulers of Oman were threatening the shores of the Persian Gulf.

No one would have thought it at the time, but the real danger came from the Ghilzai Afghans. After their rebellion in 1704 was suppressed, their leader, Mir Wais, was held captive at the Safavid court, where he gained insights into the weaknesses of the regime. Doubtless this knowledge encouraged his young son, Mahmud, to take on the apparent might of the empire. In 1719 Mahmud sensed the Safavid weakness when the governor fled as he advanced on Kirman: on this occasion a revolt in Qandahar forced him to hurry home. In 1721 he advanced again, failed to take Kirman and Yazd, but nevertheless continued to march in the direction of Isfahan. On 8 March 1722, on the plain of Gulnabad, Mahmud's force of 18,000 men faced a Safavid force of 42,000, including the great asset of heavy artillery. By evening, the Safavid forces had retreated in disarray to Isfahan, victims of the failure of their generals to co-ordinate their command. There began the agony of a long siege; thousands died of starvation, disease and failed attempts to escape. Eventually, in October Husain capitulated to Mahmud. On 23 October, Husain announced his abdication in favour of Mahmud, fixing with his own hand the jewelled plume of heron's feathers, the symbol of monarchy, on Mahmud's turban, and two days later rode into the city at Mahmud's left hand.

Thus, the era of Safavid glory came to an end. To his credit, Husain had continued to support the work of the royal library workshops. There were major buildings in his name – a new palace in Isfahan and a pleasure house at Farahabad – moreover, his mother paid for the last great work of Safavid architecture, the Chahar Bagh madrasa, caravanserai and bazaar complex, built between 1706 and 1714. This apart, Husain was a major part of the problems bringing about Safavid decline – a ruler ill-prepared

THE HAREM OF SULTAN HUSAIN

'It was a great burthen to the State to maintain the "Haram" [harem] in the degree to which it had risen under this prince, who had trebled the expense of it to which it was in the time of his predecessors: none of them came near what we have seen of this kind in his reign, either for the vast number of women, with whom he had filled his 'Haram', or for the extraordinary luxury and splendour in which he maintained them. His first care in the beginning of his reign was to cause a general search to be made for all the handsome women in Persia and to order them to be brought to his "Haram". ... he boasted publicly that he would spare no cost to outstrip the most voluptuous kings that ever were in the world. ... Each of these women had her particular eunuch and chambermaid and, as to the expense of the toilet and provisions, it had no bounds. ... Besides what he laid out upon them in the "Haram", he gave them a considerable portion when they went forth to be married ... the Shah bestowed women not only on his courtiers, but also on the inferior offices of his palace and his very cooks.'

Fr. du Cerceau, *Chronicle of the Carmelites*

The Chahar Bagh Madrasa, Isfahan, viewed from the west. Built between 1706 and 1714 by the mother of Shah Sultan Husain, it was known as the Madar-i Shah Madrasa and was the last great religious building of the Safavid dynasty. Attached to it was a caravanserai and a bazaar to help pay the expenses of the Madrasa. The mother of the Shah patronized the construction of religious buildings, as Timurid and Mughal women did. What was significant about this complex was its size and therefore the wealth and power of women in the Safavid harem.

for government, along with the excessive influence of the harem, the growing influence of the ulama, the corruption of the administration and the decay of the army. Sultan Husain was held in prison until 1726, when he was executed on the order of Mahmud's successor, Ashraf.

THE GHILZAIS AND REMAINING SAFAVIDS 1722–73

GHILZAI RULE LASTED NO MORE than seven years and experienced great difficulty in imposing itself over most of Iran, which slipped into chaos. For many years after the fall of Sultan Husain there was no doubting the prestige of the Safavid name, and the fear that it instilled in the minds of those who usurped the throne. Support for the Safavid prince, Husain's son, Tahmasp, from the citizens of Qazwin led to a murderous spree from Mahmud in Isfahan; he killed nearly 300 notables, 200 of their sons and 3,000 Iranians of the royal guard. The escape of a second Safavid prince, Safi, led **Mahmud** (1722–25) personally to behead every other prince he could find. Mahmud was murdered in 1725 and succeeded by his nephew **Ashraf** (1725–29), who began his reign by executing all Mahmud's supporters and his own Afghan supporters, and by blinding his brother. In 1726, the fear that the imprisoned Sultan Husain might be the focus of Ottoman support, led Ashraf to have the former Shah decapitated. Unsurprisingly, Ashraf's rule was insecure; in 1729 he was defeated by Nadir Quli Beg Afshar (Nadir Shah; p. 208) and executed in 1730.

During the seven years of Ghilzai rule, 18 Safavid pretenders made claims and, during the reigns of the early Afsharids (see below), a further 12. Some claimants were real Safavid princes. **Tahmasp II** (1722–32), Sultan Husain's crown prince, escaped to Qazwin where in November 1722 he had himself proclaimed Shah. He lived a fugitive existence in northern Iran until he teamed up with Nadir Quli Beg Afshar, a most able general who had defeated Ashraf, restored Tahmasp to the throne at Isfahan, and then in 1732 overthrew him as a drunken incompetent, after he was defeated in battle by the Ottomans. Such was the Safavid charisma, however, that Nadir still thought he needed a puppet and placed Tahmasp's eight-month old son, **Abbas** (1732–36) on the throne, where he lasted until 1736. The last Safavid puppet was **Ismail III** (1750–73), who was primarily a front for Karim Khan Zand (p. 214).

MAHMUD SLAUGHTERS THE NOTABLES AND SOLDIERS OF ISFAHAN

'He invited on 25.1.1723 some 300 notables to a banquet, where all except some 25 were slain barbarously on their arrival at the palace, their dead bodies after being stripped were flung out into the Maidan naked. Two days later he had two hundred youths, sons of leading men, slaughtered in a field outside the city – 'like hares', wrote the chronicler. On 31.1.1723 it was the turn of the soldiers of the guard, some three thousand Persians, who had previously sworn allegiance to the new monarch and were being regaled on pilaf and meat: while they were eating their arms were taken from them and they were put to death in the courtyard of the palace by Afghans. All February soldiers of the ex-Shah were sought out, and killed wherever they were found.'

Fr. Krusinski, *Chronicle of the Carmelites*

THE AFSHARIDS
1736–96

Nadir Shah
1736–47

Shah Rukh
1748–50, 1750–96

Nadir Shah, who, in a career of remarkable conquest, restored Iranian power in the world. However, he treated his people so brutally that they were happy to see him die.

NADIR SHAH	
Born	Sultan Husain),
16 November 1688	name unknown
Father	(daughter of Abul
Imam Quli Beg	Faiz of Bukhara)
Mother	*Sons*
?	5, including Riza
Wives	Quli, Nasr Allah,
Name unknown	Imam Quli
(elder daughter of	*Enthroned*
Baba Ali Beg of	Spring 1736
Abiward), name	*Died*
unknown (younger	20 June 1747,
daughter of Baba Ali	murdered by his
Beg of Abiward),	troops
Raziya Begum	*Buried*
(daughter of Shah	Mashhad

Nadir Shah

His eldest son ... when governor of Hamadan, had pulled down a house belonging to a poor citizen, in order to widen the Maidan, where he played games on horseback ..., this being done without Tahmasp Quli Khan's [Nadir Shah's] consent. When the general returned from his last attack on Baghdad, on the owner of the house making complaint to him personally, Tahmasp Quli Khan had his own son strangled on the spot in dispute. After the execution ... the son showed signs of life and was revived: the news was taken to Tahmasp Quli Khan, who again gave orders for his son to be killed.

Fr. Leander, *Chronicle of the Carmelites*

THIS RUTHLESS MAN, who for much of his life was a brilliant leader of men, was born on 16 November 1698 in the fortress of Dastgird, in the north Khurasan uplands. He was an Afshar, a Turkman tribe which the Safavids, for security reasons, had moved from Azarbaijan to Khurasan. Nadir Quli Beg's early life seems to have been spent suppressing robbers to aid the merchants on the Khurasan trade route. He moved on to become a junior officer in the forces of the royal governor of Abiward,

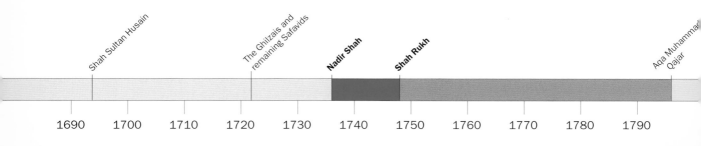

Shah Sultan Husain

The Ghilzais and remaining Safavids

Nadir Shah

Shah Rukh

Aqa Muhammad Qajar

1690 1700 1710 1720 1730 1740 1750 1760 1770 1780 1790

NADIR SHAH'S CRUELTY IN ISFAHAN

'It was … two years ago, i.e. 28.12.1745, the first time that the tyrant entered Isfahan after he had usurped the crown of Persia: it was the day of the (Holy) Innocents, and indeed that second Herod, more cruel than the first, without putting it off for a moment, on the very day of his entry at once opened the courts of his injustice, in which he alone sat as accuser, witness and judge, avarice serving as his counsel, tyranny as his authorities, his own arbitrary will as the law. He at once began the horrible butchery by having slaughtered under various pretexts a quantity of the chief persons of the country, among the principal of whom were the governor of Isfahan and the mayor of [New] Julfa, commonly called the 'Kalantar'. It was a sight to see in all parts of the city, and especially in the great Maidan [square] numbers of people of every grade tortured by the royal officials in order to extract money from them in accordance with the orders of the tyrant. To cut off noses, ears, put out eyes, mutilate members, to make all the toe-nails drop off under blows of the bastinado – these were ordinary affairs ….'

Bishop of Baghdad, *Chronicle of the Carmelites*

succeeding in marrying the governor's daughter, while his widowed mother married the governor. In the early 1720s he assumed control of the fortress of Kalat, a local strong point, and, as central power broke down, used diplomacy and force to neutralize or eliminate rivals. A successful leader, he quickly built up forces to challenge for the rulership of Khurasan.

In the mid-1720s Tahmasp II, who had been courting the Qizilbash chief Fath Ali Khan Qajar of Mazandaran, realized that Nadir Quli Khan was probably the man to help him regain his throne in Isfahan. The two men met and Tahmasp renamed Nadir 'Tahmasp Quli Khan' ('The Slave and Khan of Tahmasp'). In 1727 the latter proceeded, with the Shah's sanction, to capture Mashhad, the major city of Khurasan. Then, after capturing Herat and strengthening his position throughout the northeastern region, he defeated the Ghilzai ruler Ashraf, placed Tahmasp on the throne in Isfahan, and cemented his position by marrying the Shah's sister.

From 1730 to 1736, Nadir used the Safavids to give legitimacy to his actions; he was a far from servile 'slave'. In 1730 he chased the Ghilzai Afghans out of Iran, asking the Mughal emperor Muhammad Shah (p. 169) to close his frontier to them as well. In the same year he recaptured Hamadan from the Ottomans. Two years later, when Tahmasp II allowed himself to be defeated by the Ottomans and conclude a treaty on humiliating terms, Nadir marched to Isfahan with a large army and, amid dramatic scenes, forced Tahmasp II to abdicate, sent him under guard to Khurasan, took up residence in the royal palace and made Tahmasp II's baby son Shah as Abbas III. 'On 28.8.1732', recorded Fr. du Cerceau in 1740, 'Tahmasp Quli Khan … ordered to be set up in the Chihil Situn [sic] a magnificent cradle, in which the infant king was laid, and at the side of the cradle were put the turban, the royal plume and a sabre. Then Tahmasp Quli Khan assembled the Mullas and Saiyids and went to prayers in the presence of all the officers of the army, after which they congratulated the [baby] Shah upon his accession to the throne ….'

THE AFSHARS

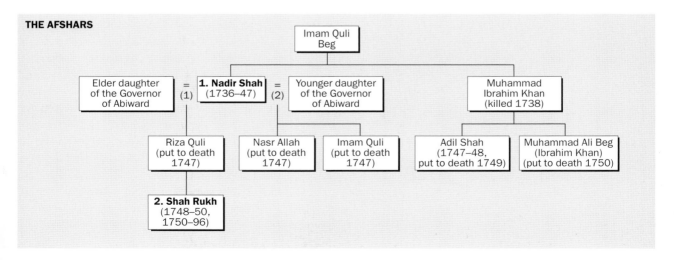

Nadir Khan is crowned Shah

In 1733, with the aim of controlling the trade route from India through Basra to the Mediterranean, Nadir campaigned against the Ottomans, capturing Baghdad. In 1734, he suppressed a rebellion in south Iran led by a man he had placed there to control the region. In the same year he fought the Russians, who were expanding southwards into Azarbaijan, and in March 1735 concluded the Treaty of Ganja, by which Iran for the first time achieved a common frontier with Russia. In January 1736 he held a great gathering of chiefs and notables of Iran on the Mughan plain in Azarbaijan to enable him to take the throne by popular acclamation. In the event it was not so easy. Nadir had his spies throughout the encampment. When one senior mulla was heard through a tent wall proclaiming that ill would befall the family which superseded the Safavids, he was strangled the following day before the whole gathering. Notables were dragged before Nadir with halters around their necks to testify to their allegiance. After three weeks, and just before the Iranian new year, Nadir was crowned Shah.

A battle scene with Nadir Shah on horseback, which is possibly by Muhammad Ali, the son of Abd al-Baig, the son of Ali Quli Jabbadar (see p. 203). Nadir Shah is said to have commanded the most powerful military force in Asia at this time.

Nadir Shah experiments with a new form of Islam

Just before his coronation Nadir proclaimed a new faith for Iran. He had two big problems. The first was the religious aura which was still attached to the Safavids and which was closely bound up with the conversion of numerous Iranians to Shiism. The second was the difficulty this caused with many of the peoples of his frontiers, Turks and Afghans, who were Sunnis. So, with the Ottoman ambassador and representatives of other religions present, he proclaimed his new Jafari faith. Iranians were to become followers of those imams whom all Muslims could accept, who included Jafar al-Sadiq, the sixth Imam. They were to stop the Shia practice of cursing the first three orthodox caliphs; Jafaris were to be recognized as a fifth school of Islam; and from now on five rather than four schools were to be acknowledged around the Kaaba in Mecca, the focus of the annual pilgrimage. The Ottomans were expected formally to recognize this extraordinary attempt to overcome the breach which reached back to the earliest days of the Islamic community, and which hindered Nadir's attempts to consolidate his realm. They refused to do so, thus robbing the idea of a crucial endorsement.

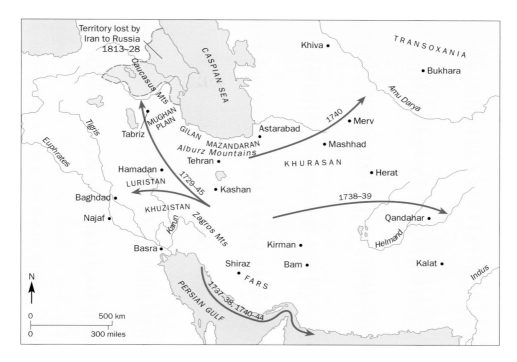

This map shows how in a formal reign of a mere 12 years Nadir Shah defeated the Afghans, crushed the Mughals, conquered the Uzbegs, invaded Oman, and asserted Iranian power in the northwest against the Ottomans.

Nadir Shah's campaigns

Now that Nadir was in charge, he devoted himself to what he did best, military conquest, primarily in search of loot. A soldier himself, he knew that well-paid soldiers were more likely to be loyal. In the autumn of 1736 he raised military pay and at the same time persuaded the merchants of Isfahan to finance a three-year expedition. In March 1737 he recaptured Qandahar, and in 1738 used the excuse of Muhammad Shah's failure to keep the Afghans under control to invade Mughal territory (see p. 170). On 24 February 1739 he defeated the Mughal army at Karnal. On 12 March he made a state entry into Delhi, and set about extracting resources, which led to resistance, a punitive massacre and systematic looting. By 27 March he had collected enough loot to be able to exempt Iran's provinces from taxes for three years, to give his soldiers their arrears of pay and to reward them with a gratuity equal to six months' pay. Before leaving, he demanded that Awrangzeb's great-granddaughter should be married to his son, Nasr Allah.

Nadir now set out to deal with his other border regions. In 1740 he captured Bukhara and Khiva, thus defeating Iran's traditional enemies, the Uzbegs of Transoxania. In 1741, following a mutiny amongst the Arab sailors whom he used to control the Gulf, he began building his own navy, ordering ships from India and having huge quantities of timber conveyed the vast distance from the forests of the Caspian to the shores of the Gulf. In 1742, he began developing a fleet on the Caspian to break the Russian monopoly on trade. In the same year he ordered Taqi Khan, one of the richest men of Shiraz, to invade Oman; unfortunately this led two years later to Taqi Khan, now a rebel, leading an invasion of southern Iran from Muscat. In July 1744, Nadir resumed his war against the Ottomans in the Caucasus, resulting in January 1747 in a peace treaty, in part sweetened by Nadir's gift to the Sultan of a dancing elephant from India. The two states acknowledged each other's boundaries, and undertook to support perpetual peace and to respect each other's religious interests. There was no mention of Nadir's Jafari faith: he had let the matter drop.

Towards the end of his life, Nadir's mind seemed to become increasingly unhinged. Some thought that it was the outcome of an assassination attempt, which led him to have the eyes of his son, Riza Quli, torn out. There is no doubt, however, that he became increasingly obsessed with taxation to the extent that not only did he perpetrate great cruelties on the townspeople of Iran but even tortured his own tax collectors. Increasingly people rose in revolt. On 16 August 1747 Fr. Sebastian wrote from Isfahan to describe how Nadir ended his days:

The cruel man came this last winter to this capital, and his wicked occupation was nothing but mutilating, strangling and burning people, and burying them alive; all this in order to extract money .... After having sated himself with cruelties the wretch went on to the town of Kirman ... and did the same there, more or less. He continued on to Mashhad, the capital of Khurasan; and there gave way to excesses and had seven very high towers made of human heads. He had buried alive two sons of Ali Quli Khan, his nephew, and the eyes put out of the mother and wife of the latter. He sallied forth from Mashhad to go elsewhere, and on the march took into his head to put to the sword all his bodyguard, consisting of 4,000 men; but they got wind of the iniquitous intention of the monarch and ten of the more courageous of them went at night into the royal tent and with their swords hacked to pieces the tyrant, and sent portions of his flesh to all parts of the country. But the head was cut off and put on top of a lance and carried in triumph for sport.

Chronicle of the Carmelites

SHAH RUKH

As to the news from Persia that empire is continually going from bad to worse; and famine reigns to such a pitch that no bread to eat is to be had. We do not know how the poor missionaries are faring, because for many months we have received no letters from them ...

Letter from Bishop Emmanuel of Baghdad, 15 January 1749,
Chronicle of the Carmelites

IT IS POSSIBLE THAT Ali Quli Khan was involved in the murder of his uncle. Certainly, he had a motive and he quickly took charge after Nadir's death, executing Nadir's surviving sons, but sparing Riza Quli's son, Shah Rukh, aged 13, on the grounds of his Safavid blood – his mother was a daughter of Sultan Husain. Two weeks after Nadir's death, Ali Quli Khan was proclaimed **Adil Shah**; immediately he had to confront two

---

SHAH RUKH TORTURED FOR NADIR SHAH'S JEWELS

'The passion of avarice was almost as strong implanted in the mind of Aqa Muhammad Khan as the love of power; and he appeared especially desirous of possessing jewels. ... The blind Shah Rukh was yet believed to possess many precious stones of great value, which he had concealed even from his sons. These were demanded by Aqa Muhammad Khan; but he denied the possession of them, and took he most solemn oaths to persuade that monarch to credit his assertion; but in vain. Torture, in all its forms, was applied, and we almost cease to pity this degraded and miserable prince, when informed, that his discoveries kept pace with the pains which were inflicted upon him. Treasures and jewels were produced, which had been sunk in wells and built up in walls; and, at last, when a circle of paste was put upon his head, and boiling lead poured into it, he, in his agony, discovered a ruby of extraordinary size and lustre, which had once decorated the crown of Awrangzeb, and was the chief object of the search of Aqa Muhammad. That monarch, we are informed, the moment he heard that this jewel was found, expressed the greatest joy; he directed the torments of Shah Rukh to cease, and accused that prince, not altogether without justice, of being the author of the great miseries, which he had suffered.'

Sir John Malcolm

View of the shrine of Imam Rida, the 8th Shia Imam, in Mashhad. The city is the holiest in Iran, a great focus of pilgrimage. It also is the site of the mausoleum of Nadir Shah. Nadir's grandson, Shah Rukh, ruled Khurasan from here for nearly 50 years. But, blinded while still a teenager, he ruled in name only; he was the tool of a faction of notables who had been close to his grandfather.

SHAH RUKH	
Born	Mirza, Imam Quli
1734	Mirza
Father	*Daughters*
Riza Quli Beg, son	?
of Nadir Shah	*Enthroned*
Mother	1748, and again in
Fatima Sultan	1750
Begum, daughter of	*Died*
Shah Sultan Husain	1796 as a result of
Wives	torture by Aqa
?	Muhammad Qajar
Sons	*Buried*
Nadir Mirza, Abbas	Damghan
Mirza, Nasr Allah	

rivals. First, there were the Qajars, a Turkman tribe transplanted in the 17th century from Azarbaijan to Mazandaran, whom he defeated. He captured the young son of the Qajar leader, the future Aqa Muhammad Shah Qajar (p. 218), whom he castrated. Second, there was his brother, Ibrahim, who, after being sent to secure Isfahan, set out to overthrow Adil. In this he succeeded, having Adil blinded. But the notables of Khurasan now stepped in, enthroning Shah Rukh at Mashhad in October 1748. Shah Rukh was supported in part because of his Safavid blood and in part because of deft use of his grandfather's treasure. Adil Shah was brought to Mashhad where he was put to death at the behest of Nadir's widow. Soon afterwards, his brother, Ibrahim, suffered a similar fate.

During 1750 there was a brief moment when some Qajar chiefs deposed Shah Rukh, replacing him with Saiyid Muhammad, the guardian of the shrine of the Imam at Mashhad, who had Safavid blood. He reigned for a few months as **Sulaiman II**, and in this time Shah Rukh was blinded. This fact did not prevent him from being put back on the throne by a faction of notables who had been close to his grandfather. He was totally dependent on them, as indeed they became on Ahmad Abdali (see pp. 171–73), a former commander of Nadir Shah's army, who was beginning to fashion what was to become modern Afghanistan. He relieved Shah Rukh of some of his grandfather's treasure, which helped him invade Mughal India. But he, his son and grandson, as rulers of Afghanistan, made a point of sustaining Shah Rukh in Khurasan as a protectorate, until in 1796 Aqa Muhammad Qajar took Mashhad and tortured Shah Rukh in search of the remainder of Nadir's treasure, after which the poor man died.

THE ZANDS
1751–94

Karim Khan Zand
1751–79

Karim Khan Zand, who, from the early 1750s, based in Shiraz, extended his authority over much of central, western and southern Iran. After the madness of Nadir's rule, he is remembered with affection for the peace he brought, the trade he encouraged and the new prosperity which developed.

KARIM KHAN ZAND	
Born	*Enthroned*
c. 1705	1751, assumed
Father	title of Commander-
Inaq Khan	in-Chief, and later
Mother	Regent
?	*Died*
Wife	1 March 1779
?	*Buried*
Sons	Originally Shiraz,
Muhammad Rahim,	then Tehran, and
Abul Fath,	finally An Najaf
Muhammad Ali,	
Ibrahim, Salih	

Opposite Karim Khan Zand amongst his courtiers. Note that he wears no signs of royal authority; he maintained his position as regent. Nevertheless, the courtiers hold themselves respectfully in his presence, amongst them Karim Khan's brother, the blind Sadiq Khan. The portrait is attributed to Muhammad Sadiq.

KARIM KHAN ZAND

Persia – or rather Isfahan and the provinces subject to Karim Khan are now quite quiet, and the living is cheap; but the country is empty of men and money. None of the Catholics who went away have been signalled as returned, for they foresee fresh disturbances and revolts on the death of Karim Khan, who ... up till now has not cared to assume the title of 'Shah', but simply that of governor ....

Bishop Cornelius of Isfahan, 5 July 1763,
Chronicle of the Carmelites

THE ZANDS WERE A MINOR TRIBAL GROUP from the Zagros mountains of western Iran, who wintered on the plains around Hamadan. Under Nadir Shah, they had been forced to move to Khurasan. As soon as Nadir was killed, their leader Karim Khan, an officer in Nadir's army, led his people back to their ancestral lands. From there he began to compete in the struggle for power which followed Nadir's death. By 1750 he was part of the tribal federation which captured Isfahan, putting a puppet Safavid prince on the throne as Ismail III. Karim Khan emerged as part of a tri-umvirate in which Ali Mardan, the Bakhtiari tribal leader, was regent,

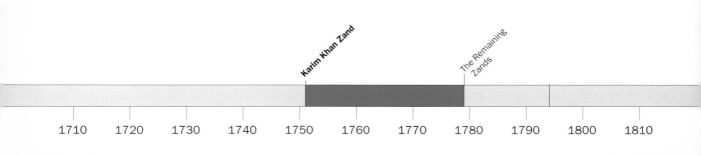

Karim Khan Zand   The Remaining Zands

1710   1720   1730   1740   1750   1760   1770   1780   1790   1800   1810

STORY TOLD BY KARIM KHAN ZAND OF HIS EARLY LIFE

'When I was a poor soldier, in Nadir Shah's camp, my necessity led me to steal from a saddler, a gold embossed saddle which had been sent by an Afghan chief to be repaired. I soon afterwards learnt, that the man, from whose shop it had been taken, was in prison, and sentenced to be hung. My conscience smote me, and I replaced the saddle exactly on the place, from whence I stole it. I watched, till it was discovered by saddler's wife, who, on seeing it, gave a scream of joy, fell down upon her knees, and prayed aloud that the person, who had brought it back, might live to have a hundred gold embossed saddles. I am quite certain', Karim used to add smiling, 'that the honest prayer of the old woman has aided my fortune in the attainment of that splendour, which she desired I should enjoy.'

Sir John Malcolm

Abul Fath, a leading notable of Isfahan, was governor of the city, and Karim Khan was Commander-in-Chief with a brief to conquer the rest of the country. Within the year they had fallen out; Ali Mardan had killed Abul Fath, and Karim Khan had chased Ali Mardan out of the city of Isfahan and taken control of Ismail III. He was now widely recognized as a power in Iran.

From 1751 to 1763 Karim Khan competed for overlordship with the leaders of the great tribes of Iran: Ali Mardan of the Bakhtiari federation, who remained a power in the Isfahan region; Muhammad Hasan of the Qajars of the south Caspian shore; and Azad Khan, a Ghilzai Afghan, who had risen to power in Azarbaijan. By 1754 Karim had eliminated Ali Mardan. Between 1755 and 1759 Karim campaigned against the Qajars. Initially he was defeated in a Qajar advance on Isfahan and forced to retreat to Shiraz. In 1757 he successfully defended Shiraz against a Qajar siege and then rolled back the overextended Qajars to the Caspian shore, taking their capital of Astarabad in 1759; he killed Muhammad Hasan, made his son Aqa Muhammad (p. 218) a hostage at court and came away with much booty. In 1762 Azad Khan, a dangerous ally of the Qajars who controlled much of northwest Iran, surrendered to Karim. By 1763 Karim had conquered all of western Iran.

From now on Karim was primarily concerned to round out his dominions. This campaign was conducted from Shiraz, which he did not leave after 1765. In 1766 his armies asserted his authority in Laristan, the large, mountainous region to the south of Shiraz. Income from trade meant that he was constantly interested in the Gulf. Although his armies were

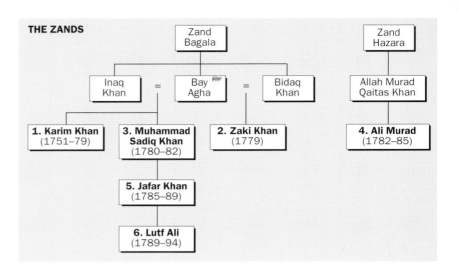

THE ZANDS

```
                    Zand                              Zand
                    Bagala                            Hazara
                       |                                 |
        +--------------+--------------+          Allah Murad
        |              |              |          Qaitas Khan
      Inaq   =    Bay Agha    =    Bidaq              |
      Khan                          Khan
        |              |              |               |
  1. Karim Khan   3. Muhammad   2. Zaki Khan   4. Ali Murad
    (1751–79)     Sadiq Khan      (1779)         (1782–85)
                   (1780–82)
                       |
                  5. Jafar Khan
                    (1785–89)
                       |
                   6. Lutf Ali
                    (1789–94)
```

This painting, attributed to Muhammad Sadiq, of two young lovers, shares some of the eroticism and sensuality of the Safavid painting of some 140 years earlier (see p. 203). From the clothes, the jewelry, the cut-glass decanter, we get a sense of what the good life in late 18th-century Shiraz might have been like. The painting is cut at the top to fit a niche.

not particularly successful in asserting Zand authority over the Imams of Oman, towards the end of his reign most of the Shaikhs of the Gulf ports recognized Zand supremacy. From 1774 Karim turned his attention to Ottoman Iraq, which led on 16 April 1776 to the capture of Basra, but he did not get the official access to the Shia shrines in Iraq for Iran's pilgrims which he sought. On 1 March 1779, in his seventies but still very active, Karim Khan died.

Zand Iran was roughly half the size of the Safavid empire at its height. Karim always remained regent and never Shah, even after Ismail died in 1773. For this he was much liked by the Iranians, with their strong Safavid prejudice. He was also respected for upholding the ways of conventional Shiism, after Nadir Shah's flirtation with quasi-Sunni Jafarism, and he would not have lost any support, except from the stricter ulama, for encouraging Sufis to return to the country. Particularly important in the popular mind were Karim's measures to restore prosperity after Nadir Shah's mad extortions and the civil wars which ravaged the land from 1722 to the early 1760s. He repopulated the land in part by bringing peace, which persuaded Shias to return from Iraq, and in part by making it clear to Christians and Jews that they were most welcome to settle. Trade was encouraged with European companies and with Indian merchants, who, for instance, had their own caravanserai in Shiraz. Some of the old Safavid bureaucratic standards were restored, cities began to flourish again, there was wealth enough for artistic patronage to help build a bridge between the traditions of the Safavids and those of the Qajars which were to come, and Shiraz was fortified and renewed as a city with many beautiful gardens. Karim Khan is remembered by Iranians as a good ruler, whose first concern was for the welfare of his people. He had his weaknesses: he enjoyed wine and opium to excess, and there was a moment when under stress in the early 1760s he became unstable and vindictive. But the enduring memory is of a humane, tolerant and wise man.

Rustam Khan Zand, the grandson of Karim Khan Zand's half brother, Zaki (r. 1779), in a painting, also cut to fit a niche, attributed to Muhammad Sadiq.

THE REMAINING ZANDS 1779–94

As soon as Karim Khan died, his kinsmen set about destroying what he had created. One, **Zaki Khan** (r. 1779), who had taken control of Shiraz, committed such atrocities on his way to confront another, who had taken control of Isfahan, that his soldiers killed him. A second, **Muhammad Sadiq Khan** (r. 1780–82), now occupied Shiraz, which was besieged by Ali Murad, yet another kinsmen. After Shiraz was captured, Muhammad Sadiq Khan and all his sons were killed except Jafar Khan, who had formed an understanding with **Ali Murad** (r. 1782–85).

The new ruler was now faced by a resurgence of Qajar power led by Aqa Muhammad, who had escaped from Shiraz the morning after Karim's death. Ali Murad campaigned vigorously against the Qajars in Mazandaran until he died in 1785. While Ali Murad was thus busy in the north, **Jafar Khan** (r. 1785–89) occupied Isfahan until a Qajar advance forced him to fall back on Shiraz. In 1789 he was killed by his own men because of his treacherous behaviour towards them. He was succeeded by his son, **Lutf Ali** (r. 1789–94), who captured Shiraz from his father's murderers and held it against Qajar assault. After many vicissitudes, in 1794 he was surprised by treachery in Kirman. Aqa Muhammad Qajar killed or blinded all the males in the city and gave 20,000 women and children to his troops as slaves. Lutf Ali was seized in the town of Bam, blinded, tortured and taken to Isfahan for execution.

Aqa Muhammad Qajar, seated, with his minister Hajji Ibrahim. Although he ruled formally for only one year, he had spent the previous 18 asserting Qajar authority over almost all Iran. Castration, aged 13, had left 'the person of this monarch', according to Sir John Malcolm, 'so slender that at a distance he appeared like a youth of 14 or 15. His beardless and shrivelled face resembled that of an aged and wrinkled woman; and the expression of his countenance, at no times pleasant, was horrid when clouded, as it very often was, with indignation.' Once Malcolm asked Hajji Ibrahim if Aqa Muhammad was personally brave. 'No doubt', the minister replied, 'but still I can hardly recollect an occasion when he had the opportunity of displaying courage. That monarch's head never left work for his hands.'

THE QAJARS
1796–1925

Aqa Muhammad Qajar
1796–97

Fath Ali Shah
1797–1834

Muhammad Shah
1834–48

AQA MUHAMMAD QAJAR	
Born c. 1734	*Enthroned* 1796
Father Muhammad Hasan Qajar	*Died* 16 June 1797, murdered by his servants
Mother ?	*Buried* Shrine of Imam Ali, An Najaf
Wife ?	
Sons None, castrated aged 13	

AQA MUHAMMAD QAJAR

If, according to your desire, I put the crown on my head, this will cause you, in the beginning, toil and hardship, as I take no pleasure in bearing the title of king, as long as I am not one of the greatest kings of Persia. This petition will not be granted but by toil and fatigue.

Aqa Muhammad's Khan's words to the notables who asked him to become Shah, Hasan-i Fasai, *Farsnama-yi Nasiri*

THESE WORDS SPEAK OF THE VIGOUR, energy and ambition of the man who united all of Iran under one ruler for the first time since Nadir Shah (p. 208). His tribe, the Qajars, had first entered Iran in the 11th century. They were one of the original components of the Safavid Qizilbash confederation, and formed a group strong enough in their homelands on the south Caspian shore to sustain their identity after the breakup of Nadir's Shah's rule.

Aqa Muhammad first appears in 1747 as a 13-year-old castrated by Ali Quli Khan, Nadir's nephew (p. 213). He appears again in 1759 when Karim Khan Zand, after his capture of the Qajar capital of Astarabad, kept Aqa Muhammad hostage at his court in Shiraz (p. 215). Here, it is said, Karim

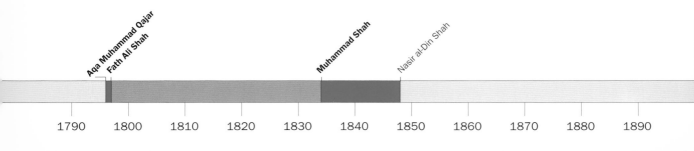

1790	1800	1810	1820	1830	1840	1850	1860	1870	1880	1890	

Khan held him in high regard, and he learned much. The day after Karim Khan's death in 1779 he fled Shiraz and set about building his kingdom. He began by confronting the internecine rivalries within his tribe, which had prevented it from achieving its full potential. Thus, in the years up to 1785 he concentrated on consolidating his power base in the lands around the south Caspian shore and the Alburz mountain region. From 1785 he moved to conquer central Iran, and in two years of great success captured both Isfahan and Tehran, the latter being made his capital. By 1794, with the absorption of Fars and Kirman, his conquest was complete.

He now turned to address the northwest, where the threat from Russia grew stronger as that country expanded southwards, and the northeast, where Shah Rukh still ruled Khurasan from Mashhad, the most holy city in the traditional lands of Iran. In 1795 Aqa Muhammad conquered Georgia, which was in alliance with Russia, perpetrating a massacre in the capital Tiflis which was the equal to that he had carried out in Kirman. After this, in 1796, he agreed to be crowned Shah, the coronation taking place on the Mughan plain, where 60 years before Nadir Shah had been crowned. He then went on to conquer Khurasan, entering Mashhad on foot as a pilgrim to the shrine of the eighth Imam, weeping and kissing the earth.

The following year, campaigning in the Caucasus to resist the spread of Russian influence, he gave orders that two servants in his private quarters who were quarrelling should be executed immediately. After intercession, he agreed that the execution could be postponed to the following day, and then unaccountably allowed the condemned men to continue to serve him. When he fell asleep, they stabbed him to death. His body rested in state for three days at the shrine of Shah Abd al-Azim to the south of Tehran, and then it was sent to Najaf to a final resting place in the shrine of Imam Ali.

FATH ALI SHAH

On extraordinary occasions, nothing can exceed the splendour of the Persian court. It presents a scene of the greatest magnificence, regulated by the most disciplined order. There is no part of the government, to which so much attention is paid, as the strictest maintenance of those forms and ceremonies, which are deemed essential to the power and glory of the monarch ....

Sir John Malcolm

FATH ALI KHAN, the son of Aqa Muhammad's brother, Husain Quli Khan, had been designated heir to the throne. On hearing of his uncle's assassination, he left Shiraz,

Over 37 years Fath Ali Shah Qajar gave Iran more peace and prosperity than it had had in a century. This painting was presented to the French envoy Amédé Jaubert on 11 July 1806 as a gift to the Emperor Napoleon. Fath Ali Shah had a large number of such paintings done to promote his power and authority. Moreover, his image was made to appear on articles of all kinds, from pen boxes to mirror backs, as a means of spreading that authority.

THE QAJARS

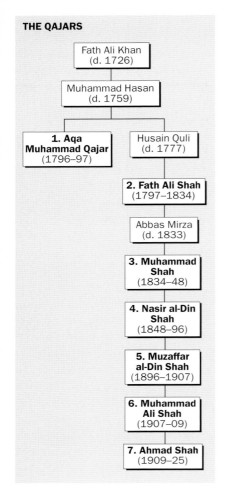

Fath Ali Khan
(d. 1726)

Muhammad Hasan
(d. 1759)

1. Aqa Muhammad Qajar
(1796–97)

Husain Quli
(d. 1777)

2. Fath Ali Shah
(1797–1834)

Abbas Mirza
(d. 1833)

3. Muhammad Shah
(1834–48)

4. Nasir al-Din Shah
(1848–96)

5. Muzaffar al-Din Shah
(1896–1907)

6. Muhammad Ali Shah
(1907–09)

7. Ahmad Shah
(1909–25)

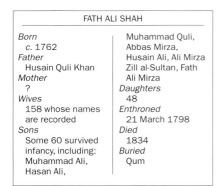

FATH ALI SHAH	
Born	Muhammad Quli,
c. 1762	Abbas Mirza,
Father	Husain Ali, Ali Mirza
Husain Quli Khan	Zill al-Sultan, Fath
Mother	Ali Mirza
?	*Daughters*
Wives	48
158 whose names	*Enthroned*
are recorded	21 March 1798
Sons	*Died*
Some 60 survived	1834
infancy, including:	*Buried*
Muhammad Ali,	Qum
Hasan Ali,	

where he was governor, and on 15 August 1797 entered Tehran. Immediately, he had to deal with risings in the northwest, as well as with his uncle's assassins, one of whom he personally cut to pieces. So it was not until 21 March 1798 that he was able to crown himself Shah in the Gulistan palace in Tehran. In his 37-year reign he was able to give Iran more peace and prosperity than it had had in a century.

Ironically, one of the reasons that Iran did so much better under Fath Ali Khan was that he was indolent. He could bestir himself when necessary, but he did not have sufficient energy for his mild cruelty and his greed to weigh heavily on his people. What energy he had was devoted to self-indulgence, not in alcohol and opium as in the case of his Safavid predecessors, but in women. He had many wives and produced, according to one source, roughly 60 sons and 48 daughters. He was moderately pious, not particularly talented and not especially brave. On the other hand, he had the style of a king, being extremely handsome, dignified and affable.

It was helpful that Fath Ali Shah looked royal because a major feature of his reign was the use of his image to project his power and majesty. In doing so he was following in the great tradition of Iranian kingship; thus, as the Sasanian kings had had their images cut into rock faces, so did he. Especially notable were the many life-size portraits of the Shah, and the decoration of palace rooms with scenes of Iranian glory, as in the Gulistan palace, all of which were designed to impress the foreign visitor. But equally, the Shah's image appeared on many objects used by society at large, such as pen and mirror cases.

Despite criticism from European visitors that the Shah's ministers were corrupt and unjust, it would appear that by the standards of the time they were able and effective. The ulama, who had come to believe that in the absence of the Hidden Imam (p. 191), the Shah's rule was illegitimate, and who aimed to stand up for the rights of the oppressed, were nevertheless on a day-to-day basis willing to work with the representative of the Crown. Moreover, there seems to have been a good number of able governors and prime ministers. Of Abd Allah Khan, who was Amin al-Dawla (prime minister) 1823–25 and 1828–34, James Fraser said: he is 'beyond all comparison the most eminent man at court for talents, probity, general popularity and attachment to his master's interest.'

Foreign relations

Arguably, two of the more significant issues of the reign were relations with foreign powers and the succession. In the case of the former, Fath Ali Shah in the early years of his reign found the French and the British competing for influence, while the Russian threat still loured from the north. The British victory over the French in the Napoleonic Wars meant that Iran now settled into the geopolitical pattern – which was to embrace it to the end of the First World War – of being steadily squeezed between the British to the south and the Russians to the north. In 1812 Iran signed a Definitive Treaty with the British, by which Iran agreed to prevent any European power from crossing its territory to invade India

Crown Prince Abbas Mirza took the lead in creating a modernized army for the Qajar state. In this painting, which may be of the battle at Sultanabad on 13 February 1812, he can be seen at the left with a pile of Russian heads in front of him. On this occasion the Qajars won; in the later war of 1826–28 they lost badly.

THE ULAMA: DEFENDERS OF THE INTERESTS OF THE PEOPLE

'The ecclesiastical class [the ulama], which includes the Mujtahids [interpreters of religious law] … and the Qazis [judges] … are deemed by the defenceless part of the population as the principal shield between them and the absolute power of the monarch. The superiors of this class enjoy a consideration that removes them from those personal apprehensions, to which almost all others are subject. The people have a right to appeal to them in all ordinary cases, where there appears an outrage against law and justice, unless when the disturbed state of the country calls for the exercise of military power.'

Sir John Malcolm

and the British agreed to pay Iran a subsidy if it was invaded by a European power. This arrangement was of little use to Iran in the war with Russia which ended with the Treaty of Gulistan in 1813. Iran had to surrender both Georgia and rights in the Caspian Sea to the Russians.

To address the Russian threat, Fath Ali Shah had an army of two distinct types: traditional formations, such as the royal ghulams (slave forces), tribal cavalry levies and militias raised by city governors, and from 1813 a new army, formed by Crown Prince Abbas Mirza, of regular cavalry and infantry regiments, trained and equipped in European style. Unfortunately, there was still much to learn. In 1826–28 Abbas Mirza led these forces in a disastrous war against the Russians, resulting in the Treaty of Turkmanchai, which saw further territorial concessions in the northwest and a large indemnity (see map p. 211).

Abbas Mirza's failure had a serious bearing on his prospects of succeeding Fath Ali Shah. Many brothers and nephews thought that now they too might have a chance. Fath Ali Shah, however, was determined that Abbas Mirza's reputation should be restored. The year 1831 saw the Crown Prince putting down disturbances in Kirman and Yazd. In 1832 he was posted to Khurasan, where he could seek glory in chastising Turkman raiders, controlling difficult chiefs and capturing the cities of Merv or Herat. But he died in 1833. Fath Ali Shah then made Abbas' son, Muhammad Mirza, his successor. In October 1834, Fath Ali Shah died in Isfahan. All were worried that this would lead to immediate civil war. The Shah was taken north in a litter and surrounded by his harem, as though he was still alive. Muhammad Mirza was instructed to hasten to Tehran. Only then was the death of the Shah announced.

MUHAMMAD SHAH

MUHAMMAD SHAH	
Born	*Daughter*
5 January 1808	Malikzada (later
Father	Izzat al-Dawla)
Abbas Mirza	*Enthroned*
Mother	January 1835
Name unknown	*Died*
(daughter of	5 September 1848,
Muhammad Khan	from complications
Beglerbegi Develu	brought on by
Qajar)	chronic gout
Wife	*Buried*
Malik Jahan of the	Qum
Quvanlu	
Son	
Nasir al-Din	

The Hajji [Aqasi] had entirely conquered the temperaments of the late shah [Muhammad Mirza]. By means of mysticism, piety and asceticism he convinced the late shah that he is one of the saints. Since the late shah by nature was ready to acquire apparent and spiritual accomplishments, he recognized the claims of the Hajji and planted the seed of his affection in his noble heart.

Jahangir Mirza, historian and half-brother of
Muhammad Shah, blinded at his accession

ON HEARING OF HIS GRANDFATHER'S DEATH, Muhammad Shah hastened from Tabriz, supported by both British and Russian envoys, to take control of affairs in Tehran. In January 1835 he was formally enthroned. The extent of British involvement is evident from their advance of £20,000 to pay for his troops, the presence of their military mission in his army and their attendance at his coronation. The first months of his reign were spent dealing with uncles and cousins who pretended to the throne. Given British assistance to Muhammad Shah, it was not surprising that they were furious when in 1837 he advanced on Herat; they said that this would expose Afghanistan and India to the Russians. The Shah, however, was merely executing his family's long-standing policy, which in the outcome failed to overcome Afghan resistance. A good part of Muhammad Shah's reign was spent dealing with the intrigues of exiled members of the Qajar royal family in Baghdad. One led to a revolt of the Aga Khan and his Ismaili Shia community in Yazd and Kirman; they were exiled to Bombay. There were also strained relations with the Ottoman empire over control of the Shatt al-Arab waterway into the Persian Gulf and the treatment of Iranian pilgrims to the Shia shrines in Iraq.

The most striking feature of the reign was the Shah's dependence on his prime minister, Hajji Mirza Aqasi. The first prime minister was the able Qaim Maqam; but within a year the Shah had him secretly strangled in the cellar of his Nagaristan palace. Aqasi, a Sufi who had been the Shah's tutor as a boy, was said to have been involved. He succeeded as prime minister and remained so for the reign. The Shah had strong spiritual inclinations and regarded Aqasi as his spiritual master; he refused to seek the guidance of the leading ulama. This was the start of the pronounced hostility of the ulama to the Qajars, which was a feature for the rest of their rule. Muhammad Shah died, aged 40, on 5 September 1848 in Tehran, from complications brought on by chronic gout.

Muhammad Shah, painted a year after his accession by Muhammad Hasan Afshar. For much of his reign, he was under the influence of his former tutor, a Sufi.

Nasir al-Din Shah
1848–96

Nasir al-Din Shah, drawn by Madame Labat in Tehran in 1844. Nasir al-Din, ruling for over four decades, had success in leading the development of Iran in an age of European imperialism.

NASIR AL-DIN SHAH	
Born	*Sons*
17 July 1831	Muin al-Din,
Father	Muzaffar al-Din,
Muhammad Shah	Amir Qasim, Masud,
Mother	Kamran, Sultan
Malik Jahan (later	Husain
Mahd-i Ulya)	*Daughters*
Wives	?
Several hundred	*Enthroned*
permanent and	21 October 1848
temporary wives,	*Died*
including: Anis al-	1 May 1896,
Dawla (chief wife),	assassinated at the
Amina Aqdas,	Shrine of Abd al-
Shukuh al-Sultana	Azim, Tehran
(a granddaughter of	*Buried*
Fath Ali Shah),	In a mausoleum
Jayran, Khanum	next to the Shrine of
Bashi	Abd al-Azim, Tehran

NASIR AL-DIN SHAH

The Shah's visit yesterday went off admirably and he is certainly vy. intelligent but I thought him very dignified. There was nothing to shock one at all in his eating or anything else .... He is delighted with England with everything here ... the Shah has produced almost a fever [amongst Londoners]...

Queen Victoria to the Crown Princess of Prussia, 21 June 1873

NASIR AL-DIN, THE CROWN PRINCE, was in Tabriz, where he was governor, when he heard from the Russian consul of his father's death. On 13 September 1848 he officially declared himself Shah. Wisely, he set about assembling a significant force before going to Tehran, which he could only do with funds raised with British help. He made the very able Amir Kabir his commander-in-chief and entered Tehran. On 21 October 1848 he was crowned. Amir Kabir was soon made prime minister, in addition to being commander-in-chief, and set out on a programme of modernization. He strengthened the army, improving its Western-style military training; he worked to reorganize central government and make it efficient; he founded the first newspaper and Western-style secondary school, the Dar al-Funun; and he tried to start modern industries, but was

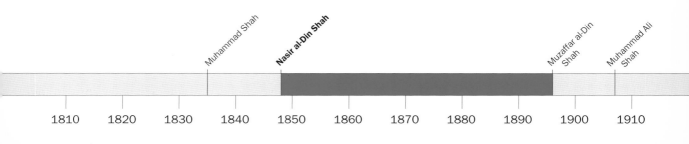

hampered by the lack of transport infrastructure and appropriately skilled labour. His activities, which attacked many areas of corruption, made him powerful enemies, from the court through to the ulama. Most important in the court was the Queen Mother, Malik Jahan, whose opposition Nasir al-Din hoped to neutralize by commanding his sister to marry the Amir. Nevertheless, the hostility against Amir Kabir grew. In 1851 the Shah exiled him to Kashan, where, in 1852, under great pressure from Malik Jahan, he had him executed. The assassins found him in his bath, shoved a towel into his mouth and opened his veins.

The opening up of Iran to the West

Two important features of Nasir al-Din's reign were the increasing presence of Westerners and Western goods and the growing influence of the ulama. Westerners sought concessions to develop various parts of the Iranian economy, while Western goods, in particular from Britain and Russia, were penetrating Iranian markets, destroying the livelihoods of bazaar merchants and artisans. The resulting socio-economic disruption was an increasingly fertile ground for opposition. In the case of the ulama several factors made them potential leaders of the opposition – the triumph of a school of thought which declared that believers must follow the most learned of the ulama, who were most likely to understand the will of the Hidden Imam; their economic strength from endowments and religious taxes; the roles they played in providing educational and legal services; and their close links with merchant and artisan communities.

The process of opening up Iran, however, was uneven. Amir Kabir's successor as prime minister, Mirza Aqa Khan Nuri, reversed his predecessor's reforms and broke relations with Britain. In 1856–57 Iran found itself defeated by Britain in a war over Herat, and in the subsequent peace had to surrender all claim to the city as well as agreeing to stop importing African slaves. After this Nuri was dismissed and the Shah began to govern himself, using a body of officials and ulama to advise him. The system did not work well. One technological innovation, however,

MALIK JAHAN, MAHD-I ULYA

Malik Jahan, the mother of Nasir al-Din, was a significant figure in the politics of the early years of her son's reign. A forceful personality and skilful politician, she dominated the harem and also strove to dominate her son. In the early years of his reign, this meant power struggles with his prime ministers. When Nasir came to the throne, she arranged the dismissal, working closely with the British, of Aqasi. She also

Malik Jahan, Madh-i Ulya, who ruled Nasir al-Din's harem and was a major player in the early decades of his reign. She is said to characterize 'the wider current of matriarchy in the Qajar elite'.

organized the opposition to Amir Kabir, in return for which he may have spread accusations of her promiscuity. 'Now in the position of queen-motherhood', she wrote to her son, 'no one is as defenceless as I am. ... This is the pledge I made in the shrine of Ma'suma [sister of the eighth Imam buried in Qum] for Mirza Taqi Khan [Amir Kabir]. Let him not harass me. If at God's threshold I am blameworthy, still He has done many great works for me. Here, too, He will not let a mother be so severely parted from her son.' For nearly two decades she maintained close relations with British envoys. Towards the end her influence declined. She died in 1873.

brought new strength to central government, though also later to the opposition – the telegraph. The impetus came from the British in India, who, after the Mutiny Uprising of 1857, wanted rapid communications with Britain. The first telegraph concession was granted in 1860, and Iran soon had a network, linking major cities to Tehran and the world beyond.

In the 1860s Nasir al-Din came under the influence of a member of his foreign service, Mirza Husain Khan, who had served in India and at the Ottoman court, and had developed a strong reforming vision. He persuaded Nasir al-Din to make the first visit by a Shah to foreign territory for peaceful purposes: he went to Iraq to see the modernization taking place there. Soon after his return in 1871, Nasir al-Din put an end to his unsuccessful system of personal rule with advisers, and made Mirza Husain Khan prime minister, with a cabinet that met weekly and ministers responsible to the prime minister. The Shah placed himself firmly behind the reforming agenda, which modernized the army, attacked corruption and sought British help in particular to raise capital to drive economic development. This led in 1872 to a massive concession negotiated by the Iranian ministers in London and Baron Reuter, founder of the news agency, giving him the right to build a railway and exclusive rights to develop factories, mines, irrigation facilities and modern transportation.

Nasir al-Din goes to Europe

In 1873 Nasir al-Din travelled to Europe, the first of three visits. His aim was to learn in order to improve the process of reform. The journey did not start well. Such was the difficulty of managing without embarrassment his heavily veiled harem in Russia that he sent the women home, including his favourite wife, Anis al-Dawla, who incorrectly placed the blame on Mirza Husain Khan. The Shah kept a diary of his visit which was dutifully published for the benefit of his people in the *Tehran Gazette* – there had been two earlier diaries of his travels to Iraq and to the Caspian provinces of Iran. The diary reveals his immense curiosity about nature and the small details of European life, and, while he readily acknowledges British progress and power, he also notices great poverty in Liverpool. A connoisseur of women, he says of London that: 'it has most lovely women. The nobleness, the greatness, the gravity and sedateness of the women and men shine out from their countenances.' But when the Shah returned to Iran in 1873 not everyone shared his enthusiasm for things European; the ulama in particular were displeased. Enormous opposition had also built up against the Reuter concession. The Shah was forced to cancel it and dismiss Mirza Husain Khan as prime minister.

The period from 1873 saw the rise of Amin al-Sultan, a father and a son bearing the same title. The father, the son of a Christian convert, rose from the lower ranks of the royal household to direct the mint, the treasury, the customs and the court. After his death in 1883, his son took over his titles

Anis al-Dawla, head of Nasir al-Din's harem in its later years and reckoned to be comparable in political influence to Mahd-i Ulya. Of peasant background, she is thought to have championed people's causes and to have criticized the Shah for his personal excesses, for instance an obsession with a shepherd boy. During the Tobacco Protest of 1891 she is said, in defiance of the Shah, to have forbidden smoking in the harem. This photograph would appear to support the judgment of Abbas Amanat that 'the Shah's refined sense of aesthetics often stopped at the harem's doorsteps, judging by the taste and outfits of his wives....'

Nasir al-Din Shah visited England twice. Here, he is received by Queen Victoria on his visit in 1873. He made a favourable impression as he moved in London society. 'The Shah's visit yesterday went off admirably', Queen Victoria wrote to her daughter the Princess Royal, 'and he certainly is vy. intelligent but I thought him very dignified. There was nothing to shock one at all in his eating or anything else … the Shah has produced almost a fever and Mr Gladstone says he can hardly get the House of Commons to sit!'

and posts, and was appointed prime minister. He knew how to keep all parties happy, both inside and outside Iran, while building up his own group of supporters. He gained much power. Along with the Shah he conducted a skilful policy of balancing Russian against British interests, and preserved his country's territorial integrity rather better than most in this heyday of European imperialism.

Opposition to the regime grows

From 1888 Amin al-Sultan began to grant increasing numbers of concessions: there were the rights to international navigation on the Karun river in Khuzistan, for which the British pressed; the Imperial Bank of Persia was opened by the British, and a compensating Russian Bank for the Russians. In 1889 the Shah returned from his third trip to Europe with several concessions signed, including one for a lottery, to which on religious grounds the ulama strongly objected and it had to be cancelled. Alongside such concessions was the growing presence of Westerners – businessmen, diplomats, missionaries, and their schools and clinics. In 1890, among the concessions, the monopoly on the production, sale and export of tobacco was granted to a British subject. This concession was felt far more immediately than the others because many landlords, merchants and shopkeepers already benefited from the tobacco trade. In the spring of 1891 mass protest began, ulama and merchants working together, making good use of the telegraph to co-ordinate activity. All Iran's major cities were involved. By December 1891 there was a countrywide boycott of tobacco, which was observed even by the Shah's wives led by Anis al-Dawla. In early 1892 the Shah cancelled the concession, incurring Iran's first foreign debt as a result of the huge compensation involved.

The growing opposition to the regime had at least two strands. On the one hand, there were the secular intellectuals, who felt that Iran was not reforming fast enough along Western lines; on the other were ulama and merchants who deeply resented the socio-economic and cultural disruption consequent on the penetration of the West. These two conflicting strands came together in the Tobacco Protest, as they were to do in all the great Iranian movements of protest up to the Revolution of 1979. A key figure in the Tobacco Protest was Saiyid Jamal al-Din al-Afghani, an Iranian who took the name Afghani to widen his appeal to the Sunni world, and who had emerged as a champion of the Muslim world against Western, and in particular British, imperialism. He was active in Egypt, India and Istanbul, as well as Iran. In 1891 the Shah forced him into exile, but he continued to oppose the regime from London. From 1892, after being invited by the Ottoman Sultan Abd al-Hamid, he continued his campaign from Istanbul. In 1895 he suggested to Mirza Rida Kirmani, one of his disciples, who had been imprisoned in Iran, that he assassinate the Shah. On 1 May 1896, as the Shah visited the shrine of Abd al-Azim to give thanks for 50 years of rule, the deed was done. The Shah's body was propped up in a carriage and taken back to Tehran, Amin al-Sultan working the dead man's arms to make it seem that he was still alive.

Muzaffar al-Din Shah
1896–1907

Muhammad Ali Shah
1907–09

Ahmad Shah
1909–25

Opposite Muzaffar al-Din Shah with his minister, Abd al-Majid, Amin al-Dawla, behind him, painted by Sani Humayun. The European dress and the almost photographic quality of the execution give a sense of the cultural distance travelled by the Qajar elite in the 19th century. Muzaffar al-Din's dismissal of Amin al-Dawla in 1906 opened the way to Iran's first Majlis (Parliament) and the writing of a constitution.

MUZAFFAR AL-DIN SHAH	
Born 25 March 1853	*Sons* Muhammad Ali Shah, plus 5 others
Father Nasir al-Din	*Daughters* 12
Mother Shukuh al-Sultana	*Enthroned* 3 June 1896
Wives Several, including: Umm al-Khakan (daughter of Amir Kabir)	*Died* January 1907 *Buried* ?

MUHAMMAD ALI SHAH	
Born 21 June 1896	*Sons* Ahmad, plus 5 others
Father Muzaffar al-Din Shah	*Daughters* 4
Mother Umm al-Khakan	*Enthroned* 19 January 1907
Wives Jahan Khanum (daughter of Kamran, son of Nasir al-Din), plus several others	*Died* 5 April 1925 at San Remo *Buried* An unconfirmed report suggests in present-day Moldova

MUZAFFAR AL-DIN SHAH

The Shah himself was utterly ignorant and illiterate, knowing nothing of either history or politics, and utterly devoid of prudence, judgment or foresight. Government and other important offices were openly sold by auction, and the Royal Signature lost all credit. He was a devout specta-tor of the Muharram mournings and t'aziyas (Passion plays), and had some knowledge of gunnery, and was passionately fond of cats. Unlike his father, he was averse from violence, bloodshed and cruelty ....

Nazim al-Islam, *History of the Awakening of Persia*

MUZAFFAR AL-DIN, NASIR AL-DIN'S SON, was not very active in his approach to government and chronically ill for much of his reign; for health reasons he made three very expensive visits to Europe. He started well, by dismissing Amin al-Sultan and appointing the reforming Amin al-Dawla as prime minister. The latter attempted to reform law, finance and education, and brought Belgians in to manage customs. Throughout he was resisted by vested interests. When in 1898 he failed to raise a loan from the British, he was dismissed and Amin al-Sultan returned to power. Amin al-Sultan extended Belgian management from customs into the rest of the financial administration of the country. The government thereby gained extra income, as it also did from two Russian loans in

Muzaffar al-Din Shah | Muhammad Ali Shah | Ahmad Shah

| 1870 | 1880 | 1890 | 1900 | 1910 | 1920 | 1930 | 1940 | 1950 | 1960 | 1970 |

exchange for concessions – which brought fear of a Russian takeover.

From the early 1900s opposition grew, particularly amongst the merchants, artisans and ulama of the cities. Revolutionary societies formed. In 1903, Amin al-Sultan was dismissed as prime minister in favour of the reactionary Ain al-Dawla. Opposition was given a major fillip by the Japanese defeat of the Russians, the first Asian victory over the West in modern times, in the war of 1904–05. The movement later called the Constitutional Revolution began in December 1905, when the governor of Tehran had some sugar merchants bastinadoed for failing to keep their prices down. This resulted in a series of popular protests which led to the dismissal of Ain al-Dawla in 1906 and the Shah's acceptance of a Majlis or Parliament in August 1906. The Majlis delegated to a committee the writing of a constitution, based on the constitutional monarchy of Belgium, which was signed by Muzaffar al-Din in December. In January 1907, he died.

MUHAMMAD ALI SHAH

That the new Shah should dislike the constitution and regard the Majlis with suspicion and aversion was perhaps natural enough, for he had looked forward to exercising the same autocratic and irresponsible powers as his predecessors had been wont to enjoy, and it could hardly be expected that he would welcome the limitations of his authority laid down by the Constitution, which limitations, it was clear from the beginning, the National Assembly intended to enforce.

E. G. Browne

Below From 1800 the development of Iran was constantly subject to the commercial ambitions and strategic rivalries of Britain and Russia. This led in 1907 to the Anglo-Russian Convention, which divided Iran into spheres of influence.

Boundary of Iran, 1920

CASPIAN SEA

RUSSIAN SPHERE OF CONTROL

Tehran

Isfahan

NEUTRAL REGION

Basra

Masjid Sulaiman 1908

BRITISH SPHERE OF INFLUENCE

PERSIAN GULF

N

0   500 km
0   300 miles

MUHAMMAD ALI, THE SON OF THE LATE SHAH, also signed the constitution in December 1906, and at his coronation, to which he pointedly did not invite members of the Majlis, he promised to uphold it. But Muhammad Ali was close to the Russians, who were unhappy about the constitutional movement, and he was moreover determined to regain what autocratic powers he could. He recalled Amin al-Sultan, who had been abroad learning about constitutionalism, as prime minister. But on 31 August, Amin al-Sultan was assassinated as he was leaving the Majlis by a revolutionary from Azarbaijan. On the same day, Britain and Russia signed a convention dividing Iran into spheres of interest; Russia took northern and central Iran down as far as Isfahan, the British the southeast region, while the southwest region remained neutral. In 1907–08 the Majlis passed reforming measures in taxation, education and the law.

Then, in June 1908, after a failed assassination attempt, Muhammad Ali staged a coup, supported by the Russian-officered Cossack Brigade, founded by Nasir al-Din in 1879. He closed the Majlis and executed the leaders of the constitutional movement. For the moment he was in control, Tabriz being the only city in the hands of the opposition. In July 1909, however, an army consisting of socialist and religious fighters from Tabriz in the northwest, and Bakhtiari tribesmen from Isfahan to the south, converged on Tehran. Muhammad Ali fled to safety with the Russians. His young son, Ahmad, was made Shah, first with the Qajar prince Azud al-Mulk as regent, and then the Oxford-educated Nasir al-Mulk.

AHMAD SHAH

The young Shah took no interest in Persian politics and was well content to leave the affairs of his country in the hands of ministers; his ruling passion was said to be the acquisition of money, of which [in 1918] he was believed to have amassed about £1 million since his accession.

Denis Wright

AFTER THE RESTORATION of constitutional government, two main parties formed in the elected Majlis – one the Democrat Party, with a progressive secular nationalist programme, and the other the Moderate Party, which represented the conservative interests of ulama and landlords. By 1910 these groups were splintering, with assassinations on both sides. Order broke down and the centre was unable to exert authority; this was to be the situation until the rise of Riza Khan. In 1911, the government brought in a team of Americans under Morgan Shuster to centralize and reform the finances. The Russians took exception to foreign officials being appointed in their sphere of influence without permission and issued an ultimatum demanding Shuster's dismissal. In a dramatic inci-

Muhammad Ali Shah, even though he had signed the constitution in December 1906, worked with the Russians to overthrow it. Eventually the constitutionalists drove him into exile in Russia.

AHMAD SHAH	
Born 20 January 1898	*Son* 1
Father Muhammad Ali Shah	*Enthroned* 21 July 1909
Mother Jahan Khanum	*Died* 21 February 1930, Neuilly-sur-Seine
Wives Several of low status	*Buried* ?

WOMEN DESCEND ON THE MAJLIS, 1911

Morgan Shuster describes in his book on his mission to Iran, *The Strangling of Persia*, how in 1911 women descended on the Majlis to resist the Russian ultimatum:

'The Persian women supplied the answer. Out from their walled courtyards and harems marched three hundred of that weak sex, with the flush of undying determination in their cheeks. They were clad in their plain black robes with the white nets of their veils dropped over their faces. Many held pistols under their skirts or in the folds of their sleeves. Straight to the Majlis they went, and, gathered there, demanded of the President that he admit them all. ... The President consented to receive a delegation of them. In his reception-hall they confronted him, and lest he and his colleagues should doubt their meaning, these cloistered Persian mothers, wives and daughters exhibited threateningly their revolvers, tore aside their veils, and confessed their decision to kill their own husbands and sons, and leave behind their own dead bodies, if the deputies wavered in their duty to uphold the liberty and dignity of the Persian people and nation.'

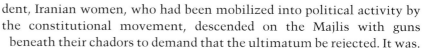

Ahmad Shah, the last of the Qajars, came to the throne as a minor and throughout his reign was in the hands of his ministers. In 1925 Riza Shah Pahlavi persuaded the Majlis to overthrow the dynasty.

dent, Iranian women, who had been mobilized into political activity by the constitutional movement, descended on the Majlis with guns beneath their chadors to demand that the ultimatum be rejected. It was.

But, as Russian troops advanced on Tehran, Nasir al-Mulk felt that he had no alternative but to dismiss the Majlis, accept the ultimatum and sack Shuster. All power was left with a conservative cabinet under British and Russian influence. By 1914 oil, which had been discovered in the southwestern region in 1906, was raising British levels of interest.

In July 1914 Ahmad was crowned Shah and ruled without a regent. He was a weak ruler and presided over a disastrous period for Iran, as foreign armies marched and counter-marched across it. Between 1915 and 1917 the Russians advanced to the outskirts of Tehran, extracted all the benefits they could from northern Iran for the Russian economy and competed with the Ottoman Turks for Azarbaijan. At the same time, the British formed the South Persian Rifles and asserted their influence in southern Iran, making a secret treaty with the Russians by which Russian interests were recognized in the Dardanelles, while the British interest in oil-bearing southwest Iran was acknowledged. The Germans played a spoiling game, supporting Iranian nationalists and mobilizing tribes.

With the armistice at the end of the First World War in 1918, the Russians and Turks left Iranian territory, and a pro-British government formed under Wusuq al-Dawla. Iran was wracked by appalling famine; many died. On 9 August 1919, Wusuq al-Dawla and the British foreign minister, Lord Curzon, signed the Anglo-Iranian agreement which virtually made Iran a British protectorate. Ahmad Shah demanded a pension for his support for the agreement. Wusuq al-Dawla and two other ministers received £130,000 each for their part in the arrangement. But there was considerable popular resistance and the Shah was forced to replace Wusuq al-Dawla. The agreement became unworkable.

Iranians now increasingly sought strong central government. This began to be achieved from February 1921 when Riza Khan, recently made leader of the Cossack Brigade (for which the British now paid), and Ziya al-Din Tabatabai, a pro-British journalist, carried out a *coup d'état*. The British told Ahmad Shah to accept the outcome; Riza became commander-in-chief, Ziya, prime minister. Within three months Riza had forced out Ziya and began building up an efficient centralized administration. In October 1923 he made himself prime minister and in October 1925 persuaded the Majlis to overthrow the Qajar dynasty. On 25 April 1926 he crowned himself Riza Shah Pahlavi. Ahmad Shah had been abroad for some time. In February 1930 he died at Neuilly in Paris.

Briefly in 1941, when the British were considering forcing out Riza Shah Pahlavi, they also considered a Qajar restoration, using Ahmad Shah's nephew, known as David Drummond, who was currently serving in the merchant navy. After the young prince had lunch with Anthony Eden and Leo Amery, the idea was dropped.

SELECT BIBLIOGRAPHY

Contemporary sources

E&D = H. M. Elliot & John Dowson, *The History of India as told by its own Historians: the Muhammadan Period*, 8 vols, London 1867–1877.

COP = W. M. Thackston (sel. and trans.), *A Century of Princes; Sources on Timurid History and Art*, Cambridge, Mass., 1989.

Afif, Shams-i Siraj, *Tarikh-i Firoz Shahi*, E&D, 3, pp. 269–373.

Allah, Niamat, *Tarikh-i Khan-Jahan Lodi*, E&D, 5, pp. 67–115.

Anon., *Tarikh-i Ahmad Shah*, E&D, 8, pp. 104–23.

——, *Tarikh-i Alamgir-Sani*, E&D, 8, pp. 140–43.

Awrangzeb, *Ruka'at-i-Alamgiri or Letters of Aurangzebe*, trans. J. H. Bilimoria, Delhi 1972.

Babur, *The Baburnama*, trans., ed., annot., Wheeler M. Thackston, New York 1996.

Badaoni, Al-, *Muntakhabu'T-Tawarikh*, trans. W. H. Lowe & George S. A. Ranking, 3 vols., reprint, Delhi 1973.

Bakhshi, Nizam al-din Ahmad, *Tabaka't-i Akbari*, E&D, 5, pp. 177–476.

Bar Hebraeus, *The Chronography of Gregory Abu'l Faraj ... Commonly Known as Bar Hebraeus*, trans. E. A. W. Budge, London 1928.

Barni (Barani), Zia al-Din, *Tarikh-i Firoz Shahi*, E&D, 3, pp. 93–268.

Begam, Gul-badan, *The History of Humayun*, trans., intro. & notes by A. S. Beveridge, reprint, New Delhi 1983.

Browne, Edward Granville, *The Persian Revolution 1905–10*, Cambridge 1910.

Chardin, Sir John, *Travels in Persia 1673–77*, New York 1988.

Chick, H. (ed. & trans.), *A Chronicle of the Carmelites in Persia and the Papal Mission of the XVIIth and XVIIIth centuries*, 2 vols., London 1939.

Clavijo, Ruy Gonzalez de, *Narrative of the Spanish Embassy to the Court of Timur at Samarkand in the years 1403–06*, trans. Guy Le Strange, London 1928.

Court, M. H. *Malcolm's History of Persia (modern) edited and adapted to the Persian Translation of Mirza Hairat*, Lahore 1888.

Dawlatshah, *see* Samarqandi

Documentos Elucidativos 1515, trans. Catarino Belo, Jon Thompson (ed.), in Thompson, Jon & Canby, Sheila R. (2003), pp. 333–37.

Dughlat, Mirza Muhammad Haidar, *Tarikh-i Rashidi*, COP, pp. 357–62.

Du Jarric, Pierre, *Akbar and the Jesuits: An Account of the Jesuit Missions to the Court of Akbar*, London 1926.

Eden, Emily, *Up the Country: Letters Written to her Sister from The Upper Provinces of India*, new intro. E. Claridge, notes by E. Thompson, London 1983.

Fasai, Hasan-i, *Farsnama-yi Nasiri*, Tehran, 1895, trans. Busse, H., *History of Persia under Qajar Rule*, New York 1972.

Fazl (Fadl), Abul, *The Ain-i Akbari*, trans. H. Blochmann, 2nd ed., D. C. Phillot, Calcutta 1939.

——, *The Akbar Nama*, trans. H. Beveridge, reprint, Delhi 1993.

Ferishta, Mahomed Kasim, *History of the Rise of the Mahomedan Power in India till the year A.D. 1612*, 4 vols, trans. John Briggs, reprint, Delhi 1989.

Fryer, J., *A New Account of East India and Persia in Eight Letters being Nine years travels Begun 1672 and Finished 1681*, London 1689.

Hadi, Muhammad, *Tatimma-i Waki'at-i Jahangiri*, E&D, 6, pp. 400–38.

Hali, Altaf Husain, *Hayat-i Javed*, trans. K. H. Qadiri & D. J. Matthews, Delhi 1979.

Heber, Reginald, *Narrative of a Journey through the Upper Provinces of India from Calcutta to Bombay, 1824–1825*, 2 vols, London 1828.

Ibn Arabshah, Ahmad, *Tamerlane or Timur the Great Amir*, trans. J. H. Sanders, London 1936.

Ibn Battuta, Shams al-Din, *The Travels of Ibn Battuta*, trans. H. A. R. Gibb, 3 vols, Cambridge 1958–71.

Jahangir, *Tuzuk-i-Jahangiri or Memoirs of Jahangir*, trans. Alexander Rogers, ed. H. Beveridge, 3rd ed., New Delhi 1978.

Jouher (Jawhar), *The Tezkereh al Vakiat or Private Memoirs of the Moghul Emperor Humayun written in the Persian Language by Jouher a confidential domestic of His Majesty*, trans. Charles Stewart, reprint, Delhi 1972.

Juvaini (Juwaini), Ata-Malik, *Genghis Khan: The History of the World-Conqueror*, trans. & ed., J. A. Boyle, intro. David O. Morgan, Manchester 1997.

Juzjani, Minhaj al-Siraj *Tabakat-i Nasiri*, E&D, 2, pp. 259–383.

Khan, Inayat, *The Shah Jahan Nama*, trans. A. R. Fuller, W. E. Begley & Z. A. Desai (eds), Delhi 1990.

Khan, Muhammad Hashim Khafi, *Muntakhabu-l Lubab*, E&D, 7, pp. 207–533

Khan, Seid-Gholam-Hossein, *The Seir Mutaqherin*, 4 vols, reprint, Delhi 1990.

Khwandamir, *Habib al-siyar*, COP, pp. 101–236.

Lahori, Abd al-Hamid, *Badshah-Nama*, E&D, 7, pp. 3–72.

Malcolm, Sir John, M. H. Court, *Malcolm's History of Persia (modern) edited and adapted to the Persian Translation of Mirza Hairat*, Lahore 1888.

Manucci, Niccolao, *Storia do Mogor or Mogul India 1653–1708*, trans. & intro. William Irvine, 4 vols, London 1907.

Marco Polo, *The Book of Ser Marco Polo, the Venetian*, ed. & trans., Henry Yule, 2 vols, London 1875.

Metcalfe, Sir Thomas, *Reminiscences of Imperial Dehli*, in M. M. Kaye (ed.), *The Golden Calm*, Exeter 1980.

Mirza, Sultan Husain (Baiqara), 'Apologia', COP, pp. 363–72.

Monserrate, S. J., *The Commentary of Father Monserrate, S. J. on his Journey to the Court of Akbar*, trans. J. S. Hoyland, London 1922.

Muhammad, Fakir Khair al-Din, 'Ibrat Nama, E&D, 8, pp. 237–54.

Mukhlis, Anand Ram, *Tazkira*, E&D, 8, pp. 76–98.

Munshi, Iskandar, *Tarikh-i 'alam-ara-yi 'Abbasi*, trans. R. M. Savory as *The History of Shah Abbas*, 2 vols, Boulder 1978.

Nizami, Hasan, *Taju-i Ma-a'sir*, E&D, 2, pp. 204–43.

Qasim (Kasim), Muhammad, *Ibrat-Nama*, E&D, 7, pp. 569–73.

Samarqandi, Mir Dawlatshah, *Tadhkirat al-shu'ara*, COP, pp. 11–62.

Shah, Nasir al-Din, *The Diary of H. M. the Shah of Persia during his tour through Europe in A.D. 1873*, trans. J. W. Redhouse, intro. Carole Hillenbrand, Costa Mesa 1995.

Shah, Sultan Firuz, *Futuhat-i Firoz Shahi*, E&D, 3, pp. 374–87.

Shuster, M., *The Strangling of Persia*, London 1912.

Spuler, Bertold, *History of the Mongols Based on Eastern and Western Accounts of the Thirteenth and Fourteenth Centuries*, London 1972.

Tavernier, Jean-Baptiste, *Travels in India*, 2 vols, London 1925.

Tytler, Harriet, *An Englishwoman in India: The Memoirs of Harriet Tytler 1828–1858*, ed. Anthony Sattin, intro. Philip Mason, Oxford 1986.

Yadgar, Ahmad, *Tarikh-i Salatin-i Afaghana*, E&D, 5, pp. 1–66.

Yazdi, Sharaf al-Din, *Zafarnama*, COP, pp. 63–100.

Modern references

Abisaab, Rula, Jurdi, *Converting Persia: Religion and Power in the Safavid Empire*, London 2004.

Alfieri, Bianca Maria, *Islamic Architecture of the Indian Subcontinent*, London & Ahmedabad 2000.

Amanat, Abbas, *Pivot of the Universe: Nasir al-Din Shah Qajar and the Iranian Monarchy, 1851–1896*, Berkeley & London 1997.

Asher, Catherine B., *Architecture of Mughal India: the New Cambridge History of India 1.4*, Cambridge 1992.

Avery, Peter, Hambly, Gavin & Melville, Charles (eds), *The Cambridge History of Iran. Volume 7. From Nadir Shah to the Islamic Republic*, Cambridge 1991.

Babaie, Sussan, Babayan, Kathryn, Baghdiantz-McCabe, Ina, Farhad, Massumeh, *Slave of the Shah: New Elites of Safavid Iran*, London & New York 2004.

Bahari, E. B., *Bihzad: Master of Persian Painting*, London & New York 1996.

Bayly, C. A. (gen. ed.), *The Raj: India and the British 1600–1947*, London 1990.

Beach, Milo, Cleveland, *Mughal and Rajput Painting: The New Cambridge History of India 1.3*, Cambridge, 1992.

—— & Koch, Ebba, *King of the World: The Padshahnama*, London 1997.

Begley, Wayne E., 'The Myth of the Taj Mahal and a New Theory of its symbolic Meaning', *The Art Bulletin*, March 1979, pp. 7–37.

—— & Desai, Z. A., *Taj Mahal: The Illumined Tomb*, Seattle 1989.

Blair, Sheila & Bloom, Jonathan M., *The Art and Architecture of Islam 1250–1800*, New Haven 1994.

Blake, Stephen P., *Half the World: the Social Architecture of Safavid Isfahan, 1590–1722*, Costa Mesa 1999.

Bosworth, C. E., *The Islamic Dynasties*, Edinburgh 1967.

Boyle, J. A. (ed.), *The Cambridge History of Iran*, Vol 5, *The Saljuq and Mongol Periods*, Cambridge 1968.

Brijbhushan, Jamila, *Sultan Raziya: Her Life and Times*, New Delhi 1990.

Canby, Sheila R., *The Golden Age of Persian Art 1501–1722*, London & New York 1999.

—— *Safavid Art & Architecture*, London 2002.

Dalrymple, William, *The Last Mughal: The Fall of a Dynasty, Delhi, 1857*, London 2006; New York 2007.

Diba, Layla S. with Ekhtiar, Maryam, *Royal Persian Paintings: the Qajar Epoch 1785–1925*, New York 1998.

Eaton, Richard M., *The Rise of Islam and the Bengal Frontier, 1204–1760*, Berkeley 1993.

Eraly, Abraham, *The Mughal Throne: The Saga of India's Great Emperors*, London 2003.

Ernst, Carl & Lawrence, Bruce B., *Sufi Martyrs of Love: The Chishti Order in South Asia and Beyond*, Houndmills, Basingstoke 2002.

Falk, Toby & Archer, Mildred, *Indian Miniatures in the India Office Library*, London 1981.

Findly, Ellison Banks, *Nur Jahan: Empress of Mughal India*, New York 1993.

Gascoigne, Bamber, *The Great Mughals*, London 1971.

Gommans, Jos, *Mughal Warfare*, London & New York 2002.

Goron, Stan & Goenka, J. P., *The Coins of the Indian Sultanates*, Delhi 2001.

Gray, Basil, *Persian Painting*, Geneva 1961.

Gupta, Narayani, *Delhi Between Two Empires 1803–1931*, Delhi 1981.

Habib, Irfan (ed.), *Akbar and his India*, Delhi 1977.

Hardy, P., *Historians of Medieval India*, London 1966.

Hillenbrand, Robert (ed.), *Persian Painting from the Mongols to the Qajars*, London 2000.

Howorth, Henry H., *History of the Mongols from the 9th to the 19th Century*, London 1888.

Islam, Riazul, *Sufism in South Asia; Impact on Fourteenth-Century Muslim Society*, Karachi 2002.

Jackson, Peter, *The Delhi Sultanate: A Political and Military History*, Cambridge 1998.

—— & Lockhart, Laurence (eds), *The Cambridge History of Iran. Volume 6. The Timurid and Safavid Periods*, Cambridge 1986.

Keddie, Nikki R., *Qajar Iran and the Rise of Reza Khan 1796–1925*, Costa Mesa 1999.

Khan, Iqtidar Alam, *Gunpowder and Firearms: Warfare in Medieval India*, New Delhi 2004.

Lal, K. S., *History of the Khaljis A.D. 1290–1320*, rev.ed., New Delhi 1980.

——, *Twilight of the Sultanate*, rev. ed., New Delhi 1980.

Lane-Poole, S., *The Coins of the Moghul Emperors of Hindustan in the British Museum*, ed. R. S. Poole, London 1892.

Lentz, Thomas W. & Lowry, Glenn D., *Timur and the Princely Vision: Persian Art and Culture in the Fifteenth Century*, Washington, DC 1989.

Lewis, B. et al. (eds), *Encyclopaedia of Islam*, 2nd ed., Leiden 1960–2004.

Loukonine, V. & Ivanov, A., *Persian Art: Lost Treasures*, London 2003.

Manz, Beatrice Forbes, *The Rise and Rule of Tamerlane*, Cambridge 1989.

Markovits, Claude (ed.), *A History of Modern India 1480–1950*, London 2002.

Melville, Charles (ed.), *Safavid Persia: The History and Politics of an Islamic Society*, London & New York 1996.

Michell, George (ed.), *Architecture of the Islamic World: its History and Social Meaning*, London & New York 1978.

Mirza, Dr Wahid, *The Life and Works of Amir Khusrau*, reprint, Delhi 1974.

Morgan, David, *Medieval Persia 1040–1797*, London 1988.

Mujeeb, M., *The Indian Muslims*, London 1967.

Nicholle, David, *The Mongol Warlords*, Poole 1990.

Nizami, Khaliq Ahmad, *Akbar and Religion*, Delhi 1989.

—— *On History and Historians of Medieval India*, New Delhi 1983.

—— *The Life and Times of Shaikh Nizamuddin Auliya*, Delhi 1991.

—— *Some Aspects of Religion & Politics in India during the Thirteenth Century*, 2nd ed., Delhi 1974.

Okada, Amina, *Indian Miniatures of the Mughal Court*, trans. Deke Dusinberre, New York 1992.

Piotrovsky, M. B. & Rogers, J. M. (eds), *Heaven on Earth: Art from Islamic Lands*, London 1988.

Raby, Julian, *Qajar Portraits*, London & New York 1999.

Rachewiltz, I. De, *Papal Envoys to the Great Khans*, London 1971.

Richards, John F., *The Mughal Empire: New Cambridge History of India 1.5*, Cambridge 1993.

Richards J. F. (ed.), *The Imperial Monetary System of Mughal India*, New Delhi 1987.

Robinson, F., *Atlas of the Islamic World since 1500*, Oxford & New York 1982.

Ross, Sir E. Denison (ed.), *Sir Anthony Sherley and his Persian Adventure*, London 1933.

Russell, Ralph & Islam, Khurshidul, *Ghalib: Life and Letters*, London 1969.

Sarkar, Jadunath, *The Fall of the Mughal Empire*, 4 vols, 4th ed., New Delhi 1991.

Saunders, J. J., *The History of the Mongol Conquests*, London 1971.

Savory, Roger, *Iran Under the Safavids*, Cambridge 1980.

Schimmel, Annemarie, *The Empire of the Great Mughals: History, Art and Culture*, London 2004.

Sims, Eleanor, with Marshak, Boris I. & Grube, Ernst J., *Peerless Images: Persian Painting and its Sources*, New Haven 2002.

Smith, Vincent A., *The Oxford History of India*, 4th ed., Percival Spear (ed.), Delhi 1981.

Spuler, Bertold, *History of the Mongols: Based on Eastern and Western Accounts of the Thirteenth and Fourteenth Centuries*, London 1972.

Stronge, Susan, *Painting for the Mughal Emperor: The Art of the Book, 1560–1660*, London & New York 2002.

Thomas, Edward, *The Chronicles of the Pathan Kings of Delhi*, 1st Indian ed., Delhi 1967.

Thompson, Jon & Canby, Sheila R. (eds), *Hunt for Paradise: Court Arts of Safavid Iran 1901–1576*, New York 2003.

Vaudeville, Charlotte, *A Weaver Named Kabir: Selected Verses, With a Detailed Biographical and Historical Introduction*, Delhi 1993.

Welch, Stuart Cary, *Imperial Mughal Paintings*, New York 1978.

—— & Masteller, Kimberley, *From Mind, Heart, and Hand: Persian, Turkish and Indian Drawings from the Stuart Cary Welch Collection*, New Haven 2004.

Woods, John E., *The Timurid Dynasty*, Papers on Inner Asia no. 14, Bloomington 1990.

Wright, Denis, *The English Amongst the Persians During the Qajar period 1787–1921*, London 1997.

—— *The Persians Amongst the English: Episodes in Anglo-Persian History*, London 1985.

Sources of quotations

Afif, Shams-I Siraj, *Tarikh-I Firoz Shahi*, E&D, 3, pp. 276, 277, 283, 286, 303, 306, 344, 368.

Anon., *Tarikh-i Ahmad Shah*, E&D, 8, pp. 112, 113, 114, 116

—— *Tarikh-i Alamgir-sani*, E&D, 8, p. 142.

Awrangzeb, *Ruka'at-i-Alamgiri or Letters of Aurangzebe*, J. H. Bilimoria trans., (Delhi 1972), pp. 29-30, 70–72.

Babur, *The Baburnama*, trans., ed., annot., Wheeler M. Thackston, New York 1996, pp. 40–42, 93, 150, 182, 206, 211, 224, 320, 329, 350–51, 358, 373, 413–24, 427.

Barni (Barani), Zia al-din, *Tarikh-i Firoz Shahi*, E&D, 3, pp. 98, 99, 125–26, 138, 140, 141, 155, 159,169, 199, 211–12, 217–18, 224, 236, 237, 263.

Begam, Gul-badan, *The History of Humayun*, trans., intro. & notes by Annette S. Beveridge, reprint, New Delhi 1983, pp. 104–05, 150–51, 169.

Browne, Edward, Granville, *The Persian Revolution 1905–10*, Cambridge 1910, pp. 116, 133–34.

Chick, H. (ed. & trans.), *A Chronicle of the Carmelites in Persia and the Papal Mission of the XVIIth and XVIIIth centuries*, 2 vols., London 1939, 1, pp. 404, 470, 471, 576, 597, 601–02, 649, 654, 657, 663.

Dawlatshah, *Tadhkirat al-Shu'ara*, COP, pp. 19, 22, 27–28, 42, 48, 56–57.

Documentos Elucidativos 1515, Catarino Belo trans., Jon Thompson (ed.), in Jon Thompson & Sheila R. Canby (eds), *Hunt for Paradise: Court Arts of Safavid Iran 1501–1576*, New York 2003, p. 335.

Eden, Emily, *Up the Country: Letters Written to her Sister from the Upper Provinces of India*, new intro. Elizabeth Claridge, notes by Edward Thompson, London 1983, p. 98.

Fazl (Fadl), Abul, *The Ain-i Akbari*, trans. H. Blochmann, 2nd ed., D. C. Phillot, Calcutta 1939, pp. 113, 122, 167, 168, 171, 176, 177.

_____, *The Akbar Nama*, trans. H. Beveridge, reprint. Delhi 1993, 1, pp. 258, 275–76, 456; 2, pp. 153, 214, 569, 835, 1245.

Ferishta, Mahomed Kasim, *History of the Rise of the Mahomedan Power in India till the year A.D. 1612*, John Briggs, trans., Delhi 1989, 1, pp. 295, 328, 343, 345; 2, pp. 41, 228; 4, pp. 141–42, 270–71.

Hadi, Muhammad, *Tatimma-i Waki'at-i Jahangir*, E&D, 6, pp. 398–99.

Hali, Altaf Husain, *Hayat-i Javed*, trans K. H. Qadiri & David J. Matthews, Delhi 1979, p. 22.

Heber, Reginald, *Narrative of a Journey through the Upper Provinces of India from Calcutta to Bombay, 1824–1825*, London 1828, 1, p. 362.

Ibn Arabshah, Ahmad, *Tamerlane or Timur the Great Amir*, trans. J. H. Sanders, London 1936, pp. 29, 206, 282–83.

Ibn Battuta, Shams al-Din, *The Travels of Ibn Battuta*, trans. H. A. R. Gibb, 2, pp. 340, 343, 3, pp. 652, 657, 660–61.

Jahangir, *Tuzuk-i Jahangiri or Memoirs of Jahangir*, trans., Alexander Rogers, ed. Henry Beveridge, 3rd ed., New Delhi 1978, 1, pp. 2, 2–3, 35, 68, 105, 308, 375; 2, pp. 52, 143, 201, 213–14, 222, 293.

Jouher (Jawhar), *The Tezkereh al Vakiat or Private Memoirs of the Mughul Emperor Humayun written in the Persian Language by Jouher a confidential domestic of His Majesty*, trans. Charles Stewart, reprint, Delhi 1972, p. 106.

Juvaini (Juwaini), Ata-Malik, *Genghis Khan: the History of the World-Conqueror*, trans. & ed. J. A. Boyle, intro. David O. Morgan, Manchester 1997, pp. 36, 607, 615.

Juzjani, Minhaj al-Siraj, *Tabakat-i Nasiri*, E&D, 2, pp. 298–99, 320, 332, 337, 345.

Khan, Inayat, *The Shah Jahan Nama*, trans. A. R. Fuller, ed. W. E. Begley & Z. A. Desai, Delhi 1990, pp. 70, 71, 147.

Khan, Khafi, *Muntakhabu-l Lubab*, E&D, 7, pp. 386–87, 407–08, 410, 428, 433, 436–37, 442, 443, 474, 485, 504.

Khwandamir, *Habib al-Siyar*, COP, p. 173.

Malcolm, Sir John, M. H. Court, *Malcolm's History of Persia (modern) edited and adapted to the Persian Translation of Mirza Hairat*, Lahore 1888, pp. 52, 55, 103, 107, 161, 208.

Manucci, N., *Storia do Mogor or Mogul India 1653–1708*, trans. & intro. W. Irvine, 4 vols, London 1907, 1, pp. 194, 330, 355, 359–60; 2, p. 320; 4, p. 100.

Marco Polo, *The Book of Ser Marco Polo, the Venetian*, ed. & trans. Henry Yule, 2 vols, London, 1875, II, 405, 478.

Metcalfe, Sir Thomas, *Reminiscences of Imperial Delhie*, in M. M. Kaye (ed.), *The Golden Calm*, Exeter, 1990, n. p.

Mirza, Sultan Husain (Baiqara), 'Apologia', COP, p. 376.

Monserrate, S.J., *The Commentary of Father Monserrate, S. J. on his Journey to the Court of Akbar*, trans. J. S. Hoyland, London 1922.

Muhammad, Khair al-Din, *Ibrat-Nama*, E&D, 2, pp. 241, 248, 249.

Mukhlis, Anand Ram, *Tazkira*, E&D, 8, pp. 84–85.

Nizami, Hasan, *Taju-l Ma-a'sir*, E&D, 2, pp. 103, 143,

Shah, Nasir al-Din, *The Diary of H. M. the Shah of Persia during his tour through Europe in A.D. 1873*, trans. J. W. Redhouse, intro. Carole Hillenbrand, Costa Mesa 1995, p. 142

Shah, Sultan Firuz, *Futuhat-i Firuz Shahi*, E&D, 3, p. 373, 376.

Shuster, M., *The Strangling of Persia*, London 1912, p. 198.

Tytler, Harriet, *An Englishwoman in India: the Memoirs of Harriet Tytler 1828–1858*, ed. Anthony Sattin, intro. Philip Mason, Oxford 1986, p. 166.

Yadgar, Ahmad, *Tarikh-i Salatin-i Afaghana*, E&D, 5, p. 7.

Yazdi, Sharaf al-Din, *Zafarnama*, E&D, 3, pp. 480, 497, 501, 502–05.

Extracts quoted in:

Amanat, Abbas, *Pivot of the Universe: Nasir al-Din Shah Qajar and the Iranian Monarchy, 1851–1896*, London 1997, pp. 136, 234.

Asher, C. B., *Architecture of Mughal India: The New Cambridge History of India 1.4*, Cambridge 1992, p. 110.

Avery, P., Hambly, G. & Melville, C. (eds), *The Cambridge History of Iran Volume 7: From Nadir Shah to the Islamic Republic*, Cambridge 1991, pp. 129, 153.

Boyle, J. A. *The Cambridge History of Iran*, vol 5, *The Saljuq and Mongol Periods*, Cambridge 1968, pp. 371, 374, 379, 390, 407, 413.

Canby, Sheila R., *The Golden Age of Persian Art 1501–1722*, London 1999, p. 144.

Du Jarric, Pierre, *Akbar and the Jesuits: An Account of the Jesuit Missions to the Court of Akbar*, London 1926, p. 205.

Eaton, Richard, M., *The Rise of Islam and the Bengal Frontier, 1204–1760*, Berkeley 1993, pp. 47–49.

Eraly, Abraham, *The Mughal Throne*, London 2003, pp. 240, 246, 276–77, 282, 302, 358, 387, 403.

Findly, Ellison Banks, *Nur Jahan: Empress of Mughal India*, New York 1973, p. 275.

Howorth, Henry H., *History of the Mongols from the 9th to the 19th Century*, London 1888, Vol III, pp. 210, 277, 290, 529, 573, 648, 696.

Islam, Riazul, *Sufism in South Asia: Impact on Fourteenth Century Muslim Society*, Karachi 2002, p. 257.

Jackson, P. & Lockhart, L. (eds), *The Cambridge History of Iran. vol. 6. The Timurid and Safavid Periods*, Cambridge 1986, pp. 272, 934.

Lal, Kishori Saran, *Twilight of the Sultanate*, Delhi 1980, p. 186.

Lentz, Thomas W. & Lowry, Glenn D., *Timur and the Princely Vision: Persian Art and Culture in the Fifteenth Century*, Washington, DC 1999, pp. 23, 32, 67, 97, 151.

Mirza, Dr Wahid, *The Life and Works of Amir Khusrau*, reprint, Delhi 1974, p. 59.

Nicolle, David, *The Mongol Warlords*, Poole 1990, pp 119, 173.

Richards, J. F., *The Mughal Empire: The New Cambridge History of India I.5*, Cambridge 1993, pp. 124–25.

Russell, R., & Islam, K., *Ghalib: Life and Letters*, London 1969, pp. 101–02.

Sarkar, J. N. *Fall of the Mughal Empire*, 2, p. 315; 4, p. 246.

Savory, R., *Iran under the Safavids*, Cambridge 1980, pp. 23, 46, 60,72, 83, 229.

Schimmel, Annemarie, *The Empire of the Great Mughals: History, Art and Culture*, London 2004, p. 261.

Smith, Vincent, A., *The Oxford History of India*, 4th ed., ed. Percival Spear, Delhi 1981, pp. 267, 288–29.

Spuler, Bertold, *History of the Mongols Based on Eastern and Western Accounts of the Thirteenth and Fourteenth Centuries*, London 1972, pp. 144, 147, 120–21, 122-23, 141–42.

Thompson, Jon & Canby, Sheila R. (eds), *Hunt for Paradise: Court Arts of Safavid Iran 1501–1576*, New York 2003, p. 73.

Wright, Denis, *The Persians Amongst the English: Episodes in Anglo-Persian History*, London 1985, pp.129, 206.

ILLUSTRATION CREDITS

a = above, c = centre, b = below, l = left, r = right

previous; **123** Photo J. D. Beglar, *c.* 1870. Archaeological Survey of India, Indian Museum; **124** Photo Christina Gascoigne; **125** *Akbar Hands his Imperial Crown to Shah Jahan* (detail). Bichitr, 1631. Gouache on paper, 29.7 x 20.5 (11⅝ x 8 1/16). Minto Album. The Trustees of the Chester Beatty Library, Dublin. Ms.7 no.19; **126** 17th century, *Akbarnama*. Bodleian Library, Oxford, Ms Ouseley. Add. 171, f. 13v; **127** From Peter Mundy's Journal, 1632. Bodleian Library, Oxford, Ms Rawl. A315, f. 40v; **128a** Photo Robert Harding Picture Library; **128c** ML Design; **128b** Photo Thalia Kennedy; **130** Miskina, Sarwan and portraits by Madhav, *c.* 1590–95. 32.9 x 19.8 (12 15/16 x 7 13/16). Victoria & Albert Museum, London, IS 2-1896 114/117; **131** Narsingh, *c.* 1605, *Akbarnama*. The Trustees of the Chester Beatty Library, Dublin. In. 03, f. 263v; **133** From a treatise by Fathallah Shirazi, in M. A. Alvi & A. Rahman, *Fathallah Shirazi*, New Delhi 1968, fig. 2; **134l** from the *Akhlaq-i-Nasiri* of Nasir ud-Din Tusi, *c.* 1590–95. Gouache on paper, 21 x 10.5 (8¼ x 4⅛). Prince Sadruddin Aga Khan Collection. Ms.39 f. 196a; **134r** Kesav the Elder and Nar Singh, *c.* 1590–95. 31.5 x 18.4 (12⅜ x 7¼). Victoria & Albert Museum, London, IS 2-1896 110/117; **135** Khem Karan, *c.* 1590–95, *Akbarnama*. 32.9 x 20.9 (12 15/16 x 8¼). Victoria & Albert Museum, London, I. S. 2-1896, 73/11; **136** British Library, London, Add. Or. 1039; **137** Photo Sonia Halliday Photo Library; **138** Bichitr, *c.* 1635, Minto Album. Gouche on paper, 20.5 x 12.7 (8 1/16 x 5). The Trustees of the Chester Beatty Library, Dublin. Ms.7 no.5; **139** Nadir az-Zaman (Abu'l Hasan) and Hashim, *c.* 1614. Gouache on paper, 18.3 x 11.6 (7 3/16 x 4 9/16). Musée Guimet, Paris. No. 3676B; **140** after Michiel Jansz. van Miereveldt, *c.* 1640. Oil on panel, 72.4 x 59.7 (28½ x 23½). National Portrait Gallery, London; **141** The Trustees of the British Museum, London; **142l** Lahore, *c.* 1598, Large Clive Album. Gouache and gold on paper, 19.4 x 11.3 (7⅝ x 4 7/16). Victoria & Albert Museum, London, IS 133-1964, f. 79b; **142r** Copy of 17th-century original ascribed to Mansur, 29.9 x 11.3 (11¾ x 4 7/16). Victoria & Albert Museum, London, IM 122-1921. Bequeathed by Lady Wantage; **143** Bichitr, *c.* 1615-18, page from the Saint Petersburg Album. Gouache on paper, 25.3 x 18.1 (9 15/16 x 7⅛). Freer Gallery of Art, Smithsonian Institution, Washington, DC, Inv. 42.15B; **144** Ascribed to Govardhan, Lahore or Agra, *c.* 1616–20, *Jahangirnama*. Gouache on paper, 32.4 x 19.3 (12¾ x 7⅝). Musée Guimet, Paris, no. 7171; **145a** Photo Thalia Kennedy; **145l** Abu'l Hasan, Jahangir Album. Rampur Raza Library, India; **145r** Attributed to Govardhan, *c.* 1615–20. Opaque watercolour, gold and ink on paper, 18.7 x 11.6 (7⅜ x 4 9/16). Los Angeles County Museum of Art, From the Nasli and Alice Heeramaneck Collection, Museum Associates Purchase. Photograph courtesy Museum Associates/LACMA, M.83.1.6; **146** The Trustees of the British Museum, S13 C56.24; **147a** Attributed to Hashim, *c.* 1620. The Trustees of the British Museum, London; **147b** Photo John Warburton-Lee Photography; **148** Bichitr, *c.* 1631, Minto Album. 22.1 x 13.4 (8 11/16 x 5¼). Victoria & Albert Museum, London, IM 17-1925; **149** Abid, *c.* 1633, *Padshahnama*, f. 94b. Image 31.8 x 20 (12½ x 7⅞). The Royal Collection, photo 2006, Her Majesty Queen Elizabeth II; **151a** British Library, London; **151b** British Library, London, Add. OR. 948; **152 & 153a** Photo Corbis; **153c&b** Photo akg-images, London; **155** Mughal School, *c.* 1660–70. British Library, London, J.64, 28; **156a** Bichitr, *c.* 1630, *Padshahnama*, f.50b (detail). 30.8 x 21.1 (12⅛ x 8 5/16). The Royal Collection, photo 2006, Her Majesty Queen Elizabeth II; **156b** Attributed to Payag, *c.* 1658. Grey-black ink, opaque watercolour, gold and metallic silver paint over white wash on off-white paper, 28.5 x 38.5 (11¼ x 15 3/16). Courtesy of the Arthur M. Sackler Museum, Harvard University Art Museums, Gift of Stuart Cary Welch, Jr.,1999. 298; **157** Mughal School, *c.* 1710. Bibliothèque Nationale, Paris, Od. 51, f. 8; **160** Unknown artist, *c.* 1635, *Padshahnama*, f. 134A. 24.6 x 40.3 (9 11/16 x 15⅞). The Royal Collection, photo 2006, Her Majesty Queen Elizabeth II; **161** Photo Robert Harding Picture Library **164** The Trustees of The British Museum, London, 1974, 0617.0.11.12; **165** *c.* 1700. British Library, London (detail). Photo Scala, Florence; **167** *c.* 1710. British Library, London, J. 24, 4; **168** Mughal school, *c.* 1712–19. British Library, London, J. 2, 3; **169** British Library, London, J. 66, 1; **171** Mughal School, *c.* 1750. British Library, London, J. 24, 2; **173** Mihr Chand, Allahabad, *c.* 1765. 24.7 x 18.1 (9¾ x 7⅛). Museum für Islamische Kunst, Berlin, Polier Album, I.4594, f. 32r. Photo bpk / Museum für Islamische Kunst, SMB / Georg Niedermeiser; **176** British Library, London, J. 66, 3; **177** Ghulam Murtaza Khan, *c.* 1810. Gouache with gold on card. British Library, London, Add. Or. 342; **178** From *Reminiscences of Imperial Dehlie*, known as the 'Delhie Book' compiled by Sir Thomas Metcalfe for his daughters; **179** Photo P. H. Egerton; **181l–r** Bishn Das. The Trustees of the British Museum, London, 1920 0917, 0.13. 2 (detail); possibly Muhammad Riza Hindi. Isfahan, *c.* 1740 (detail). Oil on canvas, 162.7 x 102 (64 1/16 x 40⅛). Given to the Victoria & Albert Museum, London, by G. F. Welsford, I.M. 20-1919; attributed to Muhammad Sadiq, Shiraz, after 1779 (detail). Oil and metal leaf on canvas, 129.5 x 276.8 (51 x 109). Collection Mrs Eskandar Aryeh; **182** Photo Alex Starkey; **183** ML Design; **184a** Steel inlaid with gold. Topkapi Saray Museum, Istanbul, no. 2/1842; **184b** Photo Dr Sheila Canby; **185** Photo Alex Starkey; **186** Rock crystal, 3.1 x 2.4 (1¼ x 15/16). Nasser D. Khalili Collection of Islamic Art, TLS 2714; **187** Lampas, 120.7 x 97.3 (47½ x 38 5/16). Metropolitan Museum of Art, New York, Purchase, Joseph Pulitzer Bequest, 1952, no. 52.20.12; **188a** *c.* 1530–40. 25.3 x 16.7 (9 15/16 x 6 9/16). Topkapi Saray Museum, Istanbul, H. 2154, f. 138b; **188b** *Shahnama*, *c.* 1530, attributed to Qadimi, f. 171b. Tehran Museum of Contemporary Art, Iran; **189** Tabriz, 1539-43, *Khamseh of Nizami*, ascribed to Mir Sayyid 'Ali. Opaque watercolour, gold and ink on paper, 32 x 18.2 (12⅝ x 7 3/16). British Library, London, Or. 2265 f. 157b; **190** Bishn Das (detail). Mughal School. The Trustees of the British Museum, London, 1920, 0917, 0.13. 2; **191** Hasham Khosorovani Collection, Geneva; **192** Gouache on card, 19.3 x 9.2 (7⅝ x 3⅝). Topkapi Saray Museum, Istanbul, H.2155, f. 19b; **193l** 1634. Watercolour, gold and ink on paper, 14.6 x 19.2 (5½ x 7 9/16). Detroit Institute of Arts/Bridgeman Art Library, London; **193r** Riza' Abbasi. The Trustees of the British Museum, London, 1920, 0917 0. 298.3; **195a** ML Design; **195c** from Cornelius de Bruin, *Travels*, 1737; **195b** Photo Roger Wood; **196al** ML Design; **196ar** from Cornelius de Bruin, *Travels*, 1737; **196b** Photo Thalia Kennedy; **197a&b** Photo Werner Forman Archive; **199** From A. Olearius, *Relation du voyage*, 1727; **200** From a *Diwan* of Baqi, 1636. Opaque watercolour, gold and ink on paper, page 28.2 x 17 (11⅛ x 6 11/16). British Library, London, Add. 7922, f. 2r; **201** Victoria & Albert Museum, London; **202** Photo Alex Starkey; **203** Mir Afzal Tuni, Iran, *c.* 1640. 11.7 x 15.9 (4½ x 6¼). The Trustees of the British Museum, London; **204** Ali Quli Jabbadar, Isfahan, *c.* 1660s–70s, f. 98a. Opaque watercolour, silver and gold on paper, 28.2 x 42.1 (11 1/16 x 16⅝). The Saint Petersburg Branch of the Institute of Oriental Studies, Russian Academy of Sciences, E14; **205** Muhammad Ali son of Muhammad Zaman, Isfahan, 1721 (detail). The Trustees of the British Museum, London, 1920 0917 0.299; **207** from Pascal Coste, *Monuments Modernes de la Perse*, Paris 1867, pl. xviii; **208** (detail) **& 210** possibly Muhmmad 'Ali ibn' Abd al-Bayg ibn 'Ali Quli Jabbadar. Isfahan, mid-18th century. Opaque watercolour and gold on paper, 22.5 x 16.7 (8⅝ x 6⅝). Museum of Fine Arts, Boston. Francis Barlett Donation of 1912 and Picture Fund 14.646; **211** ML Design; **213** Photo Bridgeman Art Library, London; **214** Muhammad Sadiq, Shiraz, *c.*1770–79. Watercolour wash drawing, 24 x 11 (9 7/16 x 4 5/16). Musée du Louvre, Paris, Section Islamique, MAO 796; **215** Attributed to Muhammad Sadiq, Shiraz, after 1779. Oil and metal leaf on canvas, 129.5 x 276.8 (51 x 109). Collection Mrs Eskandar Aryeh; **216** Attributed to Muhammad Sadiq, Shiraz, *c.* 1770–80. Oil on canvas, 149.8 x 96.5 (59 x 38). Collection Mrs Eskandar Aryeh; **217** Muhammad Sadiq, Shiraz, *c.* 1779. Oil on canvas, 147.3 x 88.9 (58 x 35). Collection Mrs Eskandar Aryeh; **218** British Library, Add. Or. 24903; **219** Attributed to Mihr 'Ali. Tehran, *c.* 1800–06. Oil on canvas, 227.5 x 131 (88 11/16 x 51⅛). Musée du Louvre, Paris, Section Islamique, on loan from the Musée National de Versailles, MV 638; **221** Artist unknown, Iran, *c.* 1815–16. Oil on canvas, 230 x 395 (90 9/16 x 155½). State Hermitage Museum, St Petersburg, VR-1122; **222** Muhammad Hasan Afshar. Tehran or Tabriz, 1835–36. Oil on canvas, 154 x 104 (60⅝ x 41). Musée du Louvre, Paris, Section Islamique, on loan from The Musée National de Versailles, MV 6700; **223** Mme. Labat. Thornton, *Images*, 18, pl. 23; **224** late 1860s photograph. I. Afshar, *Ganjina-yi ' Aksha-yi Iran*, Tehran, 1992; **225** Bahram Kirmanshahi, Tehran, 1857. Oil on copper, 36 x 25.5 (14 3/16 x 10 1/16). Musée du Louvre, Paris, Section Islamique, MAO 776; **226** Photo by Nasir al-Din Shah, 1871; **227** *The Graphic*, Vol. VIII, no. 187, 28 June 1873, p. 604; **229** Sani Humayun. Tehran, early 20th century. Oil on canvas, 125 x 80 (49¼ x 31½). Private Collection; **231b** Sub-Lieutenant David Drummond RNVR, alias Prince Hamid Mirza Qajar.

INDEX

Page numbers in *italic* refer to illustrations.